Germany's New Politics

Parties and Issues in the 1990s

Edited by

David P. Conradt, Gerald R. Kleinfeld,
George K. Romoser, Christian Søe

Berghahn Books
Providence • Oxford

Published in 1995 by

Berghahn Books
Editorial offices:
165 Taber Avenue, Providence, RI 02906, USA
Bush House, Merewood Avenue, Oxford, OX3 8EF, UK

Library of Congress Cataloging-in-Publication Data
Germany's new politics/edited by David P. Conradt ... [et al.].
    p.   cm. -- (Modern German studies ; vol. 1)
    Includes bibliographical references.
    ISBN 1-57181-032-3 (cloth : alk. paper). -- ISBN 1-57181-033-1
(paper : alk. paper)
    1. Elections--Germany. 2. Germany. Bundestag--Elections, 1994.
3. Germany--Politics and government--1990- I. Conradt, David P.
II. Series: Modern German studies (Providence, RI) ; vol. 1.
JN3972.A95G47   1995   95-31588
324.943'0879--dc20   CIP

British Library Cataloguing-in-Publication Data
A CIP catalogue record for this book is available from
the British Library.

Printed in the United States on acid-free paper.

CONTENTS

INTRODUCTION

G ermany has held its first federal election since the euphoric year
of unity. More than that, there were nineteen different major
elections in 1994—enough for the pundits to speak of the "Superwahljahr" (super election year). It was the first time Germans had so
many ways to express their views on the direction of their united
country in a changed Europe and a changed world. Unification has
been far more costly than anyone expected and brought tenacious
problems. What has emerged? Where is Germany heading? Not long
ago, an American diplomat referred to the new "Berlin Republic" as
the successor to what we had come to call the Bonn Republic. It is
the politics of this emerging Berlin Republic that all Americans
ought to become familiar with, as Germany settles in to becoming a
regional great power with global significance. Most Germans themselves would be more modest in asserting this, but that is the nature
of today's Germans.

Germany's New Politics is an introduction to politics in a new/old
environment. It is continuity amidst change, as political scientists are
fond of saying. The authors seek to combine election analysis with a
study of the political framework and the shifting balance of forces
within what is clearly the most powerful country in Western Europe.
Speaking for themselves, they explain the Bundestag election campaign and issues, look at the political parties and their roles, and
finally analyze the economy and foreign policy.

Germany's New Politics is also a testimony to the long history of
transatlantic cooperation in studying electoral politics. Since 1961,
the year in which sustained public opinion research on German elections developed its short-range plans and long-range intentions,
many of us, represented by chapters in the current volume, have
been privileged to be part of this endeavor. Often it has been only
as observers, but from time to time as researchers and authors,
whether for German or American audiences. Always the Americans
represented in the current book—along with others who did not
take part in it—have sought to be interpreters of German affairs in
English-speaking countries, "multipliers" of knowledge about postwar Germany through contacts with students and colleagues, and
often with a general public interested in lectures and discussions
about Germany. For the many opportunities given us by German

colleagues and friends, some represented in this volume, as will be duly noted, the editors and authors are most grateful.

Throughout this volume, we have used English words for German federal states, and have referred to the new federal states as East, and to the "old" federal states as West. This convention will gradually disappear, but it is useful in this particular election. For the East, we have sought to include data for the section of Berlin formerly within the German Democratic Republic whenever this is possible.

After the customary disclaimers that we authors are responsible for any errors, and not any of those who have helped or assisted us in this and past projects leading to the present book, we want to thank some individuals for their help. We are very grateful to the German Federal Press and Information Office and the German Information Center for financial support towards publication. This crucial assistance, showing a useful cooperation between scholars and those who can help in research, came at the right time. In particular, we want to thank Wolfgang Gibowski, Deputy Chief of the Press Office in Bonn, and Georg Merten, Director of the German Information Center in New York. Both bodies, with their knowledgeable, helpful, and supportive civil servants, have aided many of us in various endeavors in the past as well. In 1994, Wolfgang Gibowski was instrumental in bringing many of the authors in this volume to Germany for an October election study tour, on the invitation of his agency. On the other hand, neither of these offices saw or asked to see any part of the manuscript before publication, and the authors are solely responsible for what has been written. Our colleague, Wolfgang Gibowski, a student of Rudolf Wildenmann, is an election researcher in his own right, and he was surprised to see that we turned right around and asked him to write on his own, as he has done for many elections in the past before entering federal service.

We also want to thank Dieter Roth, of the Forschungsgruppe Wahlen, for supplying many of us with useful election data for many years, and Wolfgang-Uwe Friedrich for supporting in-depth research by American experts on Germany through the Traveling Workshops of the Deutsch-Amerikanischer Arbeitskreis, one of the most valuable resources for continued study on German affairs and transatlantic relations. Originally aided by the Federal Ministry for Intra-German Affairs, the workshops have been supported since unification by the Federal Press Office.

The authors express their special appreciation to Ursula Hummert, secretary and editorial assistant at the *German Studies Review*, for her tireless, really tireless, efforts in typesetting and structuring the volume.

It is with sadness that we mourn the loss of our friend and colleague, H. G. Peter Wallach, a political scientist whose research and human kindness made him a valued colleague and friend to all who came in contact with him. He was with some of us during that last election trip in October 1994. We dedicate this book to Peter.

CONTRIBUTORS

Hans-Georg Betz is Assistant Professor of European Studies at the School of Advanced International Studies.

Clay Clemens is Associate Professor of Government at the College of William and Mary.

Irwin L. Collier, Jr., is Professor of Economics at the Free University of Berlin.

David P. Conradt is Professor of Political Science at the University of East Carolina.

Wolfgang-Uwe Friedrich is Privatdozent at the University of Hildesheim.

Wolfgang G. Gibowski is Deputy Director of the German Federal Press and Information Office.

Mary N. Hampton is Assistant Professor in the Political Science Department at the University of Utah.

Gerald R. Kleinfeld is Professor of History at Arizona State University.

Michael Minkenberg is Assistant Professor at the Center for European and North American Studies at the University of Göttingen.

George K. Romoser is Professor of Political Science at the University of New Hampshire.

Klaus Schoenbach is Professor of Communication at the University of Music and Theater, Hanover, Germany.

Holli A. Semetko is Associate Professor of Political Science and TV/Radio/Film at the S. I. Newhouse School of Public Communications and the Maxwell School of Citizenship and Public Affairs.

Stephen J. Silvia is Assistant Professor of European Studies at American University.

Christian Søe is Professor of Political Science at California State University, Long Beach.

Helga A. Welsh is Assistant Professor in the Department of Politics at Wake Forest University.

1

THE 1994 CAMPAIGN AND ELECTION

AN OVERVIEW

DAVID P. CONRADT

O n 16 October German voters selected the membership of the national legislature (Bundestag) for the thirteenth time since the founding of the Federal Republic in 1949. For the electorate in the five new states of the former German Democratic Republic (GDR), it was only the second national election and the first since the social and economic upheavals of unification began in early 1991. The year 1994 was a very busy year for voters. In addition to the Bundestag election, deputies to the European Parliament were chosen in nationwide balloting in June, state parliaments in eight of the sixteen Länder were elected throughout the year, and local government elections took place in nine of the states.

This chapter will first examine the institutional framework within which the electoral struggle takes place, giving particular attention to the complex German electoral law and its impact on the parties and voters. Secondly, the major trends in German voting behavior since the 1980s will be discussed. Thirdly, the 1994 strategies of the major parties and the campaign themes will be analyzed. I conclude with a brief discussion of the results and their implications for the parties and the political system.

The Institutional Framework and the Electoral Law

Elections to the Bundestag must be held at least every four years but can be held sooner if the government loses its majority and requests the federal president to dissolve parliament and call new elections. This has occurred twice: in 1972, when the Brandt government, through the defection of several FDP and SPD deputies, lost its majority, and the opposition was unable to secure a majority for a new government; and in 1982, when the new Kohl government called for elections to legitimize the parliamentary developments that ended thirteen years of Social Democratic-Liberal rule. Elections to the various state parliaments are held every four or five years, but special elections can be called earlier.

For elections to the national parliament, the Republic is divided into 328 constituencies with an average size of about 240,000 residents and 165,000 registered voters. Each district must be a contiguous whole, while respecting state (Land) and, if possible, county (Kreis) boundaries. The size of each district must not deviate by more than one-fourth from the national average. There is thus considerable variation in district size, especially in the five new states in the East.

The Basic Law, as amended in 1970, grants universal suffrage and the right to hold public office to citizens eighteen years of age or above. Germany has automatic registration based on residence records maintained by local authorities. If a citizen has officially reported his or her residence in the constituency (it is required by law to do so), he or she will automatically be placed on the electoral register, provided that the age requirement is met. Before election day, the citizen will then be notified of registration and polling place.

The Electoral Law

The German system has been termed a "personalized proportional law" with half of the 656 parliamentary deputies elected by plurality vote in single-member districts and the other half by proportional representation from Land party lists. Each voter casts two ballots—one for a district candidate and the other for a party. The party vote (second ballot) is more important because it is used to determine the final percentage of parliamentary mandates a party will receive. The seats won in the district contests are then *deducted* from this total. Thus, the more district mandates a party wins, the fewer list seats it will receive.

This latter provision makes the law essentially a proportional system with several exceptions which can be important, and in 1994 they certainly were. Indeed, the 1994 election was the first in which all of the complexities of the electoral law, adopted in 1956, came into play at the same election. Specifically, the 5 percent clause, the three direct mandate waiver of the 5 percent clause, and the provision for excess seats (*Überhangsmandate*) all played a role in 1994.[1]

THE 5 PERCENT CLAUSE

To discourage small splinter parties, which were generally held to be a negative factor in the Weimar system, a 5 percent second ballot minimum was required in order to participate in the proportional payout. The 5 percent clause has been a factor at every federal election since 1957. Usually, it is the FDP or, since 1983, the Greens who are in danger of falling below the magic mark, thus providing journalists and commentators with a standard campaign story line.

THE THREE-MANDATE WAIVER

The suspension or waiver of the 5 percent clause for any party that succeeds in winning at least three district or direct seats has not been a factor since 1957, the first election that the current law was in force, when the Deutsche Partei (DP)—a north German ally of Adenauer's CDU—won six districts and thereby received an additional eleven list mandates for a total of seventeen seats or 3.4 percent, its second ballot percentage. The DP's success at the district level was due largely to support from local Christian Democratic organizations who encouraged their voters to split their ballots.

In 1994 this provision was the key to the hopes of the Party of Democratic Socialism (PDS), the heir to the former ruling Communist party of the German Democratic Republic. If the party could win in at least three districts, it would share in the second ballot proportional distribution. By concentrating its resources, the PDS did indeed win four seats in the former East Berlin and received an additional twenty-six mandates (or 6.5 for each district victory) from the second ballot distribution. Thus, a vote for the PDS candidate in one of these four East Berlin districts was worth 6.5 times more than a first ballot vote for the parties that did surmount the 5 percent hurdle barrier.

THE EXCESS MANDATE (ÜBERHANGSMANDATE) PROVISION

Until 1990 the excess mandate provision was a little-known and relatively inconsequential component of the electoral system. It is designed to affirm the integrity of the district or "personal" dimension of the law: any party that wins more districts in a given state than it would be allotted under proportionality is allowed to retain these "extra" seats, with the Bundestag enlarged accordingly. Before unification the largest number of excess mandates was five in 1961, and in several elections there were none at all. But in 1990 the CDU won six such seats, and in 1994 the number increased to a record sixteen—twelve for the Christian Democrats and four for the Social Democrats. Because of this provision, the government's "true majority" of only two seats grew to ten when all the first district ballots were counted, and the Bundestag was "enlarged" from 656 to 672 members.

Excess mandates are associated with small, below-average-in-size electoral districts and three-cornered races, in which a party can win a plurality with far less than 51 percent of the vote. Both of these characteristics in 1990, and above all in 1994, were found largely in the new eastern states. As table 1.1 shows, most three-cornered races, defined as those in which the winning party secured less than 40 percent, took place in the East and most of the smaller districts (defined as the difference between a state's proportionate share of the electorate and its proportionate share of the seats, i.e., the more a state's share of the seats exceeds its share of the electorate, the smaller on average the districts) were located in the East. A third possible factor that may be specific to the East could have been the greater role of personality in the eastern district elections. At state elections in Saxony and Brandenburg in 1994 the respective minister-presidents, Kurt Biedenkopf (CDU) and Manfred Stolpe (SPD), led their parties to absolute majorities, a rarity in western Germany, with the exception of Bavaria. Neither candidate was as successful at European, local, or national elections in their states. Their state campaigns were apparently not distorted by European or national issues.

One indirect means to examine this thesis is to compare the first and second vote spread for the winning party and candidate in the western and eastern districts. A greater spread in the East could indicate more personality voting. This was not the case, however; the average difference between the first and second ballot in the 248 western districts was 3.9 percent as compared to 2.4 percent in the East. Winning first ballot candidates in the West thus tended to run ahead of their party by a greater margin than their counterparts in the East.

Shortly after the election the Greens petitioned the Federal Constitutional Court, challenging the constitutionality of the excess mandate provision.[2] The party argued that the electoral law violates the "political" equality principle according to which each vote should have the same value or *Erfolgswert*.[3] The Greens did not propose that the court invalidate the 1994 election, but rather that additional seats be awarded to the parties which did receive excess mandates in 1994, and that the excess mandate provision of the law be changed before the next election. The essence of the Greens argument is that, thanks to the excess mandates, it took fewer voters to elect a CDU or SPD member than those deputies belonging to the other parties that did not receive a direct mandate.

TABLE 1.1

CORRELATES OF EXCESS MANDATES, 1994

State	No. of Excess Mandates	Three-Cornered Races	District Size*
Baden-Württemberg	2 (CDU)	0	-0.43
Bremen	1 (SPD)	0	0.01
Mecklenburg-West Pom.	2 (CDU)	4	0.44
Brandenburg	3 (SPD)	1	0.62
Saxony-Anhalt	2 (CDU)	5	0.46
Thuringia	3 (CDU)	3	0.56
Saxony	3 (CDU)	1	0.68
Berlin	0	3	-0.30
Bavaria	0	0	-0.43
Saarland	0	0	0.21
Hesse	0	0	-0.34
Rheinland-Palatinate	0	0	0.23
Schleswig-Holstein	0	0	0.12
Hamburg	0	0	0.10
North Rhine-Westphalia	0	0	-0.08
Lower Saxony	0	0	-0.14

*Proportion of seats above or below (-) proportion of population.

In a parallel action a law professor, Dr. Hans Meyer, filed a protest with the Bundestag's election control committee arguing that the excess mandate provision violates the electoral equality principle. In his published commentaries on the current law, Meyer has also contended that the three direct mandate clause is unconstitutional. At the 1994 election this latter provision distorted the outcome to a greater extent than the excess mandate clause (sixteen excess mandates for the CDU and SPD versus twenty-six extra seats for the PDS).

Voting Trends

For most of its history, the Federal Republic's electorate has been one of the most moderate and predictable of the Western industrialized societies. Responding to postwar economic prosperity and social stability, German voters rejected parties and movements at the extremes of the left-right ideological spectrum and by the early 1960s had concentrated their support in two large parties, the Christian Democratic Union (CDU) and the Social Democrats (SPD), and one third party, the centrist Free Democrats (FDP). These parties had differentiated sociodemographic bases: the Christian Democratic core was composed of rural and small-town Catholics, farmers, and businessmen; Social Democratic support was centered among unionized industrial workers in urban areas; and the Free Democrats received the bulk of their vote from the secular, educated middle- and upper-middle-class voters dissatisfied with the Catholicism of the CDU and the socialist image of the SPD.

Campaign issues and themes focused on pragmatic economic and security problems—unemployment, stable prices, law and order, health and welfare programs—all of which fit into the traditional left-right ideological schema. Elections were won and lost in the center of this electorate.

By the 1980s, however, significant changes had taken place in this traditional pattern. The two major parties had lost support; turnout had declined; ticket-splitting had increased; the influence of class and religion on voting behavior had declined; "new politics" issues, such as the environment, disarmament, and civil liberties, had become salient to increasing numbers of voters; and in 1983 a new party, the Greens, broke the twenty-year monopoly of the three "old" parties on parliamentary representation.

Figure 1.1 documents one of these trends: the decline in party identification. Since 1980 the proportion of the electorate with a "strong" or "weak" preference for a specific party has dropped from 77 percent to only 48 percent, with the largest drop taking place among voters with a "strong" attachment to a political party. In the West, the proportion of voters with no identification with any of the parties has increased from 13 percent in 1980 to 32 percent by 1993. Among eastern voters, almost half in 1993 reported no identification with a party.

Germans are more interested in politics than ever before, but as this increases, so does their disinterest in traditional parties and politics and their willingness, at least at the state level, to "throw the rascals out" via the ballot. By the 1990s almost 60 percent of voters reported that they had an "interest" in politics as compared to less than 30 percent in the 1950s. Yet, membership in the major, established political parties has been in decline for the past fifteen years.[4]

Voters have also been less inclined to return incumbent governments. At state and national elections held from 1949 to 1987, the voters in the West had 110 opportunities to remove a government and replace it with the opposition, but they did so in only five elections. Since 1987, with twenty-one chances to remove a government, the voters have done so seven times.[5]

FIGURE 1.1

PARTY IDENTIFICATION, 1980–1993

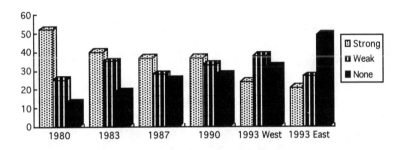

Q. In Germany many people, over a long period of time, will favor a certain political party, even though they will once in a while vote for another party. How about you: do you favor, generally speaking, a specific party? How strong, or how weak, all in all, is your preference for this party?

Source: Forschungsgruppe Wahlen

The post-1990 unification process has further complicated this pattern. The traditional demographic relationships in the West noted above have yet to become apparent in the East. At the March 1990 Volkskammer election and the December federal election, for example, the bulk of manual workers supported the Christian Democrats and not the Social Democrats. The new eastern voters are also more likely to change their party preferences in the short run than their western counterparts. After the 1990 election in the West, the victorious Christian Democrats experienced a 6 to 10 percent drop in support and fell behind the Social Democrats for most of the interelection period. As the October 1994 election approached, however, the gap narrowed. In the East the pattern was quite different. The Christian Democrats, between December 1990 and October 1993, dropped from 42 percent to 20 percent in the polls while the SPD jumped from 24 percent to 38 percent. But at the 12 June European and local elections, the CDU/CSU rebounded with gains of 10 to 15 percent over its standing in public opinion polls two to three months earlier. Fluctuations of this magnitude are simply unknown in "mature" Western electorates. The eastern voters lack the firm demographic and/or organizational moorings of class, religion, family, friends, and work environment that still characterize most—but by no means all— western German voters. They are still floating, issue voters with few ties to labor unions, churches, and business and professional associations. They are more likely to respond to short-term changes in the economic situation than are experienced western voters.

Party Strategies and Campaign Themes

THE CHRISTIAN DEMOCRATS (CDU)

Soon after the 1990 victory the Union's electoral fortunes, as measured in polls and state elections, declined sharply. The announcement in February 1991 that the costs of unification would indeed require tax increases prompted a "tax lie" campaign by the opposition which bore fruit at state elections throughout 1992 and 1993. It was not until the June 1994 European Parliament election that the CDU could reverse two years of electoral decline. That victory was presaged by steady improvements in the party's standing in public opinion polls since early 1994 and by public perceptions of an improving economy. Between February and June 1994, the proportion of the population that saw the economy as moving in the right direction rose from 26 percent to 55 percent.[6] By the European election the CDU was seen as more competent to deal with the country's economic problems in both East and West than the SPD.

As in 1990 the CDU campaign began and ended with the chancellor. His experience, wisdom, and commitment to traditional values were contrasted by party campaigners with the young, ambitious, but inexperienced Scharping who was charged by the Union with playing games with the voters in terms of the SPD's possible coalition partners, his plans for new taxes, and his ecological experiments. But above all Kohl was projected as *staatsmännisch*. The official calendar provided ample opportunities: visits to Germany by Presidents Clinton and Mitterand, the fiftieth anniversary of the July 20th attempt on Hitler's life, the G-7 Naples summit, Germany's assumption of the EU's commission chair, the departure of Russian troops from the East and Western forces from Berlin, and new plant openings in the East.

Prior to the election Kohl had effectively removed many of the potential policy obstacles to his reelection. The asylum issue was largely defused by the 1993 constitutional amendment restricting the right of political asylum. By 1994 asylum applications had dropped by over 60 percent. The tax increases agreed to by all parties, except the Greens and PDS, in the 1993 Solidarity Pact did not take effect until January 1995. In the East, the unpopular Treuhand had largely completed its privatization task (and left a DM275 billion bill).

Kohl's standard speech highlighted the accomplishments of his governments since 1983: three million new jobs between 1983 and 1990, a decline (until unification) in government spending relative to GNP, an 18 percent real gain in income, and, in the East, four million new telephone lines since 1990 as compared to only 1.8 million in forty years of socialism. Since unification (he never tired of telling his eastern supporters), the average pension increased from DM500 a month to DM1250. For all Germans, the chancellor presented a final election offering: long-term nursing care insurance.

When in the East, the chancellor's position toward the GDR's Communist past was carefully tailored to the wishes of the great majority of former GDR citizens. His statement that he wished the *Stasi* documents would "go to the devil" and his oft-repeated confession that he could not honestly say how he would have behaved had he lived under the Communist dictatorship were designed to appeal to the great majority of GDR citizens who adapted and accommodated themselves to the regime. The West CDU, however, supported a complete review of the *Stasi* files.

THE FREE DEMOCRATS

The FDP's fortunes steadily declined throughout the interelectoral period. At three state elections in 1991, it averaged about 8 percent of the vote. In 1992 the party's average vote at two state elections dropped to less than 6 percent. At the ten state elections since 1992, the party had failed to surmount the 5 percent barrier, i.e., it had lost ten straight state elections. This string of losses began with the departure in May 1992 of its long-time leader and coarchitect of unification, Foreign Minister Hans-Dietrich Genscher. Genscher was the most popular political leader in the Federal Republic and critical for the party's electoral future. While the unpopular decisions of the Kohl government and the poor economy also played a role in the party's decline, the Genscher factor stands out.

At the outset of the campaign, the FDP was in its most precarious position since the 1983 election, which followed the party's switch in coalition partners from the SPD to the CDU. Could the party survive without Genscher? His successor, Foreign Minister Kinkel, has not been the *Wahllokomotive* that his supporters and mentor had hoped. This could already be seen at the 1992 state parliamentary election (Landtagswahl) in Baden-Württemberg, his home state, where he was showcased, but failed to bring the party any significant gains.

The FDP's message was simple: the only way to avoid the twin evils of a "red-green" or Grand Coalition was to vote FDP. The major unknown in this scenario was the leadership question, that is, Kinkel's campaign ability or lack of it. Kinkel was the least popular FDP leader since polling on this question began in the mid-1950s. Part of the FDP's appeal has always been to have a popular, or at least respected, personality at the top of the ticket: Genscher (1990, 1987, 1983, 1980, 1976), Walter Scheel (1972, 1969), Erich Mende (1965, 1961), and Reinhold Maier (1957, 1953). In the heat of the two-party struggle, the calm, *sachlich* FDP leader has gained in stature as a reasonable alternative or corrective to the major parties.

Organizationally and psychologically, the mobilization of a mass electorate has never been an FDP strong point. The party's élitist *Selbstbild* came through in May when the first draft of its program declared that the FDP wanted to be known as the party of the *Leistungsträger* and the *Besserverdienenden*. A few days later this formulation was changed somewhat to "avoid misunderstandings."

Following the debacles at the European Parliament election and the Landtagswahl in Saxony-Anhalt (26 June 1994), the party changed its *Werbekonzept* to a straight-forward, no-new-taxes approach: "*Gegen Steuern—gegensteuern.*" This replaced the ill-fated *Besserverdienenden* theme. The new approach did the party little good, as seen by its abysmal performance in Saxony, Brandenburg, and Bavaria a few months later.

In the campaign's final phase the FDP, at least in North Rhine-Westphalia, trotted out Genscher and Count Lambsdorff and launched its usual ticket-splitting (*Zweitstimmen*) appeal. To charges that it was a mere *Anhängsel* of the Union, the party pointed to the Post and Bahn reforms, the Lufthansa privatization, and the loosening of the *Bundesanstalt für Arbeit's* monopoly on the labor market. None of these issues excited many voters, but together with massive help from Christian Democratic splitters they hoped that the FDP would gain enough to put the party over the 5 percent mark.

THE OPPOSITION: SOCIAL DEMOCRATS

The SPD attempted with Rudolf Scharping, their fifth candidate since 1983, to avoid its fourth consecutive loss. He was, of course, not the first choice of the party élites, who would have preferred either Oskar Lafontaine or Björn Engholm, both of whom self-destructed after 1990.[7]

Until early in 1994 the outlook for Scharping was very promising. The party had moved back into the center of the political spectrum and was more united than it had been for almost twenty years. After three straight losses, the party appeared willing to pay the price in terms of compromise on policy and leadership questions. This was shown in 1993 when the SPD consented to the restrictive asylum law and the Solidarity Pact. In the early going, Scharping did well on the campaign trail. He ran a Clinton-style campaign emphasizing jobs, jobs, jobs. (In January 1994, unemployment reached the four million mark [about 10 percent], the highest level since the end of World War II.) Scharping's course even received the imprimatur of the ultimate SPD centrist, Helmut Schmidt. At his mid-March seventy-fifth birthday banquet in Bonn, Schmidt announced that there finally is *"ein SPD mit der es geht. Und einer mit dem es geht."*[8]

The SPD's *Wahlprogramm* reflected this middle-of-the-road approach. Its centerpiece was the replacement of the universal 7.5 percent surtax on incomes (*Solidarzuschlag*), scheduled to take effect in 1995, with a 10 percent tax limited to those single tax payers with gross incomes of DM60,000 or more, or married taxpayers with gross incomes above DM120,000. The 7.5 percent surtax was part of the bipartisan Solidarity Package approved by most of the Social Democrats in March 1993. The party estimated that 80 percent of the taxpaying public would not be affected by its proposed tax.[9]

Originally, Scharping apparently wanted the upper limits for the tax set at DM50,000/100,000, but opposition from within the SPD caused him to accept the higher figure. The confusion over this question provided the governing parties with an opportunity to criticize the whole program as another example of socialist envy and to dispute the contention that most taxpayers would not be affected. Scharping had to expend substantial resources during the campaign on defending his tax program.

At the March 1994 state election in Lower Saxony, however, Scharping's strategy appeared to be successful. The SPD was able to cut into the CDU camp and captured about 10 percent of the

Union's 1990 support and about 20 percent of the FDP's electorate (a much smaller group).[10] State level factors and especially the far greater popularity and recognition of SPD minister-president Gerhard Schröder, a sometime rival of Scharping, also played a major role in the SPD's victory.

Scharping's problems began shortly after the Lower Saxony victory when he apparently confused "gross" with "net" income in announcing his tax plan. His original minimum of DM50,000 (single)/DM100,000 (married) was later changed to DM60,000/DM120,000 after strong protests from several trade unions. But Scharping explained that the DM50,000 referred to "net taxable income" which would be about DM60,000 before standard deductions. The CDU and FDP jumped on this gaffe, pointing to yet another example of how Social Democrats did not understand economic issues. His problems continued in May when he sharply criticized the newly elected federal president, Roman Herzog, following his election in Berlin. Disappointed that the FDP had not gone over to the SPD's candidate, Johannes Rau, Scharping vented his anger at Herzog. Gerhard Schröder felt compelled to publicly remind him that Kohl, not Herzog, was the opponent.

Apart from the improving economy, Scharping's campaign was hindered by the lack of a strong, central, and unifying theme or issue. The plan to stress jobs and an economic upturn (*den Aufschwung wählen*) had been rendered less credible by the recovery, and the party had little to put in its place. Opposition parties and especially those on the center-left both need issues that can mobilize the committed and win over the undecided who are usually somewhere in the center of the political spectrum.

Why, for example, did the SPD in March agree to the *Pflegeversicherung* (long-term nursing care) compromise, which broke the postwar consensus on parity in financing social welfare programs? Six months before the elections the SPD agreed that the costs of the program were to be financed largely by employees and not employers. Workers will have to give up one and probably two of their paid holidays in addition to an increase in social security contributions to finance the program. If the party had rejected it as antilabor, the SPD would have had an ideal campaign issue with considerable attraction for voters in the middle: manual workers, and lower-level white-collar workers. They could have blamed the absence of a law on the CDU and its pro-business orientation.

THE OPPOSITION: ALLIANCE 90/GREENS

In 1990 the West German Greens—their leaders, activists and many of their voters—failed to understand the political impact of the unification issue and were not returned to the Bundestag. By 1994 with the euphoria of unification long gone and united with their eastern German equivalent—the Alliance 90/Greens party—the Greens were well positioned to reverse the 1990 defeat. With the Realist wing of the party, led by Joschka Fischer, now in control, the party since 1990 was able to demonstrate in several state-level coalitions—Lower Saxony, Hesse, and until 1994 Brandenburg—that it was able to govern. Moreover, environmental issues continue to trouble more than enough voters to put the party over the 5 percent mark. An added plus for the Greens in 1994 was the SPD's move to the center. The party hoped to pick up some voters from the SPD's left wing, which has been alienated by Scharping's ultrapragmatic course.

At the European and local elections on 12 June the Greens—both East and West—did very well with 10.1 percent of the national vote (11 percent in the West and 7 percent in the East). The strong showing in the West came largely at the expense of the SPD. Throughout the campaign the Greens urged the SPD to commit to a coalition with them, arguing that the real center of the electorate was now held by the young, postmaterialist service class. Following the European Parliament election in June, there was little doubt among party leaders that the Greens would return to the Bundestag.

But during the campaign it became evident that there was a growing division within the party between its western and eastern wings: the postmaterialist, middle-class, affluent western German Greens have little understanding for their eastern counterparts. The core of the eastern group is the Alliance 90, the former dissidents who played such a critical role during 1989–90 in the collapse of communism. The eastern Germans are still deeply concerned about coming to terms with the Communist past, including a vigorous investigation and, if possible, prosecution of Communist officials. The widest gulf between the two groups, however, occurs over the question of how to deal with the resurgent former Communist party, the PDS. The western Greens, with no personal experience of living under Communist rule, would like the party to reach out to former Communists especially the rank and file who were relatively innocent of any association with the abuses of the Communist regime. The Alliance 90 remains deeply suspicious of the old Communists and rejects any cooperation with them.

THE OPPOSITION: THE PARTY OF DEMOCRATIC SOCIALISM

The specter at the German party feast was the PDS/LL (Party of Democratic Socialism/Left List), the successor to the SED, the former ruling Communist party in East Germany. At local elections in early 1994 in Brandenburg and at local elections on 12 June in the other four eastern states, the party showed substantial strength. While now proclaiming itself free of its Communist past, the PDS has gratefully assumed the SED's treasury and organizational infrastructure. With 131,000 members (90 percent of whom were in the SED), it is still the largest party in the old GDR.[11] Its membership still extends into almost every nook and cranny of the country.

The party's successes on 12 June (in some East Berlin precincts it achieved Communist-era results of about 85 percent!) and at subsequent state elections in Saxony-Anhalt, Brandenburg, and Saxony were due primarily to its image as the only purely "eastern" alternative available to GDR voters who want to send a message to the dominant *Wessis*. It articulates the sense of "*Entwertung*" and neglect felt by many eastern Germans. One western German reporter sent to a PDS Hochburg, the East Berlin suburb of Hohenschönhausen (also known as "*Stasi*-City"), found another explanation that social scientists would term "relative deprivation":

> In the old days only the 'others', the *Stasi*-Kinder, had fresh fruits and vegetables (bananas, oranges, tomatoes) in their lunch boxes. Today we all have that. But it's no fun to have bananas when everyone has bananas. Therefore they still vote PDS, it's that simple.[12]

In short, bananas or even GTI's are not enough: dignity, status, recognition of "their" history and culture by the West are now the critical "goods" demanded by many eastern Germans.

To enter the Bundestag the PDS needed either 5 percent of the all-German vote *or* three direct district victories. The party strategy was geared toward the latter. It identified about twenty districts in the East where it believed it had a chance at a plurality on the first ballot. Toward the latter stages of the campaign it focused its resources on several districts in the former East Berlin: Marzahn/ Hellersdorf, Hohenschönhausen, Neu-Brandenburg, and Berlin-Mitte. Victory in just three of these districts would pay huge dividends for the party, for it would then share in the proportional payout of the second ballot votes, i.e., it would receive far more than three seats.

Campaign Themes

THE REVIVING ECONOMY

As in the United States in 1992, the 1994 German election campaign was focused on domestic issues, particularly the economy. In survey after survey during the eighteen months preceding the vote, voters in the West overwhelmingly considered unemployment to be the most important problem. Of course, in the East it has been the number one problem almost since unification in 1990, as the number of employed eastern Germans dropped from 9.5 million to 6 million. While in past elections—especially those of 1987 and 1990—noneconomic issues such as the environment, "law and order," or "peace" (missiles, disarmament) have equalled or surpassed economic issues in importance, this was not the case in 1994.

Until early 1994 the public's view of the economy was generally very negative. But beginning in February, public perceptions of economic improvement jumped dramatically; the Forschungsgruppe Wahlen , for example, found that from February to May the proportion of the electorate that believed the economy was improving doubled from 26 percent to 52 percent.[13] As figure 1.2 shows, by October almost 70 percent of western voters and 60 percent of those in the East agreed that the economy was "on the way up."

FIGURE 1.2

PERCEPTION OF THE ECONOMY
FEBRUARY–OCTOBER 1994: EAST—WEST
(PERCENT ECONOMY IS IMPROVING)

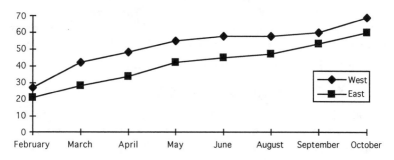

Source: Forschungsgruppe Wahlen

This belief reflected in fact some positive economic news. New industrial orders began a steep rise in December 1993; by April 1994 productivity was up by 4 percent; real growth in the first quarter of 1994 was at an annualized rate of 2.1 percent. In the new states, investments in 1994 exceeded DM160 billion, and a real growth rate of almost 8 percent was expected. Most economic institutes revised their 1994 estimates of all-German growth from 1–1.5 percent to almost 3 percent.

Inflation was also down, especially in the East, and dropped to 2.7 percent overall by the fourth quarter. In the West, the April 1994 level of 2.9 percent was the lowest since 1991. Even the Bundesbank cooperated by lowering the discount rate to 4.5 percent and the Lombard rate to 6 percent. These positive economic developments, however, had little downward impact on unemployment, which hovered at around 9 percent.

The chancellor and his party were the major beneficiaries of this perceived economic upturn. By April 1994 Kohl, who had trailed Scharping in polls since the SPD leader became the party's chancellor candidate in mid-1993, was within four points of the challenger. Two months later the chancellor had a ten-point advantage which he was never to relinquish.

In the East, Scharping in February held a 62–30 percent advantage over the chancellor. It disappeared by August. Support for the CDU also increased from only 30 percent in March to 42 percent by June, a level which then remained fairly constant until the October election. In February only 29 percent of the electorate expected the government to win the election; by June 1994 about 70 percent expected the coalition's reelection.

Most of this Kohl comeback occurred between March and the June 1994 European election. The Social Democrats were able in late summer to stop the hemorrhaging and, with the help of its new team approach, to stabilize its support at about the 36 percent mark it maintained until the election.

THE SAXONY-ANHALT GAMBIT AND THE RED STOCKINGS

Following the disastrous European Parliament election in June, the SPD campaign showed signs of self-destruction that characterized the 1983, 1987, and 1990 efforts. Gerhard Schröder began sniping from Hanover, the trade unions showed signs of writing Scharping off, and the Young Socialists called for a more confrontational approach and an unabashed alliance with the Greens. The party and especially Scharping were in dire need of a win that would turn around his loser image in the media. (The numerous Landstagswahlen in 1994 leading up to the October national vote became, in a sense, the functional equivalents of the American presidential primaries.)

In Saxony-Anhalt the party appeared poised for such a victory. The CDU/FDP coalition government was badly weakened by major scandals which had resulted in the resignation of much of the government. (Since 1990 the Land had gone through three minister-presidents.) The SPD's *Spitzenkandidat*, Reinhard Höppner, was one of the few indigenous Ost-SPD leaders with a fairly good record and reputation; he was more popular than his opponent Christoph Bergner. Until the reversal of the national trend in March–April, the SPD had held a large lead in the polls.[14]

At the 26 June election, the SPD secured 34 percent of the vote, only 5,000 votes less than the CDU (34.4 percent). The Union dropped 4.6 percent from its 1990 total while the SPD gained 8 percent—a substantial swing. The FDP saw its proportion of the vote collapse from 13.5 percent in 1990 to only 3.6 percent in 1994. Thus, the combined government proportion dropped from 52.5 percent to only 38 percent. The PDS was the big winner with 19.9 percent (7.9 percent over 1990) while the Alliance 90/Greens were at 5.1 percent.

A Grand Coalition with Bergner as minister-president seemed the only possible outcome given the pariah status of the PDS and the departure of the FDP. While the combined SPD-Alliance 90 vote (39.1 percent, 41 seats) was slightly larger than that of the CDU (34 percent, 37 seats), the "red-green" alignment was well short of a majority in the Landtag. However, in a surprising move (even to some leading SPD figures), Höppner announced that he was forming a minority government with the Greens that would be tolerated by the PDS. It is still unclear who was responsible for this decision, but many observers see the influence of Günter Verheugen, the party's general secretary and chief campaign strategist.

Publicly, the CDU was livid, charging that the SPD had broken the forty-five-year-old consensus among the "democratic" parties prohibiting any coalition with anti-system extremist parties such as the neo-Nazis or Communists.[15] The CDU launched a new ad campaign denouncing the Social Democratic alliance with the "Red Stockings," the old Communists. The SPD responded to CDU attacks on its Saxony-Anhalt decision by questioning the democratic commitment of the Christian Democrats in the eastern state. As a "block party" in the Communist-dominated national front, it was an integral part of the Communist system. The only *unbelastete* democratic parties in the East, according to the SPD, are the Social Democrats and the Greens, the new parties founded during the Revolution of 1989–90, and they therefore should build the government. The Christian Democrats could further their own "democratic maturation process," the SPD argued, by accepting this new government and becoming a loyal opposition. Privately, SPD strategists contended that the party had little choice but to form a government with the Greens, since a Grand Coalition so close to a national election would have undercut the party's entire strategy.

CDU campaign strategists viewed the SPD's Saxony-Anhalt decision as a "gift from heaven." The Union now had what was considered a gripping theme that could be used to counter the SPD's "it's time for a change" campaign. While the "Red Stockings" message was not limited to the West, as some party strategists proposed, but was also directed at the East, its major purpose was to divide the western German Social Democrats. Kohl and other CDU leaders never tired of citing Kurt Schumacher, the first postwar leader of the SPD, who after 1945 termed the Communists *"rotlackierten Fascisten"* (red-lacquered fascists). "How could this old and honorable democratic party, the Social Democrats, cooperate with this discredited band of ex-Communists?" asked CDU speakers rhetorically in their standard campaign speeches. The CDU ran a series of TV spots arguing that the new SPD leadership had betrayed the party's rank-and-file electorate by the decision to cooperate with the ex-Communists. These spots were considered by CDU planners as among the most effective of the campaign.

But was the "Red Stockings" theme as effective as the campaign strategists and party leaders believed? Thus far, there is no evidence that this campaign produced any net gains for the Union. Indeed, some analysts, including several from the CDU camp, have argued that in the East the campaign actually helped the PDS by giving it added notoriety and enhancing its image as the only party that had the interests of the East as its sole concern. The ex-Communists could point to the thunderous denunciations coming from Bonn as proof that their message was getting through to the movers and shakers in the West. Significantly, CDU campaigners in the former GDR downplayed the theme. Almost three-fourths of voters in the East, according to polls, did not see the PDS as a "danger to democracy."[16] Even most (55 percent) Christian Democratic supporters in the East did not consider the PDS to be a threat to the democratic system. In the West, opinion on this question was more evenly divided, with 41 percent of western voters perceiving the PDS as a danger, while 49 percent did not. Finally, it should be noted that the big CDU gains in the polls and the European Parliament election took place *before* the "Red Stockings" media blitz. The proportion of voters who expected the CDU to win did *not* change significantly between June and October.

But irrespective of its net electoral impact, the Saxony-Anhalt decision certainly gave the party's leaders, campaign planners, and activists an issue they could relate to with gusto in an otherwise dull campaign. This helped to energize and rally the party faithful, even if it did little to mobilize the undecided voter.

Conclusion

The 1994 election produced mixed results for all parties, large and small. There was neither a clear winner nor a clear loser. The ruling coalition returned to power, but with a greatly reduced majority. To carry their small and weakened partner, the Free Democrats, over the 5 percent line, the Christian Democrats had to give up about 4 percent of their vote to the Liberals. The Social Democrats, with 36 percent of the vote, finally ended their string of three straight declines in national elections. But they nonetheless lost their fourth straight national election and failed to transfer their 1993–94 successes at the state level to the Bundestag in Bonn. The SPD offered the electorate only a weakly defined programmatic alternative to the government, and its leader was unable to compete on even terms with the chancellor once the campaign heated up.

Among the small parties, the Free Democrats with only 6.9 percent of the vote, due mainly to splitting by CDU voters, did return to the Bundestag, but on the same election day they lost another three state elections in the Saar, Mecklenburg-West Pomerania, and Thuringia, as well as the local elections in North Rhine-Westphalia. It is now a party without a state and local base, or in the more colorful image of some journalists, a "mermaid party" (*Damen ohne Unterleib*).The Greens became the first party ever to return to the Bundestag following a failure to clear the 5 percent hurdle. But the party, having overcome its Realist vs. Fundamentalist cleavage, must now deal with a potentially more divisive issue—the relationship between its western and eastern wings. Unlike 1990, the eastern Greens owe their reelection to their western counterparts; in the five eastern Länder the Alliance 90/Greens failed to surmount the 5 percent barrier. The PDS achieved its goal of returning to the parliament, but the party remained insignificant in the West and is still largely a regional protest movement.[17]

The ambiguous outcome of the 1994 electoral marathon was underscored a few weeks after the election when Chancellor Kohl succeeded by only one vote in becoming the first chancellor since Adenauer to be elected four times. The government's weakened position was also reflected in the absence of any major policy initiatives for the new legislative term. As the Federal Republic approaches its fiftieth anniversary, the transformation of its politics and party system continues.

Notes

1. As in past elections, most voters did not understand this system. Only 30 percent, in one survey, correctly identified the second ballot as more important than the first; 14 percent believed the first was more important than the second (a not entirely incorrect answer for PDS voters in some eastern Berlin districts); 58 percent stated that the two ballots were equally important; while the remaining 8 percent of the sample knew nothing about the system. Institut für Demoskopie survey cited in *Frankfurter Allgemeine Zeitung*, 5 October 1994, p. 5.

2. *Frankfurter Allgemeine Zeitung*, 4 November 1994, p. 5. In February 1995 the Court dismissed the petition on technical grounds.

3. The CDU needed 65,940 votes for each of its Bundestag seats as compared to 69,859 for the Greens, 69,316 for the FDP, and 68,913 for the PDS. The SPD, which was also the beneficiary of four excess mandates, needed 68,021 votes. The CSU, which received no excess mandates, had a ratio of one seat for every 68,543 votes.

4. Wilhelm Bürklin, "Verändertes Wahlverhalten und der Wandel der Politischen Kultur," in Wilhelm Bürklin and Dieter Roth, eds., *Das Super Wahljahr* (Cologne: Bund Verlag, 1994), 27–53.

5. Dieter Roth, "Was bewegt die Wähler?" *Aus Politik und Zeitgeschichte* 11 (18 March 1994): 1.

6. For many activists, however, the turning point took place earlier at the February 1994 Parteitag in Hamburg. At this gathering Kohl succeeded in rallying the party faithful from the pessimism that had accompanied the Union's free fall in the polls, especially in the East.

7. Lafontaine's prospects for a second try at the chancellorship were dealt a severe blow in 1992 when it was revealed, largely through the efforts of *Der Spiegel* and the writings of Professor von Arnim, a frequent critic of party finance, that he had taken advantage of some very generous provisions of the Saarland's pension laws. While still serving as minister-president of the state, Lafontaine was already receiving a pension for his previous stint as mayor of Saarbrücken. The law under which Lafontaine was being doubly compensated had been intended for his predecessor

who had to leave his post because of ill health. Neither the state parliament nor Lafontaine proposed any changes after the Social Democrats came to power. While insisting that he had done nothing wrong and was the victim of a media defamation campaign, Lafontaine did eventually reimburse the state treasury DM228,000. His troubles continued later in the year when the press discovered that one of his aides had an extensive criminal record. Lafontaine's chances for a second candidacy were also hindered by his very low level of support in the former East Germany. During the 1990 campaign, Lafontaine left little doubt that he opposed the rapid unification of the two states. His general lack of emotional commitment to unity contrasted to the optimism of Chancellor Kohl during the campaign.

8. Scharping's pragmatism was in sharp contrast to Lafontaine's blatant courting of the new social movements. Some typical Scharping quotes: "the strongest party will always find a partner" (*Der Spiegel*, 9 May 1994, p. 27); "15 percent of the electorate swings between CDU and SPD, but only 4 percent between Greens and SPD." (The Greens were grateful for the 4 percent.) Such unabashed pragmatism was too much for even the most realistic Greens. Ludgar Volmer, chief party spokesman, called Scharping's program a return to the Helmut Schmidt era. Less tactful Greens referred to the SPD candidate as "Kohl with a beard."

9. *Frankfurter Allgemeine Zeitung*, 28 April 1994, p. 5.

10. Forschungsgruppe Wahlen, Election Day Survey, "Wahl in Lower Saxony," *Berichte der Forschungsgruppe Wahlen*, 17, 17 March 1994, p. 36.

11. Almost three-fourths of the party's 131,000 members are retired! Only 7 percent of the membership is under thirty-five. Central Institute for Social Science Research, Free University of Berlin 1994 survey cited in *Frankfurter Allgemeine Zeitung*, 6 August 1994, p. 2.

12. Evelyn Roll, "PDS wählen, damit es jeder sehen kann," *Süddeutsche Zeitung*, 18 June 1994, p. 3.

13. Forschungsgruppe Wahlen, *Politbarometer*, June 1994, p. 4.

14. This has been a recurrent problem for the Social Democrats in the East. The party lacks an organizational infrastructure in the new states. Since the SPD ceased to exist in 1946, the traditional relationship between workers and the party must be rebuilt. The SPD had only about 26,000 members in the new states as compared to 87,000 for the CDU. On the SPD's problems in the East, see the excellent article by Stephen J. Silvia, "Left Behind: The Social Democratic Party in Eastern Germany After Unification," *West European Politics* 16, no. 2 (1993): 24–48.

15. The PDS/LL does have a faction that may qualify for the extremist label. The "Communist platform" group views the Federal Republic as a "bourgeois parliamentary representative democracy" whose basic structures are designed to coopt and corrupt its "participants." The goal of the party, according to the platform group, should be to "drive this system to the limits of its development in order to demonstrate that this 'dictatorship of money' cannot solve the fundamental problems of people and must lead to the downfall of humanity. Only then can majorities be found for another system." *Frankfurter Allgemeine Zeitung*, 8 August 1994, p. 8.

16. Basis Poll, September 1994. I am grateful to Wolfgang Gibowski for making these data available.

17. Most analysts found that the party's vote was related to the following demographic and attitudinal characteristics: above average education, a nostalgia for the old GDR, a feeling of being discriminated against by the West, and strong support for the ideological principles of socialism. For an excellent analysis of the PDS vote, see Jürgen W. Falter and Markus Klein, "Die Wähler der PDS bei der Bundestagswahl 1994," *Aus Politik und Zeitgeschichte* 51–52 (23 December 1994): 22–34.

2

POLITICS, LEADERSHIP, AND COALITIONS IN GERMANY, 1994

GEORGE K. ROMOSER

Reasserting Leadership: Helmut Kohl and 1994

One of the central results of the election of 16 October 1994 may well be an underlining of the importance of Article 65 of the Basic Law—the *Richtlinien* article which puts the federal chancellor in charge of "determining, and being responsible for, the general policy guidelines" of the federal government. The narrow margin by which the Christian Democratic Union/Christian Social Union/ Free Democratic Party coalition triumphed in the federal election, and the narrow majority in the Bundestag through which Helmut Kohl retained office as chancellor, tell us only part of the significance of the election. For example, the personalization of the federal campaign probably strengthened Kohl's hand for governing by redramatizing his leadership image after its erosion in the trying years since unification in 1990. He moved alertly after 16 October to exploit the revived "chancellor bonus."

Since the founding of the Federal Republic in 1949, the concern for moderation and stability has contributed to a slowness of the policymaking process in (West) German government. The consensus and corporatist patterns have reflected and intensified this trait. Since 1990, however, the increasingly evident difficulties in achieving the inner reunification of Germany have inspired apprehensions and more than one prediction about imminent and significant changes in various dimensions of German political life. "There is obviously a crisis in the German system of party government.... The 1990 election was a ... respite from the fundamental political and economic problems that now face the Federal Republic as a result of unification."[1] Such assertions may often confuse political and economic problems with a "crisis" of the party system of government. The resultant picture may be overdrawn, because it is made with too little reference to the strong elements of stability in the German political system. It also only partly addresses the topic of how political power is exercised. The limitation of electoral and party research alone is evident in the above quotation. The "Superwahljahr" of 1994 has had an impact, of course, but elections are but one of the ingredients in the German political scene. They are an important ingredient, to be sure, and reflect significant developments, but they must be analyzed in relation to social, psychological, economic, and structural developments. The study of elections must be placed in a broad perspective.

Less than one year after widespread predictions of his political demise, when the German government had been described as "staggering in circles,"[2] the fact that Helmut Kohl triumphed in the federal election of 1994 is perhaps a sign of electoral volatility. On the other hand, it also reflects a strong element of stability in the polity. Moreover, the scant, but adequate, plurality for the government parties was a personal triumph for Kohl, showing the impact of concepts and practices of political leadership developed by the chancellor and some of his colleagues and aides.

This approach combines strict attention to the cultivation of influence within the Christian Democratic parties with an analysis of how to exercise power in a society with strong orientations toward stability. Despite substantial, and probably increasing, signs of political fragmentation in Germany, then, the Superwahljahr 1994 turned out to be less dramatic than many had anticipated. The shape and management of change, at least in the current legislative period before 1998, will be formed by forces which include the conservative parties as senior partners, rather than as a defeated minority. This fact is undoubtedly the central result of 1994, although the erosion of their electoral strength—particularly of the CDU rather than the Bavarian CSU—is evident. The institutional roots of German politics tap deeper than the party roots.[3]

Nevertheless, Helmut Kohl has repeatedly shown himself to be adept at combining influence in his party with utilization of the powers of government. It has become almost a cliché to say that he has long been underestimated as a political leader. He has been declared politically dead on numerous occasions since he ascended to the chairmanship of the CDU in 1973. The cover of the 15 January 1979 issue of *Der Spiegel*, for example, featured a hefty portrait of "Kohl kaputt." The accompanying article wrote of his "dismantling" by alleged friends as well as enemies in the CDU. To be sure, occasional "positive" covers and articles (*Der Spiegel*, 19 November 1990, soon before his victory in the 1990 federal election, showed a giant Kohl towering over the united Germany, with the title "The Happy Giant: Why Kohl is Successful") interrupted the flow of negative characterizations, reflected again in the 6 December 1993 issue, just as the Superwahljahr was about to start. This cover, the rear of Kohl's head positioned as if he were departing, announced, "The End of an Era: Kohl's Power Disintegrates." Even more moderate commentators in the media and elsewhere most often echoed such sentiments. The negative judgments of Kohl's political strength probably reached their most intense point in the autumn of 1993 and the early winter of 1993–94. They coincided with a continuing low standing in opinion polls. "The disappointment of the electorate, especially in the new states in the eastern part of Germany, was great after the federal election of 1990, and began early in 1991."[4]

This period between the last two Bundestag elections was indeed, at least until the spring of 1994, a time of stress for Germany's politics and Kohl's leadership.[5] At the same time, it was—especially starting in early spring 1994—a period of exceptional demonstration of Kohl's political talent. All in all, the 1991–94 period could be seen as an exaggerated recapitulation of his earlier political career, from startling lows in the polls to substantial recovery.[6] Arguably, some of Kohl's problems were of his own making. These included his underestimation of the financial and psychological difficulties of reunification, and his style of party leadership. The latter was at one and the same time his great strength and long-range weakness. The "flourishing landscape" that he had promised for the former GDR in the 1990 election campaign became a phrase to haunt him, though he professed to shrug it off, while he aimed to be still in the process of making the prophecy come true. In fact, by October 1994 his reputation as a competent problem-solver, at least in comparison with his challenger, Rudolf Scharping, was well established. Yet throughout the 1991–94 period, the position of the CDU in the Länder disintegrated in both electoral results and party recruitment, leading to an SPD dominance in the Bundesrat and significant questions about the future, "post-Kohl" direction and the leadership of the CDU. Kohl's dominance of the party has inhibited the development of strong party figures at the provincial level or challengers at the federal level. Those who sought to mount a challenge in earlier years were outmaneuvered by the chancellor. At the same time, as party chair, Kohl centralized much policymaking, and his mastery of party affairs has stood him in good stead at the time of Bundestag elections.

Kohl's latest and most impressive recovery was rooted in several circumstances, all of which are instructive for the understanding of political leadership in Germany. In the 1989–90 period of rapid change, the collapse of the GDR, and the reunification of Germany, Kohl was "at the right time at the right place." Kohl had never been a "popular" chancellor, certainly not in the sense of Konrad Adenauer or Willy Brandt, but he became in that crucial period a national symbol, partly by accident, partly by his deft grasp of the opportunities. He understood that national unity could be achieved and made himself the manager of reunification from the beginning. His Ten Point Plan of November 1989, vague as it was, and as foggy as the future course of events appeared at the time, nevertheless lifted him in public consciousness out of the the ordinary run of politicians, creating an impression of statesmanship. In effect, he revived a sort of "chancellor bonus" in 1989 and 1990, on a different basis than that ascribed to Adenauer. In 1990, Kohl became the central figure of the election campaign and elicited support as the national leader in a time of rapid change. Indeed, it is likely that this strength continued under the surface even during the most confusing days of the post-unification era, for example, in 1992, with its plethora of knotty problems and disturbing events, ranging from violent attacks on foreigners to waves of strikes in the public sector, foreign criticisms of Bonn's alleged new assertiveness in international affairs, growth of extremist voting, and cuts in health benefits. This new type of "chancellor bonus" might well rest, not simply on the "normal" give-and-take of politics, on who appears the most worthy of confidence among contending leaders, but upon factors of reassurance seen in the leader in a time of change, especially startling change.

The disappointments following reunification have already been noted. Kohl's relative success in 1994 indicates that it would be an error, at least in Germany, to deduce from such disappointments a weakening of the leader's capacity to elicit trust. Similarly, the much described "German malaise" and *Parteiverdrossenheit* (alienation from political parties) which seemed to reach their peak in Germany in the past few years, may actually be turned to advantage by a political leader who inspires confidence and trust, like a rock amidst a swirling storm.[7] The point may be put more mundanely: Helmut Kohl emerged as an embodiment of "the nation" in 1989–90. He took on this new role, which went beyond that of being a skilled party tactician and on-again, off-again inspirer of confidence, as the deliverer of future prosperity. Might he be "Bismarck in a cardigan," as he was at least once termed while enunciating his stubborn confidence in triumph. A lightning-rod symbol certainly fits: grumbles and complaints assail him, but he still inspires more confidence than other political figures at the crucial moments. A study of January 1994 found that alienation from parties had "as a counterweight, especially in the East, that more and more people place their hopes in the strong politician at the top, who attacks problems and sees them through." "Fifty-eight percent in the former GDR and 53 percent in the West agree with the assertion that such a politician is needed in order to deal with unemployment or crime, for instance."[8]

To be sure, other influences were at play in 1994 to enable Kohl to achieve at least a relative recovery from the problems of 1991–93. Moods of deep pessimism about the economy started to change in late 1993, first among the business élites, then widening in the spring of 1994 to broader circles. Another significant factor was the degree to which high-level issues of the post-unification period were addressed by the government, in at least two major instances with the aid of the major opposition party, the SPD. In November 1992, for example, the SPD moved to cooperate with the CDU/CSU/FDP government on new, stricter regulations for asylum seekers. These restrictions took effect on 1 July 1993 and substantially quieted the explosive issues associated with asylum seekers and the role of foreigners in Germany—to be sure, without settling the remaining, but less high-profile, problems of qualifications for citizenship. The government and SPD also worked out a joint plan for long-term nursing home health coverage, under the goading of long-time Labor and Social Minister Norbert Blüm, like Kohl himself from the "social" wing of the CDU. There were other signs of consensual politics with the Social Democrats, especially when the issues did not involve foreign policy matters of German involvement in out-of-NATO-area peacekeeping. Moreover, in July 1994 the Federal Constitution Court interpreted Article 24 of the Basic Law as permitting out-of-area involvement under certain restrictions. This was a defeat for the SPD, but also a benefit to Kohl's election campaign by weakening the issue in the political arena, at least for the immediate future. "Anti-crime" legislation, on the other hand, was passed in late September 1994 with support from the SPD. Perhaps significantly for the future, the consensual arrangement with the Social Democrats was worked out after the SPD-controlled Bundesrat had earlier rejected a stricter law passed by the governing coalition in the Bundestag.

Terrorist antiforeigner incidents in 1992 led to strong concerns abroad, particularly in the United States, but also at home. Substantial criticisms of alleged inadequate government responses to the extremists helped move the Kohl coalition to a series of cooperative and independent efforts to address both the image problem and the reality of the threat from the radical-right. Citizen demonstrations against terror were basically nonpartisan, but the government also moved to a "law and order" agenda, notably through efforts to undermine the milieu of the far-right, which stretched from parties such as the Republikaner to "skinhead" and neo-Nazi terrorists. The naming of the conservative leader of the CDU in the Hessian Parliament, Manfred Kanther, as interior minister in July 1993 symbolized a harder line towards crime and political extremists. His appointment was clearly in response to polling information which identified these issues as citizen concerns.[9]

Kohl's leadership is but part of the panorama of German politics, but it tells us a good deal about how to organize and analyze the political forces at work. Moreover, Kohl and his advisers have addressed the topic of effective leadership under today's conditions several times in the last few years. Though their comments may be viewed partly as an *ex post facto* homage to the chancellor's performance in 1989–90 and later, they have another dimension which illuminates the role of political leader, as distinct from party or interest group or legislative maneuvering, on the German scene.

Wolfgang Bergsdorf, already cited, was for many years head of the domestic section of the Federal Press Office, an important part of the chancellor's central office (*Bundeskanzleramt*), and a man in the inner circle of Kohl's advisers. He has written extensively on the language of politics. That which Bergsdorf terms the "linguistic presentation of politics" is a central example of the "surroundings" of contemporary politics, according to Bergsdorf. Politics today, writes Bergsdorf, is sort of a contest in political communication between leaders and the media. Effective leaders have to "exercise communicative discipline in the interest of general policy objectives," but this need conflicts with the "insatiable desire for news," i.e., "a rapid turnover of topics and personalities." Alluding to Max Weber's ideas about "enthusiasm, a sense of responsibility, and a sense of proportion" as traits needed by political leaders, Bergsdorf finds the contest between communicative discipline and the voracious consumption of news "an extreme challenge [which] modern democracy poses for political leaders."[10]

According to Weber, there is a need to maintain "proportion," and a "reflective distance between oneself and political reality," but, Bergsdorf comments, "political leadership in a pluralistic democracy is not possible without damage to personal prestige." Even apparent political victories "have a Pyrrhic nature." "The better a great problem is solved, the less the political accomplishment is perceived." This phenomenon is related to the economic notion of declining marginal utility. Among other things, the "Pyrrhus principle" means that the leader, in developing consensus, does not give most, if any, of the engaged interests a high level of satisfaction, and thereby creates a kind of general disgruntlement, even with a successful compromise.

Bergsdorf and Wolfgang Schäuble, now the chancellor's heir apparent and CDU leader in the Bundestag, seem to share certain perspectives. For example, in early 1989 Schäuble pointed out that Helmut Schmidt's government collapsed, but that Schmidt was popular across party lines, while Kohl's government "with many successes, has at the same time much criticism." His conclusion was that governing was different than popularity, and that all a leader can do is "follow a procedure of trial and error within a legislative period, pushing to the limit the existing capacity of the majority."[11]

These German theorists of political leadership pursue their analysis beyond media impacts. They refer to the fragmentation and individualization of cultural, social, and political positions in contemporary Germany. Schäuble, for example, writes of "a field, in principle, of infinitely pluralistic interests." And yet they reject the view of "ungovernability," at least thus far. In their perception, Kohl was primarily a victim of the *Zeitgeist* that was a product of years of affluence which appeared to be in danger of being lost due to the costs of unification. Solidarity is threatened for many reasons, including the loss of a sense of the state as a protective community rather than just a supplier of services, and the weakening of the idea of "the personal element in politics," i.e., the "leadership task in politics."[12]

It is difficult to believe that Helmut Kohl does not share many of the sentiments sketched here. For reasons of political prudence or an unspeculative mind, he is rarely heard expounding them so directly. However, under the impact of the disappointment in the public after 1990 and in tune with the views of advisers, he began openly to complain of a German "egotistical cult of self-fulfillment," and of a lack of "solidarity," "unity," and "lively patriotism," themes developed in greater detail in a book published by Schäuble in June 1994, soon before the federal election, and blessed by the chancellor at a Bonn reception.[13] Later in the campaign, Kohl seemed to tone down the more strident aspects of his 1993 speeches in favor of phrases such as "completing the unification of Germany internally." Yet, it would be unconvincing to assert that Kohl simply took up certain themes to try them out, then dropped them because they made little impact. The second part of such an assumption might well have been correct, but the bringing up of the themes noted rested on an idea that modern political leaders, to be effective, have to combine "'combativeness' and 'compromise;' in emotional terms, [these] are a unit."[14] The "communicative discipline" noted above, however, seems to contain a strong element of reticence in use of inflammatory terms, and this has usually been Kohl's approach. Cultivating a spirit of unity and combativeness in one's own group (party) is one objective which permits compromise with others later on.[15]

The October 1994 Election Results

The ideas sketched above provide an overview and a framework for understanding the election campaign at the federal level in 1994, the patterns of the subsequent coalition negotiations, and the workings of the reshaped government and opposition. The combination of a personalized election campaign, in which Kohl was the dominant leader, with the imperatives of consensual or "coordination" democracy has become essential for government stability in a time of fragmenting trends in the party system and, to some extent, in society in general. The political face of Germany is essentially that of a somewhat concealed balancing act between centripetal and centrifugal forces, with the role of the leader the central focus. At the same time, the leader as "manager of coordination," once a government is installed, is both "strong" and "weak." This figure comes to the governmental leadership role through a process of personalization, as has been seen ("profiling" of the candidate as leader), yet must also, as chancellor, attend to the increasingly precarious status of his position, as fragmentation and pluralism increase.[16] The remaining "giants," the *Volksparteien*, tend to be drawn closer together, yet there is also a sense in which the smaller partner of a giant in a coalition acquires some control over the larger partner, as will be illustrated below. Thus, the leader must play a sort of two-faced game of accommodation, both towards the major opponent and the pygmy partner.

In retrospect, there was clearly no alternative leader to Kohl in the 1994 electoral contest. That is, there was no one who could be identified by sizeable groups of voters as a likely performer of the balancing act described above. An indication of the problems of the Social Democrats and their chancellor candidate, Rudolf Scharping, was given by the creation of a "troika" of Scharping and the prominent SPD politicians Oskar Lafontaine and Gerhard Schröder in late summer, to represent the campaign and the aspirations of social democracy to power. While this may well have originated in an effort by Scharping to bring his sometimes independent colleagues under more campaign discipline, it achieved little resonance in the public. It may even have been seen by some as an indication of divisions among the Social Democrats, and of the inexperience of Scharping.[17] Scharping, fourth SPD chancellor candidate since Helmut Schmidt left office in 1982, lacked a reputation for leadership. He developed no clear thrust to his campaign, other than the notion that it was time for a change. In fact, the comment by some that Scharping "was running a Bill Clinton-like" campaign was not far from the mark: trying to appeal on behalf of something "new," against the old and worn out.[18] Aside from the apparent fashionableness of this approach—before the steep decline of Clinton's popularity—it probably held little promise, given the immense differences between German and American voters and the structures and institutions of the two societies. The word "new" lacks in Germany the psychological resonance it has in the United States.

An analysis of the SPD in the Superwahljahr is provided elsewhere in this volume. However, a few further points should be highlighted here, in the context of the focus on leadership and coalitions. The SPD remains indisputably one of the two major parties in Germany. Its results in the October federal election reversed the relationship of 1990 with the CDU and made it again the largest vote-getting party at the federal level (quite aside from its current strength in the second chamber, the Bundesrat). In 1994 it obtained 36.4 percent of the crucial party list vote, as compared with only 34.2 percent for the CDU. Of course, the addition of the CSU vote from Bavaria, 7.3 percent, up from 7.1 percent in 1990, made the CDU/CSU the largest vote-getting alliance. Over the last few years, moreover, given the death of Franz Josef Strauß, the perpetual maverick from Bavaria's CSU, and the key position held by CSU head Theo Waigel as minister of finance in Bonn, tensions between the CDU and CSU have eased and positive collaboration has improved. Nevertheless, the SPD results were hardly disastrous, even given a decline of its share of the vote in the East. Candidate Scharping received respectable personal popularity ratings, but was judged by the electorate more competent than Kohl only in the area of reducing unemployment. In the last few weeks of the campaign, Scharping seemed better able to mobilize traditional SPD voters, and in the simultaneous state election in Mecklenburg-West Pomerania, the party strengthened itself to the point that it would later enter a Grand

Coalition with the CDU in the state legislature. The differentiated picture of SPD strength in the East is typical of discrepancies between the performance of all parties in West and East.[19]

The real national problems of the Social Democrats as potential leaders lie in several areas other than incremental electoral gains or even the successes at the state levels in the last several years. Its coalition possibilities are now more limited than those of the CDU, for aside from the recent declines of the FDP overall, the "left-liberal" segment of that party has largely eroded since 1982, and the PDS on the left is not now a viable partner in any guise to offer the voters. The creation of a minority government of SPD and Alliance 90/Greens "tolerated" by the PDS in the state of Saxony-Anhalt reinforced images of disunity within the party, a negative factor for gaining support in German elections. As coalition partners, then, the SPD is left with the Alliance 90/Greens. Even that card is becoming less strong, since the specter of an alternative "black-green" coalition has emerged as elements within the two seemingly incompatible camps tenuously approach one another. As a theoretical possibility, the *Ampel* (traffic light) coalition of SPD, FDP, and Alliance 90/Greens exists—indeed, it became a mathematical possibility on 16 October. But the condition of the FDP itself undermines the possibility.

In any case, the keys to understanding the SPD's problem in capturing governmental power do not lie in the coalition blockages, the party's lack of consensus on its own leadership, or any particular missteps during the 1994 campaign on state coalition politics or on tax and budget issues, or even Rudolf Scharping's confused handling of the latter in March 1994 speeches and media appearances. Kohl and the CDU had their errors in the recent campaign, as well. The clumsy handling of the federal presidential election race in its early stages, and the chancellor's curious comments late in the Bundestag campaign about not running again in the future are examples of lapses of judgment. What the SPD lacked was a persuasive theory of leadership which had a bridge to political reality, to contrast with Kohl's imagery of unity, perseverance, and stability. In effect, the opposition to Kohl and the government coalition, whether SPD, Alliance 90/Greens, PDS, or anything else, was a strong indicator of pluralism, but a diffuse machinery to set against an "establishment" which had long been in power. The emphasis on programmatic statements in the SPD has a long history, but also always an air of unreality. After the 1994 election, a conservative SPD leader, Friedhelm Farthmann, chairman of the SPD in the state legislature of North Rhine-Westphalia, sought to correct this gap by advocating yet another program, albeit one unburdened by past issues, and showing "social openness." The only "other way" for the SPD to play a decisive role in the future, according to his analysis, is "the American solution, i.e., no programmatic differences between the big German umbrella parties any longer: political competition directed only towards who has the most convincing personality to offer."[20] His analysis is flawed with respect to the United States. It also underestimates the *blending* of an "image of competence with a few broad programmatic points, which the CDU/CSU presented in the 1994 campaign."[21]

The negative view of such a combination sees the Christian Democratic campaign as entirely "empty," sunk in slogans, such as the Tina Turner hit "Simply the Best" (used frequently in CDU "spots"), and tied in with "media moguls and TV stations" trivializing all issues.[22] Such critiques are common in intellectual circles, yet offer few starting points for effectively combining issue orientation with some degree of political power. Historically, the SPD has attained power only after previously being in coalition with the CDU/CSU (1966–69). From this position, it attained enough experience and share in power to act the governmental rather than oppositional role—that is, to insist on leadership as well as programmatic points, even when the latter were placed in second position. This, of course, was especially true with Helmut Schmidt as chancellor, given his self-confidence as a manager. Among other events during his 1973–82 chancellorship, however, generational and socioeconomic changes took place "at the grass roots," along with new versions of reformist zeal. The rise of the Greens in the early 1980s contributed to pressures from the new forces in the SPD to move the party more to the left, and the resulting tensions inside the SPD and the SPD/FDP coalition helped undermine Schmidt's government. However, the posture of reformist movements or groups in a pluralistic setting seems always to be associated with difficulty in achieving a majority or, at least, some kind of working plurality. With the rise of new reformist or protest movements on the left, the erosion of Kohl's CDU (however much it made a recovery from the low point of 1992–93) did not primarily benefit the SPD. As "the" opposition, the Social Democrats garnered few laurels in the 1994 federal election. In the East in particular, they lost ground to the PDS, and often the choice between CDU and PDS was a clearer distinction than between CDU and SPD. Nor did the SPD play the role which Helmut Kohl so masterfully exhibited in the Hamburg CDU party convention of late February 1994, when he articulated the emotional but convincing generalities about Germans pulling together.

The Victorious Coalition and the Future

A path has been opened for the SPD to relive its entry into a Grand Coalition with the CDU/CSU, but this is only one of the possibilities engendered by the Superwahljahr 1994. The SPD had hoped for an insistence by the electorate on change, and its campaign essentially amounted to an appeal in that direction. The result of the federal election, at least, showed that the assumption and appeal were unsuccessful. The main opposition party did not replace the main governing party. Other forms of change have taken place, and even cautious observers believe "that change is in the air in Bonn," that is, in governing. "We stand before interesting and disquieting times for the creation of stable majorities."[23]

The SPD aimed, as its electoral calls late in the fall campaign emphasized, for "full political responsibility." The Christian Democrats maintained the claim to political leadership in a political terrain increasingly fraught with pitfalls. Yet, as almost all analysts agree, Germany's reunification has somehow changed the country politically, without the full contours of the alterations being easily predictable. Due to the strong conservatism of the country's institutions and society, the changes might turn out to be less than some now predict. This essay has tended to stress those elements of continuity and those evidences of leadership in managing change which exhibit the stability of the society and of its political tendencies, not only in the fundamental sense of institutions, but also in day-to-day politics. Yet, there can be little doubt that the party system is undergoing some degree of change, given the decline of the FDP, the strength of the PDS in the East, the retooling of the Alliance 90/Greens as a potential governmental participant, and the difficulties of the two "giants" in sustaining voter loyalty or choice. Only the meager results for the Republikaner and other right-wing groups in 1994 testified to a reduction in fragmentation.

Issues and directions in the smaller parties are examined in other contributions to this volume. As far as leadership and existing or potential coalition roles or impacts of these groups are concerned, it is sensible to connect such topics with brief sketches of the coalition negotiations following 16 October and with the agenda and workings of the new government installed after Helmut Kohl's reelection as chancellor in the Bundestag by 338 of 672 votes, a bare majority.

Formal coalition negotiations among the CDU, CSU, and FDP were unusually brief, lasting only three weeks. Substantively, the coalition agreement simply postponed details on numerous points.

However, the FDP won concessions against the expansion of electronic surveillance (*grosser Lausch-angriff*) to combat crime, but not on its advocacy of a system for dual citizenship or a specific date for ending the new 7.5 percent "solidarity subsidy" added to income taxes on 1 January 1995 to fund enormous aid for the East. The FDP lost control of two ministries in a cabinet reduced in size by two to a total of seventeen. A so-called "Super Ministry" on education, research and technology, dubbed a "Futures Ministry," was assigned to the forty-three-year-old CDU "comer," Jürgen Rüttgers.

After a triumphant appearance (and reelection as party chairman) by Kohl at a CDU convention in late November, and a raucous FDP gathering in early December, at which party leader Klaus Kinkel, still the German foreign minister, was apparently on the verge of giving up his party chairmanship after shouts from the floor to resign and conflicting evidences of support or nonsupport from other FDP notables, the extended Christmas and New Year's holiday pause was upon Germany.

Returning to the theme at the start of this essay, one way to gain an overview of the new political situation is to focus on the question: Who governs? This again emphasizes the strong role of the chancellor and of the institutional and political weight of an established government. Some speak of "muddling through." This is not necessarily the same as "addressing issues," as critics demand. Survival of the government is not always the same goal as addressing problems. As was argued some decades ago, "chancellor democracy" is a kind of answer to a typical "German problem of the state." That problem is how to combine democratic parliamentary control with stability.[24] This theme may not be outdated. On the other hand, considerable caution is needed by the current government to remain in power. The FDP not only suffered constant losses in 1994 state elections, in effect losing most of what remained of its grass roots, but there are unresolved issues in the party concerning leadership, the image of leadership or lack of it, and future aims in a programmatic sense. After the federal election, a conservative group, centered in Berlin, became active. Since the party has lost a good part of its former left wing since 1982, only the rather small and disunited center of the FDP can moderate the more conservative rumblings. The FDP is a weak coalition partner, but at the same time has a peculiar power in that Kohl cannot afford to be placed in the position of losing its support, either through its final collapse, or even through an attempt to transfer power to a successor before the next scheduled federal election in 1998. There can be no certainty that a CDU/CSU successor to Kohl would be supported by all FDP deputies in the Bundestag.

Kohl, Schäuble, and others in the CDU show signs of having at least two alternative strategies to that of working with—or enduring—the FDP in the federal coalition. The first is that of moving towards a Grand Coalition with the SPD before 1998, and the second, partly under the goading of some reformers in the CDU who are worried about its weak organizational status in many states, is to stick it out until 1998, with or without the FDP, but with Kohl staying at the helm.

In this second scenario, the constitutional requirement of a "constructive vote of no confidence" to replace a chancellor is very relevant. Other relevant factors include the emerging flirtation between sectors of the CDU and the Alliance 90/Greens, the ongoing disunity of the political opposition, and the internal revitalization of the party structures. Given these factors and the continued aid of a stable CSU, which now seems content in its Bavarian homeland, the CDU could have a strong chance of moving from the Kohl era to a new age of Christian Democratic dominance.[25]

The alternative of a Grand Coalition is probably more likely than any other for the CDU, other than the present government surviving through the Bundestag term. As indicated earlier, the SPD's best route to power is probably still through a prior Grand Coalition, in order that it may attain a share in the all-important governing function in Germany. Under some circumstances, its interests could intersect with those of important forces in the CDU, though cooperation with the CSU would be a problem. While some voices argue that this "deal" is already in the works,[26] it seems more likely that the CDU/CSU would prefer to stay with the present coalition to the very last moment, should this not damage its own options. The tangled leadership question in the SPD, with Scharping by no means entirely solid in the saddle, creates problems for establishing a Grand Coalition. And there is always the question of who would be chancellor under such an arrangement. Kohl is unlikely to leave the scene before 1998, as noted above, and his position is in no way comparable to that in 1966 of Ludwig Erhard, the only chancellor who had to bow out because of divisions and his own weakness. Again, despite its disarray, the FDP is found to be in a key role, though for different reasons than in the past. Its very disarray creates great uncertainties about a possible withdrawal by its ministers from the cabinet, or disappearance of the party, or both.

Despite the potential of changed dynamics in Bonn, the emphasis being placed since October on problem solving and consensual agreement in advance of formal governmental actions, that is, by a form of consensus building cutting across party and interest group lines, is evident. Both CDU/CSU leaders and Scharping and Gerhard Schröder from the SPD are involved. Despite frequent complaints by critics about paralysis and the failures of the federal government to address important problems, the overall record is at least mixed in this respect: "In the past two years ... radical and painful changes have been introduced without any trace of industrial unrest ... it is still possible to build consensus and compromise in the most unpromising circumstances. Which gives grounds for optimism that it may be much too soon to be worrying about the onset of political paralysis."[27] In the SPD, Schröder, a disappointed contender for the party leadership against Scharping, particularly cultivates industry ties in the energy area. He is apparently a proponent of a Grand Coalition. Along with Scharping, and to a lesser extent Lafontaine, Schröder appears to be seeking an access to power rather than confrontation, first of all through participation in consensual deliberations, and sooner or later through more formal governmental power. The trend towards policymaking outside the Bundestag seems accentuated by 1994. It remains to be seen whether the *Vermittlingsausschuss* (Reconciliation Committee) between Bundestag and Bundesrat will seek expanded power under its new chair, Oskar Lafontaine, given the dominant SPD role in state governments. This committee is one to observe carefully for its future role in the mixed conflictive-cooperative relationship between the government and the SPD.

If a major thorn for the CDU/CSU is the weakness of the CDU in state parliaments, and thus in the Bundesrat, the SPD must be concerned with the future role of the PDS, which may seek to establish itself nationwide, to the left of the SPD and Alliance 90/Greens. There are tensions among Social Democrats on whether to maintain strict isolation from this successor to the ruling party of the GDR, or to seek somehow to influence it. As long as the SPD accents its search for governmental power, and a Scharping-Schröder duo—with the less certain participation of Lafontaine—tends in the direction of a sort of informal Grand Coalition, the PDS will, in turn, tend to be isolated. However, the situation in the East has many unpredictable elements. Regional strongholds of parties may be a permanent feature of the German political landscape, as with the PDS in 1994, complicating the creation of stable majorities in Bonn or, in a few years, Berlin.

Finally, German foreign policy is another potentially unpredictable ingredient in the new German scene. "Germany is ... back,"
in the eyes of a keen foreign observer.[28] It is creating ties and relationships in various directions. Kohl made the further development
of the European Union, and Germany's participation in it, a key
theme of his campaign. However, there are still serious doubts
among many Germans, mostly on the left, about their country's
international role. They are skeptical about the propriety of participation, whatever the Basic Law says, even in assisting the UN in out-
of-area situations. Scharping has shown interest in sharing or
attaining power by his posture on such matters also. In December
1994 he sought to place pressure on Lafontaine and on Heidemarie
Wieczorek-Zeul, another prominent Social Democrat, who was also
a contestant against Scharping for party chair. He sought to bring
them around to the possible use of German missiles to defend the
withdrawal of UN forces from Bosnia, a position supported by the
government. The SPD is far from united on such topics, the Alliance
90/Greens even less so. Party squabbles about Germany's role at
times of international crisis, and in Europe, may well be accentuated
in the next several years.

Overall, then, what of "Germany's new politics" from the perspective of leadership questions and political constellations and coalitions? New is that some doors have been opened for a variety of
changes. It is not yet clear, however, how much short-term change
will actually move through these doors, and whether such changes
will be dramatic in effect over the long term. There are still structures
and practices which act as brakes on rapid or radical change.

Notes

1. Russell J. Dalton and Wilhelm Bürklin, "The German Party System and the
   Future," in Russell J. Dalton, ed., *The New Germany Votes* (Providence: Berg
   Publishers, 1993), 251, 252.

2. *The New York Times,* 21 January 1994.

3. Cf. for example M. Rainer Lepsius, "Die Prägung der politischen Kultur der
   Bundesrepublik durch institutionelle Ordnungen," in Lepsius, *Interessen, Ideen
   und Institutionen* (Opladen: Westdeutscher Verlag, 1990), 63–84.

4. Matthias Jung and Dieter Roth, "Kohls knappster Sieg," in *Aus Politik und Zeit-geschichte* B51–52, (23 December 1994): 4. Rather than cite a multitude of sources, including personal conversations and observations in Germany over the past several years, in connection with this brief survey of the roles of party leaders and candidates, reference is made here to sources such as the above-cited issue of *Aus Politik und Zeitgeschichte* (which also contains analyses by Renate Köcher of the Institut für Demoskopie, "Auf einer Woge der Euphorie," Jürgen W. Falter and Markus Klein, "Die Wähler der PDS bei der Bundestagwahl 1994," and Ursula Feist, "Nichtwähler, 1994"), the other chapters in the present volume, and the study by the Bereich Forschung und Beratung of the Konrad Adenauer Foundation: *Die Bundestagswahl vom 16.Oktober 1994: eine erste Analyse* (Sankt Augustin: KAS), 17 October 1994.

5. Cf. the study by one of Kohl's circle during this period: Wolfgang Bergsdorf, *Deutschland im Stress* (Bonn: Verlag Bonn Aktuell, 1993); a summary of some of the points in this volume, in English "Germany under Stress," in *German Comments* 30 (April 1993): 41–47.

6. "Noch zu Beginn des Jahres wurde ich als Auslaufmodell, als Dorfdepp der Nation gehandelt. Jetzt auf einmal bin ich ein Phänomen."—Helmut Kohl, interview in *Deutschland-Magazin* 26, no. 10 (1 October 1994): 7.

7. Cf., Günther Rieger, "'Parteienverdrossenheit' und 'Parteienkritik' in der Bundesrepublik Deutschland," and Christof Ehrhart and Eberhard Sandschneider, "Politikverdrossenheit: Kritische Anmerkungen zur Empirie, Wahrnehmung und Interpretation abnehmender politischer Partizipation," in *Zeitschrift für Parlaments-fragen* 25, no. 3 (August 1994): 441–58, 459–71.

8. Elisabeth Noelle-Neumann, *Die Demokratie geht rückwärts* (Allensbach: Institut für Demoskopie), 19 January 1994; summary also in *Frankfurter Allgemeine Zeitung* (FAZ), 19 January 1994. Note that the study shows support for "democracy" in general, revealing only distinctions in appreciation of parties vs. "leaders."

9. The profile of Kanther in *Der Spiegel* 47, no. 28 (12 July 1993), though written in the usual *Spiegel* jargon, is instructive.

10. Bergsdorf in *German Comments* 30 (April 1993); "Political Leadership as a Challenge of Communication," *German Comments* 18 (April 1990): 78–84.

11. Ibid.; Bergsdorf, "Vom Guten des Schlechten, *"Die Politische Meinung,* 243 (March–April 1989): 33; Wolfgang Schäuble "Erfolgreich regieren: Politikvermittlung und politische Führung," *Die Politische Meinung,* 242 (January–February 1989): 10ff.

12. Cited and partly quoted in *Der Spiegel* 47, no. 8 (22 February 1993) (on the "Zeitgeist"); Schäuble, *Und der Zukunft zugewandt* (Berlin: Siedler Verlag, 1994), 102–6, 176, 177.

13. *Und der Zukunft zugewandt.* On the reception with Kohl presenting the book to the public: *Frankfurter Rundschau,* 21 June 1994 ("Schäuble wirft den Deutschen Sattheit und Vollkasko Mentalität vor"). On Kohl's speeches, for example, see the indicated issues of the *Bulletin* of the Presse- und Informationsamt der Bundesregierung: "Die Rolle der Meinungsforschung in der freiheitlichen Demokratie," 12 May 1993; Standortbestimmung Deutschlands für die Herausforderungen der 90er Jahre," 27 January 1993; "Neue Prioritäten für

die Zukunftsgestaltung Deutschlands," 17 May 1993; "Neue Weichenstellung zur Gestaltung der Zukunft," 12 July 1993.

14. Bergsdorf in *German Comments* 18 (April 1990):82–83.

15. Cf. the data in Renate Köcher, "Auf einer Woge der Euphorie," *Aus Politik und Zeitgeschichte*, B51–52 (23 December 1994): 20–21, on voter preference for candidates who they believe have great influence within their parties.

16. On the concept of "coordination" as key to the German chancellor's governmental role in recent years, see several writings by Wolfgang Jäger, e.g., "Eine Lanze für das Kanzlerwahlverein," in Manfred Mols et al., eds., *Normative und institutionelle Ordnungs-probleme des modernen Staates* (Paderborn: Schöningh, 1990), 96–110, and *Wer regiert die Deutschen? Innenabsichten der Parteien-demokratie* (Zürich/Osnabrück: Fromm Verlag, 1994). New life for the "chancellor bonus" in the event of any shift toward a more pronounced multiparty system was foreseen by Gordon Smith in "The Resources of a German Chancellor," *West European Politics* 14, no. 2 (1991): 54–55.

17. Renate Köcher in *Aus Politik und Zeitgeschichte* B51–52 (1994): 21.

18. Erwin Scheuch, quoted in dpa telex despatch, 14 October 1994.

19. In addition to sources already cited for election figures and analyses, these writings should be noted: Dieter Oberndörfer, Gerd Mielke, and Ulrich Eith, "In den Siegesbechern der Parteien finden sich Wermutstropfen," *Frankfurter Rundschau*, 21 October 1994; Konrad Adenauer Foundation, *Bundestagswahl … 16. Oktober 1994*.

20. "Die Streitfragen werden verdeckt," *Frankfurter Allgemeine Zeitung*, 2 December 1994.

21. "Candidates have now become objects of identification, and flexible 'Ersatz-Parties,' but always with a 'policy-mix' tailored to the key political figure," Oberndörfer et al., in *Frankfurter Rundschau*, 21 October 1994.

22. Günter Hofmann, "Der Kanzler von der Sonnenseite," *Die Zeit*, 9 September 1994. In an earlier article, however, the same author finds the Social Democratic leaders no real alternative, being "lax and lame." Gunter Hofmann, "Die Enkel sind alt geworden," *Die Zeit*, 30 April 1993.

23. Heinrich Oberreuter, *Superwahljahr '94: Beobachtungen* (Passau: Selbstverlag, 1994) (Radio and press commentaries, 1994), 36–37. Professor of political science at the University of Passau, Oberreuter is now also director of the Academy for Political Education in Tutzing.

24. Karl Dietrich Bracher, quoted in Karlheinz Niclauss, *Kanzler-demokratie* (Stuttgart: Verlag W. Kohlhammer, 1988), 283.

25. Cf., for example, "Annäherung der CDU an die Grünen?" *Frankfurter Allgemeine Zeitung*, 14 November 1994; "Den Übergang regeln," *Der Spiegel* 50 (13 December 1994); Thomas-Kielinger, "Die unfertige Gesellschaft," *Rheinischer Merkur*, 14 October 1994. Minister-President Kurt Biedenkopf of Saxony, the most successful CDU politician at the state level in Germany, West or East, and a possible Kohl successor if West-East tensions intensify, is a major voice on economic and social restructuring, though kept at arm's length from Bonn by his long-time rival Kohl.

26. Cf., "Die SPD kann kommen," *Der Spiegel* 1 (2 January 1995): 18–21.

27. Christopher Parkes, "In Search of a New Consensus," *Financial Times* (21 November 1994): 10.

28. W. R. Smyser, "Dateline Berlin: Germany's New Vision," *Foreign Policy* 97 (winter 1994–95): 152. "The old nostrum about Germany as an economic giant but a political dwarf is embarrassingly out-of-date."

3

FOUR YEARS AND
SEVERAL ELECTIONS LATER

THE EASTERN GERMAN POLITICAL LANDSCAPE
AFTER UNIFICATION

HELGA A. WELSH

In 1990, at the time of German unification, it was generally agreed that the new Germany would be more than the sum of its parts. Now, more than four years later and after several elections, patterns of change have become more concrete.[1] The "super election year" of 1994 with nineteen elections, of which two were held in all of Germany and an additional nine in the former German Democratic Republic (GDR) alone,[2] sheds new light on unification dynamics and their impact upon the electoral and party landscape in Germany.

I will first outline some of the political, social, and economic changes that have taken place in eastern Germany since unification. Against this background, I will proceed to analyze the political landscape in the eastern part of Germany as it unfolded during the elections of 1994. My goal is twofold: to highlight the political situation in the former GDR and to emphasize those electoral developments that are of significance to policymaking in the unified Germany. Progress toward what I term consolidated unification has stressed the persistence of East-West differences. But, although party landscapes are changing, basic features of the party system and of conflict resolution have been reinforced by unification and by the elections of 1994.

The Former GDR: Between Transition and Consolidation

The recent regime transitions in Central and Eastern Europe extended far beyond the political realm and coincided with economic and social system transformation and, in some cases, even national reconfiguration. The decision-making overload was daunting, as were the perceived, as well as real, time pressures.[3] Mass mobilization, which propelled regime change in much of Central and Eastern Europe, proved to be short lived and was followed by a decrease in high levels of active public engagement in the political process. Above all, however, transition periods were marked by high levels of uncertainty in public and private lives. All post-Communist countries in Central and Eastern Europe have been affected by these transition dynamics. The former GDR is no exception, although unification has made it a special case. As a result, pressure to "catch up with modernization"[4] was more pronounced than in the rest of the region, as was the degree of uncertainty. Finally, the commanding authority of the West in political and economic matters added a special dimension to decision-making procedures, identity formation, and institutional changes.

Political transition periods have beginnings and they have ends. In the case of eastern Germany, the question of what constitutes the end of the transition phase is rather different than in the rest of Central and Eastern Europe. Since few doubted the democratic nature of the newly unified Germany and the implementation of democratic structures, progress toward consolidation is primarily measured according to the successful integration of the two Germanies. In other words, the transition is only accomplished once the goal of formal unification (the institutionalization of a democratic political system) *and* a certain degree of integration between the two Germanies have been achieved. Integration, however, implies more than assimilation; it also accepts the recognition of differences. Even if one assumes gradual, but steady, economic and social assimilation, it is worth asking whether it will be accompanied by similar changes in the political environment.[5]

Relatedly, there is a case for saying that consolidation has been reached once a relatively high degree of stability and gradual change have become the prevailing modes of operation. I argue that after the early years—during which life in the former GDR was characterized by high dependency on the West and an unusual degree of uncertainty regarding most aspects of life—signs of consolidation increasingly manifest themselves. Thus, the second all-German federal elections coincided with consolidated unification which, after the crisis of unification, is characterized by moves toward a more gradual approach toward the integration and normalization of relations between the two parts of Germany.

The initial phase of unification was marked by a high degree of uncertainty, particularly in the economic sector: in October 1994, 13.3 percent of eastern Germans were unemployed (western Germany: 7.9 percent), not counting those who were part of state-sponsored retraining measures. Between 1989 and 1993, the working population declined from 89 percent to 58 percent, falling slightly below employment levels which are customary for the western part of Germany.[6] Compared to other modern industrial societies, the GDR had a disproportionate number of people who were employed in industrial and agricultural sectors as opposed to the service sector. In the industrial sector alone, only one of three workers is still employed, and the number of people working in the agricultural sector has plummeted from 9.9 percent in 1989 to 3.9 percent in 1993 (western Germany: 3 percent).

As a result, a high degree of professional mobility was required of eastern German citizens. Traditionally, and in contrast to work habits in the United States, this is not one of the strong traits of German professional culture, East or West. According to one survey, in 1991–92, 22 percent of employees changed their vocation, 21 percent their place of work, 14 percent started retraining measures, 11 percent changed their job within the same place of work, 20 percent worked fewer hours, and 26 percent were unemployed at one time or another.[7]

Despite these dramatic changes and the accompanying assimilation in occupational structures between eastern and western Germany, the distinctions are still important, reflecting the substantial contrast in economic organization prior to 1989 (see table 3.1).

TABLE 3.1

OCCUPATIONAL STRUCTURE IN GERMANY (EAST AND WEST) (IN %)

	Blue-Collar	White-Collar	Self-Employed
Germany (East)	44.1	50.0	5.8
Germany (West)	35.7	54.0	10.3
Berlin	30.4	60.9	8.7

Source: *Statistisches Jahrbuch 1994 für die Bundesrepublik Deutschland*, 116.

Although it is to be expected that economic dislocation results in spillover effects into the social sphere, the actual reverberations greatly surpassed expectations. The sheer magnitude of political and economic changes created pressures of psychological and sociological adaptation, as well as everyday living problems. Between 1989 and 1990 marriages declined by 22 percent and by 50 percent between

1990 and 1991. The birthrate saw an equally drastic downturn; at the end of 1993 it was at a level less than half of that in 1989 while the rate in the West had remained basically unchanged. Such drastic demographic changes are normally only associated with wartime experiences.[8] More recent data indicate a slow process of "normalization," although it will take considerable time to return to the pre-unification levels (see table 3.2).

TABLE 3.2

MARRIAGES AND BIRTHS IN THE NEW FEDERAL STATES
AND BERLIN (EAST)

Year	Marriages	Births
1989	130,989	198,922
1990	101,913	178,476
1991	50,529	107,769
1992	48,232	88,320
1993	49,257	80,548

Source: *Zur wirtschaftlichen und sozialen Lage in den neuen Bundesländern. Vierteljahreszeitschrift.* Ed. Statistical Federal Office, Wiesbaden (August 1994).

Initially, high levels of migration from East to West and low numbers from West to East characterized the situation in Germany. For example, in 1990, 338,700 easterners came to the West, but only 35,600 westerners moved eastward. However, within three years the migration rate—which initially had acted as a major incentive to advance the timetable for unification—declined substantially. In 1993, only 53,450 more people moved westward compared to those settling in the East.

The unmodified transfer of the western model in 1990 was conditioned on a broad institutional consensus in the West and insufficient opposition to this model in the East.[9] In addition, it has been argued that—contrary to the notion that periods of change unlock possibilities for considerable institutional renewal—the intense uncertainty of a situation may prompt retention of old patterns.[10] Although formal organizational structures were quickly put into place, they were often little more than institutional shells whose functioning, it was reasoned, depended on expert assistance from the West. Since unification, at one time or another, approximately 20,000 civil servants from the West have been employed in the East. In general, the higher the position in the administrative sector, the greater the likelihood that this position is occupied by a western German. Between 1990 and 1994, three out of five eastern German prime ministers were western

Germans, as were the majority of justice, economics, and finance ministers. Since 1993, the employment of western German administrators in the East has been declining substantially, although its overall magnitude is difficult to estimate since many civil servants have taken permanent positions in the East.[11] For example, in the first half of 1993, 8,337 western German civil servants provided assistance in the eastern part of Germany. In Mecklenburg-West Pomerania almost 3,000 had been employed between 1990 and 1993. Of those, nearly two-thirds returned to their original place of work in the West, but 677 decided to settle in the East.[12]

In general, élite change in the eastern part of Germany has been far-reaching. The new political élite shares few commonalities with the old one: it is substantially younger (on average the parliamentarians in the new Länder are less than fifty years old), is primarily trained in technical (as opposed to "ideological") professions, and has little previous political or administrative experience.[13] This is correct even considering that the percentage of politicians who had been card-carrying members of the previous bloc parties and the SED is high, in particular among eastern German state parliamentarians.[14] But in the majority of cases, their political involvement had been restricted to the local level which carried little political responsibility and can hardly be considered training ground for state or national leadership positions.

The somewhat fragile, evolving nature of political circumstances in the first four years of parliamentary activity in the new federal states revealed itself through relatively frequent changes in government compositions and in party affiliation. Especially affected was Saxony-Anhalt: between 1990 and 1994, the position of prime minister switched hands three times, and only two ministries were headed by the same individual over the entire period. Twelve MPs changed their party affiliation, some repeatedly; six parliamentarians resigned because of documented *Stasi* affiliation. Continued electoral volatility and intraparty differences led to a substantial turnover rate among state parliamentarians in the state elections in 1994: for example, in Brandenburg only forty-seven of eighty-eight incumbents were reelected, and in Saxony-Anhalt approximately one-third of parliamentarians were replaced.[15]

Elections and Party Development

One way progress toward political consolidation can be measured is with reference to the degree of party concentration. Compared to other countries in the region of Central and Eastern Europe, the level of party fractionalization is notably lower in the former GDR. However, this is not primarily the outcome of indigenous processes, but the result of adoption of the western German party system.

On the one hand, the relative ease with which the main features of the western German party system became established in a matter of months in the new federal states is notable.[16] This is evident in the considerable overlap in political actors, the dominance of the two major parties, CDU and SPD, and the rejection of right-wing parties such as the Republikaner in East and West in national elections.[17] On the other hand, despite patterns of similarity, many differences endure, and others are becoming more pronounced.

The elections of 1994 emphasized the continued structural weakness of the political parties in the East and the accompanying repercussions, such as shortages of candidates to run for elections at the local level. Notable membership decline among the former bloc parties[18] and the inability to attract new members to the newly constituted parties, such as Alliance 90/Greens and the SPD, are characteristic of the former GDR. The membership decline also holds true for the PDS, although its organizational infrastructure, including the number of members, still surpasses those of the other parties (see table 3.3).

TABLE 3.3

PARTY MEMBERSHIP DEVELOPMENT IN THE
EASTERN STATES OF GERMANY

Party	December 1990	December 1993
CDU	109,709[a]	83,794
FDP	106,696	29,754
PDS	284,632	131,406[b]
Alliance 90/Greens	2,037	2,715
SPD	24,400	26,000

[a]December 1991.
[b]The figures for the PDS include Berlin (1993: 23,633 members) and the western federal states (1993: 1,180 members).

Source: Compiled by the author according to data provided by state and national party headquarters.

Difficulties in membership recruitment can be traced to distrust of political parties, fostered by over forty years of SED socialism, the freedom of not having to join a party, and the lack of identification with the new or substantially reorganized political parties. In some parties, membership also entails pressures toward active political involvement. For example, in the SPD more than 40 percent of its members in the new Bundesländer hold at least one political office and among Alliance 90/Greens the percentage is still higher. Comparable problems of weak institutionalization can be observed at the level of interest group representation.[19] As in other aspects of political development, some similarities with the other post-Communist countries can be discerned since problems of establishing institutions of political pluralism are common across the region.[20]

As in practically all aspects of political life, western advisers have played and continue to play an important part in the party development in the eastern part of Germany. In the West, party structures are entrenched to the point that the power of the political parties has been criticized for its pervasiveness in all aspects of political life. In this environment of party dominance it has been interesting to observe their difficulty to influence significantly the institutionalization of the parties in the East.

Unification and the Elections of 1994

From a strictly numerical point of view, nationwide elections are determined by western Germans since eligible voters from the West outnumber those from the East by a margin of 4 to 1. But eastern Germany's impact on the elections of 1994 was significant. In the months prior to the national elections of 1994, communal elections had taken place in all five new states, and state elections in all but Thuringia and Mecklenburg-West Pomerania, whose state elections were held simultaneously with the federal elections. The results revealed important electoral shifts that were to influence the national elections in October as well.

At the beginning of 1994, the chances for the governing coalition of CDU/CSU and FDP to win the elections in October continued to look as dim as they had for the last three years—in considerable measure because of the sharp decline of approval in the new federal states: in July 1993 only 20 percent of eastern Germans would have voted for the CDU; the FDP remained relatively constant at 6 percent. But within a short period of time, electoral fortunes changed. During the spring and summer of 1994 it became clear that the federal elections of 1994 were preceded by an increasingly positive outlook on the part of many easterners; the perception that "the worst is over" contributed to the overall degree of electoral stability for the CDU in relation to 1990.[21]

The time seemed opportune for the governing coalition; since
1992 economic growth rates in the eastern part of Germany have
been positive (10 percent in 1992, 7 percent in 1993, 9 percent in
1994).[22] In October 1994 the general economic situation in the
eastern part of Germany was evaluated with the greatest optimism
since unification. Twelve months earlier, 58 percent of eastern Germans had judged the economic situation as poor; now the number
had declined to an all-time low of 32 percent.[23] Unemployment figures and income differences between East and West were declining
slowly but continuously in 1994.[24] The perception of overall economic upswing—even if it not directly related to personal better-
ment—governed the attitude of many eastern Germans during the
summer and fall of 1994. But only the CDU profited, while the fate
of the FPD started to settle below the crucial threshold level of 5
percent. At the same time, many remained disappointed with the
process of unification and the overall political and economic circumstances, and they sought political change. The major electoral shift
during 1994 favored the PDS, not the SPD.

The electoral outcomes of 1994 are notable for the dominance of
the two major parties and by marked East-West differences regarding
the roles of smaller parties. Eastern Germans have added the post-
Communist PDS to the political landscape, although its future continues to be uncertain.[25] By doing so, they brought attention to the
lingering effects of unification and to certain stipulations of the German electoral law that had been given only passing attention in the
past. According to the electoral provisions, a party that fails to overcome the electoral threshold level of 5 percent for Germany as a whole
can still be represented in parliament if it secures at least three directly
elected seats.[26] Accordingly, four members of the PDS (one more than
required) who were directly elected in the eastern part of Berlin[25] were
sufficient to assure the presence of PDS members in the Federal Diet.

Once the PDS stopped nothing short of gaining 19.9 percent in
the state elections of Saxony-Anhalt (which constituted an increase
of 7.9 percent in comparison to 1990) in June 1994, benign negligence toward the party by most western politicians quickly became
keen interest. The attitude of the established political parties toward
the PDS became a major factor in coalition strategies, and national
electoral campaign tactics in Germany changed noticeably. The federal elections campaign—which otherwise lacked significant sources
of disagreement—shifted to a crusade against the former Communists, in particular as far as the ruling CDU was concerned. The success of this strategy remains doubtful: the PDS's meager election

result in the West with 1 percent of the total vote was to be expected. The 19.8 percent of eastern Germans who voted for the PDS seemed unimpressed by the political campaign against former Communists and voted for it in spite of it, or maybe partly because of it. In many ways, the vote for the PDS can be described as one of protest and identity manifestation, not one of nostalgia for some sort of GDR socialism. The regional character of the vote for the PDS remains the clearest indication of the differences between the East and the West.

The year 1994 proved to be one of electoral defeats for the FDP. Its weakness as a programmatic party that has little more to offer than being a convenient coalition partner became apparent throughout 1994. At the end of the year, the FDP remained a national power only because of its support in the West, much of it borrowed from the CDU.[28] A coalition partner in all five states in the East in 1990, the Liberals fell below the 5 percent threshold level in state and national elections four years later. There is little doubt that the substantial decline and hence the rejection of the FDP in all states in the East highlighted the electoral weakness of the Liberal party in all of Germany. No other party has drawn more pronounced and different evaluations between the eastern and western electorate,[29] and no other party has seen a more dramatic membership decline than the FDP.

East-West Comparison of Voting Behavior

As far as the elections of 1994 are concerned, scholarly interest in the new federal states centers especially on the impact of party development on electoral outcomes, the reasons for electoral choices (and here the relationship between party identification and issue voting), and causes and consequences of electoral volatility. Electoral results are determined by a combination of party identification rooted in class differences, by long-term political party identification, and by perceptions of the current political situation and thus by political events and the belief in the capability of political leaders. In West European politics, it has long been taken for granted that party identification (based on social criteria and traditional loyalty), although declining in overall significance, still serves as a reliable predictor of electoral outcomes. But it has been argued that in the context of eastern Germany, the "level of nonidentification with any of the political parties" remains "probably the most important difference between East and West Germany."[30] Thus, the trend toward weaker partisan bonds and a decline of traditional socioeconomic ties to specific parties—which has already been visible in the West since the 1980s—has been reinforced by the electoral behavior of the eastern Germans.[31]

The social profile of eastern and western voters differs in particular in two important respects: class and religious affiliation. As outlined earlier, despite far-reaching changes in the last several years, the proportion of blue-collar workers in the East remains higher than in the West, and the proportion of independent entrepreneurs remains much below the western level. As far as religious affiliation is concerned, the differences between the two parts of Germany are striking. Fifty-five percent of eastern Germans claim no religious affiliation (western Germany: 10 percent) and only 7 percent belong to the Catholic church (western Germany: 41 percent). In theory, this could have had grave consequences for the CDU, which traditionally has found most support among the religious middle class and, in particular, among Catholics and the self-employed.

In 1990 the electoral success of the CDU in the new federal states stunned political observers and the interested public. But the anticipated drastic decline in voting support that seemed certain in 1992 and 1993 did not materialize in 1994; the CDU lost only 3.3 percent of votes in the former GDR (western Germany: -2.3 percent). In contrast to western Germany, where the SPD emerged as the party with the most votes, the CDU remained the strongest party in the eastern part of Germany.

Most workers in the former GDR continue to favor the CDU, although it should be noted that between 1990 and 1994 the percentage of working-class votes has shifted somewhat to the SPD. At the time of the Volkskammer election in March 1990, 47 percent of workers backed the CDU-led "Alliance for Germany," and nine months later the CDU was able to increase this share to 50 percent. In 1994, 41 percent of workers remained loyal to the CDU, whereas 35 percent voted for the SPD (1990: 25 percent). In the West, however, workers continue to prefer the SPD: every second working-class vote was cast for the Social Democrats (CDU: 35 percent). In East and West, the majority of voters who claim a religious affiliation is drawn to the CDU. However, the differentiation between Protestant and Catholic votes remains insignificant in the East but powerful in the West, where the SPD is stronger among Protestants and the CDU among Catholics.

But the surface of continuity and gradual change is misleading, as is easily revealed if one compares electoral outcomes across several elections. For example in Saxony, the CDU gained 38.1 percent in the elections to the European Parliament and 39.2 percent in the communal elections in June, but 58.1 percent in the state elections of September, and 48 percent in the federal elections in October. In Brandenburg, the SPD won 36.9 percent in the elections to the European Parliament in June, 54.1 percent in the state elections in September, and 45 percent in the federal elections in October 1994. Contrast this, however, with the voting pattern in Mecklenburg-West Pomerania and in Thuringia where the fluctuation of votes for the CDU was contained within a much more restricted range.

Electoral volatility even within relatively short time periods is an indicator of the increased importance of "personalized votes" in eastern Germany, in particular in communal and state elections. Regional "czars," such as Manfred Stolpe (SPD) in Brandenburg and Kurt Biedenkopf (CDU) in Saxony, account for much of the spectacular success of their respective parties, and when their own offices were at stake in the state elections of September 1994, the voters championed them. This support influenced the other elections, but to a lesser degree. In those states where the personality factor was less dominant, such as in Saxony-Anhalt or Mecklenburg-West Pomerania, electoral volatility was less noticeable.

The fact that thirteen of the sixteen "excess" seats (*Überhangsmandate*)[32] to the national parliament were gained in the East—which in many ways made the continuation of the Kohl government feasible—may indicate a significant split between first and second votes in selected districts of the former GDR where particular candidates were given preference over their parties.[33] However, these occurrences were in fact quite isolated. In contrast to the United States where the personalized aspect of voting is favored by the electoral law and the nature of the party system, German voting behavior traditionally has been centered on party lines.[34] In lieu of strong party identification in the East, it is therefore hardly surprising that the personalized aspect of the proportional electoral law in Germany has recently received wider attention. This trend may have been further strengthened by the ideological similarities of the two major parties, CDU and SPD.

For several years, the term *Politikverdrossenheit* ("disenchantment with politics") has helped to explain such phenomena as the emergence of new social movements, the weakening of voting alignments, and the decline in party membership and in voter turnout. Although nobody expected a continuation of the 93.6 percent participation rate reached at the time of the Volkskammer election of 1990, few were prepared for a decline to the 74.5 percent turnout rate in the former GDR just eight months later at the first all-German federal elections. What remains important, however, is the continued East-West difference in voter turnout. In the West it climbed slightly from 78.6 percent in 1990 to 80.6 percent in 1994, whereas 72.9 percent voted in the eastern half of Germany, which constitutes a slight decline of 1.6 percent in relation to 1990. A lower electoral turnout in the East is generally observable at the regional and local levels as well.

The generally lower voting morale in the East is linked to a higher degree of alienation from the political system. But the level of political participation as seen in electoral activities should not be correlated too closely with political stability or interpreted solely as an indicator for approval or disapproval, in particular since no longitudinal data are available for comparison.[35] Decline of political participation is not limited to the former GDR, but has become a trademark of post-Communist politics in general where a highly mobilized public initially set the framework for the regime transfer, and then retreated once again into the private realm. Though a voter turnout of 72.9 percent is low for standards which were established in the western half of Germany, in international comparison it is still considered quite high, even among established democracies.

East-West Differences and the "New" Germany

Regional political differences within Germany are no novelty; in the "old" Federal Republic the differences between the predominantly Protestant North and the Catholic South have been persistent, as have urban-rural differences. North-South differences exist in the former GDR as well, and in some ways they mirror the greater support of the political left in the North, whereas the CDU is strongest in Saxony and Thuringia which have historically been hailed as strongholds of the political left. Unification has added yet another dimension to regionalism.

During the most recent national elections, the former GDR has asserted its distinctiveness in more than one way. It remains to be seen whether the PDS will continue as a regional party; its increased influence goes well beyond its reelection to the federal parliament since it is represented in all state parliaments and most communes in the former East Germany.[36] The split among the parties to the political left (SPD, PDS, Alliance 90/Greens) affords new possibilities of coalition building and increased electoral competition. The posture toward the PDS, the question of membership of former SED members in the established parties, and East-West issue cleavages are becoming more pronounced within the SPD, but its divisive potential also impacts the other parties. Different partisan choices have their roots in diverse political preferences. Although basic democratic value orientations are shared in both parts of Germany,[37] a fuller understanding of political attitudes in the unified Germany demands further inquiry. Despite a broadly based acceptance of democratic norms in both parts of Germany, substantial disparities in political opinions exist. Satisfaction with democracy characterized the attitude of 66 percent of western Germans and 41 percent of eastern Germans. In 1994, 71 percent of eastern Germans endorsed taking an attitude of normality toward the PDS, while only 44 percent of western Germans concurred. The electoral rule according to which three direct mandates allow for representation in the national parliament was endorsed by 73 percent of eastern Germans but only by 37 percent of western Germans. In the East 44 percent agreed with the model of the minority government in Saxony-Anhalt in which the SPD and Alliance 90/Greens can govern only with the tangible support of the PDS or the CDU; only 15 percent in the West approved of this move.[38]

The electoral results of 1994 have revealed that, far from an electoral adjustment, further differentiation is characteristic of electoral politics in the new Germany. The extent to which stable partisan bonds are beginning to emerge is uncertain: were eastern Germans behaving only rationally when they voted for the "party of unification" in 1990, and in 1994 for the party which was perceived as most capable of dealing with the economic problems in the East? Or did they vote according to a diffuse party loyalty which they had gained via indirect exposure to the western German political parties prior to unification and via subsequent direct exposure? Arguments can be made for either interpretation,[39] both in 1990 and in 1994. The continued strong support for the CDU, although declining somewhat, may point to already existing diffuse forms of partisan identification. It may, at the same time, indicate the inclination of many eastern Germans to vote for the party that promises continued economic improvements.

However, looking at the electoral results of the other parties, substantial reorientations have taken place between 1990 and 1994. The SPD was able to garner 7.2 percent more votes than in 1990, and the PDS increased its percentage by 8.7 percent. At the same time, the FDP lost 9.4 percent and Alliance 90/Greens 1.4 percent. This indicates major shifts among parties and weak partisan bonds. Contrary to many expectations, consolidation in unification, then, may be marked by the acceptance of differences between the two parts of Germany and not the expectation of continued assimilation in all aspects of life. Although there are signs toward consolidated unification and of shared political attitudes, tangibly different political opinions in the two Germanies continue to exist. However, this may be indicative of consolidation as well: the pressure toward assimilation is declining, and a new assertiveness in the East is emerging.

Despite these variations, there is evidence that one distinct feature of policymaking in Germany may have been reinforced by unification, one which acts as a powerful mechanism for conflict resolution between East and West. Although the decision-making process leading to German unification has deviated in some ways from the usual pattern of inclusive negotiation, it has since reverted to the more customary traits of cooperative federalism and opposition.[40] This tendency has been reinforced by the current power distribution between the two houses of parliament. In the Federal Diet, the CDU/CSU and FDP coalition government is able to rule with a slight majority of ten votes, but in the Federal Council the roles are reversed since the SPD holds forty-one votes and the CDU only ten. Seventeen votes belong to federal states that are currently being ruled by Grand Coalition governments; traditionally they abstain from voting. Differing majorities in the two houses of parliament make cooperation in policymaking imperative, as does the persistent need for coalition government at the national level and in most federal states.

The history of power-sharing arrangements is quite different in the different parts of Germany: in the western case it is related to neocorporatist arrangements and insistence on decentralized power structures; in the eastern part it has been reinforced by the common and successful experience of roundtable negotiations. A tendency toward inclusive government was one of the early features of parliamentary activity in the East, and its decline in recent years has been lamented by many.[41] Although many have observed that unification has changed the face of Germany, a case can be made that many features will indeed remain the same, even if they have evolved somewhat in the process.

Notes

1. For an early account, see Manfred G. Schmidt, "Political Consequences of German Unification," *West European Politics* 15, no. 4 (1992): 1–15. See also Peter Pulzer, "Unified Germany: A Normal State?" *German Politics* 3, no. 1 (1994): 1–17.

2. The territory of the former GDR is commonly referred to as the new federal states (Bundesländer). In addition to the all-German elections, in 1994 all new federal states held state elections as well as, with the exception of Brandenburg, communal elections. Communal elections in Brandenburg took place in December 1993.

3. Rose and Haerpfer aptly use the term "simultaneity of stress" to describe the situation. See Richard Rose and Christian Haerpfer, "Mass Response to Transformation in Post-Communist Societies," *Europe-Asia Studies* 46, no. 1 (1994): 3–28.

4. See Jürgen Habermas, *Die nachholende Revolution* (Frankfurt am Main: Suhrkamp, 1990).

5. For a critical assessment of the provision of the Basic Law which postulates "uniformity in standards of living beyond the borders of a federal state" (art. 72), see Meinhard Miegel, "Wie realistisch und wünschenswert ist die Angleichung der Lebensverhältnisse in West und Ost," *BISS public* 4, no. 14 (1994): 5–9.

6. As an aggregate group, more eastern than western Germans (in particular women and elderly) are interested in employment. It explains, at least partly, the higher percentage of unemployed and the greater disinterest to accept part-time as opposed to full-time jobs in the East. See *Der Spiegel* 46 (14 November 1994): 123–24.

7. *Sozialreport 1992. Daten und Fakten zur sozialen Lage in den neuen Bundesländern* (Berlin: Morgenbuch Verlag, 1993), 92–93.

8. Wolfgang Zapf, "Die Transformation in der ehemaligen DDR und die soziologische Theorie der Modernisierung," *Berliner Journal für Soziologie* 4, no. 4 (1994): 295. See also Nicholas Eberstadt, "Demographic Shocks in Eastern Germany, 1989–93," *Europe-Asia Studies* 46, no. 3 (1994): 519–33. It should be noted, however, that these demographic changes are not only related to social and economic uncertainty, but also to newly available possibilities which may make the postponement of marriage and birth desirable. See *Süddeutsche Zeitung*, 27 December 1994, p. 4.

9. See Hans-Ulrich Derlien, "German Unification and Bureaucratic Transformation," *International Political Science Review* 14, no. 4 (1993): 331.

10. See Roland Czada, "Schleichweg in die 'Dritte Republik.' Politik der Vereinigung und politischer Wandel in Deutschland," *Politische Vierteljahresschrift* 35, no. 2 (1994): 245–70.

11. Others will, in all likelihood, return when additional monetary incentives for employment in the East cease on 1 January 1995.

12. See information provided to the author by the *Staatskanzleien* of Thuringia and Saxony-Anhalt, as well as by the Ministry of the Interior of Mecklenburg-West Pomerania.

13. See my paper "Political Elites in Transition: The Case of Eastern Germany," delivered at the annual meeting of the American Political Science Association, 1–4 September 1994, New York, New York.

14. Thomas A. Baylis refers to former Communist party members who occupy positions of influence in post-Communist administrations across Central and Eastern Europe as the "lower nobility." See his comparative assessment of post-Communist élites, "Plus Ça Change? Transformation and Continuity Among East European Elites," *Communist and Post-Communist Studies* 27, no. 3 (1994): 315–28.

15. At the national level, the rate of reelection for incumbents in the Federal Republic is 78 percent. See Bernhard Boll and Andrea Römmele, "Strukturelle Vorteile der Amtsinhaber? Wahlchancen von Parlamentariern im internationalen Vergleich," *Zeitschrift für Parlamentsfragen* 25, no. 4 (1994): 544.

16. See Michaela W. Richter, "Exiting the GDR: Political Movements and Parties Between Democratization and Westernization," in M. Donald Hancock and Helga A. Welsh, eds., *German Unification. Process and Outcomes* (Boulder, Colo.: Westview Press, 1994), 93–137.

17. The Republikaner have not been able to garner substantial support in the new Bundesländer. But, as is well known, lack of support for right-wing political parties is not accompanied by a similar lack of right-wing activities. For further details, see the chapter by Michael Minkenberg in this volume.

18. In 1990, the CDU merged with the German Peasant Party (DBD), the newly established Democratic Awakening (DA), and the German Social Union (DSU). The FDP incorporated the FDP-East, the German Forum Party, and the former satellite parties LDPD and NDPD.

19. For example, between 1992 and 1993 the membership in the German Trade Union Federation in the eastern states declined by 14.3 percent (western Germany: 3.2 percent). For a general discussion of this problem, see Bernhard Boll, "Interest Organisation and Intermediation in the New Länder," *German Politics* 3, no. 1 (1994): 114–128.

20. See, for example, Paul G. Lewis, "Democratization and Party Development in Eastern Europe," *Democratization* 1, no. 3 (1994): 391–405.

21. See Richard Hilmer and Rita Müller-Hilmer, "Die Stimmung stimmt für Kohl," *Die Zeit*, 7 October 1994, pp. 6–8.

22. However, even at those impressive growth rates—which are mainly due to western transfer payments—it will take at least until the end of the decade to make up for the enormous decline in economic output between 1989 and 1991. For a more detailed analysis, see Irwin Collier's chapter in this volume.

23. See Forschungsgruppe Wahlen, *Politbarometer*, div. issues.

24. Income differentials between East and West declined by approximately 2 percent during 1993, although sectoral differences are important. In the public sector, wage differences had been reduced to 20 percent but, to take one example, in the textile industry it still lingered at around 44 percent.

25. For a detailed analysis of the PDS, see the chapter by Gerald R. Kleinfeld in this volume.

26. For the first all-German elections in 1990, a one-time exception had been negotiated. Accordingly, representation in the national parliament was secured once a party reached the threshold level of 5 percent in eastern or western Germany.

27. Put differently, 257,541 votes in East Berlin were sufficient to assure the return of the PDS to the national parliament.

28. For more details, see the chapter by Christian Søe in this volume.

29. Max Kaase and Hans-Dieter Klingemann, "The Cumbersome Way to Partisan Orientations in a 'New' Democracy: The Case of the Former GDR," in M. Kent Jennings and Thomas E. Mann, eds., *Elections at Home and Abroad. Essays in Honor of Warren E. Miller* (Ann Arbor: University of Michigan Press, 1994), 123–56.

30. Kaase and Klingemann, 137.

31. Hans-Joachim Veen and Peter Gluchowski, "Die Anhängerschaften der Parteien vor und nach der Einheit—eine Langfristbetrachtung von 1953 bis 1993," *Zeitschrift für Parlamentsfragen* 25, no. 2 (1994): 184–85.

32. For an explanation of "excess seats," see the section on electoral law by David P. Conradt. In 1990, the CDU had gained all six "excess seats" in eastern Germany.

33. In the aftermath of the elections, the fact that far fewer votes are necessary to secure a direct mandate as opposed to one that is gained through the normal channel of the second vote has drawn considerable attention. Alliance 90/Greens have brought the issue to the attention of the Federal Constitutional Court which is expected to rule on the constitutionality of the "excess seats" in 1995.

34. In a recent study Max Kaase concludes that in Germany, "There is no evidence now available that candidate factors are growing in importance in explaining voting choices." But he argues against generalizing his finding at this stage of political development and cites the central role of the political élite in political transitions, such as the one in eastern Germany. Max Kaase, "Is There Personalization in Politics? Candidates and Voting Behavior in Germany," *International Political Science Review* 15, no. 3 (1990): 211–30.

35. Christof Ehrhart and Eberhard Sandschneider, "Politikverdrossenheit: Kritische Anmerkungen zur Empirie, Wahrnehmung und Interpretation abnehmender politischer Partizipation," *Zeitschrift für Parlamentsfragen* 25, no. 3 (1994): 440–58; and Klaus Armingeon, "Gründe und Folgen geringer Wahlbeteiligung," *Kölner Zeitschrift für Soziologie und Sozialpsychologie* 46, no. 1 (1994): 43–64.

36. According to Lothar Bisky, the PDS has been able to win approximately 6,000 seats in different representative institutions during 1994. See *Süddeutsche Zeitung*, 27 December 1994, p. 6.

37. For the most recent analysis, see Russell J. Dalton, "Communists and Democrats: Democratic Attitudes in the Two Germanies," *British Journal of Political Science* 24, no. 4 (1994): 469–93.

38. These figures were taken from *Politbarometer* (ed. Forschungsgruppe Wahlen, Mannheim) and reflect political opinions during the spring and summer of 1994.

39. See Thomas Emmert, "Politische Ausgangslage vor der Bundestagswahl 1994. Entwicklung der Parteien, Themen und Kandidaten in Ost und West," in Wilhelm Bürklin and Dieter Roth, eds., *Das Superwahljahr. Deutschland vor*

unkalkulierbaren Regierungsmehrheiten? (Cologne: Bund, 1994), 56–57; Kaase and Klingemann, "The Cumbersome Way to Partisan Orientations," 139; Carsten Bluck and Henry Kreikenbom, "Die Wähler in der DDR: Nur issue-orientiert oder auch parteigebunden?," *Zeitschrift für Parlamentsfragen* 22, no. 3 (1991): 495–502.

40. Unification negotiations during 1990 were dominated by the Chancellor's Office and the Ministry of the Interior; the decision-making process neglected in particular the Länder governments and the parties in the national parliament. For a detailed analysis, see Razeen Sally and Douglas Webber, "The German Solidarity Pact: A Case Study in the Politics of the Unified Germany," *German Politics* 3, no. 1 (1994): 18–46.

41. For further details, see my paper "Political Elites in Transitions."

4

THE MEDIA AND THE CAMPAIGN IN THE NEW GERMANY

HOLLI A. SEMETKO AND
KLAUS SCHOENBACH

Introduction

With German unification in 1990, the media and party systems also merged. Since unification, there have been important developments in the media system that may have implications for German politics and public opinion about political parties, leaders, and issues. We discuss the developments in the German media landscape since 1990 and the political parties' communication strategies in the 1994 Bundestag election. We also assess how TV news coverage of politics developed over this period by comparing coverage in 1990 and 1994 during the "hot phase" of the Bundestag election campaigns.

Developments in the German Media System

TELEVISION AND RADIO

Until the 1980s, broadcasting in West Germany was based entirely on a public service model, funded primarily by license fees. Television consisted of the ARD (the first national channel) and its regional affiliates, and the ZDF (the second national channel). Radio comprised about forty regional services and one nationwide service (Deutschlandfunk). The first commercial broadcasting channels were established in early 1984 after considerable political debate. They are funded entirely by advertising. While the new private radio stations are confined to a specific locale or region, private television channels were defined as national in scope. In 1990, the year of the first all-German election, four commercial TV services were German-based organizations and provided general appeal programming: RTL (at that time called RTLplus), SAT.1, Pro7, and Tele5. There were also some foreign channels available, including Music Television (MTV) and Sky's Super Channel. Originally, the private channels were available only via cable, but nowadays most households in the East and West receive at least RTL and SAT.1 over the air.

Prior to the 1990 Bundestag election, the broadcast system in the eastern part of the country had remained for the most part in its original form. In addition to DFF1 and DFF2—the two national (East German) public service television channels—only a small proportion of the public was able to receive RTL and SAT.1, the two most popular private channels in the West. Most eastern viewers in 1990 had to choose from only four TV services: ARD, ZDF, DFF1, and DFF2. In early 1991, legislation did away with the old centralized television system in the East, and two new regional broadcast organizations with corresponding channels were introduced, as DFF1 and DFF2 disappeared. These still are MDR (Mitteldeutscher Rundfunk) for Saxony, Saxony-Anhalt, and Thuringia—which is also responsible for MDR3, the regional television channel that is affiliated with ARD—and ORB (Ostdeutscher Rundfunk Brandenburg) which, like MDR and every other regional affiliate in the country, provides a regional window in the ARD's programming between 6 and 8 p.m. in the evenings. Finally, Mecklenburg-West Pomerania, the fifth of the new Länder, joined the NDR (Norddeutscher Rundfunk), which continued to serve Lower Saxony, Hamburg, and Schleswig-Holstein. East Berlin is now served by the formerly West-Berlin-based SFB (Sender Freies Berlin). The new regional public service channels are funded by license fees and advertising, in the same way that the older public service channels are funded. As are all regional public broadcasting outlets in the country, these are organized or administered under the umbrella of the ARD.

In the four years since 1990, the public service channels lost considerable ground to the private ones, as audiences turned more frequently to the latter for both entertainment and news programming. As a consequence, the advertising revenue rates for the public channels dropped significantly. This had the most impact on the ZDF television service which receives a larger portion of its operating budget from advertising than from license fees in comparison with ARD. The additional channels that have gained audiences include DSF (which is like the sports channel ESPN), VOX (a general appeal channel like RTL), N-TV (the German news channel like CNN),

Pro7, Kabelkanal and RTL2 (mostly for movies), and Premiere (a pay movie channel).

In addition to many new private radio stations (up from about forty throughout Germany in 1984 to 250 by 1994), instead of one national public service radio station in the country as a whole (Deutschlandfunk), there are now two. The new station—Deutschlandradio—consists of former East German DS Kultur and of RIAS1 (formerly the United States-administered radio station in Berlin). Radio has become a more important medium for news and information over the past decade because of its ability to reach people not reached by other news media (particularly adolescents) with at least small amounts of such information.

So by 1994, citizens living in the eastern part of the country had a much wider range of TV channels than in 1990. As in 1990, eastern Germans in 1993—the latest available figures—spent more time watching TV than western Germans. This was, on average, almost three-and-a-half hours (209 minutes) daily for people fourteen years of age and older, whereas in the West it was under three hours (168 minutes).[1]

Whereas the public service channels are equally popular in both parts of the country, the greater amount of time spent by eastern Germans in front of the TV set is mostly due to viewing private channels and RTL, SAT.1, and PRO7 in particular (table 4.1).

TABLE **4.1**

AVERAGE AMOUNT OF TIME SPENT VIEWING TV CHANNELS
AMONG GERMANS IN EAST AND WEST, 1993 (MINUTES PER DAY)

TV Channels	West	East
ARD1	31	30
ZDF	33	31
ARD3	13	18
SAT1	24	37
RTL	30	44
DSF	2	2
PRO7	13	24
Others	22	23

Source: Adopted from Darschin and Frank (1994), 100.

The shift towards the private channels is also apparent in the viewership of the news programs. Since 1991, ZDF's main evening news program "*heute*" dropped from 13 percent per day of people fourteen years and older in Germany to 11 percent in 1993, ARD's

"*Tagesschau*" from 16 percent to 11 percent.[2] This decline in viewership of the public channels was not entirely compensated by the
increase in the reach of the private channels' news programs, however. There has been a slight but obvious decline in viewership of
main evening news programs overall.

THE PRESS

Readership of daily newspapers in Germany has been declining,
although slowly, and this trend has not diminished since unification.
The young, in particular (under thirty), are less likely to become
habitual readers of newspapers than previous generations. Magazines, however, have—as a whole—been gaining readers as the number of titles has expanded.

Since the 1990 election there are four more weekly print maga-
zines or newspapers dealing with political issues. In 1990 there were
Der Spiegel and *Die Zeit, Rheinischer Merkur, Deutsches Allgemeines
Sonntagsblatt,* and *Stern.* By 1994, *Focus* and *Tango* were added
(both magazines in the format of *Der Spiegel*), as were *Die Woche* and
Wochenpost (both weekly newspapers).

In the East, the process of the concentration of the press has continued and is particularly striking: eighty separate daily newspapers at
the time of unification are now down to eighteen. There are approximately 1,700 newspapers in Germany as a whole but only 136 with
separate and distinct editorial structures. The remainder are local or
regional variations of a newspaper.[3]

Journalists and Journalism

In 1992–93, when the first representative survey of journalists in
united Germany took place, 82 percent of journalists in the East had
lived in the GDR prior to 1989. Only 18 percent were "imported"
from the West. Those who came from the West did not necessarily
hold the top positions.[4] The proportion of western German journalists among the newsroom élites—editors-in-chief and department
heads—is only a little more than one-fourth (28 percent). Eastern
German journalists tend to be younger, more often female, and better educated than western German journalists. They are as fond of
their work as the western Germans. They are more likely to believe
that their audience is well informed, interested, self-confident, and
tolerant than their counterparts in the West, and they do not seem to

be dissatisfied with the changes of the media system since unification. Their most common complaint is the increased "formality" of social relations in the newsroom.[5] For example, they can no longer expect to use the informal "Du" when speaking with colleagues, which had been the custom prior to 1989, and they believe they now need to dress more formally on the job.

But there are major differences between journalists in the East and West in terms of their role definitions. Eastern German journalists are more reluctant than their western counterparts to use illegitimate information-gathering techniques, such as, for example, paying for information, using confidential documents, or pressuring informants.[6] But eastern Germans are significantly more often driven by "missionary" attitudes than western German journalists, and see themselves more often as educators and advocates for their audiences.[7] In western Germany, on the other hand, recent research shows that "missionary" attitudes, although present, were never predominant and that they have diminished even further in the 1990s.[8]

The Parties' Election Communication

The 1990 Bundestag campaign was the second national election campaign in which the parties were permitted to purchase advertising on private television and radio, but for the most part the parties still relied on the free airtime made available to them by the public service channels.

Restrictions apply to the airing of ads.[9] They are confined, for example, to the "hot phase" of the campaign, which is generally three to six weeks before election day. The beginning of this phase is determined by agreement between the parties and the broadcasting organizations. TV ads on the public channels are not to exceed two minutes in length. Unlike the ads in other European countries, such as Britain or the Netherlands, which often feature "talking heads," German TV ads frequently take the form of highly professional commercials of the "Coke Is It!" type. On public broadcasting, each party contesting the election is granted at least one free ad, and additional spots are determined by the parties' level of representation in the Bundestag. The number of extra spots is roughly proportional to the number of seats the party holds in the Bundestag, though an effort is made to balance the number of spots given to the two largest parties, the CDU and the SPD. Similar rules apply to the availability of free advertising time on public service radio. On commercial television and radio, there are fewer restrictions.

In 1994, some parties used a not insignificant portion of their campaign budgets to purchase time on the commercial television channels. Overall, the CDU and the SPD each spent between 60 and 70 million marks on their entire campaigns. This compares with 8 million spent by the CSU, 11 million by the FDP, 8.5 million by the PDS, and 5 million by the Alliance 90/Greens.[10] SPD and CDU/CSU received sixteen free TV spots per party on ARD and ZDF together, while less than half of these were made available to the smaller parties (PDS, FDP, and Alliance 90/Greens). In addition, the SPD purchased twenty-four spots on RTL and twenty-four on SAT.1, twenty on PRO7, twenty-one on RTL2, and forty-seven on all the other commercial TV channels combined, which is as much as the CDU bought on these channels. The FDP paid for up to ten spots daily on N-TV, the news TV channel, and, rather than purchasing spots on other channels, the small party put funds into 25,000 posters lining the streets in major cities.

The Greens campaign was deemed to be the most technically professional of all the parties: for example, posters were created by desktop computer and delivered on disk to the precincts where they could be varied to suit the local circumstances.[11] The Greens concentrated their campaigning on target constituencies which they identified by studying election results for the party since 1985.

But a party did not need to spend four years "in the desert" (out of the Bundestag) to learn how to make full use of advanced campaign technology. The CDU, for example, distributed its party program on computer disk, as well as in a political data bank with information and arguments to support it. It even produced a computer game on disk, *Kennste Deutschland?* (Do you know Germany?), for the next generation of voters. A national computer network made it possible for information and updates to be sent out regularly to party activists in the local precincts. The PDS was also very effective in concentrating its efforts on the Berlin precincts where it eventually won direct mandates. It also focused its advertising messages on younger voters in its posters and television spots across the country.

Presidential Style Campaign Imagery

In 1990 the CDU and SPD campaigns concentrated heavily on the chancellor candidates Helmut Kohl and Oskar Lafontaine, and the

FDP remained in the shadow of a towering Hans-Dietrich Genscher. This trend continued in 1994 in party posters and billboards, as well as print ads and television spots.

Rudolf Scharping dominated SPD posters and the party's TV ads, though the three-person leadership (popularly known as the "troika") of Scharping, Oskar Lafontaine (the prime minister of Saarland), and Gerhard Schröder (the prime minister of Lower Saxony) also played an important role in party strategy. Scharping, however, even appeared to dominate the one SPD TV spot that featured the "troika"—it caused a minor furor in the conservative British tabloids because the choice of background music was "Land of Hope and Glory."

In an attempt to further develop the image of Rudolf Scharping for the German public, the SPD also borrowed from the British Labour Party's well-known 1987 election TV broadcast, "Kinnock," in which photos and home movies from then Labour leader Neil Kinnock's childhood and family provide an emotionally gripping glimpse of the man, his life, his wife and children. The German 1994 "Scharping" ad includes his mother talking about Rudolf as a child and his wife telling us how the couple first met, as well as home movies of their three daughters as toddlers, before we see the leader himself meeting and talking to voters. References to the party's key issues—jobs, the environment, social fairness, and the redistribution of wealth—were also common in the SPD's personalized TV spots.

The CDU concentrated heavily on the chancellor with few or sometimes no words in their posters. One of the most widespread ones was simply a smiling Helmut Kohl amidst a crowd. Another, poster with the face of a smiling and confident Kohl had the caption "*Ohne Bart*" ("without beard"). The double meaning refers to both his challenger's beard as well as the idea that Kohl is a modern, not old or old-fashioned, leader. The German metaphor "*etwas hat einen Bart*" means that something is out-of-date and is often used in reference to an old joke that everyone knows.

In one of the CDU's more innovative posters, the possibility of Communists in the Bundestag was visually depicted with a red sock held on a clothesline. It relayed the idea that the PDS consists of old SED cadres who, after the Wall came down, were referred to in a demeaning way as "*rote Socken.*" The PDS later adopted this label, and members proudly wore little red sock pins on their lapels.

The CDU's TV spots largely featured the chancellor and his presence at the helm during the process of unification and the subsequent economic progress. There were numerous testimonials to Kohl's popularity from voters on the street as well as his international reputation with film of Kohl and President Bill Clinton, Queen Elizabeth, and President François Mitterrand. Clinton was seen speaking German to an audience in Berlin in a number of the CDU ads—*"Amerika steht an Ihrer Seite! Jetzt und für immer!"* or *"Berlin ist frei!"* (America is on your side, now and forever. Berlin is free!)—and there was also the occasional flashback to John F. Kennedy's *"Ich bin ein Berliner"* speech, as well as Ronald Reagan saying "Mr. Gorbachov, open this Gate!"

The CDU's policy themes, and how these differed from the SPD's, were aired in short TV spots beginning with *"Tatsache ist!"* (Fact is!) which the party had to change to *"Fakt ist!"* for transmission in the East when it learned that easterners were more accustomed to this word. The CDU's main attack ads, however, were reserved for the PDS. A number of campaign observers later suggested that the attention given to the PDS by the CDU may have actually helped the small party attract protest votes.

The FDP ran a campaign about itself rather than any particular substantive issue. The party focused on its role as a powerbroker and as a voice in government. Its main poster claimed "This time everything is at stake," and photos of Foreign Secretary Dr. Klaus Kinkel and former Foreign Secretary Hans-Dietrich Genscher dominated the party's billboards. The theme "Everything is at stake" was also the focus of the party's TV spots in which different colored balls were used to depict the potential outcomes in the Bundestag (red-green, black-red, or black alone) if the FDP was missing, and how crucial it is for the future stability of the country to have the FDP (the blue and yellow ball) in the government. The spot also noted that the party stands for new ideas, the rights of minorities, culture, and the free market. Viewers were told "Without a strong FDP, you can't be sure" and asked "What would Germany be without the Liberals?" before the spot's final message "For a stable government vote Kohl/Kinkel."

The western German Greens and their Alliance 90 counterparts from eastern Germany chose not to use their free time on ARD and ZDF with party-produced spots. They were the only party to enter the Bundestag without an ad campaign that featured at least their most popular spokespersons, e.g., Joschka Fischer and Ludger Volmer.

Instead of party-produced TV spots, they initiated a competition for citizens to submit short films or videos on the theme of

"*Ausländerfeindlichkeit*" (hatred of foreigners) and racism. The five best amateur videos were aired on the public service channels, among them:

The fifth runner up: a diatribe against cows, with the voice-over by a shouting angry man who described cows as "lazy do-nothings who eat grass all day long so that the sheep have none," accompanied by film of big-eyed, bell-clad cattle grazing in the fields.

"*Holzköpfe*" (Wood Heads)—which refers to stupid or stubborn people—showed a maker of wooden dolls in his workshop painting some black and some white. When the dolls were left alone in the shop at night, they would fight and break one another. The message at the end of the film was "How long do we want to go on like this?"

"Stand Up Now!" showed a couple of skinheads harassing a Turkish man sitting at a bus stop until the man got up and left. Then the white German man with a newspaper sitting on the end of the bench stopped reading, suddenly stood up, and walked away giving a look of disgust at the way the Turk had been treated while the skinheads, sitting together with all the weight at the other end of the bench, tipped over and fell off.

The winner of the short film competition was entitled "*Hitzköpfe*" (Hotheads) and depicted rows of different colored matchheads standing upright with background music changing from a Strauss Viennese waltz to rock'n'roll as the matches were lit, to Mozart's "Requiem" as they became engulfed in flames. The message at the end was "*Lass dich nicht anstecken*" (Don't let yourself become inflamed).

The PDS followed the example of the personalized campaigns of the SPD and the CDU with posters featuring their leader, Gregor Gysi, whose face was seen on billboards around the country. One of the party's most amusing posters, aimed at young voters, showed a young couple, eyes closed, about to kiss, with the caption: "First kiss, eyes closed. First vote, eyes open." Gysi also featured in the party's "hip hop"-style, upbeat TV spots, where he played on the shame factor associated with support for the PDS. He told viewers "Vote for the PDS!" then with his hand to his mouth he whispered "I won't tell anyone!" Other posters featured prominent PDS-related candidates including writer Stephan Heym and the former minister under the Modrow government Christa Luft, who were among the four direct mandates won by the PDS in 1994.

Potential Effects of Party Advertising

Does party advertising, in its various forms, influence public opinion and electoral outcomes at all? Research suggests that it can, but effects vary by medium, across parties, and from one election to another.[12] In 1990, exposure to the CDU and SPD TV spots did not show a significant impact on public opinion about the chancellor candidates.[13] Instead, public sympathy—at least with Oskar Lafontaine—was influenced only by exposure to the party's posters in the final weeks before election day. This effect was also positively and significantly associated with perceptions of Oskar Lafontaine as competent.[14] The SPD's ads in newspapers, again in the final days before the 1990 Bundestag election, helped Oskar Lafontaine to be perceived as a "winner."[15] On the other hand, the CDU's many posters of Helmut Kohl in 1990 did not significantly influence public perceptions of the chancellor during the final weeks of that campaign. Instead, regular television news coverage of Helmut Kohl's activities as chancellor, rather than as the CDU's chancellor candidate in 1990, did more to enhance public sympathy for him.

The Visibility of Bundestag Elections in the News

In addition to the use of party posters, press advertisements, and TV spots, the parties plan their campaign activities around news deadlines. Much of what goes on during the six weeks before election day is aimed at television and the press. In 1994, as in 1990, there were numerous political discussion programs aired during prime time on the public service channels in the final weeks before election day. These were often in a panel format with representatives of the main political parties taking questions from journalists or from an audience in the studio. The chancellor candidates were also interviewed by leading political journalists on the public service channels during prime time, often following the main evening news.

1990: The "Boring" Election

Our study of the news and its effects on public opinion during the "hot phase" of the 1990 Bundestag election campaign included content analysis of main evening television news coverage of politics on

ARD, ZDF, RTL, and SAT.1 and DFF1 in the East, as well as political news in fifteen newspapers across the country.[16] One of the most remarkable findings from the content analysis was the relatively small amount of attention paid to this historic Bundestag election in the news. The number of TV news stories that actually mentioned the election was rather small (11 percent), and an even smaller portion of TV news stories about politics had the national election as a topic of its own in the story (3 percent). Stories that at least mentioned the election were more numerous in the press (19 percent), but the election actually surfaced as one of the topics in only 6 percent of press stories.

Moreover, in terms of its content, main evening TV news about the election in Germany was not what viewers in the United States or Britain would expect from their news programs during campaigns with colorful political rallies and politicians on the campaign trail meeting electors or kissing babies. In German TV news, these types of stories were far from common. In 1990, we found almost no coverage of "pseudo events" of this kind, and opinion poll coverage in main evening news was also rare. In the final days of the campaign, Helmut Kohl and Oskar Lafontaine were simply not depicted on the campaign trail. The public service and private channels were similar in their lack of emphasis on the campaign and the election in the main evening news programs.

"Regierungsbonus" and "Kanzlerbonus" in 1990

This did not mean that the political parties were not evident in the news, however. The governing parties continued to govern and attracted a great deal of media attention in so doing. Based on all political coverage in main evening TV news and the fifteen newspapers in our 1990 study, it is clear that the parties of government held a "bonus" in terms of the amount and prominence of coverage. Table 4.2 shows the visibility of the government and opposition parties, as well as the two chancellor candidates (we coded up to ten politicians per story) in the news in 1990, based on all political news stories on television and in the press. The percentage indicates the proportion of stories in which a politician or a party was mentioned. On main evening television news in the West, for example, Helmut Kohl was mentioned in 22 percent of stories compared with only 6 percent that mentioned Oskar Lafontaine. In addition, 52 percent of western TV news stories mentioned other CDU/CSU politicians compared with only 38 percent that mentioned other SPD politicians. There were no significant differences between the public service and private television channels on this point. When we take only stories that mentioned the election, we see that the opposition's visibility increases, but it still does not equal that of the government politicians, as table 4.3 shows.

TABLE 4.2

POLITICIANS AND PARTIES IN POLITICAL NEWS,[a]
1990 BUNDESTAG ELECTION CAMPAIGN (IN PERCENT)

| Politicians/Party | TV News | |
	West Germany[b]	East Germany[c]
Helmut Kohl	22	16
CDU/CSU	52	49
FDP	22	22
Oskar Lafontaine	6	5
SPD	38	38
Alliance 90/Greens	11	14
N[d]	(1,135)	(391)

[a]All stories in which the political actor or party mentioned. Up to ten actors or parties were coded for each story. 1 October–1December 1990.
[b]ARD,ZDF, SAT.1, RTL.
[c]DFF1.
[d]All political reports.

TABLE 4.3

POLITICIANS AND PARTIES IN ELECTION NEWS,[a]
1990 BUNDESTAG ELECTION CAMPAIGN (IN PERCENT)

| Politicians/Party | TV News | |
	West Germany[b]	East Germany[c]
Helmut Kohl	39	44
CDU/CSU	59	59
FDP	24	29
Oskar Lafontaine	20	24
SPD	43	49
Alliance 90/Greens	26	20
N[d]	(123)	(41)

[a]Election was mentioned in the story. Up to ten actors or parties were coded for each story. 1 October–1 December 1990.
[b]ARD, ZDF, SAT.1, RTL.
[c]DFF1.
[d]All political reports or stories in which the election was mentioned.

The so-called "Regierungsbonus" therefore meant that the politicians of the incumbent coalition and the chancellor himself appeared more often than opposition politicians in the final eight weeks before election day. A longer-term content analysis from April to December 1990 of a sample of prestigious and regional newspapers, TV news, and material from the wire services also shows a clear "Kanzler-bonus," with Helmut Kohl mentioned in general political coverage sometimes as much as six times more often per media outlet than Oskar Lafontaine, and concluded: "the total reporting is clearly dominated by the ruling coalition."[17] The opposition parties in 1990, therefore, were less well placed for getting their politicians into the news before polling day.

TV Journalists' Professionalism in 1990: Nonevaluative News

Visibility would no longer be a bonus if the extensive coverage about a political party or politician was negative. The vast majority of stories on main evening TV news in 1990 during the "hot phase," in fact, did not contain any explicitly positive or negative evaluations of the political actors.[18] The Regierungsbonus and the Kanzlerbonus in 1990 were largely only bonuses of visibility and should not be under-stood as referring to a favorable or unfavorable tone in coverage. They may, nevertheless, have represented a major hindrance to the opposi-tion parties' ability to communicate to voters via the news media.

One of the most remarkable effects we found in 1990 was that significant changes in public opinion about the incumbent coalition may have been a consequence of politicians' visibility in the news. In other words, simply depicting a party more often in the news influ-enced public evaluations. As we argue elsewhere:

> This is not a problem of ideology or partisanship, or the personal political preferences of TV news executives. The Regierungsbonus existed on all TV news channels. If the parties of government were to change, it is potentially just as likely that such an advantage would begin for the new party or parties in power. This is a problem of pro-fessionalism and how it is interpreted during an election campaign. German TV news reporters behaved professionally in 1990. They rarely injected their political sympathies into their reporting. They separated facts from opinions. They for the most part did not evaluate politicians and parties. The flagship TV news programs were virtually free of any explicitly positive or negative evaluations of politicians in words and in pictures. The news focused, as always, on the activities of the important and influential policymakers.

It was the combination of this professionalism alongside the routine political news that made mere visibility a bonus in 1990. A scandal or a running negative news story could have diminished or eliminated a visibility bonus, but there were virtually none in 1990. These circumstances, in combination with a general professional hesitation to use evaluative or critical comments in the coverage, meant that visibility was a bonus in 1990.[19]

Was 1994 Different?

Anyone who experienced both campaigns became aware of the greater excitement in 1994. It was perceived as a very close election in the final weeks before voting day. The advantage that the SPD held in the polls in early 1994 had diminished considerably by the summer, and there was much speculation about the form that a coalition government might take under various outcome scenarios. There was, therefore, much more at stake during the 1994 campaign than there had been in 1990, when the result was virtually certain months before voting day.

We replicated our 1990 content analysis of main evening news on ARD, ZDF, RTL, and SAT.1 in 1994 in the last six weeks before election day, from 29 August through 15 October. As before, all television news stories mentioning German politicians or political parties were included. Our findings show that 1994 was indeed different from 1990 in important ways, but in other respects it was also similar.

One important difference: the election itself was far more visible in the main evening television news in 1994. A full 25 percent of all television news stories about politics mentioned the election in 1994, compared with only 11 percent in 1990. The 1994 election was also mentioned in more political stories on the private channels than the public service channels: 35 percent on RTL, 29 percent on SAT.1, 21 percent on ZDF, and 18 percent on ARD. Opinion polls and election forecasts, included in these percentages, were also more prominent, though they accounted for only a small portion (less than 10 percent) of stories on all channels. Even when the election result appeared to be very close, and the competition between the CDU and the SPD remained intense right up until election day, German election news on TV nevertheless remained far behind the United States in its emphasis on the "electoral game," that is, the polls or horse race.[20] This is an admirable quality.

German TV news about politics during the six weeks before election day in 1994 was also largely devoid of positive or negative evaluations of politicians. Only approximately 11 percent of all evaluations made in political news stories were directional, that is, positive or negative or some mixture of the two. There were no significant differences between the public service and private channels on this point. In other words, reporters almost always used neutral or descriptive terms to discuss politicians' activities and statements, and this was also the case in 1990. They also rarely injected positive or negative evaluations by politicians or other partisans into their stories. In this respect, German news in 1994 was very much like that in 1990.

Another similarity is in the extent to which the parties of government continued to be highly visible on the main evening news about politics during the final weeks of the campaign—although the visibility gap between government and opposition parties was not as great as it had been in 1990. Table 4.4 shows, for example, that across all four television channels Helmut Kohl was seen in 20 percent of stories compared with 12 percent for Rudolf Scharping. Fifty percent mentioned other CDU/CSU politicians compared with only 40 percent for the SPD. There was some variation across channels, with a greater visibility gap between the CDU/CSU and the SPD on the public service channels than on the private ones. In 1994, as in 1990, therefore, the governing parties continued to govern during the final weeks of the campaign and still attracted substantial amounts of television news coverage in so doing.

TABLE 4.4

POLITICIANS AND PARTIES IN POLITICAL NEWS,[a]
1994 BUNDESTAG ELECTION CAMPAIGN (IN PERCENT)

TV News

Politicians/ Party	ARD	ZDF	SAT.1	RTL	Total
Helmut Kohl	18	16	19	28	20
CDU/CSU	57	51	44	44	50
FDP	19	23	29	26	24
Rudolf Scharping	9	11	12	16	12
SPD	39	41	38	43	40
Alliance 90/Greens	8	10	10	14	10
PDS	9	10	14	10	11
N[b]	(183)	(193)	(172)	(124)	(672)

[a]All stories in which the political actor or party was mentioned. Up to ten actors or parties were coded for each story. 29 August–15 October 1994.
[b]All political stories.

As in 1990, however, the Regierungsbonus and the Kanzlerbonus were again largely only bonuses of visibility and should not be understood as referring to a favorable or unfavorable tone in the coverage.

In 1990, the Kanzlerbonus and Regierungsbonus had diminished in stories that mentioned the election. In 1994, however, both bonuses disappeared. As table 4.5 shows, in stories that mentioned the election in 1994, Rudolf Scharping was actually mentioned more often than the incumbent Helmut Kohl, and, on all channels, other SPD politicians appeared more often than other CDU/CSU politicians.

TABLE 4.5

POLITICIANS AND PARTIES IN ELECTION NEWS,[a]
1994 BUNDESTAG ELECTION CAMPAIGN (IN PERCENT)

TV News

Politicians/ Party	ARD	ZDF	SAT.1	RTL	Total
Helmut Kohl	36	23	29	44	32
CDU/CSU	50	50	44	56	50
FDP	31	35	48	49	41
Rudolf Scharping	42	35	31	42	37
SPD	64	67	71	63	64
Alliance 90/Greens	28	27	25	29	27
PDS	28	21	25	19	23
N[b]	(36)	(47)	(52)	(41)	(177)

[a]Election was mentioned in the story. Up to ten actors or parties were coded for each story. 29 August–15 October 1994.
[b]All political stories in which the election was mentioned.

Conclusion

The fact that TV news coverage of politics was largely devoid of positive or negative evaluations of politicians means that in comparison with Britain and the United States, Germany is at the high end of the continuum in terms of objectivity and neutrality in political reporting, with the United States at the low end, and Britain, closer to Germany than the United States, in between.[21] The excitement of the 1994 race did not lead German reporters to become more evaluative or critical of politicians' statements or activities. They continued to report the news objectively, and, for the most part, avoided mixing facts with opinions, just as they had in 1990.[22] This is in stark contrast to campaign reporting in the United States, which has become significantly more evaluative over the past thirty years and, in 1992, was particularly negative about George Bush's election campaign and record as incumbent.[23]

German TV news reporters and editors used professional standards and criteria of newsworthiness to cover politics and the election in 1994 as in 1990. They paid much more attention to the election campaign in 1994 because it had all the characteristics of a newsworthy story. It provided drama, excitement, and conflict. The closeness of the race made it a more interesting election, in sheer news value terms.

This reliance on news values was also true in 1990, though it led to a different result. The fact that in October the majority of the public believed the incumbent coalition would win the December 1990 election, according to one TV news producer, actually had an impact on television news reporters who "were not willing to fight" to bring stories about the 1990 election into the bulletin.[24] An observation study at ZDF in the 1990 campaign led us to conclude that television reporters took a "conventionally journalistic" approach to covering the campaign.[25] News values were almost always the primary criteria for the selection and placement of news stories during the campaign. The perception that the 1990 election result was a foregone conclusion suggested that the campaign was uninteresting for reporters and their audiences.

That said, German TV news nevertheless stands apart from American and British news at election time because of the continued visibility bonus for the chancellor and the incumbent parties of government. The visibility bonus for the government in general political reporting meant that the opposition parties could not rely on the news media for balanced visibility at election time, a time when in other democracies the media make special efforts to provide equal coverage of the leading parties and candidates.

In Germany, however, our comparison of 1990 and 1994 suggests that only when the election campaign appears to be a close contest does the opposition have a greater opportunity to be seen in the news. In election-related stories, the parties of government and opposition were on relatively equal footing. But in nonelection news, the government parties continued to retain a visibility bonus. Professionalism in the final weeks before voting day in Britain and the United States is understood differently by television news reporters, who strive to provide a "balance" of news about the top candidates and parties (although in the United States this is often also evaluative news).[26]

In Germany in 1990, in what was a "settled" election, we nevertheless found in our panel survey of voters that visibility alone had a favorable influence on public evaluations of certain leading politicians and parties of government. In 1994, in what was a very close race, the lack of a panel study to assess media effects on individuals' opinions allows us to only speculate about whether the greater visibility of the SPD in election-related news actually had a favorable effect on public evaluations of Rudolph Scharping and his party.

Acknowledgments

We want to express our thanks for a Goldsmiths Award from the Joan Shorenstein Center on the Press, Politics and Public Policy, Kennedy School of Government, Harvard University, and to the German Federal Press and Information Agency in Bonn for providing support for the 1994 study. The 1990 study was partially supported by a research fellowship to Dr. Semetko from the German Marshall Fund of the United States. We greatly appreciate the research assistance of Felix Bullinger on the 1994 election study.

Notes

1. Wolfgang Darschin and Bernward Frank, " Tendenzen im Zuschauerverhalten," *Media Perspektiven* 3 (1994): 98–110. For a discussion of viewership at the time of the 1990 Bundestag election, see Holli A. Semetko and Klaus Schoenbach, *Germany's "Unity Election:" Voters and the Media* (Cresskill, NJ: Hampton Press, 1994).

2. Darschin and Frank, 107.

3. See, for example, Walter J. Schütz, "Der Zeitungmarkt in den neuen Ländern," in Bundesverband Deutscher Zeitungverleger, ed., *Zeitungen '91* (Bonn: BDZV), 106–18.

4. Beate Schneider, Klaus Schoenbach, and Dieter Stuerzebecher, "Journalisten im vereinigten Deutschland. Strukturen, Arbeitsweisen und Einstellungen im Ost-West-Vergleich". *Publizistik* 38 (1993): 353–82. See also Frank Boeckelmann, Claudia Mast, and Beate Schneider, eds., *Journalismus in den neuen Ländern: Ein Berufsstand zwischen Aufbruch und Abwicklung* (Konstanz: Universitätsverlag, 1994).

5. Beate Schneider and Klaus Schoenbach, "Journalisten in den neuen Bundesländern: Zur Struktur und zur sozialen Lage des Berufstandes. Ergebnisse der Sozialenquete über die Journalisten in den neuen Ländern der Bundesrepublik Deutschland" in W. A. Mahl, ed., *Jounalisten in Deutschland: Nationale und internationale Vergleiche und Perspektiven* (Munich: Oelschlaeger, 1993), 35–56.

See also Beate Schneider, Klaus Schoenbach, and Dieter Stuerzebecher, "Westdeutsche Jounalisten im Vergleich: Jung, professionell und mit Spass an der Arbeit," *Publizistik* 38 (1993): 5–30.

6. Beate Schneider, Klaus Schoenbach, and Dieter Stuerzebecher, "Journalisten im vereinigten Deutschland: Strukturen, Arbeitsweisen und Einstellungen im Ost-West-Vergleich," *Publizistik* 38 (1993): 353–82.

7. Beate Schneider, Klaus Schoenbach, and Dieter Stuerzebecher, "Journalisten im vereinigten Deutschland."

8. Klaus Schoenbach, Dieter Stuerzebecher, and Beate Schneider, "Oberlehrer und Missionare? Das Selbstverständnis deutscher Jounalisten," in Friedhelm Neidhardt, ed., *Öffentlichkeit, Öffentliche Meinung, Soziale Bewegungen* (Opladen: Westdeutscher Verlag, 1994), 139–61.

9. Klaus Schoenbach, "Mass Media and Election Campaigns in Germany," in F. J. Fletcher, eds., *Media, Elections and Democracy* (Toronto and Oxford: Dundurn Press, 1992), 63–86.

10. Gunhild Freese, "Wellenreiter statt wellenmacher. Wahlwerbung: Den Kampf um die Stimmen haben sich die Parteien mehr als 150 Millionen Mark kosten lassen," *Die Zeit* 42, 14 October 1994, p. 27. All information in this paragraph pertaining to advertising was cited in this article by Freese.

11. Ibid.

12. Wolfgang G. Gibowski, "Wieviele Wählerstimmen kann man mit Wahlwerbung gewinnen?," in J. Jeski, E. Neumann, and W. Sprang, eds., *Jahrbuch der Werbung in Deutschland, Österreich, Schweiz 1990* (Düsseldorf and New York: ECON Verlag, 1991). See also Semetko and Schoenbach, Germany's "Unity Election."

13. Semetko and Schoenbach, 116. See also Klaus Schoenbach and Holli A. Semetko, "Medienberichterstattung und Parteien Werbung im Bundestagswahlkampf 1990," *Media Perspektiven* 7 (1994): 328–40.

14. Semetko and Schoenbach, *Germany's "Unity Election,"* 118–19.

15. Ibid.

16. Ibid. To learn more about how German coverage of politics during election campaigns compares with the most recent general election in Britain, see Holli A. Semetko, Margaret Scammell, and T. J. Nossiter, "The Media's Coverage of the Campaign," in Anthony Heath, Roger Jowell, and John Curtice, eds., *Labour's Last Chance? The 1992 Election and Beyond* (Aldershot, U.K., and Brookfield, Vt.: Dartmouth, 1994), 25–42. Effects of the British press on voters is discussed in John Curtice and Holli A. Semetko, "Does It Matter What the Papers Say?", in Heath, Jowell, and Curtice, eds., *Labour's Last Chance?*, 43–64.

17. Barbara Pfetsch and Ruediger Schmitt-Beck, "Communication Strategies and the Mass Media in the 1990 German Election Campaign." Paper presented at the April ECPR Joint Sessions of Workshops, Leiden, The Netherlands, 19. See also Barbara Pfetsch and Katrin Voltmer, "Geteilte Medienrealite? Zur Thematisierungsleistung der Massenmedien im Prozess der deutschen Vereinigung," in Hans-Dieter Klingemann and Max Kaase, eds., *Wahlen und Waehler: Analysen aus Anlass der Bundestagswahl 1990* (Opladen: Westdeutscher Verlag, 1994),

509–42. See also Ruediger Schmitt-Beck and Peter Schrott, "Dealignment durch Massenmedien?", in Klingemann and Kaase, eds., *Wahlen und Wähler*, 543–74.

18. Semetko and Schoenbach, *Germany's "Unity Election,"* 51ff.

19. Ibid., 131–32.

20. See, for example, Thomas E. Patterson, *Out of Order: How the Decline of the Political Parties and the Growing Power of the News Media Undermine the American Way of Electing Presidents* (New York: Knopf).

21. See Holli A. Semetko, Jay G. Blumler, Michael Gurevitch, and David H. Weaver, *The Formation of Campaign Agendas: A Comparative Analysis of Party and Media Roles in Recent American and British Elections* (Hillsdale, N.J.: Lawrence Erlbaum, 1991).

22. About this journalistic norm in Germany, see Klaus Schoenbach, *Trennung von Nachricht und Meinung: Empirische Untersuchung eines journalistischen Qualitäts-kriteriums* (Freiburg and Munich: Karl Alber, 1977).

23. Patterson, *Out of Order.*

24. Semetko and Schoenbach, *Germany's "Unity Election,"* chapter 5. We note that in 1990 this was also in part a reflection of disappointment in the opposition leader, Oskar Lafontaine, whose public support had lagged well behind Helmut Kohl's since May 1990, when the SPD was split by Lafontaine's insistence that the party seek to prevent the passage of the unification treaty in the Bundesrat. According to this same TV news producer, who was not an SPD man himself, "even SPD journalists were not willing to fight for Lafontaine." Those who were more sympathetic with the SPD, however, suggested that the likelihood of Helmut Kohl's victory provided a "chilling effect" that discouraged public service journalists who were sympathetic with the opposition from making the case for bringing in more news about the SPD's campaign activities, 66.

25. Semetko and Schoenbach, *Germany's "Unity Election,"* chapter 5. See also Jay G. Blumler, Michael Gurevitch, and T. J. Nossiter, "The Earnest versus the Determined: Election Newsmaking at the BBC, 1987," in Ivor Crewe and Martin Harrop, eds., *Political Communications: The General Election of 1987* (Cambridge: Cambridge University Press, 1989), 157–74.

26. Holli A. Semetko, "'Balance' as a Culturally Relevant Concept: TV News and Elections in Cross-National Comparative Perspective." Paper prepared for the Joan Shorenstein Center on the Press, Politics and Public Policy, Kennedy School of Government, Harvard University.

5

WOMEN AND THE
1994 GERMAN ELECTIONS
DISSATISFACTION AND ACCOMMODATION

MARY N. HAMPTON

S ince unification and the first all-German elections of 1990, the
integration of former West and East Germany has been a top
political priority. The very narrow victory of the CDU/CSU-FDP
over the SPD, the impressive showing in the eastern states of the
PDS, and the rejuvenation of the Greens party in the western states,
all reflect the fact that united Germany is still a polity in transition.
While continuity was maintained in the victory of the conservative-
liberal coalition, the advances made by the SPD and the challenge to
the mainstream parties posed by opposition parties were important
indications of change. The SPD improved its showing in 1990, but
it lost important votes in the East and West to parties perceived as
more oppositional.

Central to the outcome of the "super election year" was the role of
women voters. Women helped reelect the conservative-liberal coalition, but female support for them was down significantly since 1990,
particularly among young women. Women in the western states supported the left-of-center slightly more than in the first all-German
election, but women in the eastern states substantially increased their
support. Very significant was the fact that women under 45 supported
the SPD and parties on the left in substantially larger numbers than in
1990 and more so than men of the same age groups.

Equally revealing of the changes through which united Germany
is moving is that there were very important regional deviations in the
voting patterns of women and men. In the eastern states, the PDS
did well, getting as much as 19.1 percent of the vote among women
from the ages of 18–34, and 18.8 percent from men of the same

cohort.[1] In the West, the PDS did extremely poorly. The success of the Alliance 90/Greens in the West mirrored that of the PDS in the East, and similarly the Greens did poorly in the East.

With these observations in mind, my objective in this paper is twofold. First, I will examine the results of the important 1994 all-German elections to determine how women voted. I will then discuss why they voted the way they did. What the elections revealed about women is in large part true of German domestic society generally: unification has spawned a process of change that is nowhere near resolution.

Second, I will analyze the institutional features of the German political system that accommodate change. The elections revealed the persistent march of German women into the halls of national power. Women candidates scored many more successful electoral gains in Germany than is true in most other Western democracies, with the exception of the Scandinavian countries. I argue that this phenomenon is due largely to the role of the German system of proportional representation (PR) and the system of federalism that encourages local and state interest articulation. The result is a political system that is relatively more successful in incorporating women's interests into the political agenda at the national center than are some other systems.[2]

The 16 October National Election: How Women Voted

While the results of the "super election year" reflected continuity in the German political system in that the CDU/CSU-FDP maintained their coalition government, that outcome was certainly not a foregone conclusion, and their margin of victory was much smaller than in the first all-German elections of 1990. From 1991 to 1994, support for the ruling coalition declined to the point that nationwide expectations throughout the spring of 1994 were for a SPD coalition victory. For example, in March 1994, 53 percent of Germans anticipated an SPD-Greens victory, while only 18 percent expected the conservative-liberal coalition to be returned. The number expecting a left-of-center victory fell to 21 percent by August 1994 and never climbed again.[3] It is generally accepted that the reasons the CDU-led coalition came back from the political grave to eke out a victory in October included the improvement of the economy and the resiliency of Helmut Kohl as a candidate and political leader. In the East and West, optimism about the consequences of unification began to grow again. These considerations do help explain the seeming continuity in German politics that emerged from the election. However, it is also clear that there were changes in the 1994 voting patterns that need to be explained.

The Decline of the Center-Right

Overall, the CDU/CSU-FDP went from 52 percent of the vote in 1990 to a little over 48 percent in 1994. That the conservative-center coalition lost proportionately more support among women than men is significant. In 1990, the CDU/CSU got 44.9 percent of the female vote, but only 42.2 percent in the 1994 election. In the western states, the CDU lost 5.3 percent of the women's vote it had in 1990, and 3.1 percent in the eastern states.[4] Even among the most stalwart conservative cohort, women over 60, support dropped from 54.8 percent to 52.6 percent.[5] It was still the only female age group that voted in the majority for the CDU/CSU-FDP.[6]

For women voters, 1983 was the peak election year for the conservative-liberal coalition from which support has since decreased. The year 1994 found support for the conservative-liberals down across the board, and reflected less support among women than men in some age groups. In fact, in every age group, the CDU/CSU lost female support compared to 1990, losing the most, 6 percent, in the 25–44 year group.[7]

In the 1990 elections, women in the 18–24 year age group supported the CDU/CSU by 34.9 percent. In the 1994 election, however, this group's support for the CDU/CSU dropped to 30.8 percent. Although the 18–24 and 25–34 year age groups are numerically smaller than the older groups, the drop in female support was enough to compel Chancellor Helmut Kohl to take strong action soon after the election to try to regain female backing. I will discuss this development below. Likewise, support among women for the coalition's FDP partner also dropped by 1994, going from 10.6 percent in 1990 to 6.6 percent in 1994.[8] The FDP recently made motions toward improving the lot of women in the party, although it continues to eschew introducing quotas.

Figure 5.1 below shows the drop in women's support for the CDU/CSU since 1983, and traces the decline in support for the CDU/CSU in the 18–24 year cohort. Figure 5.2 illustrates the relative increase in women's support for the left-of-center and opposition parties.

FIGURE 5.1

A COMPARISON OF WOMEN 18–24 YEARS OF AGE VOTING FOR
CDU/CSU AND ALL WOMEN VOTING FOR CDU/CSU

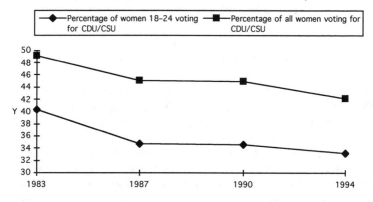

FIGURE 5.2

PERCENTAGE OF ALL WOMEN VOTING FOR SPD AND PERCEIVED
OPPOSITION PARTIES (GREENS AND PDS)

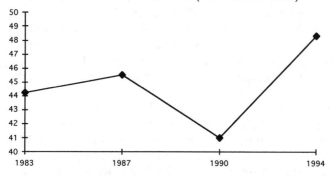

The Rise of the Left-of-Center and Perceived Opposition Parties

Figure 5.2 illustrates the pattern of women's voting behavior since 1983 vis-à-vis the left-of-center and opposition parties, including the SPD, Greens, and the PDS. The success of the left-of-center and opposition parties in the East and West is important in itself. After a dramatic loss of favor in the unification election year, support for these parties has since climbed among all women. The SPD improved its standing in 1994 compared to 1990. It went from 33.8

percent to 36.4 percent of the vote. In the western states, the gain of the left-of-center party among women picked up on the tilt in that direction that first emerged in the 1980 elections. For example, comparing the 1976 and 1980 elections, the CDU/CSU lost ground among women voters in every age group, going down overall from 48.8 percent to 43.7 percent, and actually revealing for the first time less support among women than among men for the CDU/CSU.[9] Simultaneously, support for the SPD among women in the 1980 elections increased across the board and was higher than among men for the first time.[10]

In the 1994 election, the SPD gained the most of any party overall since the first all-German elections, picking up 7 percent in the eastern states and 1.9 percent in the West since 1990.[11] Among women, the party increased its overall standing by more than 2 percent, improving on its 1990 showing in every age bracket, with the biggest gains coming in the 18–24 and 45–59 year-old groups.[12] Increased female support for the SPD showed the largest gap ever between women and men in the 18–24 year-old age group: 36.7 percent of the women and 32.7 percent of the men of this cohort voted SPD. Similarly, in the 25–34 year-old group, women supported the SPD with 42.5 percent, while the men of that cohort did so by only 36.7 percent.[13] The SPD received its highest proportion of female voters from this group.

Despite the SPD's successes, however, it must be noted that they lost many votes to the Greens and PDS. For example, the SPD gave up about 250,000 votes to the Alliance 90/Greens and around 146,000 votes to the PDS.[14] The phenomenon reflected the tendency of some voters in the West and the East to view the SPD as a status quo party, rather than as a force for real change. Thus, those dissatisfied with, harmed by, or desiring to change the status quo, often turned to what they perceived as the real opposition or protest parties. In the West, those voters went to the Alliance 90/Greens, and in the East they went to the PDS.

The Greens and the PDS gained ground among women voters since 1990, and women supported the Greens more than men in every age group. The opposition parties did much better with the 18–34 age group than with any other group. This group increased their support of the Alliance 90/Greens by going from 11.4 percent in 1990 to 15.8 percent in 1994.[15] The PDS received 5.5 percent from the 18–24 year-old cohort overall, with much more support coming from young women in the eastern states than in the western areas.[16]

Results for the 25–34 age group are similar. The Greens made noticeable gains here, going from 10.5 percent in 1990 to 14.2 percent in 1994. The PDS got 5.6 percent from this group.[17] Interesting to note again is the fact that in both of these younger age groups, women voted more heavily for the left-of-center and protest parties than did men of the same groups.

Regional Differences Between Women Voters

Regional differences were prominent among German voters generally and women in particular. To a large degree, the elections revealed the continued rift between East and West. For example, in polls taken in October and November before the elections, unemployment was the top priority in both East and West. However, in the eastern states, 80 percent of respondents in November listed it as their top concern, compared to 60 percent among Germans in the West. Questions of stability and order figured as the second concern for 21 percent of eastern respondents, followed by issues surrounding unification (11 percent), and rent and housing concerns (10 percent). For westerners, the second concern was immigrants (18 percent), followed by environmental concerns (10 percent), and then pension and health care issues (10 percent).[18]

These divergent priorities reflect the losses and insecurities felt by former citizens of the GDR and their resentment at the costs of unification. It also shows that former citizens of the FRG realize the advantages they have had and wish not to lose through unification, and shows their resentment at having to pay such a high financial price for unification. I will address this continued East-West divide as it is reflected among women, especially since many have argued that the biggest losers in unification were East German women. Of importance is the clash of "postmaterialist" values typifying many German women of the old FRG and "materialist" values held by many women in the new states. I accept here Ronald Inglehart's definitions of these terms, where materialist values address basic human "needs for physiological sustenance and safety," while the postmaterialist set of needs concern "esteem, self-expression, and aesthetic satisfaction."[19]

Important is the fact that in both East and West, the beneficiaries of dissatisfaction were often the SPD and opposition parties, rather than what were perceived as the status quo parties. This trend is demonstrated by comparing the electoral results among women voters depicted in figures 5.3–5.6.

FIGURE 5.3

TRENDS IN WOMEN VOTERS' SUPPORT FOR MAINSTREAM POLITICAL PARTIES IN WEST AND EAST

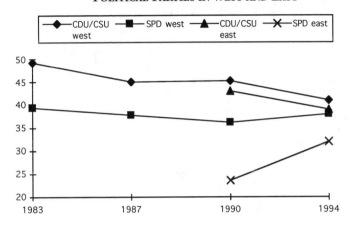

FIGURE 5.4

TRENDS IN WOMEN VOTERS' SUPPORT FOR PERCEIVED OPPOSITION PARTIES IN WEST AND EAST

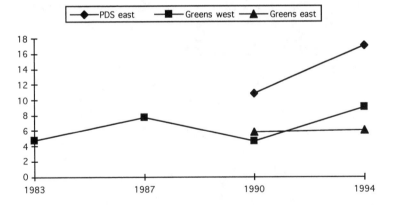

The figures illustrate that the beneficiaries of decreased female support for the conservative-liberal coalition in 1994 were the SPD, the party that warned of the costs of unity in 1990, and the opposition parties (PDS, Alliance 90/Greens).

Figures 5.5 and 5.6 show the loss of CDU/CSU votes among women even more vividly by looking first at western and then eastern women voters to illustrate the successes of the SPD and perceived opposition parties.

FIGURE 5.5

RISE IN WOMEN VOTERS' SUPPORT FOR LEFT-OF-CENTER AND
PERCEIVED OPPOSITION PARTIES IN THE WEST AS MEASURED BY
PERCENTAGE OF VOTES RECEIVED

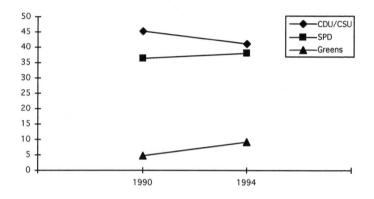

FIGURE 5.6

RISE IN WOMEN VOTERS' SUPPORT FOR LEFT-OF-CENTER AND
PERCEIVED OPPOSITION PARTIES IN THE EAST AS MEASURED BY
PERCENTAGE OF VOTES RECEIVED

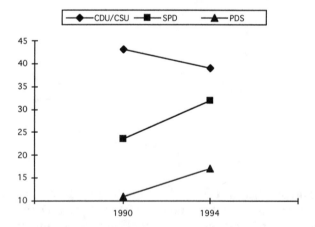

All four figures (5.3–5.6) illustrate the decline in support among
women voters for the CDU/CSU, the parties most associated with
unification. In the East, there was a backlash among women against
the euphoria over unification manifested in the 1990 election. In the
West, the CDU/CSU lost support to the SPD, but the Greens

received proportionately the biggest gains among women in 1994 compared to the 1990 elections. There are a number of possible explanations for this phenomenon, which I will discuss in more detail below. Briefly, the Greens represent the most postmaterialist party in the system. Perhaps because of this, the party did not increase its support base much in the eastern states, largely because it was unable or unwilling to tailor its postmaterialist, clearly western priorities to voters in the new states. In contrast, in the aftermath of unification, western German women showed a preference to maintain some of those priorities, such as an emphasis on environmental issues, which I cited above as placing third on the list of overall western German concerns. Second, the Greens have led the way in recruiting women into its ranks and have consciously focused on women's issues and concerns since the early 1980s. These considerations helped them in the 1994 election among western women.

With the exception of Saxony, the left-of-center and opposition parties won majorities in the new states.[20] It should be instructive to the SPD that they gained proportionately more votes in the 1994 election among eastern German women than among women in the western states. The reasons for that are likely manifold. One important explanation is that the SPD was able to win a substantial number of female votes among traditional social democratic sectors: union workers and the unemployed.

Eastern Germans voted overwhelmingly more for the PDS than did western German voters, giving the party over 17 percent compared to just over 1 percent in the West. The party increased its support in the eastern states substantially since 1990, when it got 11.1 percent.[21] There were great differences between eastern and western German women when it came to the PDS. Among women in the eastern states, the PDS got 17 percent, a large jump from the 10.9 percent results of 1990. Interestingly, the PDS made its most noticeable gains among the youngest age groups, especially in the 18–24 and 25–44 age groups.[22] In the 18–34 year-old group, the PDS actually scored slightly better with eastern women than with their male counterparts.[23] Eastern German women voters between 18–34 gave 19.1 percent to the PDS, while only 1.2 percent of western women in that cohort did so. In the 35–59 age group, 15.3 percent of eastern German women voted for the PDS, compared to 0.9 percent in the West. Even in the over-60 female group, there was a big regional gap, with just over 12 percent of eastern Germans going for the PDS, in contrast to a mere 0.2 percent in the West. Eastern German women voted proportionately less for the Alliance 90/Greens than women in the West.[24]

Clearly the PDS did best in East Berlin, where it received about a quarter of the votes. However, the appeal of the party was more broadly stroked. Not only did it do well among the unemployed in the eastern states, getting about a quarter of that cohort's votes, it also did well among those who felt the most negative about their own economic positions and the general economic outlook. The PDS did very well among those who had the least trust in the institutions of the federal government, including the system of law.[25]

These categories clearly included many eastern German women. As I will discuss below, women in the eastern states lost much of their economic security through unification, and were also confronted with cultural and social challenges from the West regarding their role as women. Women in the eastern part of Germany have been most prone to feel like the losers in unification, and thus fit perfectly the profile of those who voted PDS due to psychological/economic reasons, or who didn't vote at all.[26] Women, particularly young women, made up much of the 27.4 percent of eastern Germans who did not vote in 1994, up from 25.5 percent in 1990.[27]

In short, East German women voted in the 1990 all-German election against their insecurities caused by the dissolution of the GDR. This time they voted against the insecurities brought on by unification with the West. The overwhelming support they gave to the CDU/CSU-FDP coalition in 1990 therefore shrank as they gave more support to anti–status quo parties. It was in some part a backlash against the false hopes and expectations raised regarding unification in 1990 by the CDU/CSU.

The post-unification situation in the new states is historically analogous to the failure of the political center in the United States during the Reconstruction era which later successfully incorporated southern interests. Resentful of northern intrusion, of carpetbaggers, and of the unification party that represented perceived Northern arrogance, the Republicans, a number of home-grown protest parties carried many southern votes. The South also proved to be fertile ground for populist politics, a possibility that exists in the eastern states of Germany today. The populist style of the PDS's leader, Gregor Gysi, has not gone unnoticed. In the case of the United States, the mainstream Democrats eventually succeeded at forging a national coalition that included the southern states by incorporating some of their regional interests into the party's national agenda. The fragile but extremely important coalition lasted well over a half-century.

Lack of Movement on Women's Issues and the Costs of Unity: Why Women Voted

Germany has made progress in advancing women's rights in recent years. However, there are still areas where the status quo does not serve women well, or where unification has actually reversed or challenged progress, especially recently in the area of economic security. I will discuss how these have affected women in the western and eastern states. They represent a cluster of issues that help explain why women voted the way they did in the October election.

Overall, despite the 1949 constitutional guarantee of equal rights between men and women,[28] the glass ceiling continues to hold women back in career advancement; monthly incomes of full-time employed women are still only about 65–70 percent of men's;[29] women are still passed over in job promotions;[30] and they are held back due to the emphasis still placed on women in child-rearing. Just over a year ago, one of Kohl's nominees for president, Steffen Heitmann, declared that a woman's proper place was in the home, and public opinion polls reveal that many Germans still believe women should play their traditional homemaking role.[31] A European Community survey from 1987 showed that German women, who represent over 40 percent of the work force, claim only 8 percent of middle management jobs and below 3 percent of top management positions.[32] A more recent survey shows that women make up 11 percent of upper level management.[33] In any case, the recent rise in unemployment has negatively affected women more than men in the workplace. Christiane Lemke notes that, "highly sex-segregated training and employment patterns limit women's choices more than men's, and women over forty-five have little chance of finding a new job."[34] She also observes that traditional family obligations contribute to employment problems for women. A head of a major German union, Monika Wulf-Mathies, is quoted as saying: "Women are the main victims of the economic crisis."[35]

Unification complicated further the concerns of women. It became quickly apparent as the Wall came down that eastern and western German women shared some interests and concerns. However, it was also obvious that they were extremely different. Thus, the German-wide problems faced by women during restructuring were complicated by the cultural and economic barriers separating West from East. As women strove to deal with these sets of difficulties, the political expression of their efforts in both regions of Germany included a decline in support for the right-of-center status quo Christian-Liberal coalition parties. They are considered more traditional on issues affecting women in the workplace, slower than left-of-center parties in recruiting women into positions of influence, and associated with the high expectations raised before and during unification

German Unification, East German Women, and the 1994 Election

Because of restructuring, unemployment among women in the former GDR is extremely high now, and the disadvantages women have compared to men in the workplace have been magnified. Women of the former GDR did not find their economic position enhanced by unification. In fact, the segregated and gendered nature of employment was reinforced by unification. The GDR guarantee of full employment dissolved, guaranteed child-care disappeared, and women were less able than men to commute to the West for job opportunities. East German women lost much in parental leave rights after unification.

Before unity, unemployment among West German women had been consistently higher than among East German women, with the differential reaching as high as 30 percent. Whereas East German women were nearing 90 percent employment by the late 1980s, in West Germany, only 58 percent of women between the ages of 25–49 were employed in 1988.[36] East German women also earned more relative to men than did West German women.[37] However, after unification and by 1991, 57 percent of working women in the East were unemployed.[38] All of this meant that East German women lost much ground in economic progress since unification; women lost their economic independence.[39] Clearly, this phenomenon had a major impact on how women in the East voted.

There are a number of other reasons that explain the heightened frustrations of women in the new states. Historically, East German women ran into the glass ceiling that exists throughout the West. Few East German women held top management positions, or tenured professor positions, and women also tended to dominate the less productive and modern sectors of the economy. Nonetheless, East German women made real advances during the 1950s through the 1970s in breaking into male-dominated professions and achieving high educational training and competence. Women constituted half of the GDR's higher education population, and universities and places of higher learning were equipped with childcare facilities. There also existed no real gap between women and men under 40 regarding formal job qualifications.[40]

However, advances by women in the GDR regarding employment opportunities and issues of equality were being challenged already in the GDR due to the rise of so-called "Muttipolitik," or "mommy politics," during the 1980s.[41] The progress made earlier became increasingly threatened in the 1980s. State policy still encouraged women to enter the work force, but the focus turned to the child-rearing role of women, thereby undermining earlier successes in dealing with issues of equality. As Myra Marx Ferree observes, "mommy politics" were meant to address declining birth rates in the GDR, and although the policies were meant "to facilitate women's ability to combine paid employment and motherhood," the result was "increasing gender segregation in occupational training and employment."[42]

Feminist groups began to mobilize to address the concerns of many East German women. In the heady months between autumn of 1989 and the spring elections of 1990, feminist groups in the GDR formed a group outside the reform coalition groups like Neues Forum in order to address specifically the perceived interests and grievances of women. Called the German Women's Federation (DFG), the group tried to influence the political and social agenda of East Germany prior to the spring 1990 elections. As the rapid changes of 1989 brought German unity close to reality, however, the group found itself and the interests they represented increasingly sidetracked. Thus, by the time unification came to dominate East German politics, progress in women's interests in the GDR was postponed.[43]

East German women have seen their lives challenged in other ways in the unification process as well. With the western absorption of the former GDR, little value was placed on the benefits the former socialist society might have offered in unified Germany. On important social issues like reproductive rights, policymakers in Bonn attempted to extend eastward West German law, which has been more restrictive than was policy in the GDR. The two German governments decided not to consider the controversial issue in the Unification Treaty of 1990 and to postpone a final decision until the end of 1992. In the interim, separate laws governing the issue were maintained in East and West.[44]

Throughout 1991 and 1992, the German Parliament worked on an all-German law concerning abortion. The parties differed on how

to draft the legislation, with the PDS and Alliance 90/Greens promoting the most liberal pro-choice position. The SPD and the FDP
were close in their reasoning, both advocating "periodic" regulation
of abortions, where women would be able to receive abortions in
combination with a counselling program. Both parties, along with
the PDS and Alliance 90/Greens, rejected the contemporary West
German "indications" law, where abortions were only legal in situations where medical or social reasons could be substantiated. Only
within the CDU/CSU did continuation of the policy, or tightening
restrictions, find some support. However, most in the CDU/CSU
voted for a cross-bench bill, one on which all parties had worked.
The more liberal bill carried the day.[45]

Upon its acceptance, however, the law was then appealed by conservative members of parliament to the Federal Constitutional Court.
The Court's findings of May 1993 moved away from the earlier
restrictive laws of the FRG, but is nowhere near the rights-based law
of the GDR.[46] The issue will continue to be a political "hot potato"
and reflect differences between eastern and western Germans.

Since unification, eastern German women have become increasingly politicized. There were early signs that they equated stability
with unification. For example, despite the DFG's great efforts in
early 1990 at mobilizing women, the CDU-led umbrella group,
Alliance for Germany, captured nearly 50 percent of women voters in
the March 1990 elections in East Germany.[47] A majority of 53 percent of East German women voted for the CDU/CSU-FDP coalition in 1990. Even then, however, polls showed that East Germans
overwhelmingly believed that women were treated more equally in
the GDR than in the FRG. In a poll that appeared in *Der Spiegel* in
November 1990, 67 percent of eastern German respondents held
that position versus only 10 percent who believed that women
received more equal treatment in the FRG.[48]

To summarize, women in the former East Germany voted in
larger numbers for the left-of-center and anti–status quo parties in
the 1994 elections than they did in the first all-German elections of
1990. The loss of what they perceived as their "relatively progressive
gender regime" and their security clearly influenced their voting in
October 1994.[49] Their objectives and dissatisfactions reflected materialist values, such as employment, basic economic stability, and family security. Analyses seeking to understand continuity versus change
in the unified German polity need to take account of the "potential
volatility in East German electoral politics" that women actualized
through their votes.[50]

West German Women and Their Changing Voting Habits

Women in the West voted heavily conservative throughout the 1960s. In this period, they were less educated, much less employed, and less politically interested and informed than were men. By about the end of the 1960s, however, their role in German politics began to change. Through the 1970s, women became increasingly educated, they entered the work force in greater numbers, and their awakening political interest was encouraged by the SPD under the leadership of Willy Brandt. Until the arrival of the Greens in the parliament in 1983, the SPD led the way in giving expression to the rise of women as a political force and in addressing their dissatisfactions. As women became more politically aware and politicized through the 1970s, their support for the conservative parties proportionately decreased.[51] This erosion of support for the conservatives was most apparent among young women.[52]

While the CDU/CSU made a comeback among women voters in 1983, some changes were irreversible. First, the wide gender gap of the 1950s, when women voted in far greater numbers than men for the conservatives, had narrowed.[53] Second, many women continued giving strong support to the SPD. What was most interesting about this election, however, was the appearance on the scene of the Greens. While men voted slightly more for the Greens than did women (5.9 percent versus 4.8 percent), women under age 34 voted over 10 percent for the new party. In addition, urban, educated women between the ages of 25–45 became increasingly dealigned, and therefore more typical of the postmaterialist voter who might support a party like the Greens.[54] With the arrival of the Greens, women's concerns would be placed prominently on the national political agenda, and where the SPD earlier represented the voice of women's evolving political expression, the Greens would now assume that mantle. The institutional aspects of the Greens' contribution to women are considered below. By 1987 all parties had followed the Greens in declaring themselves serious about improving women's representation in the Bundestag and in their respective party organizations.[55]

The West German political system experienced its own infusion of Muttipolitik in the 1980s, as politicized West German women began debating what course women's representation should follow. In contrast to the earlier feminist emphasis on equality for women in the workplace and on emancipatory politics, new groups of women in and outside of the parliament began promoting politics based on the interests of motherhood and family. While obviously not reflecting the state-driven policy of the GDR's Muttipolitik, it became clear in the West German context that women's issues remained electorally contestable.[56] West German policy overall was in some ways much more conservative regarding the role of the family and the woman's role therein than was East Germany's policy.[57] However, what was clearly different was that the introduction of the Greens into West German politics made postmaterialist values politically salient. The new emphasis on the environment, peace issues, and women's issues reflected the concerns of an increasingly educated and affluent society, and would necessarily begin to change the context of the political debate and, over time, offer new opportunities for women.[58]

Recently, the parties have been competing with one another in trying to reform the German workplace model, an issue at the heart of women's concerns in both East and West. The SPD has been competing with the PDS and the Alliance 90/Greens over how far to push women's interests, but all parties, including the CDU/CSU-FDP, are now adovcating more flexibility in Germany's workplace model so that women and men will begin to share more of the family and child-rearing experiences, and that both thereby divide the costs of increased unemployment among the work force. The SPD has also argued for a policy that would promote women in situations where the man and woman are equally qualified. The PDS and Alliance 90/Greens go even further in calling for the promotion of women until they have reached 50 percent of all positions.[59]

Innovation and the Forces of Change

The conventional wisdom concerning the German political system is that it is incrementalist. While there is much truth to the claim, it is also apparent that the German party and electoral system is capable of accommodation and innovation. As the rise of the Greens showed during the 1980s, the system of PR allows for a greater measure of change through institutional accommodation than the winner-take-all, or first-past-the-post, system as found in the United States.

The evolution of new and smaller parties is also accommodated by the dominant role played by state and local politics in Germany, where these parties can establish and organize themselves and gain national attention.[60] Both institutional attributes of the German political system encourage the ideological diversity and the political responsiveness of the major parties. This ability to accommodate changing interests is reflected in Germany's adaptation to increased demands from women for participation and representation.

The German PR system propels parties to innovate more than is true in the winner-take-all systems. First, parties in PR systems are obliged to nominate candidates representative of a cross section of the populace. Second, because the party leadership has the ability to influence directly the nomination process, they can enact change quickly once they have decided upon a course. Illustrative of this phenomenon are the decisions taken by the Greens, then the SPD, and just recently by the CDU, to enforce through quotas the promotion of women as party candidates and in official party positions.[61]

Central to the innovative nature of the German electoral system is the fact that a minor party can reach the political center after passing the 5 percent hurdle, attract a public following, raise political issues to new prominence, and thereby force mainstream parties to respond. The introduction of the Greens into the West German national political system in the 1980s forced the major parties to innovate on issues concerning the environment, nuclear energy, weapons and waste, and women. After the Greens arrived on the national scene, they addressed directly such issues as sexism in the German Bundestag and gender equality.[62] The proportion of women in the Bundestag jumped considerably thereafter. In 1983, the year the Greens entered parliament, the proportion of women in the Bundestag was 9.8 percent. By 1987, it was 15.4 percent. The increase was due largely to greater numbers in the Greens faction.[63] As Eva Kolinsky notes, although the Greens won just over 8 percent of the vote that year, it claimed about one-third of the women members.[64]

The number of women in the German Bundestag has continued to climb. Ironically, it was the conservatives who first responded to the new focus placed on women's issues. In 1985, just a short time after the Greens appeared in parliament, the CDU's party congress focused on women's concerns. In an attempt to regain flagging female support, especially among young women, the CDU concluded that singing the "praise of the family, of home, hearth and children, without recognizing that the modern woman also wanted to work and be socially and financially independent" was counterproductive.[65]

In 1986, the Greens prescribed a 50 percent quota for all party organization and party candidate positions to be filled by women.[66] Following the lead of the Greens, the SPD determined in 1988 to increase the proportion of women who stood as party candidates by establishing a quota of 33 percent. The SPD increased their quota to

40 percent for party office posts in 1992.[67] Tracing these policies helps explain the increase in Greens membership and support among western German women and the fact that the SPD has been compelled to follow suit since it was losing members to the Greens.[68]

As shown above, women voted as a group in the October elections more for the SPD, the Alliance 90/Greens, and the PDS than they did for the ruling party coalition. Younger women heavily supported the Alliance 90/Greens, where women now make up 59.2 percent of the party faction (twenty-nine out of forty-nine deputies). Women make up 33.7 percent of the SPD's faction (eighty-five out of 252 representatives), up from 27.2 percent in the last parliamentary cycle. Scharping named nineteen women to be members of his proposed government cabinet and personal advisors, meeting the 40 percent requirement. Women make up 40 percent of the PDS faction (twelve of thirty members).

In contrast to the left-of-center parties, women make up only 19.2 percent of the FDP (9 out of 47) and 14.3 percent of the CDU factions (42 out of 294).[69] However, the autumn election results had an immediate impact on the CDU. In November 1994, a month after his narrow victory, Kohl determined that the CDU's poor showing among women, and especially younger women, demanded that the party change course. In a striking and bold move, Kohl therefore recommended that the CDU adopt a quota system wherein women would receive 30 percent of all party posts, and whereby 30 percent of party candidates at all levels would be women. By a narrow vote (416–361), and despite prior hostility to the left's embrace of quotas, the party endorsed the measure.[70] That leaves the FDP as the only party that refuses to incorporate a quota system, although the party has been actively pursuing ways to increase women's representation short of that option.

While the 1995 proportion of women in parliaments worldwide dropped from about 15 percent to 10 percent (between 1988 and today), the proportion of female Bundestag members increased from 20.7 percent to 26.3 percent in the 16 October elections, or 177 of the 672 members.[71] By way of comparison, women are even more visible in the Scandinavian political systems, holding nine of fifteen ministerial posts in the newly formed Social Democratic government in Sweden.[72] Women also now hold 41 percent of the Swedish parliamentary seats, an increase of 8 percent over the 1990 results.[73]

German women made great advances when compared to the American election results. Women gained only one seat in Congress in the national elections of November 1994. Their proportion of representation remains at 10 percent, or fifty-five of the 535 members. As figure 5.7 shows, women have advanced in the Bundestag much more rapidly than they have in the U.S. Congress.

FIGURE 5.7

PERCENTAGE OF WOMEN AS TOTAL MEMBERSHIP IN GERMAN BUNDESTAG AND U.S. CONGRESS

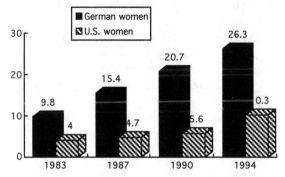

Sources: Lemke; *Week in Germany;* and Harold M. Stanley and Richard G. Niemi, "Vital Statistics on American Politics," *Congressional Quarterly* 4/e (1994): 203.

As Tina Hoffhaus and Eva Kolinsky argue, the accommodational aspects of the German PR system have been most reflected by the party list, or second vote component, of the electoral system, where women have had success as candidates. Women candidates are not selected or elected as often as district candidates in constituency seats, or according to the first vote that is closer to the winner-take-all system. Statistically, all parties have placed women as list candidates more often than as district candidates. Over the years, women elected by the list have outnumbered successful district candidates by far more than a 2:1 ratio; in some election years it has been as high as a 4:1 ratio.[74]

Some of the reasons that parties have been less likely to place women as constituency candidates include the tendency to attribute traditional and stereotypical roles to women, the likelihood that women will have less name recognition than men, and that they are less likely to come from a profession that is held in high public regard. Women will likewise be less secure in their political careers than men because they are still the main homemakers and child-rearers.[75] Even here, however, the Greens have begun the process of change with their 50 percent quota goal for women in all political positions and at all levels.

Thus, it is clear that German parties are responding to the cluster of women's demands and interests. The election in October 1994 illustrated a number of significant institutional aspects of the German political system. The regional differentiation in female support for opposition and minority parties reflected once again the crucial role that PR and federalism play. The election confirmed the importance of women voters for all parties. It revealed that the result of women's voting behavior in the October elections directly affected CDU policy regarding women and gender issues.

Finally, the institutional mechanisms in the German system that accommodate change on women's issues will likely be reinforced at the European Union (EU) level. Recent institutional recommendations by the European Parliament have advocated more female representation at the Europewide level. If successful, the push will undoubtedly reinforce such policies at the national levels.[76]

Conclusion

The 1994 elections revealed that just below the surface of continuity reflected by the CDU/CSU-FDP October victory, there is volatile movement in German politics. The role of women in the new Germany is central to that dynamism. The election revealed that women are increasingly dissatisfied with the policies that have been promoted and pursued by the ruling coalition. In both the eastern and western states, women showed their dissatisfaction by voting in large numbers for left-of-center and opposition parties. Particularly prone to such voting behavior were women in the younger age groups.

The consequences of women's actions over time have had a strong impact on party behavior. Because of the German PR system, parties have often been compelled to respond to changing demands. The immediate effect of the 1994 elections has been to sharpen party concerns for women. The poor showing of the CDU/CSU among women inspired the recent party decision to establish a quota for filling positions with women. The relative success of German women at entering national office was definitely reflected in the October elections. In sum, the October results of the "super election year" reflected simultaneously an increase in women's dissatisfactions with the political status quo and the relative responsiveness of the German political system to those dissatisfactions.

Notes

1. *Focus Wahl-Spezial,* 18 October 1994, p. 26.

2. For an excellent discussion of the German PR system as compared to the British electoral system, see Tina Hoffhaus, "Wahlsysteme und Frauenrepräsentation," *Aus Politik und Zeitgeschichte* B45 (5 November 1993): 22–29.

3. Renate Koecher, "Auf Einer Woge der Euphorie," *Aus Politik und Zeitgeschichte* B51–52/94 (23 December 1994): 16–21, esp. 19.

4. *Focus Wahl-Spezial,* 27.

5. Forschungsgruppe Wahlen e.V., No. 7, 13–15, 18, 105; "Fortsetzung: Bundesrepublik Deutschland," Infratest Burke GmbH Berlin, 30.

6. Forschungsgruppe Wahlen e.V., No. 7, 13–15, 18, 105. See also *Focus Wahl-Spezial,* 18 October 1994, p. 26.

7. Infas, 16 October 1994.

8. Forschungsgruppe Wahlen e.V., No. 7, 13–15 (Mannheim: Institut für Wahlanalysen und Gesellschaftsbeobachtung, 1994), 18. I thank Mr. Dieter Roth for sending me this material. See also "Fortsetzung: Bundesrepublik Deutschland," Infratest Burke GmbH Berlin, 31. I thank Fritz Morris for his help in acquiring this material and am especially grateful to Frau Rita Mueller-Hilmer for sending it to me.

9. "Fortsetzung: Bundesrepublik Deutschland," Infratest Burke GmbH Berlin, 30; David P. Conradt, *The German Polity,* 5th ed. (New York: Longman, 1993), 126.

10. Conradt, *The German Polity,* 5th ed., 126.

11. *Focus Wahl-Spezial,* 25; "Super Election Year 1994 Reports," No. X, Part I. Washington, D.C.: American Institute for Contemporary German Studies Documentation Center, in cooperation with the Forschungsgruppe Wahlen E.V., 1994). I thank Christian Søe for getting this material to me.

12. Infas, 16 October 1994.

13. Matthias Jung and Dieter Roth, "Kohls Knappster Sieg," *Aus Politik und Zeitgeschichte* B51–52/94 (23 December 1994): 3–15, esp. 9–10.

14. *Focus Wahl-Spezial,* 25.

15. Forschungsgruppe Wahlen, 18; Infratest, 33.

16. Roth, "Kohls Knappster Sieg," 10; *Focus Wahl Spezial,* p. 26.

17. Forschungsgruppe Wahlen e.V., No. 7, 13–15, 18. See also "Super Election Year 1994 Reports."

18. *Politbarometer* 11/94 (Forschungsgruppe Wahlen e.V., Mannheim), 4.

19. Ronald Inglehart, *Culture Shift in Advanced Industrial Society* (Princeton: Princeton University Press, 1990), 68.

20. Ursula Feist, "Nichtwähler 1994," *Aus Politik und Zeitgeschichte* B51– 52 (23 December 1994): 35–46, esp. 36.

21. *Focus Wahl-Spezial,* 18 October 1994, 25–26; EMNID (Bielefeld, 1994), 15.

22. Infas, 16 October 1994, p. 96; *Focus Wahl-Spezial*, 26.

23. *Focus Wahl-Spezial*, 26.

24. *Focus Wahl-Spezial*, 18 October 1994, p. 26. "Fortsetzung: Bundesrepublik Deutschland," Infratest Burke GmbH Berlin, 30.

25. Jürgen W. Falter and Markus Klein, "Die Wähler der PDS bei der Bundestagwahl 1994," *Aus Politik und Zeitgeschichte* B51–52 (23 December 1994): 22–35, esp. 29–30.

26. Feist, "Nichtwähler 1994," 36, 38.

27. Ibid., 39.

28. See Hanna Schissler, "Women in West Germany from 1945 to the Present," in Michael G. Huelshoff et al., eds., *From Bundesrepublik to Deutschland: German Politics After Unification* (Ann Arbor: University of Michigan Press, 1993), 117–36, esp. 119. After the efforts of people like the SPD's Elisabeth Selbert, the West German Basic Law declared simply: "Men and women are equal."

29. Friederike Maier, "The Labour Market for Women and Employment Perspectives in the Aftermath of German Unification," *Cambridge Journal of Economics* 17, no. 4 (December 1993): 266–94, esp. 272–73.

30. A recent example of this occurred in June 1994 when the German Trade Union Council passed over a woman for a lesser known man as chair. See Brandon Mitchener, "A Woman's Fight for German Labor," *International Herald Tribune*, 13 June 1994.

31. Christel Lane, "Gender and the Labour Market in Europe: Britain, Germany and France Compared," *The Sociological Review*, no. 2 (May 1993): 274–301, esp. 279.

32. Charlotte Bach, "Minding Their Own Businesses," *The Guardian*, 12 June 1992, p. 24.

33. "Women Still at a Disadvantage, Government Study Finds," *The Week in Germany*, 28 October 1994.

34. Christiane Lemke, "Old Troubles and New Uncertainties: Women and Politics in United Germany," in Michael G. Huelshoff et al., eds., *From Bundesrepublik to Deutschland: German Politics After Unification* (Ann Arbor: University of Michigan Press, 1993), 152.

35. Monika Wulf-Mathies, quoted in Michael Christie, "German Women Kick Up a Row Over Sex Discrimination," Reuters World Service, 8 March 1994, LEXUS-NEXUS.

36. Christel Lane, "Gender and the Labor Market in Europe: Britain, Germany and France Compared," *The Sociological Review* 41, no. 2 (May 1993): 274–301, esp. 282.

37. Schaffner Goldberg, "Women on the Verge," 40–41.

38. See Lemke, "Old Troubles and New Uncertainties," 151, 152. There is some disagreement on women and employment statistics. Myra Marx Ferree cites the figure of women working in the GDR prior to 1989 as 91 percent, and the number of unemployed women in 1991 standing at 61 percent of total unemployed. Myra Marx Ferree, "The Rise and Fall of 'Mommy Politics': Feminism

and Unification in (East) Germany," *Feminist Studies* 1 (spring 1993): 89–115; statistics on 91, 104.

39. Marx Ferree, "The Rise and Fall of 'Mommy Politics,'" p. 104; Lemke, "Old Troubles and New Uncertainties," 152; Schaffner Goldberg, "Women on the Verge," 35–44.

40. Marx Ferree, "The Rise and Fall of 'Mommy Politics,'" 91–92; Gertrude Schaffner Goldberg, "Women on the Verge: Winners and Losers in German Unification," *Social Policy* 22 (fall 1991): 35–44, esp 35–39.

41. Marx Ferree, "The Rise and Fall of 'Mommy Politics,'" 93.

42. Ibid., 93. See her full discussion of the two stages of policy toward women and employment, 91–98.

43. Ibid., 98–103.

44. See discussion in Gabriele Czarnowski, "Abortion as Political Conflict in the Unified Germany," *Parliamentary Affairs* 47, no. 2 (April 1994): 252–67.

45. Czarnowski, "Abortion as Political Conflict in the Unified Germany," 263–65.

46. Ibid., 265–67.

47. Lemke, "Old Troubles and New Uncertainties," 160.

48. "Spiegel Umfrage Über West-Deutsche und Ost-Deutsche im Vergleich (II)," *Der Spiegel* 47(19 November 1990): 113–27; findings on 119.

49. Lane, "Gender and the Labor Market in Europe," 294.

50. Christopher Anderson, "Political Elites and Electoral Rules: The Composition of the Bundestag, 1949–1990," in Christopher Anderson et al., eds., *The Domestic Politics of German Unification* (Boulder: Lynne Rienner Publishers, 1993), 73–96, quote on 86.

51. Frank Louis Rusciano, "Rethinking the Gender Gap: The Case of West German Elections, 1949–1987," *Comparative Politics* 24, no. 3 (April 1992): 335–57, esp. 348–53.

52. Eva Kolinski, "The West German Greens: A Women's Party?" *Parliamentary Affairs* 41, no. 1 (January 1988): 129–39, esp. 136–37.

53. Rusciano, "Rethinking the Gender Gap," 353.

54. Kolinski, "The West German Greens," esp. 136.

55. Ibid., esp. 129.

56. Ibid., esp. 145.

57. See the interesting discussion comparing West German, British, and French policies in Lane, "Gender and the Labor Market in Europe," 274–301.

58. See Rusciano's discussion in "Rethinking the Gender Gap," esp. 348–53. See also Inglehart, *Culture Shift,* esp. chapters 9–10.

59. Renate Wolter, "Nachdenken über die Quote," *Frankfurter Allgemeine Zeitung,* 8 October 1994, 3; Kolinsky, "The West German Greens," 147.

60. Conradt, *The German Polity,* 5th Edition, 189–202.

61. Tina Hoffhaus, "Wahlsysteme und Frauenrepräsentation," 22.

62. Lemke, "Old Troubles and New Uncertainties," 155.

63. Ibid., 147–66.

64. Kolinsky, "The West German Greens," 133.

65. Ibid., 146.

66. Ibid., 130.

67. Lemke, "Old Troubles and New Uncertainties," 157.

68. Hoffhaus, "Wahlsysteme und Frauenrepräsentation," 29.

69. Tom Heneghan, "Kohl's CDU for Women's Quota, Tough on Bihac," Reuter Textline, 28 November 1994, LEXUS; "Christian Democrats Re-Elect Kohl as Party Leader, Approve Proposal to Help Women Rise Through the Ranks," *The Week in Germany*, 2 December 1994; "Women are Big Winners in German Elections—More Female Deputies," Deutsche Presse-Agentur, 17 October 1994, LEXUS-NEXUS.

70. See Marjorie Miller, "Kohl's Party Sets Quota for Women," *Los Angeles Times*, 29 November 1994. I thank Christian Søe for suggesting I read this article. See also Heneghan, "Kohl's CDU for Women's Quota"; "Germany: Kohl's CDU Wants Quota for More Women in its Ranks," Reuter Textline, 18 November 1994, LEXUS-NEXUS. To avoid the left's approach, the CDU calls the quota a quorum and has determined that another third of the party's faction must be men.

71. The statistics come from a UN report cited in *The Week in Germany*, 28 October 1994, 2; and from "Women Were Big Winners in German Elections—More Female Deputies," Deutsche Presse-Agentur, 17 October 1994, LEXUS.

72. Richard Murphy, "Absence of Women at EU Summit Shocks Swedes," *The Reuter European Community Report*, 10 December 1994, LEXUS.

73. Andreas Doepfner, "Schweden: Hoher Frauenteil in Schwedens Reichstag," *Neue Zuercher Zeitung*, 20 September 1994, Reuters Textline, 21 September LEXUS.

74. Hoffhaus, "Wahlsysteme und Frauenrepräsentation," 23–25; Kolinsky, "The West German Greens," 130–31. See also Anderson, "Political Elites and Electoral Rules: The Composition of the Bundestag, 1949–1990," esp. 74–75.

75. Hoffhaus, "Wahlsysteme und Frauenrepräsentation," 25–28. See also Marcia Lynn Whicker et al., "Women in Congress" in Lois Lovelace Duke, ed., *Women in Politics: Outsiders or Insiders?* (Englewood Cliffs: Prentice Hall, 1993), 136–51.

76. Murphy, "Absence of Women at EU Summit Shocks Swedes"; Janet McEvoy, "European Union Prepares for the Battle of the Sexes," Limited Reuters World Service, 22 August 1994, LEXUS.

6

GERMANY'S GENERAL ELECTION IN 1994

WHO VOTED FOR WHOM?

WOLFGANG G. GIBOWSKI

The German general election, held on 16 October, was the highlight of a marathon election year in 1994. The results of the election confirmed once again the long-standing observation that incumbent German governments do not normally lose general elections. In the history of the Federal Republic of Germany, no opposition leader has ever succeeded in replacing the incumbent chancellor as a direct result of a general (i.e., Bundestag or federal parliament) election. (Thus far, the only change of government to come about after a general election was in 1969, but this was due to a change in coalition partners rather than to the results of the election.) However, of all the general elections held since 1949, the governing party has never had such a small lead over the opposition parties as is the case after this year's election: 48.3 percent for the CDU/CSU and FDP, as opposed to 48.1 percent for the SPD, Greens, and PDS. The fact that this has resulted in a majority of ten seats is due only to the peculiarities of the German electoral system, under which "additional seats" may occur in specific circumstances.

Any analysis of the results of general elections must always be twofold: on the one hand, an analysis of the factors that bring about consistency in individual voting patterns for a large proportion of the electorate—something which has always been evident in western Germany—and, on the other, an explanation as to what current political influences are responsible for any changes in voting patterns.

The reunification of Germany has brought about significant change in this regard. As such, an election analysis typical of the western part of the country will be applied to western and eastern

Germany separately, with a view to bringing out differences in voting patterns among western and eastern Germans. In answering the question "Who voted for whom?" an attempt will be made to determine voting patterns in the relevant groups of German society. To begin with, however, let us take a look at current political influences.

A Mega-Election Year in Retrospect

At the beginning of 1994 very few people in Germany believed that the CDU/CSU and FDP coalition government would win in the October general election. Most of the polls agreed that the mood of the electorate was very critical of the government and its leaders. According to a representative survey carried out by Infas in January 1994, 74 percent of the people polled in the western part of Germany and 79 percent of those interviewed in the eastern part of the country felt that the government was doing rather a bad job of carrying out the tasks with which it had been entrusted. At the same time, a survey carried out by Emnid showed that 55 percent of Germans in the western part of the country and 56 percent in the eastern part did not agree with Helmut Kohl's policies. This was consistent with the results of a poll conducted by the electoral research group Forschungsgruppe Wahlen, which showed that 55 percent of those polled thought that the opposition was likely to win the general election, as opposed to 25 percent who still had confidence in the Kohl government. Somewhat later, in February, Infratest Burke came to the conclusion on the basis of surveys representative of the whole population that 60 percent of the German electorate wanted a change of government.[1]

Given the results of the polls available at the time, it was logical to assume that most of the population wanted to see a change of government. The critical mood among the population was not surprising. Too much had occurred in Germany and Europe in recent years for this not to have had any influence on the mood of the population.

Reunification was welcomed by almost all Germans, both in the western and eastern parts of the country.[2] However, the economic consequences of unification were far more serious than had at first been assumed. While economic progress was being made in the new states, it had become apparent that the process of harmonizing living standards was going to take far longer and cost considerably more than had initially been thought. It soon became evident that the annual financial transfer requirement from West to East had reached the enormous level of DM150 billion. The consequences of the global economic recession, together with the economic, political, and military impact of the collapse of the former Soviet Union, had created a climate of fear and insecurity. In western Germany there was increasing fear that the ecological effects of these changes would worsen living conditions which, for most people, had thus far been good. In the East, doubts were being raised as to whether the new system would keep the economic and social promises it had made. Although annual financial transfers had taken on dimensions that would previously have been inconceivable, at the end of 1993 some 78 percent of the people living in the new states still felt Bonn was doing too little to bring living conditions into line with those in western Germany whereas, in the West, 70 percent of those polled felt that Bonn was doing exactly the right amount or was even doing too much.[3]

The constant flow of asylum seekers, which was a further problem, particularly for western Germans, had receded in the second half of 1993, but the social and political consequences of this issue continued to be felt. There was a sense of stress and worry in both parts of the country, and it is hardly surprising that such a situation should give rise to sharp criticism of the government. This was, indeed, the political mood at the beginning of 1994.

In its January poll, the electoral research group Forschungsgruppe Wahlen found that support for the CDU/CSU in both western (31.5 percent) and eastern Germany (26.6 percent) was lagging decidedly behind that for the SPD, which enjoyed ratings of 46 percent in the West and 36.4 percent in the East. The FDP had the support of 5.7 percent of the electorate in the West and 4.4 percent in the East, while the Greens could boast figures of 10.8 percent (West) and 4.8 percent (East) respectively. The right-wing extremist Republikaner party had the support of 2.6 percent of the electorate in the West and 1.4 percent in the East, whereas the PDS, the renamed former SED, had the support of 18 percent of the voters in the East. At this point then, opinion polls were showing a clear majority of voters in favor of the opposition parties.

Factors that Determined Changes in Voting Trends: The Political Issues, the Leading Candidates, the Parties, and Tactical Voting

Voters lacking a firm identification with a particular party, the so-called floating voters, are the ones most likely to alter their political preferences because of current political events. According to the Ann Arbor model, there are three areas where current political events can help political parties to gain votes:[4] the party's supposed ability to solve problems which the floating voter regards as important, the voter's perception of the party's leading politicians, and his or her perception of the external image of the party. Ultimately, it is the combination of these factors that determines how a voter casts his or her vote. In this respect, it is a question of how well a leading candidate is accepted within his or her party and how convincingly parties and leading candidates are in getting their views across on the main issues of the day.[5]

In a political system like that of the Federal Republic of Germany, whose social and institutional structures make it almost a foregone conclusion that general elections will result in a coalition government, deliberations on possible coalitions and the tactical voting that ensues as a result of this are a significant complement to the Ann Arbor model. Tactical voting means that voters arrive at their decision by considering how best to achieve or avoid a particular combination of governing parties. Tactical voting is common among those voters who want to see a particular coalition in government. In the 1994 general election this would have been one of the two possible coalitions, i.e., either the CDU/CSU and FDP, or the SPD and the Greens. Depending on the expected outcome of the election—which is why opinion polls are important in this respect—voters of this kind may choose to vote for two parties in the coalition in question so as to put their vote to optimum use. The factors determining voting behavior described above must be seen as a package in which the personal element is of paramount importance. After all, policies do have to be conveyed to the electorate. Addressing major issues and problems has a limited effect, however, if the message is put across by an unpopular politician. A popular politician, on the other hand, can compensate for any problems his or her party might have, at least for a certain period of time.

In Germany, however, the popularity of a leading politician does not automatically convert to votes for his or her party. In 1980, for example, over 60 percent of voters said that they would prefer to see the reelection of the incumbent chancellor, the SPD's Helmut Schmidt, and only 29 percent expressed support for Franz Josef Strauß, the CDU/CSU challenger.[6] This preference for Helmut Schmidt cannot have been decisive in determining the outcome of the election since the CDU/CSU ended up with 44.5 percent of the votes cast and the SPD with "only" 42.9 percent.

But if approval or disapproval of a candidate cannot be directly translated into votes, why are leading candidates so important for their parties? One must not forget that the main reasons for changes in voting behavior are intertwined in a very complex manner and that the significance of individual factors is difficult to determine. Within this complex structure, the role of a leading politician is to put abstract policies into concrete terms for the voters. Because of the contradictory opinions they hear from experts, some voters are unable to make up their minds about certain issues in a rational manner. The more sophisticated political issues become and the more difficult it becomes for voters to understand foreign policy, economic, and technical decisions, the more individual voters need to reduce the complexity of the political process by relying on the expert capabilities of their political representatives. The popularity of a leading politician is thus a reflection of how much competence the voters think he or she possesses. A popular politician will have fewer problems explaining his or her stance on a political issue than one who is less popular. Voters will give a popular politician personal credit for political successes in his or her special field, but will not do this in the case of a less popular politician. This is where the connection between politicians and their parties becomes evident. The popularity of leading politicians is not only valuable to their parties because they are able to attract votes, but also because they can convey the message of party policy to the electorate.

The Issues in Election Year 1994

As noted above, political issues and problems cannot be considered in isolation. One must also consider them in the context of how they were highlighted and dealt with by leading politicians and/or by the government and the opposition.

The 1990–94 parliamentary term was rich in issues and headlines. The monthly surveys of the electoral research group Forschungsgruppe Wahlen show that for voters in the West two issues were of particular importance: concerns about unemployment and the problem of asylum seekers and foreigners. The second issue, in particular, had been a major item on the agenda for several years. In the course of 1991, a total of 256,000 asylum seekers and 220,000 ethnic German resettlers from eastern and southeastern Europe arrived in Germany. Despite their German origin, ethnic resettlers are regarded by the native population for the most part as foreigners. The year 1992 saw the arrival of another 430,000 asylum seekers and more than 230,000 resettlers. As a consequence of this seemingly uncontrolled flood of asylum seekers, in September 1991 the topic "asylum seekers and foreigners" was, for the first time, ranked at the top of the list of important political issues by 50 percent of those polled, and it remained at the top of the list until July 1993. Only when the asylum laws were amended, a measure agreed upon by both the government and the opposition, did the influx of asylum seekers begin to decrease and the issue begin to lose importance in the eyes of the population. In the meantime, violent demonstrations against foreigners had led people, both in Germany and abroad, to speak of a general hostility towards foreigners among the German population. This impression was reinforced by the actions of right-wing groups using Nazi symbols and shouting anti-Semitic slogans.

There are, however, clear differences between the attitudes of such groups and those of the rest of the population. In western Germany, where the people have worked and lived with foreigners for over thirty years, a clear majority of over 60 percent said that they found it perfectly acceptable for Germany to have so many foreign residents. Well over 80 percent of Germans in both the East and the West were in favor of granting the basic right of asylum for victims of political persecution, as is laid down in the constitution or Basic Law. This overwhelming support for the granting of asylum by Germany remained constant during the period when the issue was high on the political agenda. At the moment, however, over three-fourths of the population is of the opinion that most asylum seekers are abusing the asylum laws.[7] This shows clearly with what complexity the issue has been examined and discussed by the population.

The heated public debate about asylum seekers gave new life to the right-wing Republikaner party, which many people had written off following unification. In April 1992 the Republikaner even managed to win seats in the state parliament of Baden-Württemberg, gaining 10.9 percent of the votes. The political success of radical right-wing parties once again brought the issue of right-wing extremism to the forefront of public discussion. However, concerns about right-wing extremism and the Republikaners faded with the gradual disappearance of the asylum issue. Other issues that were regarded as important, such as inflationary tendencies in the economy or environmental protection, remained of limited significance, even when observed over longer periods. Since autumn 1993, however, unemployment has been the dominant issue, even in the West. Prior to that point, views on what constituted the key issues on the political agenda had differed between East and West. Now this difference no longer existed.

FIGURES 6.1 AND 6.2

THE MOST IMPORTANT ISSUES (IN PERCENT)

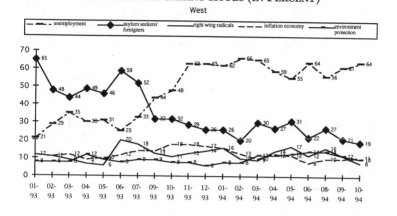

West

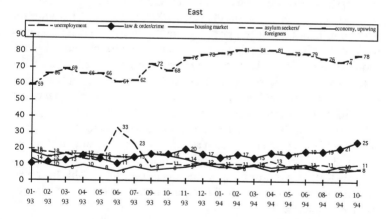

East

Data: Monthly Polls† of the Forschungsgruppe Wahlen e.V. Mannheim; Graphics: BPA.

As figures 6.1 and 6.2 show, since unification the political agenda in the new states has been dominated by the threat of unemployment.[8] This issue also gained in importance throughout 1994. Law and order was also seen as an important issue in the East, but in the West it was of marginal importance. The asylum issue was of lesser significance in the East and quickly faded in the West following the 1993 amendment. Environmental protection ranked third on the political agenda in western surveys. In the East, it was still regarded as largely irrelevant.

On the whole, the lists of issues in both eastern and western Germany are characterized by everyday concerns: bread-and-butter issues dominate; nonmaterial issues are attributed only peripheral importance in the West and none at all in the East. At the beginning of the election year, it was uncertain what issues would be taken up by the parties and the leading candidates in their election campaigns.

Leading Candidates and Perceived Party Competence

Perceptions and approval ratings of the two leading candidates, Chancellor Helmut Kohl and SPD challenger Rudolf Scharping, at the beginning of 1994 reflected the political mood at the time. In an approval-rating scale ranging between +5 and -5 and involving ten of the country's most important politicians, Helmut Kohl received an average rating of -0.3 in the western states and an average of -0.6 in the East. The western rating was the worst, the eastern rating the second worst ever recorded (January 1994).[9] Rudolf Scharping, on the other hand, was given good approval ratings, receiving averages of 1.1 (West) and 1.2 (East). At the same time 52 percent of those polled wanted to see Rudolf Scharping become the next chancellor, as opposed to 34 percent who preferred Helmut Kohl. In the spring of 1994 the approval ratings for the chancellor and his challenger remained unchanged with Scharping in the lead. Further polls in March showed, however, that a majority of the electorate perceived Kohl as being more energetic, a stronger leader, a man better suited to head a government, and, in particular, superior in representing German interests in dealings with other countries. Kohl, however, was still seen as less able than Scharping to resolve the country's economic problems.

Scharping's lead in this area of economic competence was unusual for a top SPD candidate. Economic competence is generally an area where the Christian Democrats have the advantage. Ever since Ludwig Erhard's successful introduction of the "social free market" economy (free enterprise with the welfare state) in the late 1940s, the public has seen the CDU as the "economic party." Kohl's deficit vis-à-vis Scharping in this area, a key issue[10] for most voters, reflected the loss of economic competence suffered by the CDU-led government since mid-1993. By January 1994, nearly 40 percent of those polled in both parts of the country felt that an

SPD-led government would be more competent in resolving the country's economic problems. Only 30 percent of western voters and 20 percent in the East believed that the Bonn coalition had this competence.[11] Clearly the CDU's deficit in the economic area had exerted a negative influence on the public's perception of the governing parties and also significantly worsened Helmut Kohl's approval ratings.

Soon after these negative ratings in early 1994, signs of an economic upturn became increasingly evident. It was the chancellor who was among the first to discern this positive trend, which he emphasized in his campaign appearances. Increasingly, the process of economic recovery became associated with Helmut Kohl and the Christian Democrats. Kohl's confidence, which was initially dismissed as campaign gesturing, proved ultimately to be well-founded.

FIGURE 6.3

PUBLIC EXPECTATIONS ABOUT THE ECONOMY
AND THE ELECTION WINNER

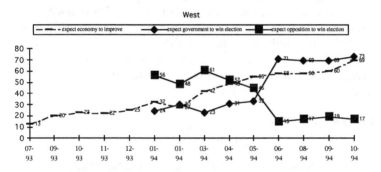

Data: Monthly polls[†] of the Forschungsgruppe Wahlen e.V. Mannheim; Graphics: BPA.

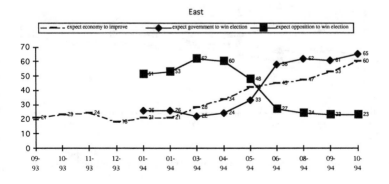

Figure 6.3 shows the relationship in both parts of the country between the electorate's perception of the economy and its expectation about the winner of the election. When asked in March 1994 whether "the economy is currently on the upswing again," 42 percent of western voters stated that it was. By May, this figure had risen to 55 percent. In the new states the trend was slower, but also positive. In March, 22 percent of those polled believed that the economy was recovering, compared with 42 percent in May. This trend with regard to economic recovery covaried with the increasing expectation that the incumbent government would be reelected. As figure 6.3 indicates, by May and June 1994 there was no longer any doubt that the Kohl government would win. This was also accompanied by significant improvement in the public's attitude about the government's economic competence. By April a majority of voters once again considered the current government to be more able in economic matters. In eastern Germany this trend was somewhat slower, but reached the same level by June.

Perceptions of an improving economy also helped the chancellor to catch up with his challenger, Rudolf Scharping, in the public opinion polls and to overtake him by election day (figure 6.4). Kohl's approval ratings on a scale of +5 to -5 rose from an average of +0.4 in May to +0.8 in June in the West and from -0.1 to +0.1 during the same period in the East. Scharping's ratings, on the other hand, declined over the same period from +1.2 to +0.4 in the West and from +0.9 to +0.7 in the East.[12]

FIGURE 6.4

PREFERRED CHANCELLOR

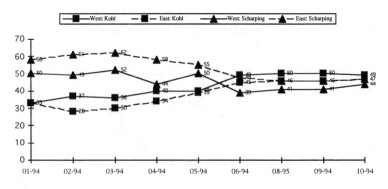

Data: Monthly polls[†] of the Forschungsgruppe Wahlen e.V. Mannheim; Graphics: BPA.

   This strong relationship between public perceptions of an improving economy and the approval ratings of Helmut Kohl and the CDU was based in fact on increasingly positive "hard" economic news. In the fall of 1993 most economic experts were predicting an economic growth rate for 1994 of only 1.5 percent; by May 1994 these same experts estimated that GNP growth had already reached 2.5 percent for the year. Exports, factory orders for durable goods, and new construction grew at a faster rate than expected.

   Yet, economic factors alone cannot explain the chancellor's comeback. Campaign events also worked in favor of the CDU and Helmut Kohl. One such development was the heated debate over who should succeed Richard von Weizsäcker as federal president. From the outset the CDU/CSU candidate, the president of the Federal Constitutional Court, Roman Herzog, had by far the best chance of winning since the governing parties held a majority in the Federal Assembly, a body composed of national and state-level parliamentarians who elect the president. The Free Democrats did at first put forth a candidate, but it was widely expected that this was largely symbolic and that the party would support Herzog in the later balloting. The SPD, and especially Scharping, created the impression that the chances of the SPD candidate for the presidency, the popular premier of North Rhine-Westphalia, Johannes Rau, were much better than was actually the case, given the SPD's voting strength. Scharping had falsely hoped that enough Free Democrats would eventually switch to Rau in the secret balloting. When the FDP indeed held firm and Herzog was elected, Scharping was bitterly disappointed and more importantly revealed his feelings in public.

   A similar pattern of dashed SPD hopes occurred at the June 1994 European Parliament election. For a time it had appeared that the SPD might be able to overtake the CDU/CSU at this poll. The improving economy and a strong Christian Democratic campaign, however, yielded a solid victory for the chancellor. The European win also revealed the growing weakness of Kohl's junior partner, the Free Democrats, who failed to surmount the 5 percent hurdle. The election confirmed the strong showing of the Greens in the opinion polls, which came largely at the expense of the SPD. The radical-right Republikaner, who had been represented in the European Parliament, failed to clear the 5 percent mark and did not return to Strasbourg. In the East, the PDS (Party of Democratic Socialism) received nearly 20 percent of the vote, but only 4.7 nationwide.

The preelection political climate was also influenced by the September state parliamentary elections in Brandenburg, Saxony, and Bavaria. At all three elections the Free Democrats fell below 5 percent, prompting widespread speculation that Kohl's junior partner might not return to the Bundestag in October. Such a result would have made it impossible for the Christian Democrats to remain the dominant coalition partner and could also threaten Kohl's chancellorship. This possibility made those voters interested in seeing a continuation of the CDU/CSU and FDP government aware of the need to vote in a manner that would promote the coalition, that is to split their ballots by voting for the Christian Democratic candidate with the first ballot and the Free Democrats with the second. Even though the CDU/CSU specifically asked voters to cast both of their votes for the Union, it was clear to tactical voters that there could only be a CDU/CSU and FDP majority if the FDP were again in the Bundestag. In the week prior to the general election, 65 percent of those polled in the West who intended to vote for the FDP actually preferred the CDU or CSU. In the East, 45 percent of the FDP voters polled indicated that in reality they were supporters of the CDU.[13]

The results of the September state elections in Brandenburg, Saxony, and Bavaria generally foreshadowed the outcome of the general election. There was strong support for the CDU in Saxony and for the CSU in Bavaria. At the same time the SPD did very well in Brandenburg so that it was not possible to say that the public mood was one-sidedly in favor of a given party. It also became apparent that the Greens were much weaker in the East than they were in the West and that the PDS had clearly become the third strongest party in the former GDR.

Who Voted for Whom?

The question "Who voted for whom?" implies a need to analyze election results in terms of demographic and social structures. From the standpoint of electoral sociology, the results achieved by the parties within various religious and professional groups is of particular interest in western Germany. In these groups there are traditional voter trends in favor of the CDU (CSU) or the SPD, resulting in both parties being able to count on a considerable reserve of loyal voters. This explains why the western German system of political parties has been so stable. At the national level, with the exception of

1972, the CDU/CSU has always been the strongest party with the SPD second. The presence of the new states automatically raised the questions as to whether the western system of political parties and patterns of voting would be able to establish itself there and the extent to which voter trends would correspond to the patterns observed in western Germany.[14]

The central question in the East is whether stable, long-term party loyalties, i.e., a personal identification with a party, are developing or have developed at the individual level, or whether voting trends are determined to a stronger degree than in the West by issues or personalities. After only two national elections, it is difficult to discern any clear patterns. At present, the most salient characteristic of public opinion in the East is its volatility.

Voter Demographics: Age and Gender

The relationships between age, gender, and party preferences at the 1994 election were consistent with past elections. Older voters tend to favor the Christian Democrats while the Social Democrats and Greens do very well among the younger age cohorts. In the case of the Greens, as table 6.1 shows, half of their voters are under the age of 34 and more than three-fourths of their voters are under the age of 45. The differences in male and female voter trends are marginal. The CDU and CSU received a slightly larger number of votes from women than from men, as did the Greens. The SPD has an almost equal number of male and female voters. The same applies to the PDS. The FDP has a somewhat higher number of male voters.

TABLE 6.1

PARTY SUPPORT BY GENDER AND AGE
RESULTS 1994 AND DIFFERENCES TO 1990 IN WEST GERMANY

			Total					
		Difference		Difference		Difference		Difference
Age group	CDU/CSU	1990	SPD	1990	FDP	1990	Greens	1990
18–24	34.2	-1.9	36.3	-0.8	6.8	-3.4	14.9	+5.1
25–34	32.2	-1.9	41.1	-0.7	5.7	-3.4	14.1	+4.3
35–44	36.4	-3.1	39.3	+1.0	7.2	-4.7	12.2	+6.1
45–59	45.6	-2.0	37.5	+3.1	8.6	-3.2	4.5	+2.6
60 and older	50.7	-2.4	34.9	+1.7	8.5	0.0	2.5	+1.8
Total	42.1	-2.2	37.5	+1.8	7.7	-2.9	7.9	+3.1

Men

Age group	Difference CDU/CSU 1990		SPD	Difference 1990	FDP	Difference 1990	Greens	Difference 1990
18–24	36.2	-1.0	34.4	-1.1	7.1	-3.3	13.4	+4.6
25–34	34.8	+0.2	38.0	-2.8	6.1	-3.3	13.1	+4.0
35–44	35.2	-3.5	40.8	+2.6	7.6	-4.2	10.7	+4.6
45–59	44.8	-1.8	37.3	+2.4	9.6	-2.3	4.2	+2.5
60 and older	50.4	+0.2	34.3	+0.3	9.7	+0.8	1.9	+1.2
Total	41.4	-1.2	37.0	+0.5	8.3	-2.3	7.7	+3.1

Women

Age group	Difference CDU/CSU 1990		SPD	Difference 1990	FDP	Difference 1990	Greens	Difference 1990
18–24	31.9	-3.1	37.8	-1.2	6.8	-3.1	16.8	+5.9
25–34	29.5	-4.2	44.5	+1.7	5.3	-3.5	15.5	+5.0
35–44	37.4	-2.8	37.4	-1.0	7.0	-5.0	14.0	+7.9
45–59	47.1	-1.6	36.6	+2.6	8.0	-3.7	5.1	+3.0
60 and older	52.9	-2.1	32.8	+0.2	8.1	-0.2	3.2	+2.5
Total	42.8	-2.5	37.0	+0.8	7.3	-2.7	8.9	+4.3

Source: Exit polls of the Forschungsgruppe Wahlen 1994 and Representative Electoral Statistics 1990.

TABLE 6.2

PARTY SUPPORT BY GENDER AND AGE
RESULTS 1994 AND DIFFERENCES TO 1990 IN EAST GERMANY

Total

Age group	CDU	Difference 1990	SPD	Difference 1990	FDP	Difference 1990	Greens	Difference 1990	PDS	Difference 1990
18–24	29.2	-3.8	25.8	+3.5	3.7	-8.1	10.4	-1.8	22.6	+11.1
25–34	31.2	-5.6	32.3	+8.2	3.4	-8.7	6.4	-2.7	23.0	+11.2
35–44	37.7	-2.5	31.6	+9.8	4.2	-10.8	3.9	-2.8	21.4	+9.8
45–59	39.5	-3.3	32.8	+8.7	3.9	-10.7	3.3	-0.8	19.0	+7.7
60 and older	45.2	-1.4	31.5	+5.2	2.9	-8.0	2.3	+0.7	16.9	+5.2
Total	38.5	-3.3	31.5	+7.2	3.5	-9.4	4.3	-1.9	19.8	+8.7

Men

Age group	CDU	Difference 1990	SPD	Difference 1990	FDP	Difference 1990	Greens	Difference 1990	PDS	Difference 1990
18–24	30.0	-3.0	23.0	+2.0	4.4	-7.0	10.2	-0.6	21.7	+10.1
25–34	35.6	-1.8	31.4	+7.8	3.9	-7.8	4.4	-3.8	18.8	+7.3
35–44	37.2	-2.7	32.9	+10.8	4.4	-10.1	4.3	-1.6	19.9	+8.0
45–59	41.2	+0.2	31.9	+6.6	4.6	-10.1	2.4	-1.0	18.7	+6.8
60 and older	35.2	-6.2	36.1	+7.4	2.3	-8.7	1.4	-0.2	23.1	+8.8
Total	36.9	-2.5	31.8	+7.1	3.9	-9.1	3.8	-1.4	20.3	+8.0

| | **Women** | | | | | | | | |
Age group	Difference CDU 1990		Difference SPD 1990		Difference FDP 1990		Difference Greens 1990		Difference PDS 1990	
18–24	25.2	-7.7	29.9	+6.2	3.0	-9.2	10.9	-2.7	25.0	+3.6
25–34	27.5	-8.7	33.7	+9.1	2.9	-9.7	8.6	-1.4	26.0	+14.0
35–44	37.9	-2.5	30.3	+8.8	4.0	-11.5	3.9	-3.5	22.6	+11.3
45–59	37.5	-6.9	32.5	+9.7	3.7	-10.7	4.4	-0.3	20.4	+9.8
60 and older	50.9	+1.2	29.3	+4.4	3.1	-7.7	3.2	+1.6	12.6	+2.4
Total	39.1	-4.0	31.0	+7.4	3.4	-9.6	5.2	-0.6	19.7	+8.8

Source: Exit polls of the Forschungsgruppe Wahlen 1994 and Representative Electoral Statistics 1990.

When we examine male and female voting patterns among different age groups, i.e., when we combine the age and gender variables, more significant differences are found. In the West among the 18–24 female group, the CDU/CSU trails only slightly behind the SPD. This is largely the result of the low level of support for the Christian Democrats among younger women (table 6.1). Among younger men, however, the CDU/CSU is actually stronger than the SPD. In the second youngest age group (25–34), the SPD has a considerable lead over the CDU/CSU among both men and women. This situation changes when we examine the over-35 age cohorts. Among these age groups the proportion of votes cast for the CDU/CSU is greater among women than among men. Among voters over 45, regardless of gender, the CDU/CSU has a clear majority. The strongest preference for the CDU/CSU over the SPD is, as always, among women over 60. The percentage of votes cast for the CDU/CSU shows a directly proportional connection with age, a factor which is much stronger among women than among men. If we compare the 1990 and 1994 results, it becomes clear that the CDU/CSU sustained its greatest losses among younger women.

The SPD attracts more votes from younger women than from younger men (table 6.1). Its strongest support is from women among the 25–34 age group. The SPD's strongest support among male voters is in the 35–44 age group. In the 1970s the SPD had much stronger support among younger voters than it does today. The Greens, who appeared on the political scene at the federal level for the first time in 1980, succeeded in attracting the support of many younger voters, largely at the expense of the Social Democrats. While the Greens vote remains centered in the youngest cohort, the party also does very well among the 35–44 age group. At the 1994 election, the Greens, in contrast to the elections of the 1980s, received more support among women in the youngest age cohort than among men.

In the new states, the situation for the CDU is almost the same as it is in the West (table 6.2). In general, the CDU receives more voter support from women than from men. However, it received the lowest percentage of votes from women under 35 and the highest percentage of votes from women over 60. The difference between the youngest and oldest group is almost 26 percent. The observations made with regard to the SPD and the Greens for the western states also apply in the East. However, the level of voter support for the Greens is considerably lower in the East than the West. The PDS is a new factor. The slight differences between the various age groups become larger when men and women voters are viewed separately. In all age groups under 60 the PDS attracts more support from women than from men. It also made its greatest gains in these groups, especially among younger women. However, PDS support among women over 60 was well below average.

Voter Demographics: Religion and Occupation

In the West the stability of the party system and voting behavior is explained by party loyalties that exist within certain major groups. These loyalties or identifications are not affected by short-run factors, such as issues and candidates. They are rooted in the social structure and the close relationship between this structure and the established parties.[15] We refer here to the strong ties, evident since the industrial revolution, between labor interests and the SPD and the equally strong relationships that existed between Catholics and the old Center Party, which were then transferred after World War II to the CDU/CSU. The majority of voters in these groups view their respective party, i.e., the SPD in the case of labor and the CDU/CSU in the case of Catholics, as being representative of their interests. As a result of social and regional mobility, these specific groups are becoming smaller, but their party loyalties are still clearly evident.

Over the past several decades, the proportion of Protestants in the West has declined from almost 50 percent to less than 40 percent of the population largely as a result of people leaving the church.[16] Since the number of Catholics was declining more slowly than that of Protestants, the Catholics were, prior to unification, slightly in the majority. In the former GDR, which was hostile to religion, only a minority of the population belonged to a religious group. (The number of Catholics in the East, however, was also very small even before the Communist era.) Reunification has now produced a rough parity between the two religions (table 6.3) and a large group (about 30 percent), above all in the East, without any religious affiliation. Since our main purpose here is to examine the differences in voting patterns among Catholics and Protestants, the voting behavior of this latter group will not be considered at this time.

TABLE 6.3

RELIGIOUS AFFILIATION, 1992 (IN PERCENT)

	Protestants	Catholics	Others/None
Germany	35.7	34.7	29.6
West Germany	38.1	42.9	19.0
East Germany	27.0	5.9	67.0

Percentage of the population (Germans and foreigners), 31 December 1992.
Source: Statistical Yearbook of Germany 1994.

TABLE 6.4

	EMPLOYED PERSONS			
	Self-Employed	Civil Servants	White-Collar Workers	Blue-Collar Workers
Germany	8.4	6.7	45.6	37.8
West Germany without Berlin	9.0	7.9	44.7	36.7
East Germany incl. Berlin	5.7	1.6	49.8	42.7

Percentage of employed persons, May 1994.
Source: Statistical Yearbook of Germany, 1994.

The current occupational structure is presented in table 6.4. Blue-collar workers, who as late as the 1950s were the largest occupational group, now comprise only about 38 percent of the work force. The proportion of self-employed persons, the second-largest occupational group in 1950, has also declined significantly.[17] Unlike religion, unification has not changed the basic all-German occupational structure. There are, of course, still considerably fewer self-employed persons in the new states.

Religion and the Party Vote

The 1994 general election confirmed once again that the CDU/ CSU attracts more voter support among Catholics than Protestants in both parts of the country. The strength of the SPD vote, conversely, is among Protestants and voters with no religious affiliation. The vote also showed that Protestants in the East react differently from Protestants in the West. The CDU secured more voter support among Protestants in the former GDR than it did among Catholics in the old Federal Republic. Those who preserved their religious affiliations in eastern Germany, regardless of whether Catholic or Protestant, were in opposition to the GDR regime, and today the majority of these persons see their values represented more by the CDU than by any other party.

As table 6.5 indicates, the Christian Democrats in 1994 sustained their heaviest losses among those eastern Germans with no religious affiliations, the secular portion of the electorate. SPD gains among eastern Catholics and Protestants came largely at the expense of the FDP and the Greens, but not the Christian Democrats.

TABLE 6.5

PARTY SUPPORT BY RELIGION, 1990–1994

West Germany

Religion	CDU/CSU 1990	Difference	SPD 1990	Difference	FDP 1990	Difference	Greens 1990	Difference	PDS 1990	Difference
Catholics	51.6	-4.7	30.6	-4.0	6.8	-2.0	6.3	+1.8	0.6	+0.5
Protestants	36.5	-3.1	43.7	+4.0	8.2	-5.1	7.8	+3.5	0.7	+0.5
Unaffiliated	28.0	+2.3	40.1	+4.9	8.3	-3.1	14.9	+3.2	3.2	+1.8

East Germany

Religion	CDU/CSU 1990	Difference	SPD 1990	Difference	FDP 1990	Difference	Greens 1990	Difference	PDS 1990	Difference
Catholics	68.5	+2.7	19.5	+8.0	2.5	-8.9	2.5	-3.8	2.9	+1.4
Protestants	53.4	0.0	28.9	+8.8	4.7	-10.7	5.0	-1.1	6.3	+4.5
Unaffiliated	27.1	-6.2	34.1	+5.4	3.1	-9.8	4.3	-4.5	28.8	+15.9

Source: Exit polls of the Forschungsgruppe Wahlen, 1990 and 1994.

The CDU/CSU did not do quite as well among Catholics with strong church ties as it did in 1990. However, the result attained is comparable with past general elections. The same applies with regard to Catholics with weaker ties to the Church. No unusual results were observed in these two groups with regard to the other parties. The CDU/CSU made gains among Catholics who are no longer churchgoers. SPD support in this group was also substantial in comparison with the last election. Among non-Catholics with church ties, i.e., in this case a very small group of Protestants, the CDU/CSU received considerably less support than in 1990, whereas the SPD made considerable gains. On the other hand, there were no changes in voter support among non-Catholics with weaker church ties or with none at all.

Overall, the religious cleavage continues to exist in the West with no significant changes. In the East, the religious cleavage is found not between Catholics and Protestants, but rather between voters with religious ties and those without. Membership in the Protestant church expresses a set of values, the party-political embodiment of which the voters will most likely find in the CDU.

TABLE 6.6

PARTY SUPPORT BY OCCUPATION
RESULTS 1994 AND DIFFERENCES TO 1990 IN GERMANY

	West Germany									
Profession	CDU/CSU	Difference 1990	SPD	Difference 1990	FDP	Difference 1990	Greens	Difference 1990	PDS	Difference 1990
Blue-Collar Workers	35.0	-4.0	49.5	+2.8	3.6	-2.4	5.2	+2.0	1.1	+0.9
White-Collar Workers	39.9	-3.1	37.7	+1.8	8.4	-3.7	9.6	+4.3	1.0	+0.7
	East Germany									
Profession	CDU/CSU	Difference 1990	SPD	Difference 1990	FDP	Difference 1990	Greens	Difference 1990	PDS	Difference 1990
Blue-Collar Workers	40.6	-7.6	35.1	+10.4	3.3	-7.1	3.3	-0.8	14.7	+7.4
White-Collar Workers	32.0	-3.9	30.7	+5.7	3.9	-10.3	5.3	-3.1	26.3	+12.7
Civil Servants	29.9	*	24.4	*	1.2	*	5.0	*	34.6	*
Farmers	59.0	*	22.2	*	1.5	*	6.5	*	9.8	*
Self-Employed	48.3	-0.5	19.7	+3.6	9.7	-10.7	2.4	-1.4	16.9	+11.9

*not asked in 1990
Source: Exit polls of the Forschungsgruppe Wahlen, 1990 and 1994.

Occupation and Labor Union Membership

The CDU sustained losses among blue-collar workers in both parts of the country, but especially in the East, with the SPD the major beneficiary. In eastern Germany, however, the CDU still received more voter support from workers than the SPD. Nonetheless, the data presented in table 6.6 seem to indicate a gradual convergence between East and West, i.e., eastern blue-collar workers are increasingly voting like their western colleagues. Note also in table 6.6 the high losses sustained by the FDP among all occupational groups in the East and the extensive gains made by the PDS across the board. Among white-collar workers, for example, the former Communists attracted nearly as much support in the East as did the CDU and the SPD. The same pattern was found among self-employed voters.

TABLE 6.7

PARTY SUPPORT, PROFESSION, AND TRADE UNION MEMBERSHIP IN WEST GERMANY (IN PERCENT)

All Respondents

	Members				Nonmembers			
	1983	1987	1990	1994	1983	1987	1990	1994
CDU/CSU	36	32	33	32	56	48	51	45
FDP	3	3	9	3	5	11	15	10
SPD	56	55	49	52	31	31	28	31
Greens	5	9	7	7	7	9	5	9
N=	278	501	272	1843	639	1204	664	4316

Source: 1976–1990: Forschungsgruppe Wahlen e. V., *Gesamtdeutsche Bestätigung für die Bonner Regierungskoalition, a.a. O.*, S. 645. 1994: Exit polls of the Forschungsgruppe Wahlen.

Blue-Collar Workers

	Members				Nonmembers			
	1983	1987	1990	1994	1983	1987	1990	1994
CDU/CSU	34	29	37	29	51	40	49	41
FDP	3	1	5	1	2	5	4	4
SPD	64	60	52	58	42	47	39	42
Greens	0	9	4	5	5	6	6	5
N=	163	300	95	933	205	358	128	1138

White-Collar Workers and Civil Servants

	Members				Nonmembers			
	1983	1987	1990	1994	1983	1987	1990	1994
CDU/CSU	41	36	31	30	61	50	47	45
FDP	4	5	11	6	4	12	19	11
SPD	48	51	47	50	26	26	27	31
Greens	7	7	8	9	9	10	40	9
N=	99	168	158	462	264	550	374	1577

Source: 1983–1990: Forschungsgruppe Wahlen e.V., *Gesamtdeutsche Bestätigung für die Bonner Regierungskoalition, a.a.O.*, 645. 1994: Exit polls of the Forschungsgruppe Wahlen.

As the data in table 6.7 show, blue-collar support for the SPD is strongest among trade union members. In comparison to 1990, the Social Democrats made strong gains among unionized blue-collar workers, its traditional proletarian core. The CDU/CSU sustained significant losses among manual workers, both among union members and nonunion members. The FDP has little support among union members regardless of whether they wear a white or blue collar.

In general, there were considerable East-West differences in voting patterns among the occupational groups regardless of union affiliations. In the West, the changes seen in 1990, when blue-collar support for the SPD declined sharply, were reversed. In the East, the Social Democratic gains among blue-collar workers suggest that voting patterns there are beginning to converge with those in the West. Thus, the SPD in 1994 did well among manual workers in both parts of the country.

Future Prospects for the Party System

This election revealed that two different party systems exist in unified Germany. In the West there are now four parties that play significant political roles: the Christian Democrats, Social Democrats, Free Democrats, and the Greens. As figure 6.5 shows, in the East there is a tripartite pattern: the Christian Democrats, Social Democrats, and the Party of Democratic Socialism (PDS). With almost 20 percent of the vote, the PDS is now the third strongest party in the former GDR. The collapse of the Free Democrats and the Greens in the East was not an accident, but rather was rooted in the structure of the eastern electorate. Both parties also did poorly in the state elections held simultaneously with the federal elections in Mecklenburg-West Pomerania and Thuringia, as well as in the state elections held in Brandenburg and Saxony in September.

Neither the FDP's pro-business liberalism, nor the Alliance 90/Greens' message of confronting the former GDR's Communist past regardless of the consequences found much resonance in an electorate focused on unemployment and highly supportive of an extensive welfare state.

The second all-German general election showed once again: 1) that the outcome of a general election does not result in a change of government; 2) that Germany can be governed only by a center coalition; and 3) that there is more competition between coalition camps than between individual parties.

However, this election also left a number of uncertainties. Five parties are represented in the Bundestag, but only two and a half of them appear to be stabilized: the CDU/CSU, the SPD, and the Greens in the West.

FIGURE 6.5

NATIONAL ELECTION 1994 (PERCENT SECOND BALLOT)

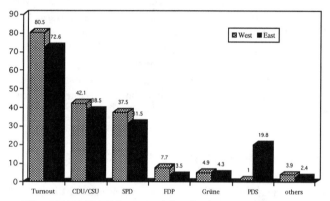

The CDU/CSU has consistently shown itself to be the strongest party, even though some voter support was lost compared with 1990. If we take into account the wear and tear this governing party has had to endure in political and economic terms over the past twelve years and if we consider the extent to which social change has damaged the party's sociostructural base, then the assessment of this election result and its comparison with past elections becomes relatively positive. This leaves aside the fact that many CDU/CSU voters cast their second vote for the FDP in order to ensure the survival of the governing coalition.

The SPD has stabilized itself as the second strongest party in both the western and eastern states. Despite all the problems it had with its leading candidates and party chairmen over the past four years, it greatly improved on its results in the 1990 election. In particular, the SPD in the East was able to make strong gains among those social groups, especially manual workers, where it had disappointing results in 1990.

The Greens in the West, following their poor performance in 1990, made an impressive comeback; they are now the third largest party in the "old" Federal Republic. They attract the support of young, alternative-minded, urban and liberal voters who have a much more realistic attitude towards many issues than some party leaders. It will be interesting to see whether the middle-class characteristics of these voters will be transferred to the larger party. In the East, the Greens were unsuccessful. In the new states the Greens are actually a combination of two different parties. In 1989 and 1990 the supporters of Alliance 90 were the advocates of a democratic new beginning in the former GDR. They did not have the strong environmental orientation of the western Greens. At least for the time being, environmental protection does not elicit nearly as much interest in the East as it does in the West. Material needs are still of foremost importance in the new states. The original civil rights activism of Alliance 90 has lost momentum as a result of reunification. A reform party of the kind that exists in other Central and Eastern European countries that formerly lived under dictatorships is not needed in Germany, since in the German context the established parties stand for democratic change. Whether the debate initiated in Magdeburg, where the SPD and the Alliance 90/Greens formed a minority government which depends upon the passive support of the PDS, has damaged the Alliance 90 group is difficult to determine. But since the June 1994 decision to form this coalition, the Alliance 90/Greens have not been successful in any of the four state elections held in the new states. The future of the Greens in the East will thus depend on the speed with which socioeconomic conditions converge with those in the West.

The FDP's situation can certainly be considered less stable than that of the Greens. The FDP has lost considerable ground, particularly in the East, but also in the West. In the new states, this is the result of the high level of voter volatility and the party's weak programmatic and leadership profile. The voters in the new states continue to react more strongly to party leaders and issues than do western voters. When Hans-Dietrich Genscher and Otto Graf Lambsdorff retired from the political scene, the FDP suddenly had no leaders with broad public appeal. In the short period before the general election, Klaus Kinkel was unable to make up for the decades of public exposure that Genscher and Lambsdorff had enjoyed. The FDP was also not perceived as a representative of eastern interests, since it had begun shortly after 1990 to resume its classic function as an alternative to the two large parties. This meant that, depending on the issue, it would sometimes vote with its ostensible partner, the Christian Democrats, but would also on occasion side with the Social Democrats. There is no tradition for this type of party function in the new states. The FDP's chances in the future will depend on the extent to which the party succeeds in finding credible leaders to communicate issues which the general public perceives as important and suited to the party. This problem for the FDP is also present in the West.

The future of the PDS seems uncertain, given the fact that its success has been limited to the former GDR. In the East the PDS received almost 20 percent of the vote; in the West a minuscule 1 percent. In the East the former Communists make use of their strong organization to address the everyday concerns of individual citizens. Nearly 40 percent of easterners are convinced that the PDS will continue to be needed as a representative of eastern interests. In the old GDR, the PDS appeals to those who have lost influence and prestige as a result of unification, not necessarily to those who have suffered material losses. In the West, the PDS attempts to project itself as a genuine left-wing party and a possible heir to the radical Greens and Alternatives. The PDS will probably survive as a regional party for the foreseeable future. In the long term, however, the party must increase its base level of support in the West to around 2 percent in order to clear the 5 percent mark nationwide. Here, a great deal will depend on the way in which the western parties, in particular the SPD, respond to the PDS. In competition with a genuine left-wing party, the SPD and the Greens would run the risk of losing left-wing voters. This would be certain to have consequences for the entire party system.

Notes

1. Infas, Indikatorenprogramm, *Die politische Stimmung in West- und Ostdeutschland, Monatsbericht Januar 1994* (im Auftrag des Presse- und Informationsamtes der Bundesregierung). Emnid, *Politik—Trends 1994, 5. Woche 1994, Bericht* (im Auftrag des Presse- und Informationsamtes der Bundesregierung). Forschungsgruppe Wahlen e.V. Mannheim, *Politbarometer in Deutschland,* January 1994. Infratest Burke Berlin, *Die Zeit,* February 1994.

2. Wolfgang G. Gibowski and Max Kaase, "Auf dem Weg zum politischen Alltag. Eine Analyse der ersten gesamtdeutschen Bundestagswahl vom 2. Dezember 1990," in *Aus Politik und Zeitgeschichte* B11–12/91, (8 March 1991): 3–20.

3. Forschungsgruppe Wahlen e.V. Mannheim, *Politbarometer in Deutschland,* November 1993.

4. Hans-Dieter Klingemann and Charles Lewis Taylor, "Affektive Parteiorientierung, Kanzlerkandidaten und Issues," in Max Kaase, ed., *Wahlsoziologie heute* (Opladen: Westdeutscher Verlag, 1977), 301–47.

5. Gibowski and Kaase, "Auf dem Weg zum Politischen Alltag," 12.

6. Ibid., 14.

7. Forschungsgruppe Wahlen e.v. Mannheim, *Politbarometer in Deutschland*, January 1992.

8. Gibowski and Kaase, "Auf dem Weg zum Politischen Alltag," 10f.

9. Forschungsgruppe Wahlen e.v. Mannheim, *Politbarometer in Deutschland*, January 1994.

10. Wolfgang G. Gibowski, "Wie wirkt sich die wirtschaftliche Lage auf das Wahlverhalten aus," in Landeszentrale für politische Bildung Baden-Würtemberg, ed., *Wahlverhalten* (Stuttgart, Berlin, and Cologne: Kohlhammer Verlag, 1991), 122–38.

11. Forschungsgruppe Wahlen e.v. Mannheim, *Politbarometer in Deutschland*, December 1993 and January 1994.

12. Ibid., May 1994 and June 1994.

13. Forschungsgruppe Wahlen e.v. Mannheim, *Blitzumfrage zur Bundestagswahl 1994*, October 1994.

14. Carsten Bluck and Henry Kreikenbom, "Die Wähler in der DDR: Nur issueorientiert oder auch parteigebunden?" in *Zeitschrift für Parlamentsfragen* 22 (1991): 495–502. Gabriele Eckstein and Franz Urban Pappi, "Die politischen Wahrnehmungen und die Präferenzen der Wählerschaft in Ost- und Westdeutschland: Ein Vergleich," in Hans-Dieter Klingemann and Max Kaase, eds., *Wahlen und Wähler. Analysen aus Anlaß der Bundestagswahl 1990* (Opladen: Westdeutscher Verlag, 1994), 397–421. Gibowski and Kaase, "Auf dem Weg zum Politischen Alltag," 3–20. Matthias Jung and Dieter Roth, "Politische Einstellungen in Ost- und Westdeutschland seit der Bundestagswahl 1990," in *Aus Politik und Zeitgeschichte* B19/92 (1 May 1992): 3–16. Max Kaase and Hans-Dieter Klingemann, "Der mühsame Weg zur Entwicklung von Parteiorientierungen in einer 'neuen' Demokratie: Das Beispiel der früheren DDR," in Klingemann and Kaase, eds., 365–96. Hans Rattinger, "Parteieignungen, Sachfragen- und Kandidatenorientierungen in Ost- und Westdeutschland 1990–1992," in Hans Rattinger, Oscar W. Gabriel, and Wolfgang Jagodzinski, eds., *Wahlen und politische Einstellungen im vereinigten Deutschland* (Bern, New York, and Frankfurt a.M.: Peter Lang, 1994), 267–314. Hans Rattinger, "Parteiidentifikationen in Ost-und Westdeutschland nach der Vereinigung," in Oskar Niedermayer and Klaus von Beyme, eds., *Politische Kultur in Ost- und Westdeutschland* (Berlin: Akademieverlag, 1994), 77–104. Holli A. Semetko and Klaus Schoenbach, *Germany's "Unity Election." Voters and the Media* (Cresskill, N.J.: Hampton Press, 1994).

15. Seymour M. Lipset and Stein Rokkan, "Cleavage Structures, Party Systems and Voter Alignments: Introduction," in Seymour M. Lipset and Stein Rokkan, eds., *Party Systems and Voter Alignments* (New York: Free Press, 1967), 1–64.

16. Forschungsgruppe Wahlen e.V. Mannheim, "Gesamtdeutsche Bestätigung für die Bonner Regierungkoalition. Eine Analyse der Bundestagswahl 1990," in Klingemann and Kaase, eds., *Wahlen and Wähler*, 639.

17. Ibid., 638.

†Data of figures: Monthly 1,000 respondents in western Germany and 1,000 respondents in eastern Germany, each representative of the population eighteen years and older.

I wish to thank Dr. Ute Molitor for her help.

7

SECOND WIND OR LAST GASP?

HELMUT KOHL'S CDU/CSU AND THE ELECTIONS OF 1994

CLAY CLEMENS

After its strong showing at the 1990 federal election only weeks after German reunification, Helmut Kohl's CDU/CSU went into a slump for several years. In 1994 the party managed a dramatic recovery and successful campaign to retain power, but the thin margin of victory created as many new questions as it answered.

To be sure, it has never paid to count the Union out. During the 1980s, chairman Kohl struck a pragmatic balance between his CDU's squabbling progressive and conservative wings. Despite the waning size and loyalty of groups that once reliably backed large "catch-all" parties, his own still managed to mobilize a broad, center-right constituency, at least at federal elections. While uncharismatic, Kohl had support among party functionaries and allies in the Union Bundestag caucus, which included conservative Bavaria's CSU, led (until 1988) by his rival, Franz Josef Strauß. As chancellor from 1982 on, Kohl also maintained good relations with longtime Foreign Minister Hans-Dietrich Genscher, whose liberal FDP assured his government a majority. But the FDP used its special role to curb both Union conservatives and progressives alike.

After the GDR collapsed in 1989, Kohl's push to unify Germany swept up the eastern "CDU," long a tool of the Communist regime. His optimistic pledges that the region would soon boom, and that Bonn's aid to it need not mean tax hikes, won broad support. At the December 1990 all-German election his Union won 44.1 percent in the West, while in the smaller East, where the CSU did not compete, his CDU garnered 43.4 percent. Given Kohl's triumph, even rivals conceded that—so long as his coalition survived—

he now had "a free hand" in the federal-level party, if not in all of its Land branches.[1]

Kohl's CDU/CSU, 1991–93: A Long Hangover

But the glow of 1990 faded quickly. Kohl's pledge that united Germany would play a larger role in world affairs was undercut by its absence from the Gulf War and differences with allies over the Balkans conflict. Like instability in Russia, these events also dashed Germany's post-unification euphoria. Kohl helped shape major new treaties on the European Union and Bonn pushed for EU expansion, but amid much horse-trading; moreover, nationally minded conservatives increasingly opposed trading the German mark for "esperanto money." At home, eastern Germany's adjustment to capitalism resulted in factory closures, joblessness, and strikes. Except among older people satisfied with generous pensions, Bonn's chancellor became persona non grata in the new Länder. Federal aid for the East rose to DM150 billion annually, and by 1992—with deficits mounting and few cuts in other subsidies—Kohl had to soften his antitax pledge. And just as growth finally began in the East, recession hit the "old" Federal Republic. Then a wave of East European refugees led to claims that German asylum laws were being abused, and brutal attacks on foreigners began attracting worldwide criticism. Kohl's government drew fire for alleged indifference to the influx *and* for the backlash. Public concern about ordinary and organized crime also mounted.

Such controversy not only damaged the government's image, but sparked internal friction as well. Fearful of losing influence now that Germany—but not Bavaria—had grown, the CSU sought to steer Bonn rightward, while the FDP demanded a centrist course. All three partners clashed over Germany's future role in military missions outside NATO. Liberals blasted the Union for resisting subsidy cuts and immigration reform. Deriding them as soft on crime and asylum misuse, Union conservatives urged tougher measures, like more use of electronic surveillance. Plans to offer long-term health care, privatize the railways, and liberalize abortion caused rifts in the coalition, even inside Kohl's CDU. Getting bills through the SPD-dominated Bundesrat increasingly required striking deals with the opposition on such issues, exacerbating intracoalition strife.

In the space of a year, eight ministers resigned. Genscher retired in May 1992, leaving Kohl more foreign policy latitude but robbing his government of a shrewd pilot. A CDU minister quit over Bonn's "shameful" inaction in the Balkans. Peccadillos forced the embittered resignations of the FDP's Jürgen Möllemann (a tiff over his replacement caused new strife) and Günther Krause, one of the CDU's few eastern stars. In 1993 the botched arrest of a terrorist led Kohl's trusted aide, Interior Minister Rudolf Seiters, to quit. Bonn's government both fed and faced rising discontent with mainstream politics, or *Politikverdrossenheit*. Journalists and, in 1992, even Federal President Richard von Weizsäcker chastised the establishment's preoccupation with perks, power, and special interests—a thinly veiled sermon against the Kohl era. Labeling the traditional parties corrupt and incompetent, ever more voters declared themselves independent or abstained from voting altogether.[2]

ILL-EFFECTS

Only three months after unification the CDU lost power in Hesse. In April 1991 it fell 7 percent in Kohl's own Rhineland-Palatinate, leading the FDP and SPD there to form a new coalition. In Hamburg, unfriendly ground, the CDU fell 5 percent in July. While it gained in Bremen that October, a radical-right, antiforeigner party won 6.2 percent—and the headlines. In April 1992 the CDU fell 10 percent in Baden-Württemberg, where it had ruled since 1946, and gained no ground in Schleswig-Holstein. In both Länder (and in Hesse's March 1993 local elections) right-wing radicals like the Republikaner topped 5 percent. Germany's party system seemed to be fragmenting, but worse was ahead. A court invalidated Hamburg's 1991 election, holding that local CDU leaders had chosen candidates undemocratically. In a new vote in September 1993, the party plummeted to a mere 25 percent. Right-wing radicals garnered 7.6 percent, the ecological, antiestablishment Greens 13.5 percent, and a small CDU breakaway group labeling itself the "'Instead Of' Party" 5.6 percent—a rare case of a protest movement profiting solely from Union losses.

Polls offered even less comfort. Kohl's December 1990 rating of 2.3 on a scale of -5/+5 evaporated; a year later he was down to 1.2, after twelve more months 0.1, and by 1993 in red figures at -0.3. As disenchantment grew in the East, CDU support there dropped from 43 percent to little more than 20 percent by 1992. In the West, the Union's approval ratings fell back to below pre-unification levels.

Such a slump undercut Kohl's faith that his Union would retain enough Bundestag seats to ensure that no centrist federal coalition could be built without it—a "strategic majority." Some Liberals hinted their party might join with the SPD, or build a three-way "stoplight" coalition that also included the Greens. Warning Kohl not to appease FDP blackmail with more policy concessions that only fueled the radical-right, some Bavarians revived Strauß's plan for the CSU to break away and become a national, right-wing party.

To be sure, most Liberals ultimately balked at dealing with the left, while CSU leaders opposed leaving the coalition, a hollow threat in any case: the CDU and FDP held enough seats to govern alone. Kohl counted on realists in each junior partner to persuade colleagues that their interests lay in making his coalition work. At a 1991 "summit" he and his top CSU ally, chairman and Finance Minister Theo Waigel, reaffirmed the need for close cooperation; Kohl also came to an accord with the FDP's new man, Foreign Minister Klaus Kinkel. Both of these men had a stake in his coalition's unity. But such accommodation only fueled the fear of some in the FDP about their party's "profile," once it began falling below 5 percent in Land elections; CSU concern about being tarnished by association with Bonn's pragmatic centrism also revived as right-wing groups gained in the polls and a scandal hit the party in 1993. Waigel's new CSU rival, Bavarian Minister President Edmund Stoiber, still urged their party to distance itself from the CDU.[3]

Over this entire controversy hung the specter of a possible CDU/ CSU-SPD Grand Coalition, like those at the Land level in Berlin and Baden-Württemberg. As early as 1991, some Union leaders claimed that a federal coalition of the two large parties could best assure post-unification bipartisanship; others saw it as a useful way to jettison the FDP. The option gained more credence as Kohl sought SPD votes for Bundesrat passage of his "solidarity" package, aid for the East (funded by budget cuts and wage restraint); long-term care insurance; health, postal and rail reform; and asylum limits. But Kohl also knew that partnership with the SPD could let it pose as a future governing party, marginalize the FDP, and feed the radical-right. While not ruling out a formal Grand Coalition, he thus dismissed it as an unnecessary risk, declaring "I wanted [a Union-FDP] coalition, and also want it to continue after 1994."[4]

DEBATING RENEWAL

If Union electoral setbacks rattled Kohl's coalition, they shocked party colleagues, who feared that years of defending government policy had worn down the CDU's own image. Conservatives demanded a harder line against asylum, crime, abortion, and European integration. Newly named Union Bundestag caucus chief and Kohl protégé Wolfgang Schäuble often sympathized with this mood. But progressives like Kohl's old rival Heiner Geissler warned the party that echoing right-wing themes to win a few points at the polls could cost its soul; they instead advised emphasizing new social programs and liberalized immigration. Kohl promised that revision of the CDU's basic program would offer a chance to discuss all such themes and shape a clearer profile, "in so far as the coalition permits it."[5]

Debate also focused on the CDU apparat. While it reemerged from a mountain of debt, membership slumped 5 percent in 1992 and another 9 percent by 1993. Even Kohl and General Secretary Volker Rühe conceded that the party needed more young and female faces, as well as greater chances for input from members.[6] But critics complained that the chancellor's own power compelled conformity, while his reliance on personal ties left ordinary members feeling excluded; many derided Rühe as "the government's second press secretary."

Most CDU Land branches were struggling to find new leaders after the retirement or defeat of longtime eminences. Baden-Württemberg's Lothar Späth, Hamburg's Jürgen Echternach, Schleswig-Holstein's Gerhard Stoltenberg, Hesse's Walter Wallmann, and Lower Saxony's Ernst Albrecht all departed, as did lackluster figures in Rhineland-Palatinate. New politicians like Hesse's conservative Manfred Kanther and Lower Saxony's young Turk Christian Wulf showed promise, but few had much immediate prospect of regaining power.

Yet such problems could not rival those in the party's new wing. Veterans of the old eastern CDU were stumbling over scandal, inexperience at democratic politics, or their own past records; from mid-1991 to early 1992, CDU minister-presidents had to step down in Saxony-Anhalt, Mecklenburg-West Pomerania, and Thuringia. Amid charges of having aided the secret police, Lothar de Maiziere—prime minister during the GDR's brief democracy—quit as deputy party chairman. New CDU colleagues who had joined the 1989 democratic revolution sought to oust *all* members with ties to the old regime, sparking strife in every eastern branch. While the chancellor's longtime rival Kurt Biedenkopf proved a popular conciliator in Saxony, Kohl's effort to fill other top CDU posts with more such western "imports" often compounded resentment.

Integrating the party's two wings was already complex enough. Many easterners were more at ease with the welfare state than market capitalism; insisting "goodwill, relative justice and [admirable] attainments" were not unknown in the GDR, they accused their new colleagues of arrogance. Westerners (in the CSU as well) often found these views naive or ungrateful and deplored "GDR nostalgia" that might turn the Union leftward. When Rühe endorsed efforts to reform CDU branches in the new Länder, many longtime party leaders there called it a "purge." And when westerners joined eastern reformers in urging that the PDS—heir to the former ruling party—be isolated, old-line CDU officials warned against "demonizing" ex-Communists with whom they had long worked.

At the CDU's December 1991 federal congress in Dresden, Kohl sought harmony by endorsing reform but not "blanket condemnation," and conceded not knowing how he might have behaved had he lived in the GDR.[7] But while Peter Hintze, the new general secretary, took up this softer line on reform, party rolls in the East shrank by 14 percent in 1992 alone, a loss of 20,000 members (a dropout rate three times higher than in the West). Some defectors joined new splinter groups, vowing to uphold the region's identity. East-West rifts over abortion and social policy widened. Complaining that colleagues in cozy Bonn could not appreciate their area's plight, eastern Bundestag deputies formed a caucus within the caucus. In late 1992 it lobbied for a "solidarity loan" and urged that 5 percent of the nation's GDP be diverted to the new Länder for fifteen years, evoking protest from western Land leaders who claimed their treasuries were already empty. To give easterners greater say, the CDU expanded the number of its deputy chair slots from one to five at the Düsseldorf congress in 1992: two went to eastern reformers Angela Merkel and Heinz Eggert, but their western supporter Rühe was rebuffed. Internal fights, integration problems, and fear that the Union was still seen as out of touch in the East persisted.[8]

Such talk raised the issue of leadership. October 1992 marked Kohl's tenth anniversary as chancellor, June 1993 his second decade as CDU chair. Since he had long held that any chief of government needed a strong party base, his announced plan to seek reelection to the first affirmed his claim on the second. But coalition and party travails were inevitably affecting his standing. At its 1992 CDU congress in Düsseldorf—where he conceded the need for new taxes and added "the fat times are past"—he was reelected chair by 91 percent, down from near-unanimity in 1990. Rather than the usual five-minute ovation, applause died out after just ninety seconds.[9]

But a challenge was unlikely. No one had Kohl's contacts and rapport with CDU functionaries. His heir apparent, Schäuble, was—despite periodic friction between them—willing to wait for Kohl's voluntary retirement. Many even wondered if the caucus chief—

wheelchair-bound since a 1990 assassination attempt—could handle higher office.[10] And while he earned broad respect, Schäuble's emphasis on family values, patriotism, and a strong state increasingly struck many progressives as opportunistic or unduly conservative.[11] Many were stunned by his idea of using the army for police purposes. But Rühe had also rubbed many the wrong way as general secretary and then defense minister; and while Biedenkopf helped shape the 1993 solidarity pact, Kohl's enmity was a barrier to his ambition. The chancellor was still secure.

LOW POINT

By mid-1993 the Union also faced a revived foe. Having used its Bundesrat majority to modify but then help pass Kohl's legislation, the SPD could present a record of moderation. After a brief leadership crisis, it had settled upon the young, confident, if wooden, Rudolf Scharping, who, like Kohl, hoped to rise from being minister-president of Rhineland-Palatinate to federal chancellor. By autumn, the SPD was ahead in surveys and launching a Clinton-style campaign for change, jobs, and law enforcement.[12]

Facing a "super election year," the Union was losing issues to rally around. Having been in power for a decade, it could not credibly call for change, and strategists had thus hoped to campaign on their record of restricting asylum misuse, right-wing violence, street crime, and the mafia; such issues dominated a lifeless September 1993 congress in Berlin. But this stance drew as much fire from Liberals as from the SPD, which was anxious to avoid appearing soft on such issues. In any case, refugee numbers were down, and playing politics with that issue was risky. Kohl voiced his usual confidence in the economy, including in the East's prospects, but conceded having misjudged how long full recovery would take; growth of only 1.5 percent was forecast for 1994. A theme he raised in late 1993—enhancing competitiveness by cutting labor costs and abandoning the "vacation society"—had little resonance. Sending unarmed units to join UN peacekeepers aroused even less support; Kohl's EU treaties faced more fire from CDU nationalists and the CSU's Stoiber than the SPD (on both policies he even had to face court challenges raised by dissidents in his own coalition).

As 1993 ended, moreover, the chancellor was mired in a mess that recalled the decline of his hero Adenauer. Set on nominating an easterner to succeed von Weizsäcker as federal president, he persuaded CDU leaders to endorse Saxony's Justice Minister Steffen Heitmann, an unknown. But the nominee's comments on confining women to traditional roles soon sparked criticism, even in the FDP and CDU. Dismissing party skeptics as disloyal troublemakers, Kohl stood by his man, but in December Heitmann withdrew. Rather than seeking a consensus choice for this nonpartisan post, Kohl (with CSU backing) then tapped western conservative justice Roman Herzog. Annoyed Liberals decided to put forth one of their own for the job.

At the same time, another eastern CDU-led government, that of Saxony-Anhalt, quit amid adverse publicity about its leaders' high salaries. A CDU successor was installed with a slim majority. And in Brandenburg at year's end, Kohl's party garnered just 20 percent of the vote in municipal elections—placing *third* behind the SPD and PDS.

With differences between the larger parties blurring and the Union at its nadir as 1993 ended, most polls showed little hope for a CDU/CSU-FDP, SPD-FDP, *or* SPD-Greens majority. A Grand Coalition seemed the most likely result of Germany's upcoming election. Kohl still downplayed that idea, though—in contrast to his disdain for past SPD leaders—he began to praise Scharping as a diligent, respectable foe. But his chances of remaining in office in a Grand Coalition still seemed slim: the SPD was not likely to serve under a chancellor it had long derided, and in any case might well demand that post for itself (at which point, rumor had it, the Union mantle would finally pass to Schäuble, Rühe, or Biedenkopf). Major change of some sort seemed inevitable in 1994.

The 1994 Campaign: Recovery, "Kohl Nouveau," and Red Stockings

When the new year began, Kohl's Union trailed the SPD by as much as six points, and he was well behind Scharping in surveys.[13] Worse still, as pollster Dieter Roth observed, in 1994 elections would shape the campaign rather than the other way around: a dozen Land and local races—all chances for Union rivals to gain further momentum—were scheduled before the 16 October Bundestag contest.

But the chancellor cherished a farmer's proverb: "In spring comes the planting, and in fall comes the harvest." Appearances notwithstanding, there was fertile soil for sowing the seeds of a comeback. New law enforcement measures might yet steal the thunder from right-wing groups like the Republikaner, or the economy might still rally. Planned visits from friends like François Mitterrand, Boris Yeltsin, and Bill Clinton would remind voters of Kohl's role as a statesman; Germany would chair the EU and bid the last Soviet troops farewell. A "chancellor campaign" thus still had potential.

Such was the calculation at CDU headquarters. Kohl's loyal General Secretary Hintze and campaign manager Hans-Joachim Reck faced more modest means than usual, DM60 million for the entire year. Choosing to cut down on costly paraphernalia and newspaper ads, they focused largely on television. Firms like von Mannstein and more cutting-edge rivals produced CDU spots, which officials screened in an "arena" modeled after the Clinton campaign's "war room." Kohl himself approved each one. Some commercials advertised a CDU information hotline. To counter Scharping's youthful image, the party produced "Kohl nouveau"—shots of the chancellor without his glasses—and the slogan "politics without a beard," underscoring the contrast with Scharping and an old adage that any outmoded idea would "grow a beard."

Facing Land *and* federal elections in 1994, CSU chief Waigel and General Secretary Erwin Huber were also ready to line up behind Kohl. Even Minister-President Stoiber—whose hard work was earning him a reputation for competence—was willing to forego his party's old tactic of mobilizing conservatives in Bavaria by sniping at the CDU and FDP. He thus stopped his attacks on Kohl's support for EU unity. Having lost a smaller share of members than the CDU, the CSU could also count on its strong grass-roots organization.[14]

Union strategists also assumed that many Germans who had been registering protest by voting for splinter parties—a few more of which emerged in 1994—would not do so when it actually came to choosing a government. After all, the electorate favored stability: no government in Bonn had ever been removed by the voters. In addition, they believed Scharping's left-leaning colleagues would undercut his effort to appear moderate, and might even talk of coalition with the Greens. Kohl, by contrast, faced the—for him—more familiar task of mobilizing a middle-of-the-road party over which he had long reigned and in which he had a firm base.

This he set out to do at a well-crafted convention in Hamburg on 21 February. Amid suspense heightened by the decision not to circulate an advance copy of his remarks, Kohl spoke for eighty-seven minutes without a text. Personifying confidence, he stressed his government's record and praised its partners. Skirting issues like unemployment or specific proposals, he characteristically struck a balance on most themes ("I do not want an authoritarian state, but I want a state with authority"). He urged Germans to overcome their worship of leisure and insecurity: "We Germans must think anew," he declared. In a personal touch, the chancellor also reflected on his own long party career. Having deleted attacks on Scharping from his speech, he nonetheless lambasted the SPD's 1990 opposition to unification. Most effective was his call for party unity: "Whoever wants different policies can argue for them here, but once we are at home [to campaign], that's it!... We're not aiming to place, but to win!" Sensing that they were launching Kohl's last campaign, delegates gave him a rousing, prolonged standing ovation. Even critics called it one of his best speeches. Other events were anticlimactic—Schäuble's sharp attack on the SPD, Geissler's pessimistic warnings, and debate on the new basic program. Delegates endorsed calls for an "*environmental* and social market economy" (despite business opposition) and a "federally organized" EU—somewhere between Kohl's "united states of Europe" and the loose confederation nationalistic conservatives favored.

But the Union still trailed its SPD rival in national polls. In early March, despite Kohl's tireless campaigning for its new leadership, the CDU in Lower Saxony had its worst showing ever. Worse still, the FDP fell below 5 percent and out of the Landtag, intensifying internal debate over its future coalition options. On the bright side, no right-wing or other splinter parties won seats.

In late March, the SPD unveiled a new economic plan, which contained what Union leaders denounced as punitive tax hikes; when Scharping then seemed unable to explain it clearly, they accused him of incompetence. While polls in early April still put the SPD at 40 percent, its lead—and Scharping's over Kohl—narrowed slightly.[15] Over the next few weeks, experts also began seeing signs of more rapid growth in the East, and—for the first time since 1992—surveys showed that more Germans, even easterners, viewed the future with optimism rather than pessimism. A majority also voiced greater confidence in the Union than the SPD on economic affairs (a mood skeptics charged was generated by Kohl's media allies). Polls showed the latter dropping slightly in both halves of Germany, while Kohl's party improved by more than 5 percent in the new Länder, and was gaining on its rival nationwide. Despite high joblessness, as well as divisions on issues like nursing insurance, and abortion, the party could now unite behind Kohl *and* a more robust economy.

While Union odds of a strategic majority were improving, its coalition options remained unclear. Having formally committed to governing with Kohl, Kinkel and FDP leaders faced charges that they had abandoned any vestige of Liberal independence. FDP unity would thus be tested in late May at the assembly to pick a new president.

After backing their own candidate on the inconclusive first ballot, FDP delegates—mostly Bundestag members—had to choose between the Union's man, Herzog, or the SPD's more popular Johannes Rau.[16] Bitterly divided Liberals narrowly voted to stand by Herzog, and thus by Kohl's coalition. Scharping's party charged that a less popular president had been chosen for tactical reasons, and even mocked his acceptance speech. But such attacks further united coalition leaders: they—and many in the media—charged the SPD with being a sore loser and insulting Germany's new chief of state.

By June, polls put the Union at nearly 40 percent, just in time for elections to the European Parliament and municipal contests in the East. Building on renewed optimism about the economy and soothing new concern about the Balkans war, CDU posters stressed "security": the picture of a family strolling through peaceful woods evoked an image of Germany as an oasis of bliss. Kohl's reputation as a European statesman also figured in the campaign, one sentimental spot telling of a couple divided for decades by the Wall who were then reunited in 1990 thanks to his policies. The chancellor campaigned vigorously in the East, often swooping into villages unannounced for beer with stunned locals. At CSU rallies he spoke before posters of himself and of Waigel and Stoiber. The CDU staffed its hotline, dispatched teams of experts throughout the new Länder, and used direct mail.

On election night, the Union reached 38.8 percent, six points ahead of Scharping's SPD; the Republikaner fell below 5 percent. A jubilant Kohl could not hide his delight, and pledged that his coalition would continue working in "a comradely way." For the first time, polls put him up on Scharping, 44 percent to 35 percent. One critic wrote, "[anyone] who takes valium instead of adrenaline each morning will have it tough against a Helmut Kohl."[17] But the FDP fell below 5 percent, while the PDS's strong showing in some eastern cities created still another cause for concern: similar success in the October election would win that party three districts, exempting it from the 5 percent threshold and earning it some twenty to thirty Bundestag seats, which—along with those of the SPD and Greens—might form a slim majority. In that case Kohl would have no choice but to seek a Grand Coalition.

Such a prospect was the backdrop to yet another election two weeks later. A favorable wind from Bonn only partly lifted the CDU in Saxony-Anhalt out of the doldrums, and its FDP ally fell below 5 percent. Rather than pursue a Grand Coalition there, however, the local SPD—with Scharping's approval—worked out a "red-green" minority government that needed a deal with the PDS. Overnight the national campaign's dynamics changed. Union leaders blasted this bargain with "Honecker's heirs." Kohl called it "a fundamental strategic change in German politics" that made the election "a decision on direction."[18] CDU and especially CSU campaigners warned that Scharping was power hungry enough to court ex-Communists and make a mockery of his moderate appeal. The CDU hatched new slogans meant to revive anti-Communist sentiment; its posters used the symbol of red socks or warned against a "popular front," while the CSU's signs even had Karl Marx's warning "I'm coming back!"

CDU officials in the East were more uneasy about this theme. Many had enjoyed careers under the old regime (a point journalists did not miss), and all needed to woo supporters who had been politically active in the GDR. Moreover, even reformists feared that voters in the new Länder, most of whom considered the PDS a legitimate party, might view attacks upon it as another case of westerners picking on easterners and their past. Strategists in Bonn thus did not press eastern branches to adopt the new theme. But the CDU and CSU did expect this new anti-Communist drumbeat to mobilize their traditional western base, preventing otherwise discontented or complacent voters from staying home in October.

That summer, Kohl's image received a further boost from visits by Yeltsin and Clinton; the American leader's remark that he "always agree[d] with Helmut" at global summits was used in CDU spots. Ceremonies marking the final withdrawal of foreign troops had a similar effect (eclipsing spats over EU integration and nuclear material smuggled from the ex-USSR). CDU and CSU leaders agreed on an election manifesto, which won quick support in each party and was unveiled by Kohl before 16,000 supporters at a Dortmund rally in late August. Without specifying how to cut unemployment, it pledged to promote growth, the environment, families, respect for law, and a larger role abroad. The chancellor declared that his main reason for running was to finish European unity—though he also conceded, "I want to know [that feeling of victory] again."[19]

Kohl's competence rating was at an all-time high; unlike Scharping, he was seen as fully in charge of his own party and enjoyed broad support among its own voters.[20] From late August onward, he attended sixty large-scale rallies, usually outdoors, and another forty events (as he noted aptly "I'm the only one who can still fill the market square"). Each was well organized, down to the brass band and twenty huge speakers to drown out hecklers. His stump speech dwelt on the positive, noting that—despite all real concerns—Germans had rarely known reason for greater joy. Without mentioning his rival by name, he assailed the "scandalous" SPD-PDS deal. "It's always fun to box the SPD about the head," he confided.[21] Unwilling to legitimate PDS chief Gregor Gysi, the chancellor rejected ideas for a televised debate among all party leaders, but also spurned a one-on-one duel with Scharping for fear of elevating the latter's profile and slighting his junior allies.

CDU posters included a simple, unposed shot of the chancellor amid admirers, with no slogan.[22] Television spots sought to make the sixty-four-year-old appear energetic, juxtaposing scenes of him with shots of dramatic events, or high-speed trains and jets—all set to Tina Turner's hit, "Simply the Best." Certain ads were targeted for eastern viewers, even with subtle changes (like using *Fakt* in place of the "western" word, *Tatsache*). A telephone bank took up to 10,000 calls nightly. Campaign material was available on computer disk or "on-line" to local party branches.

Kohl's picture even appeared regularly in the CSU's newspaper, rare in past years. With Bavarian Land elections looming, its leaders campaigned as his loyal allies—while still periodically sniping at the FDP or CDU branches that "coddled" the PDS. The CSU stressed family, growth, order, and innovation; its posters appealed for votes "so that Germany [would] remain stable." Stoiber, whose growing appeal was expected to hold the party's absolute majority, even made a Clinton-style bus tour of Bavaria with Waigel.[23]

Some final Land elections sent mixed signals. Popular SPD Minister-President Manfred Stolpe crushed the Brandenburg CDU, while the party in Saxony under Biedenkopf won a record 58 percent. But both cases showed that voters wanted strong, trusted leaders. Two weeks later a similar "bonus" helped Stoiber's CSU keep its absolute majority. As Kohl noted, such "personalization" of elections would also be felt in the national race (and at an upcoming Land contest in Thuringia, where the CDU counted heavily on Minister-President Bernhard Vogel's appeal).

But the PDS also showed well in both eastern Länder, and the Liberals fell below 5 percent in all three races. By warning against a Grand Coalition or even an absolute CDU/CSU majority, last-minute FDP ads nervously courted "second" votes from those who wanted a "stable Kohl-Kinkel government"—an effort to attract Union supporters. While calmly noting that his party had "no votes to lend," the chancellor added confidently "the louder the death knells, the more certain the FDP [was] of making it."[24] With only days left, Kohl caused a final flap by hinting that he might serve only until 1996, sparking immediate speculation about a succession fight and highlighting the Union's relative lack of depth. The chancellor's lead over Scharping began leveling off, as did the Union's lead over the SPD. With the PDS all but certain of winning seats, the outcome thus remained far from certain.[25]

Phoenix or Lame Duck? The CDU and Its Election Result

Early election-night projections delighted CDU/CSU supporters. Their party stood at 42 percent, well up on the SPD, and only a two-point drop from 1990; its FDP ally was at nearly 7 percent, down somewhat, yet safely in the Bundestag. But the result represented a near total erosion of Kohl's old 134 seat majority. Moreover, PDS success exempted it from the 5 percent hurdle, meaning the left as a whole would win nearly as many seats as Kohl's coalition, especially once CDU/CSU-FDP totals slid to 41.5 percent and 6.6 percent, respectively. With his margin apparently down to one seat, he told cheering supporters, "We have won the second all-German elections," and quoted Adenauer—"a majority is a majority." Schäuble agreed that a "slim victory is better than a clear defeat." But while the coalition lead again widened a bit overnight thanks to several "surplus" seats, it was a close call, and the CDU/CSU's worst showing in a national election since 1949. To be sure, Union voters who defected did so largely to help the FDP keep above 5 percent, and despite such a large "loan," the CDU/CSU had bested its SPD rival in the West. The CDU had finished first in four of six eastern Länder in Bundestag balloting, as well as in both of those that had held Land elections the same day; the CSU had won 51 percent in Bavaria, taking all but one directly elected seat. With just 1.9 percent nationwide, the Republikaner remained—as Kohl said—an "insignificant splinter party."

There was thus grounds for satisfaction. After all, without playing the risky "foreigner issue," Kohl's Union had deflected SPD calls for change by exploiting the electorate's faith in and desire for security in economic, domestic, and foreign affairs—areas where polls showed that voters gave Kohl and his party higher marks. In power for a decade, it had nonetheless sold a message of change and put Scharping's SPD on the defensive for dealing with the PDS. One CDU strategist said, the SPD "gave us the future and the past." *Politikverdrossenheit* kept turnout down but had not hurt the Union.

Older, Catholic, agrarian, and traditional middle-class voters, as well as a sizable share of eastern workers, had remained loyal.

But while Kohl's Union thus held a plurality, his government had been weakened. With half of its vote "on loan" from the CDU/CSU and few core supporters left, the FDP faced the charge of having become a mere appendage of the Union, and more Land-level setbacks loomed. Kinkel pledged fidelity to Kohl's coalition, but critics argued that—now more than ever—he had to win concessions from the Union on Liberal issues like immigration and taxes. Some hinted that alternatives like a "stoplight" coalition with the left should not yet be ruled out, or gave signs of defecting to the SPD themselves.

A factor likely to further fray Liberal nerves was the CSU's new strength: it now had more seats than any party but the CDU and SPD. Kohl's government would thus need the Bavarians: any even theoretical prospect of a CDU-FDP coalition was gone. Boasting that CSU influence had never been so great in a decade, Waigel warned the Liberals against new demands. To be sure, mindful of the FDP's fragility, he did not demand that they give up the Foreign Ministry, foreswore "bullying," and denied doubting Kinkel's reliability. But intraparty rivals were already urging that he use the CSU's new leverage to curb Liberal influence, pressure sure to cause more friction.[26]

Then there was Union weakness in the Bundesrat, further eroded by fresh CDU losses in Mecklenburg-West Pomerania and Thuringia, where Grand Coalitions had become necessary. Using their majority in the federal chamber, SPD-led Länder could continue forcing Kohl and Schäuble's Bundestag caucus to bargain in advance or seek deals in the reconciliation committee, further isolating the FDP.

Insisting he was no "fair-weather" chancellor, Kohl pledged to continue his coalition, adding jovially, "I'm an old marriage partner of the FDP since first becoming [a] minister-president." Noting precedents set by past SPD chancellors, he claimed that governing with a slim majority could help "discipline" a coalition: its members would be less tempted to make "excursions" if so doing might actually cripple the government. Moreover, on many issues—enhancing competitiveness, trimming social programs, playing a larger role in world affairs—the Union and Liberals still agreed. But while Kohl was not going to make life hard for the Liberals, neither was he willing to let their plight block policy.

In talks on rebuilding Kohl's government after the election, the FDP kept three major cabinet posts and won concessions on law enforcement measures. But it had to give up two portfolios and compromise on taxes, spending, and immigration. Kohl also insisted that the new legislative program set vague, general goals, so that all partners could claim victory—but also leaving room for later deals with the SPD. Four deputies, assumed to be Liberals, balked at voting to install him in the formal Bundestag election on 15 November. Had a late-sleeping CDU deputy arrived just two minutes later, the chancellor's one-vote margin would have disappeared altogether.

Thus, even while Kohl was safe for four more years, making him the first chancellor since Adenauer to serve a fourth term, many believed the frustration of dealing with so thin a majority would only grow. They suspected his era would culminate in a formal Grand Coalition, with him presiding over foreign policy—to finish his work on European unity—while Bundestag leaders hashed out domestic legislation with the SPD. Some Union colleagues even favored that prospect, expecting easier agreement with the SPD on issues like long-term nursing and health care. Others feared such bipartisanship would, as in 1966–69, only burnish the opposition's credentials and help it regain power with the Greens. But the only way around such a fate seemed to be an unexpected FDP recovery, or the hope that Schäuble (or an undiscovered rival), would take over in 1996 or 1998, chart a new course, and revive Union fortunes.

Thus even while the Kohl era survived, a postmortem on its demise was beginning. To be sure, despite warnings that parties like his Union were dinosaurs, it still commanded over 40 percent of the vote and as yet faced no real right-wing threat. On the other hand, his entire coalition had won a smaller share of the vote than the Union alone in 1983; at the Land level his CDU was in shambles and, Schäuble aside, it lacked strong future leaders. For the CDU/CSU, Kohl's legacy appeared to be an impressive record of success, but success purchased at a price still to be fully paid.

Notes

1. Späth cited in *Der Spiegel [DS]*, 19 November 1990.

2. One prominent study skewered the CDU/CSU. Erwin K. and Ute Scheuch, *Cliquen, Klüngel und Karrieren* (Reinbek: Rowohlt, 1992).

3. Hans-Jürgen Leersch, "Die CSU: eine neue Form der Bayernpartei," *Aus Politik und Zeitgeschichte* 5 (January 1992): 21–28.

4. *Frankfurter Allgemeine Zeitung [FAZ]*, 12 February 1993.

5. *AZ*, 23 April 1991.

6. Rühe declared the situation in some areas "catastrophic." Only 6.6 percent of its members were under thirty; one in four local branches had no members in that age group. Over half of all party officers were over fifty and less than 5.5 percent under thirty; just 1 percent of Land parliamentarians were in their twenties. *Die Welt*, 22 July 1991.

7. CDU, *Protokoll: 2. Parteitag der CDU Deutschlands*, Dresden, 15–17 December 1991, pp. 25–45, 114.

8. Clay Clemens, "Disquiet on the Eastern Front: The Christian Democratic Union in Germany's New Länder," *German Politics* 2, no. 2 (August 1993): 199–223.

9. "Helmut Kohl's Hour of Need," *The Economist*, 31 October 1992; CDU, Bundesgeschäftsstelle, *Protokoll: 3. Parteitag der CDU Deutschlands*, Düsseldorf, 26–28 October 1992, pp. 16–39.

10. Kohl had privately hinted at his preference in early 1991, noting "everything points to Schäuble," but then and thereafter refused to make this a public endorsement, stressing it was not a current question. *Süddeutsche Zeitung [SdZ]*, 15 April 1991.

11. Above all, he urged Germans to have more children. Wolfgang Schäuble, *Und der Zukunft zugewandt* (Berlin: Siedler Verlag, 1994). For a sharp assault on Schäuble from a Geissler ally, see Warnfried Dettling, *Das Erbe Kohls: Bilanz einer Ära* (Frankfurt: Eichhorn, 1994), 118–59. Even conservatives criticized the "crown prince." Heinrich Basilius Streithofen, *Ist die CDU noch zu retten? Bilanz und Perspektive einer Volkspartei* (Munich: Herbig, 1993).

12. "Prima Klima für die SPD," *DS*, 25 October 1993. At that stage the Union, at 33 percent in an Emnid survey, fell behind the SPD, 39 percent.

13. Allensbach gave the Union 33 percent, the SPD 38 percent. *FAZ*, 19 January 1994; Emnid put the party at less than 20 percent in two eastern Länder. *DS*, 21 February 1994.

14. The new year also eased CDU Land-level woes. Young reformers Angela Merkel and Carola Hartfelder were in their first months as chairs in two troubled eastern branches, Mecklenburg-West Pomerania and Brandenburg. In North Rhine-Westphalia, two young politicians, Norbert Lammert and Helmut Linssen, were waging an amicable contest for the leadership. Party members in this, the CDU's largest branch, would pick the winner in a mail ballot—an effort at democratizing internal decision making. Kohl ally Johannes Gerster became consensus choice to head his party in Rhineland-Palatinate.

15. Allensbach survey, *FAZ*, 13 April 1994.

16. FDP support for Social Democrat Gustav Heinemann as president in 1969 had ushered in a new Social-Liberal federal government.

17. Robert Leicht, "Angezählt ist nicht ausgezählt," *Die Zeit*, 17 June 1994; Kohl in *FAZ*, 14 June 1994.

18. *FAZ*, 26 August 1994.

19. *FAZ*, 15 August 1994.

20. Emnid showed that 65 percent of Germans considered him decisive, and 55 percent rated him competent. *DS*, 1 August 1994. Two-thirds felt he had great influence in his party, while only a quarter said the same of Scharping. *FAZ*, 28 September 1994. While only two of three SPD voters wanted Scharping as chancellor, 82 percent of Union supporters backed Kohl for the job. *FAZ*, 31 August 1994.

21. *FAZ*, 12 October 1994; *SdZ*, 13 October 1994.

22. An SPD supporter who appeared in the picture sought to block its use as campaign material, but the party had purchased all rights to the photograph. The man spurned an offer of money.

23. The CSU general secretary wrote of a "renaissance of the personality-election." Germans, he added, were weary of "unclear majorities" and "coalition-tactical games." Erwin Huber, "Konsequenzen für Bayern," *Bayernkurier [BK]*, 17 September 1994.

24. *FAZ*, 13 September 1994.

25. On election eve, Emnid gave Kohl a 45 percent to 33 percent lead in the West and a 40 percent to 29 percent edge in the East. *DS*, 26 September 1994.

26. *FAZ*, 18 October 1994; Theo Waigel, "Worum es jetzt geht," *BK*, 29 October 1994. One CSU leader called his party the "real winner" and warned the FDP against "left-liberal arrogance." Erwin Huber, "Volksfront abgewehrt, Koalition behauptet," *BK*, 22 October 1994.

8

THE SOCIAL DEMOCRATIC PARTY OF GERMANY

STEPHEN J. SILVIA

Introduction

Only minutes after the polls had closed throughout Germany on 16 October 1994, it became inescapably obvious to all that the Social Democratic Party of Germany (Sozialdemokratische Partei Deutschlands [SPD]) had lost its fourth general election in a row. Yet the very next day, a calm and relaxed Rudolf Scharping—the SPD's chairperson and candidate for chancellor—expressed his complete satisfaction with his party's electoral effort and announced, "We will govern in 1998—or sooner!"[1] Was Mr. Scharping merely exhibiting the good sportsmanship and bravura that people expect from politicians, or did he have good reason to make such a bold claim so soon after nationwide defeat?

The following essay answers this question by investigating developments within the Social Democratic Party since the first postwar all-German election of 1990. It shows that Rudolf Scharping does indeed have grounds to believe that the SPD is on the upswing. Internal reforms designed to promote grass-roots participation within the SPD have helped to reconstitute a stable party leadership and to dampen party infighting for the first time in over a decade. This change was crucial to the Social Democrats' success in narrowing considerably the parliamentary advantage of the Christian Democratic Union (Christlich Demokratische Union [CDU]), its Bavarian sister party, the Christian Social Union (Christlich Soziale Union [CSU]), and the liberal Free Democratic Party (Freie Demokratische Partei [FDP]) in the most recent federal elections from 134 to ten seats.

This change has already enhanced the power of the SPD. Social Democratic victories in state (Land) elections over the past few years allowed the party to gain control of the Bundesrat (i.e., the upper house of the German federal parliament) even before the October 1994 federal election. This permitted the SPD to delay legislation and to block constitutional amendments. The considerable narrowing of the conservative coalition's majority in the Bundestag as a result of the 1994 election tipped the balance on the joint Bundestag-Bundesrat reconciliation committee (*Vermittlungsausschuss*) in favor of an opposition party for the first time in the history of the Federal Republic. This shift gives the Social Democrats a far greater say than any previous German opposition party over the ultimate contents and fate of all future bills.

Despite substantial progress over the past few years, the Social Democratic Party of Germany still has several difficult obstacles to overcome in the next four years before the party will once again be in a position to attain power at the federal level. Specifically, the SPD must complete internal reform without alienating large segments of its diverse membership, sharpen its foreign and economic policies without triggering internal dissent, and, most important, develop a strategy to raise the party's attractiveness in eastern Germany at the expense of the former Communist party, the party of Democratic Socialism (Partei des Demokratischen Sozialismus [PDS]). If the SPD manages to make solid progress in these three areas, there is a good chance that a Social Democratic chancellor will lead Germany into the new millennium.

The large strides that the German Social Democratic Party made over the past four years in a highly turbulent environment demonstrate that the SPD is capable of advancing under adversity and despite short-term setbacks. Losing the 1990 federal election ranked among the largest of these defeats.

The SPD in the Aftermath of the 1990 Federal Election

The 1990 election was an unmitigated debacle for the Social Democrats. The SPD received only 33.5 percent of the vote, which was its lowest share in a national election since the 1950s, and only 24 percent of the eastern Germans cast ballots for the party. The poor result had several immediate causes. First, the Social Democratic Party had badly mishandled unity. This is ironic, given that the SPD pioneered détente with the German Democratic Republic (GDR) in the late 1960s. Yet, implicit within the SPD's *Ostpolitik* was the belief that *only* an evolutionary mellowing of the existing Communist regime rather than a social upheaval would advance human and political rights in the German Democratic Republic. When revolution rather than reform suddenly welled up throughout the GDR during the fall of 1989, the SPD leadership was caught completely by surprise and embarrassed by a now useless set of contacts to a deposed and discredited Communist élite. Moreover, many "postmodern" Social Democrats in western Germany found the intrinsically nationalistic dimension of German unity inherently distasteful, and thus wanted nothing to do with it. This made forging new contacts in the GDR difficult, to say the least.[2]

Second, the SPD was structurally disadvantaged in eastern Germany, which in turn hurt it in the 1990 election. In 1946, Soviet authorities, in collaboration with the Communist Party of Germany (Kommunistische Partei Deutschlands [KPD]), forced the Social Democratic Party in the eastern occupation zone into a merger with the KPD, creating the pro-Soviet Socialist Unity Party (Sozialistische Einheitspartei Deutschlands [SED]), which dominated East Germany until 1989. In practice, this merger eliminated the Social Democrats as a political force in the East, putting them under the control of the Communists.[3] The SED leadership allowed the remaining non-Communist parties east of the Elbe—including a Christian Democratic and a liberal party—to remain nominally independent, but subordinated these parties by forcing them into an "antifascist national bloc." These so-called "block parties" were allowed to recruit members, to maintain offices, and to sit in the East German Parliament, so long as they did not challenge the SED's preeminence in the GDR.

Once Communism collapsed in the GDR, the western Christian Democratic and liberal parties used the organizational resources and memberships of their eastern "cousins" to spread eastward quickly. The SPD, in contrast, had no established eastern "cousin" with offices and a substantial rank-and-file as a partner in the East. It instead had to be content making the most of a small band of dissidents centered around the Lutheran church who had formed a fledgling "Social Democratic Party in the GDR" in October 1989.[4]

Third, the Social Democratic Party's new Basic Program, approved in Berlin on 20 December 1989, was ill-suited for the changed circumstances of the first postwar all-German election. The party's new program, which was five years in the making, replaced the famous 1959 SPD Bad Godesberg Basic Program. The Berlin Basic Program was nonetheless obsolete from the start because (despite a few cosmetic changes added at the last minute) it was written by and for western Germans. Yet, even in western Germany, the program failed to resonate with party members and the larger populace. Unlike the Godesberg Basic Program—which attracted hundreds of thousands of new party members and millions of new voters, and offered an attractive and convincing set of policies for reorganizing the German economy and society—the Berlin Basic Program reads like a series of dry, abstract compromises among the various factions of the SPD and garnered the party no new members or voters.[5]

Fourth, the Social Democrats' lead candidate, the Saar prime minister, Oskar Lafontaine, proved to be the wrong candidate at the wrong time. Before unification, Lafontaine's combative style and market-based proposals for renovating the German economy to promote a postindustrial, high-technology, environmentally sound economy seemed to be the right formula to defeat a tired-looking Kohl government. German unification, however, reinvigorated Kohl and shifted the political debate radically. Unification became the central theme. Helmut Kohl, the man who dared to push for rapid unification while the SPD dithered, promised that no one would be worse off owing to unification. Oskar Lafontaine, in contrast, crisscrossed the country complaining about unification's high cost. Despite Lafontaine's accuracy (even he underestimated the true price of unity), his negative, "postnational" message did little to inspire either eastern or western voters to support the SPD in an election in which nationalism was the dominant theme.[6]

Finally, infighting also marred the Social Democrats' 1990 federal campaign. The fact that Lafontaine became the SPD's candidate for chancellor despite a nearly universal distaste for him among major Social Democratic constituencies underscored the shortcomings of the party's traditional closed-door method of choosing a leader, which consisted of a handful of the party's top leaders selecting a candidate from amongst themselves and then submitting that choice to a party convention.

Over the years, Oskar Lafontaine had managed to sour his relations with almost every important constituency of the SPD. The German labor movement, traditionally among the SPD's strongest supporters, was displeased with Lafontaine. A few years earlier, Lafontaine had scored points with the business community by criticizing organized labor's drive to reduce working time while maintaining the level of weekly pay. Consequently, labor leaders only perfunctorily supported Lafontaine's 1990 campaign. Lafontaine alienated his party's left wing by leaving it in the mid-1980s to adopt largely laissez-faire economic policies tinged with a strong environmental emphasis. He also angered the SPD's right wing during the early 1980s when he publicly assailed the character of Helmut Schmidt. The former SPD chancellor settled this score in 1990 by predicting two weeks before the election that Lafontaine would lose, adding "he deserves it, too."[7]

The depth of the 1990 electoral disaster produced the widespread belief within the Social Democratic Party that the SPD badly needed new leadership. A consensus quickly formed within the party hierarchy that the prime minister of Schleswig-Holstein, Björn Engholm, was the best choice. In May 1991, an SPD convention in Bremen elected Björn Engholm to succeed Hans-Jochen Vogel as party chair. This marked a momentous transition in both generation and style. Engholm, like Lafontaine, came from the "grandchild" (*Enkel*) generation of the SPD, in other words, the third generation to rise to the top of the party since the end of World War II. Unlike Vogel, whose aloof and pedantic manner earned him the moniker "schoolmaster" (*Oberlehrer*) within the SPD, Engholm was a suave, convivial, and self-confident *bon vivant*. His proponents described him as a compromiser and a listener who put forward a modern, sophisticated public image for the party. Engholm's detractors from within the SPD's traditionalist wing, on the other hand, derided him as an inexperienced vacillator from the hedonistic "Tuscany wing" of the SPD.[8]

The Social Democratic Party headquarters, which was long ago nicknamed the "barracks," has always been known for its rigid hierarchy and Byzantine political intrigue. Björn Engholm had spent virtually none of his political life there and shared the view of most observers that the claustrophobic environment of the barracks had become an important source of the party's electoral difficulties. Engholm believed that the SPD could only recover if the party continued to "dare more democracy" and increased grass-roots participation by members and nonmembers alike. He, therefore, made his acceptance of the post of SPD chair conditional both upon the party agreeing that he would also remain prime minister of Schleswig-Holstein (so as to have an independent power base) and on the party's approval of a resolution sanctioning a thorough organizational "modernization" of the Social Democratic Party by the year 2000.[9]

Engholm underscored his determination to change the SPD's internal climate and practices by appointing an outsider, Karl-Heinz Blessing, as the party's new general secretary. Blessing was an unconventional choice; he was in his mid-thirties and had no previous SPD experience beyond membership and participation as a volunteer in a few local activities. Before coming to Bonn, Blessing had served as the right-hand man of the president of the powerful metalworkers' union, where he had a strong reputation for innovative thinking and strategic acumen. Since Engholm would remain in Schleswig-Holstein, Blessing became the top party officer in Bonn.[10]

Soon after taking office, Blessing assembled a working group to launch the "SPD 2000" organizational modernization project that had been approved at the party's Bremen convention. The working group began the first phase of its activities by distributing a detailed questionnaire to all party members and by sponsoring a series of open discussions on party reform. These discussions focused on the strengths and weaknesses of potential innovations, such as replacing the SPD's hierarchical structure of standing committees with ad hoc project groups, relying on primaries to choose Social Democratic candidates for external offices and on internal direct elections to fill top arty posts, and allowing nonmembers to participate in SPD affairs.[11]

In 1992 Björn Engholm deftly used a more open and "dialogical" approach to help resolve one of the most vexing and explosive problems confronting the Federal Republic in the early 1990s, that is, the rapid acceleration in the numbers of asylum seekers entering Germany since the fall of the Berlin Wall in November 1989. Article 16 of West Germany's 1949 constitution (*Grundgesetz*) granted asylum to all who could prove that they were victims of political persecution. All applying for asylum could enter Germany and remain there at the taxpayers' expense until their case had been heard. The authors of this provision intended it to be a means for the new Federal Republic of Germany to make amends for the National Socialist years. Few at the time worried about abuse of Article 16 since Germany was still heavily scarred by war damage and long-distance transportation was slow and expensive.

In the early years of the Federal Republic, Europeans fleeing Communist oppression were the primary applicants, and once the Berlin Wall was built in 1962, the number of asylum seekers slowed to a trickle. During the 1960s and early 1970s, Germany made it relatively easy for migrants to gain work permits in a bid to end a persistent labor shortage. Hence, few bothered to go through the more bureaucratic process of applying for asylum. When unemployment soared as a result of the two oil shocks of the 1970s, Germany quickly ended the open migration policy. Still, in the 1980s, the Federal Republic became a magnet for asylum seekers because Germany's affluence and liberal asylum laws combined with a dramatic reduction in transportation costs and an upsurge in political oppression (particularly in the Middle East and northern Africa) to make the Federal Republic a particularly attractive destination not only for the genuinely persecuted but also for those seeking a better material life. By the end of the decade, close to 200,000 people were applying for asylum annually in western Germany. The collapse of communism in Europe and the outbreak of war in the Balkans quickly raised the number of asylum applicants for 1992 to 600,000, which completely swamped the system.[12]

Some observers charged that the Kohl government cynically chose to allow the flood of asylum seekers to inundate the system rather than allocate more resources to absorb the larger numbers, despite the huge strain this put on German society, because it wanted to amend the constitution in order to restrict the right to asylum. Yet Article 16 could only be amended with the assent of the SPD, because all constitutional changes in Germany require a two-thirds vote in parliament, which the Kohl government did not have. Allowing the system for processing refugees to break down put pressure on the SPD to assent to the government's desire to toughen the article, which the Social Democrats had flatly rejected on several occasions before the latest crisis had arisen. This put the SPD leadership on the spot. Few could deny that Germany had proved socially incapable of absorbing such large numbers of new asylum seekers, but others—particularly those on the SPD's left wing—saw acquiescing in an amendment to the article on asylum as denying the restitution that Germany still owed the world for its Nazi past.[13]

By the fall of 1992, the SPD leadership had largely agreed that amending Article 16 was unavoidable. In the past, the SPD executive committee would have announced this decision after having made it in private, and dissidents within the party would have denounced this as undemocratic, further fragmenting the internal architecture of the party. This time, however, Björn Engholm decided to take the unusual step of calling for a special party convention to be held in mid-November to vote on the matter. Old guard Social Democrats could not comprehend why Engholm took this step. For example, Willy Brandt, the legendary long-time SPD leader and former German chancellor, upon hearing of Engholm's decision, said, "That's crazy—there are things too important for a party convention." Under Brandt's leadership in 1966, the SPD even decided to enter a Grand Coalition government with the Christian Democratic parties without holding a special party convention. Nonetheless, Engholm pressed ahead.[14]

The Social Democratic Party leaders used the weeks before the special party convention to travel to local SPD meetings throughout the country in order to argue their position. Although these gatherings more often than not sparked impassioned debates, in the end they proved instrumental in assuring passage of the resolution on asylum. Many SPD members were simply pleased that the leadership bothered to take the trouble to listen to local concerns. The meetings also made clear to the SPD leaders the most common objections to their initial proposal so that they could adjust it. Consequently, when the special convention finally met, the vast majority of the delegates voted to support amending Article 16, thereby ending the debate over the topic. Björn Engholm had proved his critics wrong; the Social Democratic Party's first experiment with open dialogue and participation had been a stunning success, greatly enhancing Engholm's position within the party and German politics in general.[15]

Within the space of six months, however, Björn Engholm resigned in disgrace as SPD chair and prime minister of Schleswig-Holstein as a result of a scandal. Engholm had first risen to power in 1986 in the wake of a particularly nasty affair in Schleswig-Holstein that culminated in the death under mysterious circumstances in a Geneva hotel room of Engholm's predecessor, Uwe Barschel. Although Engholm had nothing to do with Barschel's death, he committed perjury in 1987 before a committee investigating campaign dirty tricks in Schleswig-Holstein in the aftermath of the Barschel affair when he denied knowledge of any dirty tricks whatsoever. When Engholm's dishonesty was revealed in 1993 by a criminal case arising out of the 1987 investigations, he resigned.[16]

Björn Engholm left an unfinished legacy. Engholm showed that participation paid off politically, but was unable to anchor it permanently in the statute books of the party. Consequently, once Engholm had stepped down, the "SPD 2000" reform program—which was never popular among insiders at the SPD barracks—fell by the wayside. SPD General Secretary Karl-Heinz Blessing stayed on for only a few months after Engholm's resignation. Nevertheless, before Blessing left, he instituted the reform that he had wanted most by organizing an internal party election, which Blessing called a primary, to choose Engholm's successor as the chair of the SPD. The election was a primary of sorts because it would all but determine who would be the SPD's lead candidate to challenge Helmut Kohl in 1994. At first, many party officials were skeptical, but like the convention to vote on the issue of asylum, the primary proved to be a great success.

Three candidates came forward: the left-wing political power broker and prime minister of Lower Saxony, Gerhard Schröder; the moderate premier of the Rhineland-Palatinate, Rudolf Scharping; and the left-wing feminist head of the SPD South Hesse district, Heidemarie Wieczorek-Zeul. The primary took place on 13 June. Fifty-six percent of the SPD membership participated. If the SPD leadership had chosen the candidate, it probably would have picked Schröder, because, although many SPD officials found Schröder to be crass and opportunistic, he was the senior candidate in terms of years in office and had accrued a long list of political favors. The SPD membership, however, chose differently. Scharping received 40.3 percent of the vote, Schröder garnered 33.2 percent, and Wieczorek-Zeul tallied 26.5 percent. A few weeks later, a special SPD convention voted overwhelmingly to make Rudolf Scharping—who just two years ago was a virtual unknown—the SPD's new chair.[17]

Rudolph Scharping and the 1994 Federal Campaign

Rudolf Scharping is the most down-to-earth of the new generation of SPD leaders. He first attained national prominence in early 1991 when the normally conservative Rhineland-Palatinate elected him prime minister. Scharping's victory was the product of a sound campaign, a lackluster incumbent, and a protest vote against the national CDU for raising taxes so soon after an election in which Helmut Kohl had promised not to do so. Once in office, Scharping quickly gained a reputation as a straightforward, hardworking pragmatist with a sharp mind and a talent for finding compromise solutions to difficult problems through private negotiations. Scharping is more provincial than urbane and an uneven speaker, but these qualities have reinforced his overall forthright image.

Soon after Scharping assumed his new position as SPD chair, he appointed Günter Verheugen to become the party's new general secretary. Verheugen began politics in the Free Democratic Party and quickly rose to become one of its national secretaries, but he left the FDP for the SPD in 1982 when the Free Democratic leadership decided to switch coalition partners and form a new government with the Christian Democrats. The new SPD leadership team decided immediately to concentrate the SPD's energies on preparing for the upcoming "super election year" of 1994. As a result, the "SPD 2000" reform project was suspended until further notice.

As 1994 began, SPD officials were quite optimistic that it would be the year that they would finally defeat Helmut Kohl.[18] The SPD had quickly recovered from the resignation of Björn Engholm and continued to outpace the CDU/CSU in the polls by a solid margin. The SPD leadership's initial strategy for the federal election was simply to emulate Bill Clinton's successful 1992 bid for the United States presidency by appealing to the center and by stressing the poor economic performance of the incumbent to the exclusion of all other issues, and then relying on dissatisfaction with the economy to put the SPD back into power. After all, Germany was in the midst of its worst postwar recession. The German economy began to contract in the last quarter of 1992, and the decline did not bottom out until the close of the following year. Moreover, in early 1991 Helmut Kohl had promised that within the space of a few years, eastern Germany would become a "flourishing landscape" of economic prosperity, but by the end of 1993 the five eastern states had displayed few signs of recovery from the dramatic collapse of socialist central planning. Thus, a middle-of-the-road campaign stressing new economic policies looked to be the best way to defeat Helmut Kohl.[19]

The SPD strategy worked at first. Scharping incessantly criticized the government's economic record and kept the federal campaign from drifting onto international topics by insisting that his positions on foreign policy did not differ at all from those of the Kohl government. Scharping embraced many of the conservative coalition's other objectives as well—including a reduction of the government's share of the total economy, a reform of the welfare state, continued investment in eastern Germany, widespread privatization, and tough new measures to combat crime—but argued that the SPD would implement these measures with more compassion and regard for individual rights than the current government. Polls in March showed that 42 percent of voters in eastern Germany and 48 percent in western Germany intended to vote for the Social Democrats. Scharping's tactics helped Gerhard Schröder win his first absolute majority for the SPD in Lower Saxony in mid-March, but then changed economic circumstances and a series of errors knocked the SPD's candidate for chancellor completely off balance.[20]

The German economy had begun to rebound at the start of 1994. Armed with hopeful statistics from the first quarter of 1994 and impressive predictions for the coming years, Helmut Kohl deftly turned the issue to his favor. Kohl conceded that the recession had been longer and deeper than he had anticipated—particularly in eastern Germany—but announced that the "delicate shoots" of economic growth were now clearly visible. Thus, it would be a serious mistake to turn power over to a novice set of leaders brandishing untested ideas when the recovery was so young and fragile. Each passing month brought fresh evidence of a robust recovery. All the while, Helmut Kohl travelled from construction site to construction site breaking ground, laying cornerstones, and cutting ribbons at new factories and infrastructure projects.[21] Meanwhile, Rudolf Scharping committed the first in a series of gaffes in March when he said publicly that the SPD wanted to raise taxes on individuals who had a *gross* income of DM50,000 (i.e., approx. $32,000), when he meant to say a *net* income of that amount. This unnecessarily stirred the latent fear among many voters that the SPD would raise taxes dramatically if it won the federal election.[22]

In late April, Scharping's top transportation adviser resigned angrily because Scharping had backed away from a party commitment to institute a speed limit for the German Autobahn and a comprehensive energy tax.[23] A month later, Scharping badly mishandled an important opportunity to embarrass Helmut Kohl by failing to block the chancellor's choice to replace the Christian Democrat Richard von Weizsäcker as Germany's new president. Although the office of the German presidency is largely ceremonial, it carries a great deal of prestige. Every five years, an electoral college made up of the members of the Bundestag, Bundesrat, and a handful of other prominent German citizens designated by the parties elect the German president, who must receive a majority of the votes cast. For the first round, each party traditionally votes for a candidate from among its ranks. Thereafter, any candidate who does not receive a minimum threshold of votes is dropped from the list and the delegates vote again. Traditionally, the president serves two terms and the Christian Democratic parties, FDP, and SPD take turns designating the eventual winner. This time, however, Helmut Kohl broke from that tradition, much to the consternation of the SPD whose turn it was, and said that his party would back its candidate to the end.

The CDU/CSU selected chief justice of the German Supreme Court Roman Herzog. The SPD chose the veteran prime minister of North Rhine–Westphalia, Johannes Rau, as its candidate, and the FDP picked civil rights advocate and head of the Friedrich Naumann Foundation, Dr. Hildegard Hamm-Brücher. Rudolf Scharping could have humiliated Helmut Kohl and driven a wedge between the Christian Democratic and Free Democratic parties if he had asked his party to cast votes for Hamm-Brücher in the second round. Since Hamm-Brücher was a civil libertarian on the left wing of the FDP, most Social Democrats did not object to supporting her. Hamm-Brücher, furthermore, would have been the first woman elected to the post. If Alliance 90/Greens joined in the vote, Hamm-Brücher would have had a majority. Rudolf Scharping, instead, ordered his party to continue to back Rau in a show of loyalty and to protest Kohl's flouting of an unwritten political understanding. Scharping's obstinacy led the FDP delegates ultimately to switch their votes to the Christian Democratic candidate, and Roman Herzog won. Scharping complained bitterly to the press about Helmut Kohl's strong-arm tactics, but he thereby merely gave the impression that he was politically inept and a sore loser.[24]

Scharping's mishandling of the presidential election completely deflated the SPD's already sagging European Parliament campaign with less than two weeks to go before the 12 June vote. The SPD's principal slogan for the European election—"Jobs! Jobs! Jobs!" (*Arbeit! Arbeit! Arbeit!*)—proved to be a disaster. It took a solid decade of painstaking work for the SPD to convince environmentally concerned voters wavering between the Social Democrats and the Greens that the SPD was interested in more than just jobs. A poster reading "Jobs! Jobs! Jobs!" with no mention of the environment undid all of that work in an instant. The onset of the economic recovery, moreover, made the SPD's slogan look out of place, despite continuing high unemployment. In contrast, the successor party to the Communist SED, the Party of Democratic Socialism, ran a first-class media campaign centered around the slogan, "Change starts with opposition."[25]

The results of the European Parliamentary election were cata-strophic for the Social Democratic Party. The SPD received only 32.2 percent of the vote, which was even lower than the party's total in the 1990 federal election. Worse still, a low turnout enabled the Party of Democratic Socialism to gain over 20 percent of the vote in eastern Germany, including an astounding 40.9 percent of the ballots cast in eastern Berlin. It thus became clear to all that the PDS could still play an important role in the October election, which would be especially troublesome for the SPD because the two parties were in direct competition for large numbers of voters. The more votes that the PDS received, the harder it would be for the SPD to form a majority coalition.[26]

The presidential and European Parliamentary elections brought to the fore the delicate issue of potential coalition partners for the SPD. Throughout the campaign, Scharping downplayed the question, repeatedly stating that in an election, all other parties are rivals, not partners. When pressed further, Scharping still refused to declare a preferred coalition partner, although he did rule out in advance both a grand coalition with the Christian Democratic parties and any coalition that included the Party of Democratic Socialism.

The Greens had gone through their own metamorphosis in the wake of German unification that had rendered them largely unproblematic as a coalition partner for most Social Democrats. Left-wing Social Democrats, such as Schröder and Wieczorek-Zeul, tried to sway Scharping and the party by announcing their preference for a "red-green" coalition before the election in order to push the party to the left, but to no avail. Scharping had no objections in principle to forming a coalition with the Alliance 90/Greens, but hesitated to take this step in advance because he wished to keep all of his options open. Talk also circulated in political circles of either a traditional "red-yellow" SPD-FDP coalition similar to those led by Willy Brandt and Helmut Schmidt, or a "traffic-light coalition" (*Ampelkoalition*) comprised of the SPD, FDP, and the Alliance 90/Greens, but the Free Democrats repeatedly stated that they were only interested in continuing the current coalition.[27]

The immediate aftermath of the European Parliamentary election marked the low point of the Scharping campaign. In June, the CDU/CSU stood significantly ahead of the SPD in the polls for the first time since the 1990 election, and support for the PDS surged to a record high in the east. Critics inside and outside of the Social Democratic Party complained about Scharping's centrist campaign strategy, arguing, "Why would anybody buy a copy [i.e., Scharping], when they already have the original [i.e., Kohl]?" The fact that Scharping and Kohl came from the same part of Germany and had identical Rhineland-Palatinate accents did not help matters.[28]

With his back against the wall, Rudolf Scharping managed to turn his campaign around dramatically at his formal nominating convention in Halle on 22 June 1994. Scharping gave a powerful performance as he presented the SPD's official party platform, which stressed job creation, improving the environment, and reforming the welfare state.[29] He concluded by asserting that far from being lost, the election was still an open race. Germany desperately needed change, and the SPD offered the kind of change that the majority of the voters wanted. During the address, Scharping also challenged Gerhard Schröder, his loudest critic within the SPD, turning to him and saying, "Dear Gerhard ... I would be most grateful if we spoke directly with one another," rather than through journalists. Afterward, the two men made peace with one another, and then 95 percent of the convention delegates formally endorsed Rudolf Scharping as the SPD's candidate for chancellor. Scharping's "miracle in

Halle," as the press called it, had singlehandedly succeeded in rein-
vigorating the party and the campaign. Scharping demonstrated his
leadership skills by presenting a positive party platform and then
directly confronting complaints about his performance. Scharping's
deft handling of Gerhard Schröder preserved SPD unity while making plain that he was in charge of the party.[30]

Within a week, new political developments tested the candidate's
tactical skills once more, but Scharping again handled it well. State
elections in Saxony-Anhalt on 27 June 1994 forced Scharping to
revisit the coalition question, but this time in a much more problematic form, because it involved the Party of Democratic Socialism.
The Saxony-Anhalt election produced no clear winner. The SPD and
the CDU each received 34 percent of the vote, the PDS came in
third with 20 percent, the Alliance 90/Greens tallied 5 percent, and
the FDP failed to reach the 5 percent threshold. As a result, neither
the SPD in coalition with the Alliance 90/Greens nor the CDU had
enough seats to form a government. After three weeks of negotiations, the SPD and the Alliance 90/Greens decided to form a minority government that tacitly relied on the toleration of the PDS to stay
in power. This step triggered a tirade of protest from the conservative coalition in Bonn. Helmut Kohl denounced the minority government as a "treasonous act" and "scandal on an enormous scale,"
adding, "in Magdeburg, the SPD betrayed its own tradition" of
resisting communism. In response, SPD General Secretary Günter
Verheugen only managed to concede, "I'm not comfortable with it,
but I can't forbid it."[31]

The formation of a minority government sparked an intense
debate within the SPD that had been simmering beneath the surface
for months. There was general agreement that the SPD should not
enter into any coalition that included the PDS, but unity ended
there. The vast majority of the SPD leadership, including Rudolf
Scharping and Günter Verheugen, preferred a strict policy of no contact with the PDS, in order to avoid the charge that the SPD was
consorting with Communists. Others, including Thomas Westphal,
the chairperson of the SPD's Young Socialists (*Jungsozialisten*
[JUSO]) youth organization, former staunch advocates of *Ostpolitik*,
such as Egon Bahr and Erhard Eppler, and the new Social Democratic premier of Saxony-Anhalt, Reinhard Höppner, criticized the hard
line, arguing that it amounted simply to repeating the same mistake
that the SPD had made with the New Left in the 1960s and the
Greens in the 1980s. These critics preferred a policy that they called
"demystification through integration," which aimed to undercut the

PDS by forming alliances with it. This would deny the PDS auton-
omy and allow the SPD to appropriate any attractive positions that
the PDS developed. Between these two extreme positions, prominent Social Democrats, such as Peter Glotz and Wolfgang Thierse,
argued that the SPD should under no circumstances cooperate with
the PDS, but should engage it in direct debates.[32]

The Social Democratic Party papered over the issue temporarily
by issuing a document called the "Dresden Declaration" on 11
August, which Scharping and the SPD heads from each eastern state
signed in the Saxon capital. The declaration was a compromise that
categorically rejected participation in any coalition government that
included the PDS at the national or state level, but permitted informal cooperation with the PDS "to implement SPD goals." The document, in other words, simply ratified what had been going on in
much of eastern Germany already while setting strict limits to the
depth of cooperation with the post-Communist party. The SPD covered its flank by following up the Dresden Declaration with a campaign poster distributed throughout the East with a picture of
Helmut Kohl giving a buss on the cheek to the former head of the
GDR, Erich Honecker. At the bottom of the poster, a caption
pointed out that 63 percent of current eastern CDU officials were
also functionaries in the eastern CDU when the party was a compli-
ant participant in the government of the former GDR. The declaration and poster helped considerably to blunt the CDU's protests, and
Rudolf Scharping managed once again to avert a split in his party.[33]

In late June, Scharping managed to stop the Social Democratic
Party's slide in the polls, but by late August, surveys showed that the
SPD had still not been able to make up the ground lost to the
CDU/CSU and the PDS earlier in the year. Scharping's electoral
team realized that only something dramatic would enable the Social
Democrats to catch up in time for the 16 October election, so they
decided to present a full cabinet drawn from the ranks of the Social
Democratic Party. In keeping with Rudolf Scharping's pledge to
reduce the size of government, the SPD cut the number of cabinet
ministries from eighteen to thirteen and the number of ministers
down to fifteen, including two without portfolio. The proposed cabinet was comprised of eight men and seven women and the average
age of the ministers was fifty. A triumvirate of Rudolf Scharping,
Oskar Lafontaine, and Gerhard Schröder headed it.[34]

Creating the hypothetical cabinet proved to be a political boon.
It demonstrated that the Social Democrats had more than enough
talent to staff a government all on its own; no other party could

make such a claim. The SPD alternative cabinet also showed the public that the Social Democrats had the confidence to compare their team with the current government. The SPD did not undertake the exercise to assert that it wished to govern alone, but creating the alternative cabinet helped to dampen further speculation about coalitions. The most controversial element of the alternative cabinet was the triumvirate. Its objective was to undercut opposition charges that Scharping was too inexperienced to become chancellor. Suggesting a triumvirate could have backfired, since it implicitly conceded that Scharping might need the extra help, but it did not because Lafontaine and Schröder were both extremely careful to emphasize their subordinate role to Scharping in a future SPD-led government.[35]

The Social Democratic Party opened the "hot phase" of the campaign with a massive rally in Dortmund on 4 September 1994 under the slogan, "Look forward to change, Germany!" The rally was a massive display of unity seldom seen in the Social Democratic Party. Former chancellor Helmut Schmidt led off the main speakers by excoriating Helmut Kohl for committing a series of "grandiose errors" that had made the lives of all Germans, but particularly those in the East, more difficult. Lafontaine, Schröder, Thierse, and Verheugen followed with blistering attacks on the government, and Scharping concluded by announcing a "One-Hundred-Day Program" outlining the measures that a new Social Democratic government would introduce to strengthen the German economy.[36]

The SPD's program included shifting the tax burden for the cost of German unification from average earners to the more affluent, an "employment offensive" relying on an industrial policy for key industries to create 700,000 jobs immediately and two million in the space of four years, increased expenditures on job training, and government subsidies to promote part-time employment at a livable wage. The One-Hundred-Day Program also proposed the construction of 100,000 new housing units, the outfitting of 100,000 existing houses with solar energy equipment, raising the monthly government support payment for dependent children to DM250 per child, the institution of purchasing preferences in public contracts for products from eastern Germany, and a comprehensive infrastructure program for the five eastern states.[37]

The SPD steadily narrowed the CDU/CSU's lead during the closing weeks of the campaign, but the Social Democrats never managed to erase the CDU/CSU lead completely. All the while, speculation mounted as to whether the Free Democratic Party or the Party of Democratic Socialism would fail to get enough votes to attain seats in the next Bundestag.

The Results of the 1994 German Election

The Kohl government narrowly won the 1994 German federal election. The CDU/CSU received 41.5 percent and the SPD 36.4 percent of the vote. This represented a 2.3 percent drop for the CDU/CSU and a 2.9 percent increase for the SPD when compared to the 1990 federal election. The Alliance 90/Greens came in third for the first time ever in a German federal election with 7.3 percent of all the ballots. The FDP finished fourth with 6.9 percent, which was a sizable drop from the 11 percent the party received in 1990. Only 4.4 percent of the electorate voted for the Party of Democratic Socialism, but four PDS candidates from eastern Berlin were elected directly to the Bundestag. Under Germany's complicated electoral law, the 5 percent threshold is waived for any party that attains a minimum of three such "direct mandates," hence the PDS also received its full share of seats.[38]

The election results had a complex impact on the SPD, improving on the whole the Social Democrats' relative position in German politics. First, although the Social Democrats lost, they managed to reverse the downward slide in their share of the national vote, which had plagued them in the previous three federal elections, dating back to 1982. That, in and of itself, elated many SPD officials.

Second, the 1994 federal election reduced the plurality of the CDU/CSU-FDP coalition in the new Bundestag from 134 to a mere ten seats. This makes governing far more precarious for Helmut Kohl and gives the SPD the opportunity to try to entice away members of the governing parties in order to undermine their majority.

Third, the Social Democrats have gained a new means to influence the legislative agenda of the Kohl government. The SPD was able to widen its majority in the Bundesrat from forty-one to forty-four out of a total of sixty-eight seats owing to the outcome of two state elections also held on 16 October. Thus, the SPD is now only one vote short of the two-thirds majority in the Bundesrat that would give it the power to kill legislation that had already passed through the Bundestag. Since 1991, the SPD has been able to use its less-than-two-thirds majority to tie up legislation by voting it down. When the Bundesrat rejects a bill passed by the Bundestag by a less-than-two-thirds majority, the bill goes to the Bundestag-Bundesrat reconciliation committee, which must produce a compromise solution. The strengthening of the SPD's majority in the Bundesrat has combined with the sharp drop in the conservative coalition's Bundestag majority to give the SPD control over the Bundestag-Bundesrat reconciliation committee for the first time since Helmut Kohl has been chancellor. Command over this committee allows the SPD to set the pace and agenda for finding compromise language to any bill the committee receives. Rudolf Scharping, who resigned as prime minister of the Rhine-land-Palatinate to become the SPD leader in the new Bundestag, has already stated that his party will use the reconciliation commit-tee aggressively to influence all future legislation. This goes a long way toward explaining Scharping's pleasure with the election results, despite his party's failure to capture the Bundestag.[39]

Rudolf Scharping can be equally pleased with the performance of his party. The SPD managed to stave off serious infighting through-out the campaign and pull together in the last six weeks of it to pro-duce a solid result. Although Rudolf Scharping's tactical adroitness, which grew day by day during the campaign, had a great deal to do with the outcome, all of the credit does not belong to him. A good share must also go to Scharping's predecessors, Björn Engholm and Karl-Heinz Blessing, because of the organizational reform that they initiated. The reforms, however, have not been institutionalized. Completing the organizational reform of the SPD will rank among Scharping's most important tasks over the next few years.

On the other hand, the 1994 federal election also revealed a seri-ous strategic problem for the SPD. Although the Social Democrats raised their share of the vote in eastern Germany between 1990 and 1994 from 24 to 30.7 percent, the gap between the SPD's share of the eastern and western vote remained large. In western Germany, the SPD received 37.8 percent of the vote, which is over seven per-centage points higher than in the East. Although the explanations of this phenomenon are multifaceted and complex,[40] the principal ben-eficiary is easy to identify: the Party of Democratic Socialism. The PDS garnered over 18 percent of the eastern vote in the 1994 fed-eral election. If the PDS consolidates its position in eastern Germany over the next four years, it will become a virtually insurmountable barrier to the SPD taking power unless the Social Democrats agree either to form a Grand Coalition government with the CDU/CSU or to drop its policy of disassociation from the PDS. The alterna-tive—namely, destroying the PDS while attracting its supporters—would be extremely difficult to achieve. One thing is certain, however. The SPD will be wrestling with the PDS and its place in German politics over the coming years.

Conclusion

In a recent book, the eminent scholar of social democracy Gerard Braunthal noted that the SPD needed to accomplish four goals before it would be ready to return to power: 1) minimize intraparty altercations, 2) project a modern image, 3) present a dynamic leadership with an appealing set of foreign and domestic policy alternatives, and 4) cope with external change and its impact on the party.[41]

Despite the defeat in the 1994 federal election, the Social Democratic Party of Germany has made great strides toward achieving these goals. Between 1990 and 1994, the Social Democratic Party accomplished the first two goals and parts of the third and fourth. After committing a quick series of missteps at the outset, Rudolf Scharping established himself as an effective leader and built on the improved internal party foundation given to him by Björn Engholm and Karl-Heinz Blessing to restore unity and common purpose to the Social Democratic Party. The SPD also made progress externally in 1994. The SPD helped to reduce the Kohl government's majority in the Bundestag to a razor-thin margin while widening the party's own advantage in the Bundesrat and taking control of the parliamentary reconciliation committee.

Nonetheless, the Social Democratic Party still has three difficult hurdles to negotiate in the coming years. First, the SPD must complete its internal organizational reforms, expanding and regularizing the participatory innovations it has already begun to use. Otherwise, difficult issues—such as the deployment of German troops in United Nations peacekeeping missions—will divide the party to a debilitating degree once again, as they did in the 1980s.

Second, the Social Democratic Party must develop new *Leitthemen* for its economic and foreign policies to replace Keynesianism and the *Ostpolitik*. This will be no mean feat, particularly given today's global *Zeitgeist* of conservatism and laissez-faire, but it is essential if the Social Democrats are to persuade enough voters that they offer a superior alternative to the Christian and Free Democrats.

Finally, the Social Democratic Party must improve its standing in eastern Germany. In practice, the SPD can do this only at the expense of the PDS. Thus far, the Social Democrats have been their own worst enemy in the East. Many western Social Democrats still remain obsessed with their own parochial concerns and regard German unity as a largely negative event. This, as eastern Social Democrat Thomas Krüger has pointed out, has prevented the party from perceiving unity as "an opportunity for a left-wing project." Krüger rightly asserts that this has been a mistake, because the PDS is ultimately not interested in the success of unity. If unity succeeds, Krüger believes, the PDS is finished. Undermining the PDS by taking a positive approach toward unity would be by far the best path for the SPD, he says, because it would enable the SPD eventually to absorb the bulk of the PDS supporters.[42]

To be sure, the three remaining difficulties discussed above are daunting. The Social Democratic Party may not completely resolve any of them. Worse still, miscalculation could cause any one of these problems to blow up in the faces of the SPD leadership, setting the party back for years. Unforeseen events could also damage the Social Democratic Party or spark a new round of party infighting, just as German unity has done. Still, if the SPD continues to make progress in the next four years at the same pace as the previous four, and if a bit of *fortuna* shines on the party in 1998, the next German chancellor could very well be a Social Democrat.

Notes

1. *Frankfurter Rundschau*, 18 October 1994.

2. Andrei S. Markovits, "The West German Left in a Changing Europe: Between Intellectual Stagnation and Redefining Identity," in Christiane Lemke and Gary Marks, eds., *The Crisis of Socialism in Europe* (Durham, N.C.: Duke University Press, 1992), 171; Wolfgang Thierse and Tilman Fichter, "Gespräch mit Wolfgang Thierse. 'Dolmetscher zwischen West- und Osteuropa,'" *Neue Gesellschaft/Frankfurter Hefte* 38, no. 2 (February 1991): 123.

3. Beatrix W. Bouvier and Horst-Peter Schulz, *"... die SPD aber aufgehört hat zu existieren." Sozial demokraten unter sowjetischer Besatzung* (Bonn: J. H. W. Dietz, 1991).

4. Hans Jürgen Fink, "Die SPD in der DDR," *Deutschland Archiv* 23, no. 2 (February 1990).

5. Gerard Braunthal, *The German Social Democrats Since 1969: A Party in Power and Opposition* (Boulder, Colo.: Westview, 1994), 351; and Sozialdemokratische Partei Deutschlands, National Executive Committee, *Basic Programme of the Social Democratic Party of Germany*. Adopted by the Programme Conference of the

Social Democratic Party of Germany at Berlin on 20 December 1989 (Bonn: Courir, 1990).

6. *Washington Post*, 30 November 1990.

7. *New York Times*, 26 November 1990; and *Zeit*, 7 December 1990.

8. "Tuscany Wing" is a derisive label applied to people in the party who wore expensive Italian clothing, drank premium Italian wines and coffees, and frequently vacationed in Tuscany (*Wirtschaftswoche*, 8 February 1991).

9. *Spiegel*, 27 May 1991.

10. *Spiegel*, 20 May 1991.

11. Karl-Heinz Blessing, ed., *SPD 2000. Die Modernisierung der SPD* (Marburg: Schüren, 1993).

12. *tageszeitung*, 23 September 1992.

13. *Zeit*, 9 October 1992.

14. *Frankfurter Allgemeine Zeitung*, 12 October 1992.

15. *Handelsblatt*, 11 November 1992; *Frankfurter Rundschau, Süddeutsche Zeitung*, 18 November 1992; and SPD-Parteivorstand, *Intern. Dokumentation. Beschlüsse und Reden. Parteitag*, no. 21, 23 November 1992.

16. *Handelsblatt*, 4 May 1993; and *Spiegel*, 26 April and 3 May 1993.

17. *Tagesspiegel*, 14 June 1993.

18. Gerard Braunthal, "The Left Parties in the 1994 Election," *German Politics and Society*, issue 34 (spring 1995), forthcoming.

19. Dieter Roth, "Patterns of Electoral Change in Germany: Past, Present, and Future." Presented at the Eighteenth Annual Conference of the German Studies Association, Dallas, Texas, 30 September–2 October 1994.

20. Forschungsgruppe Wahlen, "Bundestagswahl 1994. Eine Analyse der Wahl zum 13. deutschen Bundestag am 16. Oktober 1994," Berichte der Forschungsgruppe Wahlen no. 76, Mannheim, 21 October 1994, 2d. ed., 47, 57–59. Konrad Schacht and Norbert Seitz, "Machtwechsel 94? Gespräch mit Konrad Schacht," *Neue Gesellschaft/Frankfurter Hefte* 41, no. 5 (May 1994): 389–93.

21. *Handelsblatt*, 2 June 1994.

22. *tageszeitung*, 22 March 1994.

23. Ibid., 2 and 3 May 1994.

24. *Frankfurter Allgemeine Zeitung*, 26 May 1994.

25. *tageszeitung*, 19 and 31 May 1994.

26. Patrick Moreau, "Gefahr von links? Die DPS auf dem Weg zur Etablierung," *Neue Gesellschaft/Frankfurter Hefte* 41, no. 8 (August 1994): 694–704.

27. *tageszeitung*, 20 and 23 June 1994; and Braunthal, "The Left Parties," forthcoming.

28. *tageszeitung*, 20 June 1994; and Forschungsgruppe Wahlen, 57–59.

29. Sozialdemokratische Partei Deutschlands, Vorstand, *Politik. Das Regierungsprogramm '94*, Halle, 22 June 1994 (Bonn: Courir, 1994).

30. *tageszeitung*, 23 June 1994.

31. *Süddeutsche Zeitung*, 27 June 1994; *tageszeitung*, 29 June 1994; *Frankfurter Rundschau*, 16 and 23 July 1994; and *Zeit*, 29 July 1994.

32. *tageszeitung*, 7 July 1994; and forum on "Dealing with the PDS," in *Neue Gesellschaft/Frankfurter Hefte* 41, no. 8 (August 1994): 675, 694–735.

33. *Frankfurter Rundschau*, 15 August 1994; *tageszeitung*, 12 August 1994; *Washington Post*, 29 August 1994.

34. *Economist*, 3 September 1994; and *Süddeutsche Zeitung*, 29 August 1994.

35. *Frankfurter Rundschau*, 30 August 1994.

36. *Frankfurter Rundschau*, 5 September 1994; *Handelsblatt*, 5 September 1994.

37. *Frankfurter Rundschau*, 5 September 1994; *Handelsblatt*, 5 September 1994; and Sozialdemokratische Partei Deutschland, Parteivorstand, *"100-Tage-Programm" der SPD. Für ein gerechtes und friedliches Deutschland* (Bonn: Courir, 1994).

38. Forschungsgruppe Wahlen, 6–14.

39. *Deutsche Presse Agentur*, 9 December 1994.

40. See Stephen J. Silvia, "Left Behind: The Social Democratic Party in Eastern Germany after Unification," *West European Politics* 16, no. 2 (April 1993): 24–48.

41. Braunthal, *The German Social Democrats*, 347.

42. *Focus*, 7 November 1994.

9

THE FREE DEMOCRATIC PARTY
A STRUGGLE FOR SURVIVAL, INFLUENCE, AND IDENTITY

CHRISTIAN SØE

The liberal Free Democratic Party occupies a unique position of
influence and vulnerability in German politics.[1] It has been a key
player in Bonn's coalition game since the formation of the Federal
Republic in 1949. In terms of the length and scope of its role as a
member of government, the FDP is still the most successful small
party at the national level of politics in Europe. Yet, for years it has
been in danger of losing the narrow electoral base that provides it
with a foothold in parliament and cabinet. Its situation improved in
1990, the year of German unification, when the FDP performed
unusually well in the old western states of the Federal Republic and
managed to attract an even higher share of the vote in the new eastern region. Only four years later, however, it became clear that the
emerging East-West divide in German party politics would have a
devastating impact on the beleaguered Free Democrats. The Bundestag contest of 1994 thus provides another opportunity to examine the FDP's increasingly endangered position of strategic advantage
within the changing German party system.[2]

The FDP's traditional role as balancer makes its electoral plight a
matter of systemic importance, at least in the short term. Its marginalization or sudden disappearance in Bonn would presumably have a
scrambling effect on the power relations among the remaining parties in the Bundestag. Another set of possible consequences would
consist of more subtle and long-term shifts in Germany's style and
direction of governance.[3] In that sense, it could be argued that some
major questions hanging over the Bundestag election of 1994 were
linked to the fate of the Free Democrats. Would the relatively simple
and centrist symmetry of power in Bonn, with the FDP as its vulnerable linchpin, be reaffirmed? Or would it give way to a new and

uncertain balance in the party system—a situation that a major pre-election study called "unpredictable" governing majorities?[4]

Facing a potential electoral disaster in 1994, the Free Democrats decided to capitalize on the theme of uncertainty by presenting themselves as a guarantee against political instability and experimentation. "This time, everything's at stake!" (*Diesmal geht's um alles!*), their main slogan proclaimed. It turned out to be difficult to get a sympathetic hearing for their case in the electorate. Many voters did not appear to find the stakes very high anyway, and few seemed to link the fate of the Free Democrats to their primary political concerns.[5] It was not the first time that the endangered party had used an all-or-nothing slogan, and the new version smacked of hyperbole as well as déjà vu. Even the most articulate Free Democrat would have found it difficult in 1994 to get a serious hearing for the argument that *everything*—such as the goal of keeping the country governable and liberal-democratic?—would be in jeopardy if the Free Democrats did not return to their customary berths in the Bundestag and federal cabinet. In interviews, some FDP leaders suggested a softer version of their party's prudential theme: "Without the Liberals, Germany would be a different republic."[6] One way or another, it was a hard sell.

"This Time, Everything's at Stake!"

It is unlikely that the Free Democrats will soon forget the "super election year" (Superwahljahr). In the unprecedented series of nineteen elections concentrated between March and October 1994, the FDP set something of a record in defeat for an established parliamentary party. It registered a rout in every one of eight state parliament contests, setbacks in nine rounds of local elections, and a fiasco in the party's summer bid for the European Parliament. Even as its narrow regional and local base disintegrated, the FDP found itself in a desperate struggle for survival in national politics. It took some effort to remember that less than four years earlier, the Free Democrats had celebrated a triumph in the first all-German Bundestag election of December 1990.

In the year of national unification, the small liberal party had recorded its best election result in almost three decades by winning 11 percent of the vote in the enlarged Federal Republic. Within the newly added eastern region, including eastern Berlin, the FDP's share of the vote in 1990 actually reached 12.9 percent, topping the best result ever achieved by the party in West Germany.[7] The Free Democrats also registered what appeared to be another success story in their party's eastward projection. As the result of a friendly takeover of four Liberal parties in the East, the FDP's small membership suddenly tripled, rising from some 67,000 to over 200,000. With its disproportionately high eastern membership, the FDP formed a sharp contrast to the makeup of the much larger but "west-heavy" Christian Democratic and Social Democratic parties.

In view of this development, some observers found in the FDP a potential for becoming the first "truly all-German party."[8] They suggested that its impressive new base in the East, along with a long record of interest in *Deutschlandpolitik,* predisposed the FDP to become responsive to the special interests of the eastern region as well as to the new needs of united Germany. As the 1994 Bundestag election approached, however, it was clear that the Liberals had failed to take advantage of these new political assets and opportunities. Their position of strength in the East had collapsed, and their modest base in the West was crumbling.

In the end, the FDP managed to pass the 5 percent hurdle. Its share of the German vote in 1994 was 6.9 percent, which was also enough to clinch the parliamentary majority required to renew Chancellor Kohl's coalition government of CDU/CSU and FDP. Yet the result gave the Liberals only a tentative new lease on life. Below the federal level of politics, they were widely reduced to a peripheral role or suffered displacement altogether. By the end of the year, the FDP was present in only seven of the sixteen state parliaments. It was a coalition member in only two state cabinets.

The East-West Divide

There were, of course, many analysts who underlined the pivotal role of the Liberals in Germany's electoral geometry. In a typical report published a week before voting day, *The Economist* pointed out that the balance of forces which would determine the composition (and, presumably, direction) of the next government majority, depended to a considerable extent on the electoral performance of two small Bundestag parties.[9] One was the liberal FDP, the experienced centrist insider and traditional coalition party. The other was the Communist-descended Party of Democratic Socialism (PDS), the new far-left outsider and regional protest party. The report assumed correctly that the Greens would have no trouble winning parliamentary representation.

The FDP and PDS, which both managed to win new parliamentary terms, had very little in common. Many of their positions were a fascinating study in contrasts that have become part of a less consensual German politics since unification. By 1994 the FDP seemed to embody many features of the "old" Federal Republic towards which the PDS expressed a studied ambivalence or sharp criticism—and against which the PDS was able to mobilize considerable eastern protest. Their very different bases of voter support reflected the new East-West divide in German politics. Thus the FDP won 7.7 percent of the vote in the West in the Bundestag election of 1994, while it received just 3.5 percent of the vote in the East. That amounted to an electoral decline of "only" 2.9 percent in the old states versus a plunge of 9.4 percent in the new eastern region, as compared to the Liberal results four years earlier. In other words, the FDP was almost wiped out as a voter party in the East where it had gloried at the time of national unification. By contrast, as Gerald Kleinfeld shows elsewhere, the PDS triumphed in the East and largely failed in the West.

One simple reason for the FDP's more western image in 1994 was the loss of its "Genscher bonus." Four years earlier, in the euphoria of national unification, the veteran foreign minister had personified an all-German profile for the FDP. In his youth, Hans-Dietrich Genscher had fled to the West from his home in Saxony-Anhalt, and the party made much of this regional connection in his busy electoral activities of 1990. In the eastern states, he became the party's electoral magnet by helping it claim a vanguard role in the *Deutschlandpolitik* that had just culminated in success. However, Genscher had stepped down as foreign minister in May 1992, and there had been no continuous effort by the FDP to revive his fading eastern appeal or translate it into electoral currency. By the time he returned to the eastern campaign trail over two years later, Genscher had lost much of his immediate political relevance there.

In 1994 voters in the East were far more concerned with the wrenching dislocations that accompanied the region's social and economic transformation than with the role of the FDP in working for German unification. For them, strong and decisive state interventions should play a part in this process. It was easy to recognize that the western-led and market-oriented FDP was not a party that responded sympathetically to such demands. Its general policy orientation and public profile found little affinity in the East, even among many members of the FDP, as will be discussed later.[10] Moreover, the party's new leaders seemed to be lackluster in comparison with some of their predecessors. They held little appeal for an eastern electorate that still lacked strong party orientations and felt more attracted to "familiar" political authority figures.

It seemed natural for western Liberals to identify with the heritage of the Federal Republic which the FDP had helped shape over the past forty-five years. Although it often made pragmatic compromises on behalf of the special interests of business, civil service, and professional élites, the FDP generally stood for less state intervention and more deregulation than any other Bundestag party. It could be counted upon to celebrate the market economy, promote entrepreneurial interests, criticize bureaucratic overreach, and laud the principle of individual achievement. Western Liberals also prided themselves on a long record of concern for the protection of individual rights and liberties against powerful state or social institutions. While their "social" and "economic" wings often disagreed about the proper role of state authority, their debate started from a shared reluctance to strengthen its power. Last but not least, the FDP was an eloquent—and by no means disinterested—advocate of the idea of coalition government as practiced in Bonn since 1949. This was a form of checks and balances which could be defended in liberal principle, even while it assigned a disproportionately large role to the FDP as the junior member of government. However, it was also a recipe for public displays of disagreement among the coalition parties which did not always play well with an eastern audience keen on more decisive action to "solve" their daily problems.

Western Liberals also came to be associated with a special concern for private property rights in the new eastern region. From the beginning, they were strong backers of the legal principle that restitution (*Rückgabe*) must have priority over compensation (*Erstattung*) in the settlement of the vexed property issues that accompanied the transition from socialism to capitalism. Even in its later, modified form, this position appeared to encourage a flood of ownership claims, often from people living in the West or abroad. Many easterners saw it as a major procedural hindrance to economic development, as well as a threat to current holders or users of these properties.

In 1994 the distance between the western leadership and the prevailing concerns in the East was nowhere better reflected than in a widely publicized blunder that led the FDP to appear to be presenting itself as "the party of higher income earners" (*Partei der Besserverdienenden*). This highly unusual self-characterization was included in the first draft of the election program approved by the party's executive committee.[11] The phrase carried more than a grain of truth and even a refreshing dose of self-irony, but it clearly violated the

German equivalent of a "political correctness" test. The press joined the FDP's political rivals in reacting with a mixture of shock and ridicule to this breach of good manners. The Liberals have traditionally identified themselves with slogans that speak of the need to "reward" individual "achievement" and "responsibility." There has never been any doubt that the FDP is more skeptical of steeply progressive taxation or other measures of income redistribution than its Bundestag rivals. Yet the party had never before appeared to identify itself directly with a definable income category. The FDP hastened to withdraw the offensive phrase from later versions of its election program. The damage had been done, however, and no amount of explanation could erase the gaffe from public memory. It was a political embarrassment to the FDP throughout Germany, but eastern members or supporters seem to have found it especially rankling.[12] Many expressed their belief that it played a role in alienating voters in the new states from the Liberals by reinforcing the FDP's image as a party of the much-resented *Besserwessis*—the "better off" and "know-it-all" westerners.

The Junior Coalition Party: A Difficult Balancing Act

In addition to the unification malaise, the Liberals also faced some more familiar problems. The stakes in federal elections are always high for the FDP, because it is vulnerable and has much to lose. Its political role in Bonn is closely tied to the relatively simple and moderate system of political parties which became an early hallmark of the Federal Republic. These parties have provided the parliamentary building blocks for stable governing majorities. Within the moderate party pluralism, the FDP has received an average of less than 10 percent of the vote in federal elections, but it has almost always been needed as a coalition partner by one of the two big parties.

The small coalition party enjoys strategic advantages, but it cannot afford to forget the limits to its power and influence in Bonn. The most important constraints on its leverage and room for maneuver stem from possible retributions by a variety of actors—disappointed supporters, party members, or coalition partners. A change of coalition partners in Bonn, for example, is fraught with political risks, as the FDP knows from the experiences of 1969 and 1982.[13] The FDP will normally make a formal "coalition decision" before the beginning of a Bundestag campaign. In the spring of 1994, after the shock of its first regional election losses, it surprised no one by making an early announcement of its intention to continue as partner of the Christian Democrats. Had it not done so, it would have risked losing CDU-oriented coalition supporters, who by then were estimated to make up more than one-half of the FDP's voters.[14]

The FDP must also avoid the opposite danger of appearing as a pliant dependent or satellite of its much larger government partner. To establish its independence without losing its political attractiveness as a coalition party, the FDP therefore tries to perform a careful balancing act between cooperation and limited conflict with its cabinet colleague. Periodically, it will make special efforts to shift away from too close an identification with the chancellor party. The issues it picks may well be matters of some principle, but the tactical angle is not to be overlooked.

Three of the most publicized cases in the early 1990s may well have harmed the FDP's political image more than they improved it. In the first of these, the Liberals decided in 1993 to test the constitutionality of German participation in NATO's surveillance flights over Bosnia as part of a UN-sponsored peacekeeping mission. The issue stemmed from a supposed constitutional prohibition of "out-of-area" action by the Bundeswehr. Politically, the FDP leadership took the position that Germany must fill an international responsibility to participate in such missions. By raising a legal challenge, however, the FDP was demonstrating its constitutional sensitivity. It was most difficult to explain that the party was politically in support of an involvement even while questioning its legality. To the relief of the FDP leadership, the Constitutional Court decided that German participation was legally acceptable if supported by a Bundestag majority. It is doubtful that the FDP gained anything politically by its constitutional query. Instead, the party's appearance of equivocation earned it considerable criticism in the media.

In a second case, the FDP tried to use the election of the federal president in May 1994 to set itself apart from the chancellor party. After Genscher had refused many pleas to become a candidate, the FDP nominated another prominent veteran, Hildegard Hamm-Brücher. Her spirited, if hopeless, candidacy attracted some media attention. It turned sour when the party leadership had her step down before the final round of voting, in order to throw FDP support behind the successful CDU candidate, Roman Herzog. The event thus turned into an opportunity for the Liberals to demonstrate coalition loyalty rather than rugged independence.

Finally, the FDP had a difficult time explaining its shifting position on a key issue in social policy. In the debate over a new state-run insurance to finance nursing care for the old and handicapped (*Pflegeversicherung*), the FDP had at first taken a very different position from both the SPD and CDU/CSU. The Liberals alone had favored a voluntary rather than compulsory insurance scheme. In the end, however, the FDP retreated in the face of what in effect had become an informal Grand Coalition of the big parties on this question. On the further issue of financing such an insurance, the Free Democrats had also backed down and accepted a cost sharing by employers and employees. Some observers suggested that the Liberals had managed to lose a maximum of respect on both sides of this issue by appearing to be meanspirited and weak-willed at one and the same time.

In 1994 it was widely felt among Free Democrats that there had been far too much "going along" with the CDU/CSU to project an "autonomous" image of the FDP. Party leaders acknowledged that many voters appeared to have difficulty identifying the FDP's contributions to government and public policy. Their attempts to correct this deficit took the form of listing a number of significant new policies in which the Liberals had supposedly been the guiding hand. One typical list included postal and railway reforms, the privatization of Lufthansa, the loosening of the authority of the federal employment bureau, greater flexibility for weekend work, an economic growth program for the East (*Aufschwung Ost*), a new crime-fighting law, and the compromise on the tightening of the asylum laws. The FDP could also credibly claim to be more adamant about savings and tax reductions than the CDU/CSU.[15] The Liberals had also adopted a position against a widely discussed proposal to combat organized crime by means of electronic surveillance. It was well known, however, that they were divided on the plan that the German left has dubbed "the great eavesdropping attack."

The FDP's blurred image is linked to structural as well as political factors. It is inherently difficult to pinpoint the party's specific policy contributions because the Liberals work within a governing coalition in which they are clearly junior partners. As a consequence, they can influence, but not really alone shape the agenda of a government headed by the much larger chancellor party. In practice, the FDP often appears to moderate rather than set direction in public policy. Liberals have therefore come up with a "functional" argument for their party's inclusion in government, portraying it as a vital "third force" in the political system.[16] It supposedly offsets the tendencies toward both inertia and power abuse that would be common in a single-party government by one of the two large parties or, even

worse, in a Grand Coalition of both. In its idealized self-presentation, the FDP acts at times as a brake and at other times as an ener-
gizer that provides the necessary balance of continuity and change in
government. The functional role, then, involves far more than acting
as a "majority-maker." It includes both dynamic and prophylactic
claims for the FDP that are not always easy to explain or demonstrate
to the electorate. The FDP hopes that they will have an appeal
among some of the many German voters who seem to prefer the idea
of a coalition government in Bonn to a single-party government on
the British Westminster model.[17]

Room at the Top: The Generational Change

The FDP has long prided itself on having provided some outstanding personalities for German government. In 1994, however, it
found itself in the unfortunate position that none of its five ministers
was a cabinet veteran with a strong public profile. Foreign Minister
Klaus Kinkel, the most prominent, was in his fourth year in the cabinet. He had begun as minister of justice in January 1991, and then
moved into his new post in May 1992. Kinkel's basic political outlook probably did not differ much from that of his predecessor, but
international circumstances had changed radically since the time
when Genscher had acquired his reputation as a masterful balancer of
deterrence and détente. Genscher could not maintain his mediating
international role after the end of the Cold War, nor could it be
transferred to his successor.[18] But Kinkel's rather dull public image
also reflected the administrative habitus he had developed in his
many years as a top civil servant. No one doubted Kinkel's integrity
or competence, but his background had honed him for neither the
political limelight nor the new role of party leader that was also
thrust on him. Although Kinkel had only joined the FDP at the time
of his cabinet appointment, he was elected to replace Count Lambsdorff a little more than two years later, in June 1993. It was remarkable that the Liberals would fill their highest position with a
newcomer. After all, Kinkel had not sought out the position, and he
made it clear that he would stay on as foreign minister. The dual role
would have been a heavy task for anyone, and Kinkel's relative inexperience in party matters was bound to be a major handicap.

Free Democrats had spoken for years about the need to prepare
replacements for their veteran leaders. When the call came, there was
a remarkable paucity of personnel. The party suddenly stood before

the problem of having yearned for a generational change but having no obvious new leaders to replace the old ones. The few potential alternatives to Kinkel had been eliminated in advance by slips of commission or omission. Best known was the politically ambitious and controversial Jürgen Möllemann, the leader of the FDP in North Rhine-Westphalia (until late 1994). He had tried to make a mark as minister in a way that is quite unusual in German politics—by tying his cabinet career to the success of a drastic reduction of public subsidy programs. It soon turned out that he could not deliver very many cutbacks, but when he did resign in early 1993, it was as the result of a relatively minor charge of misusing his office. Möllemann remained in the Bundestag and continued to create publicity for himself. A very different contender for the party leadership would have been Wolfgang Gerhardt, the quiet and widely respected head of the FDP in the state of Hesse. He had characteristically failed to make a political move in time.

Irmgard Schwaetzer, the minister of housing and construction, was in many ways the most experienced FDP politician in the cabinet. Her post inevitably made Schwaetzer the focus of resentments sparked by housing and rent problems in the East. She had made a determined run for the FDP leadership against Lambsdorff in 1988, but she lacked the necessary backing to revive her candidacy when he prepared to step down in June 1993. This had become evident a year earlier when opponents in the parliamentary party managed to sabotage her internationally reported nomination to succeed Genscher in the foreign ministry.

The intraparty intrigues that surrounded this and other personnel changes added to the FDP's negative appearance as a *Pfostchenpartei* or careerist "perk party." In the aftermath of Genscher's replacement, the party's standing in the polls slipped markedly for the first time since unification. At the beginning of 1993, it sagged further in the wake of events linked to Möllemann's resignation. Thereafter, the FDP stayed in a negative evaluation zone (on a plus five to minus five scale) in the monthly polls taken by the Election Research Group.[19] On this widely disseminated poll measurement, the image of Klaus Kinkel at all times stayed in a low but positive zone—far behind the towering position of Genscher, but well ahead of the low and negative position of his party.

A third Liberal in the cabinet was the new and youthful justice minister, Sabine Leutheuser-Schnarrenberger. She was an outspoken civil libertarian and that ensured her both support and opposition within the party, especially on questions involving law enforcement powers. Her "social-liberal" wing of the FDP has a long tradition of seeking to maximize individual liberties, but there has always been another, more conservative tendency in the party that emphasizes the countervailing requirements of social order.

The last two FDP cabinet members were even more recent newcomers. Günter Rexrodt had replaced Möllemann at the beginning of 1993, and a year later Karl-Hans Laermann succeeded the only eastern Liberal in the cabinet, Education Minister Rainer Ortleb. Each of these changes had again been accompanied by factional maneuverings that reflected poorly on the party. Neither minister had made a strong public impression during his short time in office. This amounted to a lost opportunity when the German economy entered a highly publicized recovery in the spring of 1994. It is remarkable that neither Rexrodt nor his party drew public recognition in the form of a "competence bonus" from this electorally crucial turnaround. Instead, the approval ratings of Chancellor Kohl and his party improved markedly from this time on, as other chapters in this volume explain.

Electoral Decline

The German system of proportional elections and the resulting form of coalition government have been the most important institutional preconditions for the FDP's significance as a "third" party. For decades it has lacked the electoral concentrations of strength that would be required to ensure parliamentary survival in a system of winner-takes-all contests. The only winning strategy for the FDP is to pass the 5 percent threshold, but even that goal is sometimes difficult to meet. At least since the late 1960s, the small party has had a very narrow core of loyal voters that comprises less than 5 percent of the electorate. The FDP is, therefore, dependent on attracting itinerant voters. At the federal level of politics, it is relatively adept at finding such ephemeral supporters, often by appealing to their tactical calculations. Beginning with the Bundestag election of 1972, the Liberals have also regularly resorted to a "second vote" campaign. They specifically solicit the second (party list) vote from supporters of the coalition in which the FDP is a member. As a result of such split-ticket voting, the FDP has consistently recorded a notably higher number of second than first votes. It is, of course, the second vote that determines the party's presence and strength in the Bundestag.

It is considerably more difficult for the FDP to attract tactical voters in state and local politics. The Free Democrats have seen much of their local and regional base erode, even while they have managed to retain a parliamentary representation at the national level. A steeply rising number of electoral defeats at the state level over the past four-and-a-half decades reflects the dismal trend (see table 9.1). Sometimes there have been recoveries, but they always turn out to be partial and impermanent. Even where the FDP retains a foothold in the Landtag, it has often become marginalized as a small opposition party. By the early 1990s, it was a member of only two state governments in the West, where it had once been a member of nine cabinets. In the five eastern states, the situation was markedly different. Here the FDP was present in all of the parliaments and served in cabinet coalitions in every state except Saxony until the election setbacks of 1994.

TABLE 9.1

FDP ROUTS IN LANDTAG ELECTIONS, 1949 TO 1994

Decade	Number of Landtag Elections	Times FDP below 5%	Percentage of FDP Routs
1950s	30	1	3.3
1960s	23	(0)	— [20]
1970s	30	5	16.7
1980s	28	12	42.9
1990–1994			
Western states	15	4	26.7
Eastern states	10	5	50.0
Total, 1949–1994	136	27	19.9

During 1991 and the first months of 1992, the FDP enjoyed fairly good standings in the opinion polls, but there was some slippage in the East that in retrospect looks ominous. The East was hard to read, however, and the only electoral tests came in the West. Here the next series of Landtag contests showed that the FDP remained vulnerable. Although the party survived all four elections in 1991, it registered somewhat lower results than four years earlier in each case. There were only two contests in 1992, and the FDP again barely passed the 5 percent hurdle. In one of them, however, the FDP registered what would turn out to be its single electoral improvement in the whole period by winning 5.6 percent of the vote in Schleswig-Holstein. That was hardly a great victory, but it was a decisive increase over the party's poor result (4.4 percent) in 1988.

The return to the Landtag in Kiel gave the FDP an additional reason to celebrate, because it meant that the party was now again represented in every state legislature for the first time since 1978. This now rare experience of parliamentary omnipresence was cut short in September 1993 when the FDP won only 4.2 percent of the vote in Hamburg. By contrast, the Greens scored an impressive 13.5 percent. The FDP's traditional status as the established "third party" had been insecure since the breakthrough of the Greens in the early 1980s. Now it was challenged by very different rivals as well. The FDP had been outperformed by right-wing parties in two state elections in 1992, and this experience was repeated in Hamburg in 1993. Here the Republikaner barely missed the electoral hurdle (with 4.8 percent), while another protest party of the more moderate right, the populist "Instead Party," was able to win representation at first try (with 5.6 percent). Even as the ultraright dipped in electoral strength during the last year before the Bundestag election, it was still able on occasion to outperform an FDP that had declined even more.

In every one of these cases, an electoral postmortem could point to specific situational reasons for the party's failure to make even a slight advance. Yet there was apparently also a larger trend at work, reflecting the FDP's structural weakness and its declining political appeal to tactical voters. As always, the state and local elections were not to be equated with the Bundestag contest. At the federal level, the FDP can draw upon some positional advantages that almost always lead to a better performance.[21] But as the election "super year" approached, the party's strategists had reason to worry about the general trend and the dangerous "loser" image it could engender for the FDP.

The Liberal Windfall in the East: Quickly Won and Quickly Lost

The electoral decline of the FDP showed up throughout the Federal Republic, but there were special reasons to worry about the party's disarray in the new eastern region. Since the five new states and east Berlin make up only about one fifth of Germany's population, representation in the Bundestag will primarily be determined by how well a party does among western voters, unless it has an unusual concentration of eastern regional strength, like the PDS. The FDP had also slipped in the West, however, and there were symbolic reasons why it could not write off the East.

The FDP's outstanding performance in the East in 1990 had benefited from some temporary advantages. When national unification suddenly came onto the political agenda, the Liberals had hurried to become the first West German party to unite with their eastern counterparts. Their unification congress in August 1990 had been carefully orchestrated to take place a few weeks before the formal dissolution of the East German republic to provide maximum political resonance in the state and federal elections that followed. The FDP had in effect taken over two tiny dissident groups as well as the much larger remains of two old "block parties." Its formal membership, which had been only some 67,000 in the old Federal Republic, suddenly rose to over 200,000 in united Germany (see table 9.2). For a while, German wits joked about the birth of a *"liberale Massenpartei."* The immediate result was a highly unbalanced membership organization, quite unlike what happened when the much larger CDU and SPD took in their smaller eastern counterparts. At the time of the merger, two-thirds of the FDP's members were located in the East which had a population that was only one-quarter as large as that of the West. That made the ratio of membership to population approximately eight times higher in the new states in August 1990. It could thus appear that the Liberals had shifted their center of gravity markedly eastward. The FDP also laid claim to other organizational resources—press organs, political bureaus, real estate and other assets—that had belonged to the two block parties. Their value was estimated in July 1990 to be about DM200 million, a figure that was later reduced to a still impressive DM90 million. It seemed like a huge inheritance for the FDP, but the new riches were not to last very long.

Only a very small number (at most about 2,000) of the new eastern members came from the two dissident parties. They were important because they provided democratic legitimation for the organizational expansion. It is remarkable that the FDP, unlike the CDU and SPD, had failed to attract a single leading eastern German dissident to its ranks in 1990. Instead, the FDP had concentrated on incorporating the remains of two block parties: the LDP (Liberal Democratic Party) and NDPD (National Democratic Party of Germany). The LDP had been founded by progressive Liberals a few weeks after Germany's capitulation in 1945, but it had later survived as an organization by becoming an integral part of the Communist-controlled political system. That had been true for the NDPD from the beginning, for it had been sponsored in 1948 by the Communist power-holders as a political home for ideologically rehabilitated former military officers and Nazi members. The two parties had a nominal membership of about 135,000 so-called "L's" and "N's" at the time of their merger with the FDP.

TABLE 9.2

FDP MEMBERSHIP DECLINE IN THE OLD AND NEW GERMAN STATES, MID-1990 TO END OF 1994

	7–31–90*	12–31–90	12–31–91	12–31–92	12–31–93	12–31–94
Old States						
Baden-Württemberg	7,440	7,496	7,309	7,117	6,904	6,863
Bavaria	6,432	6,385	6,187	5,890	5,739	5,463
West Berlin**	2,600	2,600	2,600	2,550	2,500	2,400
Bremen	618	598	622	624	615	600
Hamburg	1,899	1,987	1,932	1,868	1,756	1,602
Hesse	7,361	7,759	7,574	7,484	7,266	6,960
Lower Saxony	7,989	7,948	8,358	8,056	7,757	7,439
North Rhine-Westphalia	20,519	20,652	20,340	20,017	19,684	19,213
Rhineland-Palatinate	5,390	5,375	5,350	5,200	5,077	5,132
The Saar	2,931	2,878	2,757	2,588	2,422	2,167
Schleswig-Holstein	3,296	3,278	3,200	3,179	3,116	3,098
Total in Old States	66,475	66,956	66,229	64,573	62,836	60,937
New States						
East Berlin**	5,444	4,412	2,412	1,170	1,299	992
Brandenburg	19,865	15,853	8,925	5,177	4,423	3,848
Mecklenburg-West Pomerania	17,744	13,154	7,994	5,826	3,755	3,220
Saxony	35,832	25,363	16,758	9,666	7,492	6,635
Saxony-Anhalt	29,151	24,171	14,289	8,394	7,254	5,908
Thuringia	28,129	28,425	20,950	7,841	6,830	6,138
Total in New States	136,165	111,378	71,328	38,614	31,053	26,741
Total Membership†	202,640	178,334	137,557	103,187	93,889	87,678
Percentage in the Old States	33	38	48	63	67	70
Percentage in the New States	67	62	52	37	33	30

*These membership figures for the end of July 1990 anticipated the FDP's unification congress in August and national unification in October 1990.

**Western Berlin membership has been estimated as eroding from 2,600, based on the December 1990 and June 1992 membership figures of 2,571 and 2,607 respectively. The estimate of eastern Berlin membership has then been derived by subtracting the west Berlin figure from the total Berlin membership.
†About 300 FDP members who reside abroad and belong to the Auslandsgruppe have not been included.

Sources: *F.D.P., Geschäftsbericht 1990–1991,* 36, for the 1990 figures. The other data were provided by the FDP party headquarters in Bonn.

After Germany's unification, there arose some tangled legal questions about the process by which these two block parties had first joined together in the spring of 1990 and then united with the FDP in August. That, in turn, raised doubts about the procedural legality of the transfer of party assets at each step, including their final transfer to the FDP. There were additional questions concerning the manner in which the block parties had acquired some of their resources in the first place. An independent investigatory commission concluded in 1993 that the FDP had no valid claim to these assets which now belonged in the public hand.[22] The Liberals nevertheless maintained a reduced claim to some of the former possessions of the LDP. Their proprietary stand received a poor press. It differed markedly from the position of the CDU, which absorbed two other block parties but relatively early abandoned claims to their remaining assets.

There were other problems associated with the FDP's eastern inheritance. After the merger, the leadership attempted to coopt some eastern members into high positions. These efforts at affirmative action led in some cases to disappointing placements, which in turn were followed by embarrassing corrections when new officeholders were replaced. The two cases which received most public attention dealt with the early retirement of the new federal minister of education, Rainer Ortleb, and the new general secretary of the FDP, Uwe Lühr, in early 1994 and mid-1993 respectively. Both had been members of the LDP, while their successors (Laermann and Werner Hoyer) were westerners. Kinkel made an effort to find another easterner for the education ministry, but it was concluded that no qualified person was available. In the four new eastern state governments where the FDP was a coalition partner until the setbacks of 1994, only a handful of eastern Liberals had gained much public recognition.

It soon became apparent that there were major differences between the eastern and western FDP members. The rough distinction between the "social-liberal" or center-left and the "economic-liberal" or center-right orientations in the West simply did not fit the outlooks of party members from the East. Many of these newcomers had political orientations that were shaped by the illiberal traditions of East Germany as well as the special social and economic problems encountered in its reconstruction. They generally turned out to be far less civil libertarian and often showed much more interest in state intervention on behalf of social services, economic stimulation or redistribution, as well as law and order. This contributed to new intraparty differences and an even more ambiguous public image for the Liberals.

The most striking evidence of the political incompatibility between many of the eastern FDP members and their western colleagues, however, can be seen in the high rate of defection by the former. At the end of 1990, there had been a loss of about 25,000 of the 135,000 newcomers. Four years later, the net loss was about 110,000, and there were fewer than 27,000 eastern members left (see table 9.2). In the same period, there had been an attrition of only about 5,500 western members. There were many reasons for an eastern German to leave the FDP, including the simple fact that the considerable privileges of block party membership had not been carried over into the Federal Republic. But the defections were also linked to a social as well as an ideological alienation from the new western-led party itself. Most eastern members had come from the LDP and missed the "warmth of the nest" *(Nestwärme)* which they remembered from its fortnightly party meetings. Their descriptions of westerners in the FDP often included references to "cold" and "quarrelsome" personal relationships.[23] Westerners, in turn, were ill at ease with the statist orientation of many of their new party colleagues. Interviews with party workers indicate that the FDP had not expected or really wanted to retain all of its huge membership in the East, but the losses were greater than had been anticipated. The massive bloodletting was bound to weaken the party's political efforts in the new states.[24]

The Campaign Strategy: From Plan to Improvisation

The FDP had already begun to prepare its campaign strategy for the Superwahljahr in January 1991. On first sight, there seems to have been nothing extraordinary about the planning, except that it began so early. As in the past, the FDP established a small campaign group headed by its federal manager at the party headquarters in Bonn. The core group, as usual, consisted of the department heads. Another regular participant was a private communications adviser with close ties to the party, who had been involved in the FDP's central campaign planning since 1978. Members of the group held monthly meetings at first, then they met weekly, and later more frequently. The overall direction lay in the hands of the party's successive general secretaries: Uwe Lühr and (after June 1993) Werner Hoyer. The FDP presidium and executive committee received occasional reports and were responsible for the review, revision, and approval of the campaign proposals. After the middle of 1993, the headquarters intensified contacts with the state party organizations in order to promote an integrated campaign, conduct regional conferences, and sponsor strategy seminars.

A closer look reveals that not all of the planning was routine. Even though they focused on the Bundestag election of October 1994, the strategists recognized that it could not be treated in isolation from the electoral marathon between March and September. They anticipated a momentum that could become decisive for the FDP. Looking back later on the disastrous turn of the electoral dynamics, the communications adviser expressed his frustrations over wasted opportunities. His unusual criticism shows that the work of the planners and their interactions with the party leadership were beset by much more than communication problems.[25] There were conceptual differences and tensions in the campaign group, but the adviser's main complaints were directed against the party leadership (the presidium and the executive committee as well as unnamed ministers and parliamentarians). They had ignored warnings about the FDP's image problems and its early electoral setbacks, and they had sidetracked recommendations for a major party reform as well as an organizationally and thematically more integrated election strategy. After its approval at the end of June 1993, the general strategy had been promptly ignored in some important points by party politicians.

The retrospective criticism has an undertone of self-justification, but it throws some light on the FDP's difficulties. The successive strategy papers show that the planners had called early attention to the party's need for a more coherent and focused self-presentation.[26] The central difficulty was really a political one. How did one mobilize consent and resources for such a strategy within an electorally weak, organizationally loose, and ideologically diverse party whose public image was primarily defined by its balancing act as junior coalition partner in Bonn?

The campaign group showed an early recognition of the growing East-West divide that would play a major role in the Superwahljahr. A strategy paper of December 1992 presented a gloomy scenario for

1994, with malaise and alienation dividing the citizenry. In this context, it was suggested that the FDP would have a real opportunity to set itself apart from the other political parties through a kind of political "liberation act" *(Befreiungsschlag)*. The FDP must address "unsparingly" a few major problems and present its distinctive approach to their resolution. Liberals should seize for themselves the topics of "achievement, the commitment to market principles, and the willingness to address the 'west-east taboo topic.'"[27] In particular, the FDP should be forthright in pointing out that the economic development of the East would take longer than had originally been expected, that western productivity must not be "taxed away," and that protectionist moves by the trade unions could delay the raising of living standards.

Such a "liberation act" never took place, as the communication adviser later rued. The efforts of the planners are nevertheless of interest to anyone who wishes to understand the small party's electoral dilemma. They all reflected a recognition that the FDP must "do something" extraordinary if it were not to become marginalized. The largely unspecified proposal for a "party reform" was not new. It merited attention along with the recommendation for programmatic renewal, but neither the outgoing FDP leadership nor their successors were predisposed to initiate such major undertakings in the short time available to them.

The Campaign: Against the Tide

The "super election year" started out with low poll standings.[28] In March, the first consequences showed up when the FDP dropped to 4.4 percent of the vote in Lower Saxony. As late as the party conference in early June, however, there appeared to be little recognition in the party of massive catastrophes to come.[29] Reality broke through a week later when the FDP won only 4.1 percent of the national vote in the European election and fell far below the Greens (10.1 percent). The Liberals trailed ignominiously behind the far-left PDS (4.7 percent) and barely nosed ahead of the Republikaner (3.9 percent). It was a small consolation that the latter two also failed in their bid for seats in Strasbourg.

There followed devastating setbacks in three eastern Landtag elections that were held in the last half of June (Saxony-Anhalt) and the first half of September (Brandenburg and Saxony). The FDP had been a government member in the first two states, and it had a substantial parliamentary presence in all three. Now the party was ejected from all of these offices when it scored results *below* 4 percent, 3 percent, and 2 percent respectively. The lockout was especially bitter in Genscher's home state, where the FDP's support plummeted from 13.5 percent to 3.6 percent. In late September the Liberals recorded another devastating defeat, this time in Bavaria, where they won only 2.8 percent of the Landtag vote and trailed both the Greens (6.1 percent) and the Republikaner (3.9 percent). As if to remove any doubt that this was the *annus miserabilis* of the Liberals, they were also widely routed in all nine statewide rounds of local elections between March and October.

In their self-presentation, the Liberals tried to promote the party in terms of its program, its function, and its leading personalities: *Programm, Funktion und Personen.* If anything had been overprepared, it was the election program. The Liberals had once again taken pride in drafting a detailed statement that would challenge the patience of the most devoted policy enthusiast. Its 141 crowded pages made it longer than the combined programs of the CDU and the SPD. Free Democrats sometimes jokingly compare their mammoth election program to a mail-order catalogue. Its main purpose is apparently to demonstrate that the party has distinctive policy positions on every conceivable issue.

The FDP provided many other printed materials as well, including the mercifully short election call *(Aufruf)*. Some of the party's most distinctive positions were in the economic and social field, where it stressed market solutions, argued for a reduction in taxation and bureaucracy, advocated deregulation and privatization, and offered its pet idea of the negative income tax *(Bürgergeld)* as an answer to the entitlement bureaucracy. The civil libertarian emphasis was also given its due, along with admonitions for tolerance and easier access to citizenship (including dual citizenship) for foreigners who were long-time residents. As always, the FDP also tried to get environmentalist attention by stressing the compatibility of ecological and market policies. If there was a basic trademark, it would be the liberal rejection of what speakers like Lambsdorff called "a blind belief in the state" (*blinde Staatsgläubigkeit*).

A party manager in eastern Berlin would later point out that the FDP had failed to consider the special concerns of the new states in its political advertising. The promotion of libertarian and entrepreneurial values had made little sense to easterners, he suggested.[30] This appears to have been a serious strategic oversight for a party which claimed in the preamble to its election program that it had "come further on the way to becoming truly all-German" than its rivals. In the East, the FDP's self-presentation served to underscore its very western image.

In addition to its policy stance, the FDP everywhere advanced its functional importance. The strategists recognized that this argument was far more relevant for the national elections than for most other contests in 1994. It often took the simple form of presenting the FDP as the indispensable majority provider by stressing that Kohl and the CDU/CSU could not "make it on their own." There was also a more sophisticated attempt to promote the idea of the FDP as a moderating and power-checking force within the government. One of the party's television spots tried to convey the functional thesis through the use of several colored billiard balls—one black (CDU), one red (SPD), and one green, as well as the blue-yellow one representing the Liberals. The colorful FDP ball was removed and restored to illustrate the need for a liberal additive to provide balance or symmetry. Its continued presence supposedly provided a guarantee against the dangers of a single-party government, a Grand Coalition, or a "red-green" alliance.

Finally, the FDP presented itself through the party's leading personnel. The personalization of the campaign did not go as far as the planners had wanted, but Kinkel was shown with the existential message—"This time, everything's at stake!"—on thousands of posters and in many other commercials. Other prominently displayed candidates included Genscher and Lambsdorff, the veteran leaders. In North Rhine-Westphalia, Möllemann's party organization ran its own special campaign, using 4,000 posters and newspaper advertisements that bore the message, "Strong heads are needed for the Land," and showed the faces of three prominent Liberals: Genscher, Lambsdorff, and Möllemann. The conspicuous absence of Kinkel was explained by pointing out that he came from another Land, Baden-Württemberg. Another commercial showed a pensive Genscher as chess player and bore the message, "A clever move: Your second vote for the FDP."

As in the past campaign years, the party directed special commercials at specific *Mittelstand* groups, and it held forums for members of the professions and the business community during the election year. Another revived tradition was a half-page political testimony signed by a group of "prominent people from culture, sport, science, and the economy" on behalf of the FDP. It appeared a few days before the election in five major newspapers, with the slogan, "Germany Needs the Liberals."

The Bavarian defeat came only three weeks before the Bundestag election. Party leaders made a strong effort to combat possible defeatism among FDP workers and supporters by pointing out that Landtag and Bundestag elections are very different. But Lambsdorff and others acknowledged publicly that the FDP now was fighting for its political existence. A few days before 16 October, the party had another wake-up call in the form of an announcement by the polling institute Forsa that the party would not make the 5 percent minimum. Other polling institutes were quick to question the conclusion, and there seemed to be a general consensus that the FDP did indeed have a reasonably good chance of returning to parliament and cabinet.

The Election Result: Conditional Survival

In the Bundestag election of 16 October 1994, the Free Democrats scraped through with 6.9 percent of the second or party vote. This amounted to a loss of 4.1 percent of the vote or almost 1.9 million voters as compared to 1990. It was the greatest setback ever experienced by the party between two successive Bundestag elections. The East-West divide set a strong imprint on the result, as noted earlier. In the East, where the FDP received just 3.5 percent of the vote, the loss amounted to 9.4 percent of the vote since the superb performance of 1990. The party fell well below 5 percent in all of the new states. In the West, by contrast, it won 7.7 percent of the vote and thus lost "just" 2.9 percent as compared to its 1990 outcome. Here it received less than 5 percent in only one state, the Saar.

The outcome could be facelifted to suggest a fairly comfortable margin of nearly 2 percent above the required minimum, and it was just large enough to save Chancellor Kohl's coalition majority. The narrow balance of power in the Bundestag also had restored the FDP's old pivotal position. Arithmetically, at least, it was possible to form a so-called "traffic light" majority, with the SPD and the Greens. But such a coalition, which has been tried in Brandenburg (1990–94) and Bremen (1991–95), would run into major political obstacles at the federal level. In Bonn, the policy differences between the FDP and the Greens on the economy and foreign policy would weigh far more heavily. It would also matter that the Greens have become a major competitor for left-liberal voters. In addition to having a greater policy affinity with the CDU/CSU, the FDP also had to consider that it owed its conditional survival to voters who wanted a continuation of the Kohl/Kinkel government.

The FDP's low vote actually overstated the party's electoral strength. The Liberals received an unusually large element of support from CDU/CSU-oriented voters who favored the coalition government rather than the FDP per se. In fact, electoral analysts calculated that such "coalition voters" made up over 60 percent of the FDP voters in 1994. As expected, the FDP benefited from vote-splitting, for it received only 3.2 percent of the first votes (compared to 6.2 percent for the Greens and 4.0 percent for the PDS). In other words, the gap between its second and first vote result was 3.7 percent, the second highest on record (in 1983 it had been even higher, at 4.2 percent).[31] The ticket-splitting on behalf of the FDP was notably stronger in the West, where tactical voting seems to be better understood.

The FDP won forty-seven seats in the Bundestag, a loss of thirty-two. There were nine new members in the parliamentary group, including Klaus Kinkel, Günter Rexrodt, and Wolfgang Gerhardt. Only seven FDP parliamentarians (15 percent) now came from the East, whereas there had been seventeen easterners (21.5 percent) before. Only eight FDP parliamentarians were women, including just one of the nine newcomers. Women thus constituted only 17 percent of the FDP parliamentary group, or even less than their previous share of 20.3 percent. It is remarkable that there was not a single woman nor a single newcomer from the East in the parliamentary group.

The FDP had lost support in all voter groups when compared to 1990. The party continued to be somewhat stronger among men (7.5 percent) than women (6.6 percent). In the age groups, the FDP was weakest among younger voters (male and female), especially those between twenty-five and thirty-four (5.3 percent). In 1990, the FDP had been weakest among voters over sixty, but this time the seniors came close to the middle-aged voters (forty-five to fifty-nine years of age), who continue to be the party's strongest supporters. The two age groups supported FDP with 7.5 percent and 7.8 percent of their vote respectively.[32]

The social dimension showed stronger and more significant differences, for the FDP continued to be a party whose supporters come overwhelmingly from the German middle classes, both "new" and "old." The FDP did best among the self-employed (14.9 percent), where it received more than twice as many votes as in the population at large. The party also did relatively well in the small group of farmers, the much larger group of civil servants, and the salaried and nonunionized administrative class of *Angestellte*, with scores of 8 percent or slightly better in each case. Administrators in highly placed positions appear to have given greater support to the FDP, as in past elections. By contrast, it continued to do poorly among all blue-collar workers (3.5 percent), and especially among unionized workers (2.2 percent) in both East and West.[33]

The Bundestag election of 1994 gave the FDP a respite, but its existential plight was by no means over. This basic message was underscored in another cluster of state and local elections that took place on the same day. Here, the FDP continued its long string of reversals. It was devastated in each of the three Landtag contests: Mecklenburg-West Pomerania (3.8 percent), Thuringia (3.2 percent), and the Saar (2.1 percent). It also recorded disastrous results in local elections in North Rhine-Westphalia. As a result, the FDP was now absent from a total of nine of the sixteen state parliaments, including all five legislatures in the new eastern states. The party was a cabinet member in only two of the sixteen state governments. It was also missing at the local level of government in many parts of Germany—and only modestly represented almost everywhere else.

Once Again: Little Party, What Now?

The campaigns of 1994 had hardly ended before Free Democrats embarked on an electoral postmortem combined with a vigorous debate about the party's future course. Their intensive self-scrutiny took place under the pressure of a political reality in which the FDP faced another round of at least four state elections during 1995 alone. This is not the proper place to review and analyze these recent developments, but it may be useful to list the most important ones until the beginning of 1995.

There were a few top personnel changes right after the election. The FDP entered Kohl's new government, but its cabinet presence was cut from five to three ministers. The survivors were Kinkel, Schnarrenberger, and Rexrodt. Irmgard Schwaetzer, who lost her ministry, stepped down from her high party positions as well. Werner Hoyer resigned from his top organizational post, but Kinkel immediately appointed him junior minister in the foreign office. He was replaced as general secretary by Guido Westerwelle, an energetic former leader of the Young Liberals. Möllemann was reelected to the Bundestag, but the special campaign in his home state had failed to give him new leverage within the party. His continued challenges to the leadership finally provoked a strong reaction from Bonn followed by Möllemann's overthrow as state party leader. There is general consensus that he will be heard from again.

The FDP shied away from an even more important change in December 1994 when Kinkel asked for a surprise confidence vote from a special party conference in Gera. The meeting had been called in the spirit of "a new beginning," but it soon turned into an acrimonious debate about responsibility for the party's political crisis. Kinkel's keynote speech on 13 December included considerable self-criticism, but it met with unprecedented hostility from many party delegates who accused him of weak leadership. There were credible reports that a deeply wounded Kinkel considered resigning, but the next day he asked for the unusual vote of confidence after an emotional speech in which he appealed for party unity. Three hundred ninety delegates (two-thirds) supported the party leader, while 185 voted against him and twenty-four abstained.[34] Kinkel declared the result acceptable, but his position as party leader had been badly shaken and remained precarious.

Without an improvement in the FDP's dismal poll standings, Kinkel could expect another challenge to his leadership at the regular party conference in June 1995. Instead, after two more routs for his party in the Landtag elections of Bremen and North Rhine-Westphalia, he chose in advance to announce his resignation from the position he had been drafted into only two years earlier. As widely expected, the 1995 party conference chose Wolfgang Gerhardt to be Kinkel's successor. Although a newcomer to the Bundestag, Gerhardt has considerable political experience as state party leader and former cabinet minister in Hesse. Unlike his controversial rival, Möllemann, Gerhardt is consensual in approach and shows little flair for seeking the political spotlight with dramatic gestures. He is acceptable to the party's different factions, but skeptical observers suggest that the small party cannot hope to regenerate without establishing a stronger profile also in its leadership.

As the party's new general secretary, Westerwelle has given priority to two major reform initiatives which have been staple topics in party discussions for years. One is an organizational renewal, including a better development of intraparty communication and "dialogue" between the Bonn headquarters and the lower party levels. Westerwelle's experience as leader of the independent Young Liberals may turn out to be a useful training for dealing with the diversity of intraparty views, sensitivities, and styles. He recognizes the special need for party reconstruction in the East, but this task will be a major challenge. He may find it necessary to mobilize as regional allies some of the remaining "L's" or "N's," who understand the special needs of the East without romanticizing their experience in the block parties. There is also a need to recruit reformers of his own generation in the new states, and that could turn out to be very difficult. Since the election, some eastern Liberals have organized an intraparty opposition that gives formal vent to their alienation from what they now call the *"West-Partei."*[35]

The second area of reform deals with a programmatic renewal. During its quarter of a century as a government partner, the FDP has largely neglected the sustained intellectual debate for which some people in the party seem to be eager and well equipped. The often-cited Freiburger Theses, adopted in 1971, are clearly a "social-liberal" product of the final years of the postwar boom. The attempt to produce a sequel, in the form of the Liberal Manifesto of 1985, failed to catch the imagination.[36] Many in the party now suggest that a short, basic programmatic statement and a new concentration on its implementation would do more for the FDP than the detailed position papers that have poured forth from the party's policy groups over the years.

Westerwelle heads a small party commission on programmatic development. He will have no shortage of opinions or formal proposals to draw upon, for the party's desperate situation has encouraged many liberal flowers to bloom. The "social-liberal" wing has been relatively weak in numbers since the coalition change in 1982, but it includes some articulate people who are demanding a more civil libertarian emphasis. Several hundred of them are linked together through the Freiburger Kreis, an intraparty discussion group with a long history under different names. There are other voices which suggest that the left-liberal field has already been occupied by the Greens and parts of the SPD. They urge the party to adopt a more conservative emphasis on social or even national order. A well-publicized initiative in this direction has come from a group of West Berlin party members around Alexander von Stahl, the former federal attorney general.[37] The deeply divided Berlin party organization seems to be a microcosm of the FDP's main factions. Here one also finds prominent social-liberals, such as Wolfgang Lüder or Carola von Braun, as well as the city-state's FDP leader, Minister Rexrodt, who like many other party members occupies a less clearly defined middle position between the two factions. In the eastern part of Berlin there is yet another tendency, represented by the dwindling number of former "L's" in the party who subscribe to a law-and-order emphasis combined with a strong social orientation.

Conclusion

The unification of Germany has brought alterations to the entire Federal Republic. After the 1994 elections, these changes are reflected more strongly in the party system, which four years earlier had been projected from West Germany into the new eastern region. Until now, however, the changes have only dented the familiar mold. The established party system has not been thoroughly revamped, and its basic shape is still the familiar one. Yet there have been some potentially important shifts in its internal composition and balance, and the FDP has born the brunt of the impact so far. That is ironic, for the Liberals had been the chief beneficiary of an electoral windfall that accompanied unification when they took pride in moving first and furthest on the path toward becoming a "truly all-German party."

The FDP's structural problems have been aggravated by the East-West divide, but they reach back over two decades to the late 1960s when the Liberals lost most of their dependable electoral base. The "super election year" was a particularly difficult hurdle for the FDP, following so close upon its change of leadership and ending, rather than beginning, with the Bundestag election. In the federal contest, the FDP is in the best position to use the functional argument for attracting the second vote of tactical coalition supporters. It would clearly have been to the advantage of the Liberals to have had the Bundestag election at the outset of the electoral marathon. Once again, however, the FDP's problems go far deeper than a whim of the electoral calendar.

Political recovery in the East will be very difficult for the Free Democrats, given their western image. It will also be problematic at the local and state levels of politics in the West, where the Liberal position had already eroded before the recent dramatic losses. It is not inconceivable that the FDP will remain a splinter party *(Splitterpartei)* at the subfederal level in much of Germany. Whether it will be able to survive and maintain its long-established strategic position at the national level will depend on developments that to a considerable extent are beyond its control. In the past, the FDP has been adept in its adjustments to shifts in the balance of forces among its larger rivals. Now it faces more competition from other small parties, as well as an apparently growing electoral belief that German politics without the Liberals is altogether thinkable.[38]

Somehow the FDP will have to persuade more voters that its presence in the Bundestag and the federal cabinet makes a worthwhile difference. It may take a stint in the parliamentary opposition to carry through a political rejuvenation, as some Free Democrats argue. Such a recourse will not be easy for this perennial government party, and it could have the unintended consequence of hastening the FDP's transition into political obscurity. The fate of the Liberals is in any case a matter of some consequence for German politics. Their disappearance would unsettle the balance of power among the remaining political parties, at least for an interval. If the functional argument is correct, their absence could also have a considerable impact on the direction and style of governance. In that sense, at least, Germany would be "a different republic" without the Liberals.

Notes

1. I am grateful to many people in Germany, including a number of active Liberals, who have been willing to inform me about the FDP and other political parties. It is not possible to name them all, but Hans-Jürgen Beyer, Rudolf Fischer, Wulf Oehme, Wilfried Paulus, Klaus Pfnorr, and Peter Schröder were particularly helpful in responding to my transatlantic requests for more information. None of them would agree with everything in this chapter. I alone am responsible for any errors of fact or interpretation. My research has been supported by a grant from California State University, Long Beach.

2. The 1980s campaigns are analyzed in my chapter, "The Free Democratic Party: Two Victories and a Political Realignment," in Karl H. Cerny, ed., *Germany at the Polls: The Bundestag Elections of the 1980s* (Durham, N.C.: Duke University Press, 1990), 110–41. The 1990 campaign is the topic of my chapter, "Unity and Victory for the German Liberals: Little Party, What Now?," in Russell J. Dalton, ed., *The New Germany Votes* (Providence, R.I.: Berg Publishers, 1993).

3. For a "thought experiment" as a way of exploring the consequences of the FDP's absence in Bonn, see my chapter "'Not Without Us!' The FDP's Survival, Position, Influence," in Peter H. Merkl, ed., *The Federal Republic of Germany at Forty* (New York: New York University Press, 1989), 317–18.

4. Wilhelm Bürklin and Dieter Roth, eds., *Das Superwahljahr. Deutschland vor unkalkulierbaren Regierungsmehrheiten?* (Cologne: Bund-Verlag, 1994). This study was published in the spring of 1994. The reference to "unpredictable governing majorities" was based on the apparent electoral vulnerability of the conservative-liberal government as a whole rather than of the FDP itself.

5. A number of polls during the summer and fall showed that many Germans (one-half or even more of those asked, in some cases) believed that the FDP would not be present in the next Bundestag. About as many appeared to find such an absence either welcome or of no importance. See "Lieber mit Liberalen," *Der Spiegel*, 19 September 1994. A very large number of respondents (68 percent in one poll) believed the FDP's political importance had declined as compared to earlier times. See "Büttel der Politik," *Der Spiegel*, 26 September 1994. One poll reported that only 15 percent of those asked in September 1994 were personally disappointed over the many electoral defeats of the Liberals in that year. See "Die politischen Schlagzeilen und ihre Nachwirkungen beim Bürger," *Frankfurter Rundschau*, 29 September 1994. On the other hand, Elisabeth Noelle-Neumann suggested that the FDP was the victim of negative reporting. She pointed out that while the FDP was the favorite party of only 4 percent of the electorate, it ranked in the second most popular spot for 30 percent of the population. Its tactical second-vote supporters would come from this group. See "Die FDP und die Versuche, sie totzureden," *Frankfurter Allgemeine Zeitung*, 21 September 1994.

6. "Bonn ohne Liberale wäre eine andere Republik," Interview with Klaus Kinkel, *Der Tagesspiegel*, 4 October 1994.

7. In the Bundestag election of 1961, the FDP had received its hitherto best result in a Bundestag election, 12.8 percent of the vote in the ten West German states which then constituted the Federal Republic. As the eleventh state, West Berlin had special status and did not vote in federal elections until after unification. A clarification may be necessary to avoid misunderstandings about the election results cited for 1990. Some political scientists have used results for "the East" that include only the five eastern states and exclude East Berlin. That leads to somewhat different electoral shares for the political parties because the electoral outcome in the former East German capital differed considerably from that of the rest of former East Germany. Thus the FDP received 13.4 percent of the vote in the five eastern states *alone* in 1990. See my chapter in Russell J. Dalton, ed., *The New Germany Votes*, 99, 124, where an editorial preference for the more restrictive electoral definition of the East prevailed. My own preference is to use the available electoral results from *the whole area* of former East Germany, including its capital.

8. For a discussion of this and other potential developments of the FDP, see the excellent analysis by Wolfram Kaiser, "Between Haiderisation and Modernisation: The German Free Democrats since Party Unification," *German Politics*, 2, no. 2 (August 1993): 224–42. For typical Liberal references to the FDP as the party which was "furthest on the way" to becoming a "genuine all-German party," see the election program for 1994, *Liberal denken. Leistung wählen*, 5.

9. "Helmut Steams On," *The Economist*, 8 October 1994, pp. 51–52.

10. The eastern German demand for a stronger state contributed to the low assessment of the FDP. See "Die Ostdeutschen wollen den starken Staat," *Neue Zeit*, 29 April 1994.

11. The FDP claims with some credibility that its formulation was misrepresented and misinterpreted. The original passage, which had been approved by the party's executive committee on 2 May 1994, had the following formulation: "We are the party of the achievers *(Leistungsträger)* and 'higher income earners' *('Besserverdienenden')* of today and tomorrow, for we want to give as many as possible the opportunity, to be 'higher income earners.'" The controversial phrase had been

set in quotation marks, as indicated. It was borrowed from the recent tax debate, where it had been introduced by the SPD as designating a minimum individual taxable income of DM50,000. The general secretary of the FDP, Werner Hoyer, has emphasized that the phrase had been meant as an ironic twist on the SPD's usage. For this explanation, see his letter to leading Free Democrats, *GS-Info-Brief,* 9 (17 May 1994): 1–2.

12. It was criticized repeatedly by eastern German delegates to the party conference in Rostock in June 1994. Many returned to the subject after the October election as well. See Lorenz Maroldt, "Die APO der Ostliberalen schimpft auf Bonn," in *Der Tagesspiegel,* 24 February 1995.

13. In 1969, the FDP abandoned its traditional coalition course and chose to form a government in Bonn with Willy Brandt's Social Democrats. In 1982, the Liberals abandoned this socialist-liberal coalition and joined Helmut Kohl's Christian Democrats in the present conservative-liberal government. In both cases, the FDP lost heavily in voters who had favored the previous coalition, before it attracted new ones who supported the change.

14. Forschungsgruppe Wahlen e.V., *Bundestagswahl 1994* (Mannheim: Forschungsgruppe Wahlen, Report No. 76, 1994), 65. In the week before the October election, 63 percent of those who intended to vote FDP reported that they were closer to the CDU/CSU.

15. See "Die FDP vor der Wahl im Herbst: Diesmal geht's um alles," *Frankfurter Allgemeine Zeitung,* 26 July 1994.

16. This point is developed further in my chapter, "The Free Democratic Party," in H. G. Peter Wallach and George K. Romoser, eds., *West German Politics in the Mid-Eighties* (New York: Praeger, 1985), 115–18.

17. In the week before the 1994 Bundestag election, only 27 percent of the respondents wanted a single-party government by the CDU/CSU or the SPD. Among the supporters of each of the two big parties, only 55 percent to 56 percent wanted "their" party to form a majority government by itself. Forschungsgruppe Wahlen, *Bundestagswahl 1994,* 66.

18. Genscher's changing role is discussed in my biographical essay on him, in David Wilsford, ed., *Political Leaders of Contemporary Western Europe* (New York: Greenwood Press, 1995).

19. See the monthly *Politbarometer* reports (Mannheim: Forschungsgruppe Wahlen e.V., 1992 to 1994).

20. The special requirements of Bavaria's election law resulted in the FDP not winning Landtag representation in that state in 1966, although the Liberals won more than 5 percent of the vote.

21. Some of the reasons for the electoral divergence between the state and federal levels of German politics are discussed in my chapter, "The Free Democratic Party," Wallach and Romoser, 170.

22. There have been numerous press reports on the subject. See, for example, *Die Süddeutsche Zeitung,* 17 December 1992, 26 March and 3 May 1994. Also *Die Frankfurter Allgemeine Zeitung,* 29 January 1993, "Unabhängige Kommission: FDP erbt nichts von Blockparteien."

23. See the article by Elke Mehnert, deputy party leader in Saxony, "Gedanken einer Ostdeutschen zur Erneuerung der F.D.P.," *Die liberale Depesche,* November–December 1994, pp. 23–24.

24. Interviews at the party conference in Rostock and at the party offices in Bonn and Berlin, June 1994. The FDP's eastern membership losses were considerably higher than those of the CDU, which had inherited two other block parties and many dissidents. A comparative study of the manner in which the FDP and CDU dealt with their eastern "inheritance" is needed. Early impressions suggest that the CDU had several advantages, including an ability and willingness to invest more resources in maintaining its network, an ideologically based greater attraction to a service-hungry eastern electorate, and a stronger political appeal of some of its leaders as authority figures.

25. For a short report on this unusual incident, see "Parteiführung: Nur schön ausgemalt," *Focus* 47 (1994): 83. The critical theses are developed at length in the internal paper, *Strategische Beratung der F.D.P.-Wahlkampfrunde seit 1981.* The author of the undated paper is Peter Schröder.

26. *Strategische Überlegungen zum Wahljahr 1994* (versions of 1 December 1992 and 27 April 1993), *Strategie für das Wahljahr 1994 für die Freie Demokratische Partei* (19 May 1993), *Strategie für das Wahljahr 1994* (August 1993), *Positionierung im Europawahlkampf* (25 February 1994). In a short and undated strategic summary from the fall of 1993, *Wahlkampf '94,* several of the fourteen points mention that the party is having difficulties in presenting a coherent and distinctive image of itself. There is a stress on the need for the FDP to present itself as "the innovative party" and to concentrate on the relatively small group of voters who are likely to find it attractive—a group which is optimistically guessed to be about 20 percent of the public.

27. *Strategische Überlegungen,* pp. 8–9. See also "Die FDP liebäugelt mit einem 'Befreiungsschlag,'" *FAZ,* 29 April 1993.

28. See the *Politbarometer* polls.

29. This observation is based on the public speeches at the party conference as well as on conversations and interviews with individual delegates.

30. Wulf Oehme, as quoted in "Polls Apart," *Financial Times,* 3 November 1994.

31. Forschungsgruppe Wahlen e.V., *Die Bundestagswahl 1994,* 16, 65–66. The difference between second and first vote results in past elections is recorded in my chapter, "The Free Democratic Party," Wallach and Romoser, 163.

32. Forschungsgruppe Wahlen e.V., *Die Bundestagswahl 1994,* 18–20.

33. Ibid., 21–24. See also Matthias Jung and Dieter Roth, "Kohls knappster Sieg. Eine Analyse der Bundestagswahl 1994," in *Aus Politik und Geschichte. Beilage zur Wochenzeitung das Parlament,* 23 December 1994, pp. 3–15.

34. "Führungskrise bei den Liberalen abgewendet," *Süddeutsche Zeitung,* 13 December 1994.

35. On the eastern opposition, see the well-informed article by Lorenz Maroldt, "Die APO der Ostliberalen schimpft auf Bonn," in *Der Tagesspiegel,* 24 February 1995.

36. It is discussed and compared with the Freiburger Theses in my chapter on the FDP in Merkl, *The Federal Republic of Germany at Forty,* 333–37.

37. Three of the most important among the many early position papers are "Anstöße zur Erneuerung" (20 November 1994) and "Europa-Nation-Staatsbürger-Ausländer" (28 and 29 January 1995), issued by the Freiburger Kreis, and "Berliner Positionen einer liberalen Erneuerung" (October 1994), signed by Alexander von Stahl and four other Berlin Free Democrats.

38. See note 5 for poll results that appear to support this conclusion.

10

ALLIANCE 90/GREENS

FROM FUNDAMENTAL OPPOSITION TO BLACK-GREEN

HANS-GEORG BETZ

The "super election year" 1994 saw the reemergence of the German Greens as a politically significant actor at the national level. After having been exiled for four years from Bonn as a result of its disastrous showing in the first all-German election in 1990, this time the party surmounted the 5 percent hurdle with relative ease. With 7.3 percent of the vote, Alliance 90/Greens—as the party has officially been known since the West German Greens formally merged with Alliance 90 in the spring of 1993—gained forty-nine seats in the new Bundestag. This assured Alliance 90/Greens its position as the third largest party in post-unification Germany.

The result of the election has confirmed that the once motley collection of protesters and antipoliticians, whose appearance in parliament had once met with hardly concealed hostility from the established parties, has become a "normal" part of the political establishment. Pre-election opinion polls in September showed that almost half of the German population had formed a favorable opinion of Alliance 90/Greens—11 percent more than held a positive view of the FDP.

The party's strong showing was a clear sign that the electoral debacle of 1990 had been a singular case, brought about by an unfortunate confluence of adverse circumstances, tactical errors, and strategic blunders. With the question of unification largely settled, the party appeared to have regained much of its appeal among its core constituency of new middle-class voters with left-libertarian, postmaterialist value preferences in the western part of the country. In the East, the results of the federal election (4.3 percent of the vote) largely confirmed the negative trend of gradual electoral decline already visible in the Landtag elections in Brandenburg and Saxony earlier in the year. The widening gap in electoral performance between eastern and

western Greens was further accentuated by the results of the Landtag elections in Mecklenburg-West Pomerania, Thuringia, and the
Saar held simultaneously with the federal election. Whereas the western Greens managed for the first time in their history to gain representation in the Saar (5.5 percent), their eastern counterparts
succeeded neither in Mecklenburg-West Pomerania (3.7 percent)
nor in Thuringia (4.5 percent) to clear the 5 percent hurdle. As a
result, by the end of 1994, Alliance 90/Greens were represented in
all but one western Land (Schleswig-Holstein, where in 1992 they
had failed to clear the hurdle by a mere .03 percent of the vote). By
contrast, in the East, the only Land in which the party was still represented in a regional parliament was Saxony-Anhalt, where the
Greens had barely surmounted the 5 percent hurdle in June 1994.

The performance of Alliance 90/Greens in the 1994 federal election thus raises at least two intriguing questions. First, what accounts
for the party's relatively rapid recovery in the West, where in 1994
the Greens came close to repeating their result of 1987? And second,
what accounts for the party's almost complete collapse of support in
the East?

The central argument behind the following discussion is that the
rapid improvement of the Greens position was largely due to an
internal process of "deradicalization" set in motion in response to
the defeat of 1990. This process was accelerated by the exposure to
the considerably less leftist Alliance 90 in the East. However, whereas
party reform and the merger with Alliance 90 changed the party's
internal makeup and organizational structures and dampened the
tendency toward programmatic excesses, they failed to transform the
nature and identity of the new party. Given the overwhelming pre-
dominance of the western Greens among the members of Alliance
90/Greens, it is perhaps not surprising that the new party retained
much of its old identity as the most authentic representative of the
experiences and values of the old Federal Republic—the prototype of
what has been characterized as a "postnational democracy" and a
"civilian power."

The 1990 Election Disaster and Its Consequences

The failure to return to the Bundestag in the first all-German election of 1990 proved to be a watershed in the development of the
German Greens. There was widespread agreement that the electoral
disaster had been the result of unfortunate circumstances, tactical

errors, and strategic blunders.[1] Perhaps the most fundamental tactical error had been the western Greens' refusal to fuse with their eastern counterparts until immediately after the election. Had the two parties merged before the election, the Greens would have received 5.1 percent of the vote. The most serious strategic blunder was the Greens' failure "to see the national implications of the East German revolution, as indicated in their futile commitment to a reformed socialist GDR."[2]

Unification radically diminished the prospect for an "ecological transformation" of the German model, which had dominated the political debate until early 1990, leaving little space for the Greens' ecological and left-libertarian demands. To further complicate things for the party, most Greens were highly critical of the rapid surge to unification or rejected its prospect altogether, either because they feared that unification might lead to the revival of traditional German nationalism and great power chauvinism, or because they feared it might entail the loss of democratic openness, freedom, and tolerance once a unified Germany started to search for a new "global role." The party's hostility toward unification was bound to alienate those Greens sympathizers who either viewed unification positively or at least resigned themselves to the inevitability of the process. The Greens' problems were further compounded by the fact that the Social Democrats chose in Oskar Lafontaine a candidate for chancellor whose campaign focused primarily on Greens issues, while his critical stance on unification was similar to the position adopted by the Greens. Not surprisingly, the Greens lost more than half a million votes—about one-third of their support of 1987—to the SPD.

However, the disaster of 1990 was only partly the result of external developments and circumstances. It also was, in part, the result of internal weaknesses and deficits which had characterized Greens politics since its earliest days, but which under the particular circumstances of 1990 proved fatal.[3] Perhaps most important was the unresolved conflict between the party's Realo faction, the undogmatic advocates of a pragmatic approach to politics, and the Fundis, the intransigent representatives of ideological purity. Although by the late 1980s the Fundis had lost much of their hold on the party, internal battles heated up once again between 1989 and 1990. The result was a wave of prominent party defections in late 1989 and early 1990. The exodus of Realos Otto Schily and Thea Bock, who both joined the SPD, was followed by that of prominent members of the staunchly anticapitalist "eco-socialist" wing around Thomas Ebermann and Rainer Trampert, who sympathized with the PDS.

The internal battles and defections only reinforced the impression of a party plagued by organized irresponsibility, self-absorption, and slow dissolution.[4]

From the perspective of 1994, the disastrous showing in 1990 was a blessing in disguise. It proved to be the "shock therapy" necessary to convince the Greens that they could not hope to survive without radical structural reforms. Joschka Fischer set the tone when he said that the Greens project could only be saved if the party managed to provide itself with an effective party organization capable of making constructive "ecological reform politics, with the right themes and the right people."[5] A first start was made at the party conference in Neumünster in early 1991. Although the pictures from the conference were once again dominated by riotous scenes of personal attacks and water pistol fights, the reformers made considerable progress. Among the most important reforms were the abolition of the rotation principle, the reduction of the size of the federal executive committee, the installation of a political manager, the reduction of the number of party speakers from three to two, and the replacement of the federal executive (*Bundeshauptausschuss*) by a states council (*Länderrat*). These reforms were designed to make internal decision-making mechanisms more effective and to increase "the role of elected state party leaders and parliamentarians in federal decision making."[6] Since most state party organizations were dominated by moderate forces, the conference represented a significant victory for the Realos, even if they failed to get a two-thirds majority to abolish the rule against the simultaneous holding of a party and an elected office.

The pragmatic reform course was further strengthened by a wave of new defections. In February, most of the hard-line fundamentalists resigned from the Greens Alternative List in Hamburg, one of the last bastions of anti-system orthodoxy. Immediately after the conference, Jutta Ditfurth, the prominent representative of radical ecological fundamentalism, announced her resignation from the Greens. With her, the last obstacle to the party's transformation into a reformed "ecological civil rights party" (as envisioned by Antje Vollmer's centrist Aufbruch group) was out of the way.

Merger with Alliance 90

The structural and organizational reform of the western party paved the way for the second important transformation of the Greens, their merger with the eastern civil rights movements. Initially, the latter had been rather skeptical about joining the western Greens. Groups like Democracy Now, New Forum, or Initiative for Peace and Human Rights were more than reluctant to give up their independence. Deeply suspicious of parliamentary politics, they were largely opposed to transforming themselves into a political party, seeking instead to continue as movements. They were "ill at ease with the 'anti-system' rhetoric and 'radical chic' that flourished among some western Greens" and appalled by the internal battles which they considered a sign of political immaturity.[7] Yet even those who deplored the "political kindergarten" atmosphere prevalent in the Greens had to recognize that there was little chance for survival as a significant political voice if they refused to join up with the Greens.[8] The merger proceeded in two stages. In September 1991 parts of the civil rights movements founded Alliance 90 as a new "political citizen movement," which then in the spring of 1992 decided to enter into negotiations with the Greens. Negotiations ended in November with the signing of an association treaty which, in turn, was approved in modified form by parallel party conferences in January 1993 in Hanover. After the merger was approved by an overwhelming majority of the membership of both parties in March 1993, the new party was officially founded at a special party congress in May in Leipzig.[9]

The merger between the two parties created several new problems. Most important of all, the relationship between the two organizations was hardly one between equals. Whereas the Greens had more than 37,000 members, Alliance 90 could count on a membership of not more than 2,700. In order to prevent ill feeling, the western Greens made several significant concessions. At least for a transition period of two years, Alliance 90 received a minimum of three seats in the transitional eleven-seat federal executive and a suspensive veto in the states council. It was also agreed that one of the two party speakers would have to come from the East. Psychologically most important, a majority of the western Greens agreed that the name of the eastern citizen movement would come first in the new party label.

A second major problem was posed by the considerable ideological differences between western Greens and eastern civil rights movements. Although the two sides largely agreed about basic Greens values, they diverged with respect to individual issues.[10] Generally, the members of the eastern movements had a considerably more favorable opinion of the capitalist system and the market economy than the traditionally much more anticapitalist Greens. In the face of massive deindustrialization in the former GDR, it was hardly surprising that they put greater stress on social questions like mass unemployment or the shortage of available housing than their western counterparts. At the same time, Alliance 90 was not prepared to go along completely with the Greens' insistence on gender equality and other feminist issues which they criticized as too "rigorous." As a result, particularly the left wing of the Greens, represented by Ludger Volmer's Linkes Forum, feared that the inclusion of Alliance 90 would mean a further erosion of the party's leftist identity.

Two issues created particular problems for the Greens: first, the easterners' insistence on the principle of an "open dialogue," i.e., cooperation with all relevant social forces across party lines to find practical solutions to pressing problems. And second, the easterners' insistence on confronting the past (*Vergangenheitsbewältigung*).[11] Ironically enough, the western Greens, for whom coming to terms with Germany's Nazi past had always been an essential issue, accused the citizen movements of being too "fixated" on their past. The citizen movements, in turn, charged the Greens of having, at best, ignored the reality in the GDR and, at worst, implicitly collaborated with the old East German regime for the sake of peace and détente. Revelations about Dirk Schneider, a former member of the Bundestag from the Alternative List of Berlin, could not but strengthen this impression. In the late 1980s Schneider had been the most vigorous proponent of recognizing the division of Germany as final. From this position he had exerted considerable influence on the Greens stance on East Germany, the East German dissident movements, and the German question in general. In early 1992 it became known that Dirk Schneider had worked for the *Stasi*. Schneider's party-internal nickname—"East Berlin's secret ambassador in Bonn"—had not been far off the mark after all.[12]

Ups and Downs in the Länder

The fact that there still were a number of unresolved problems, however, should not detract from the fact that at the beginning of 1994 the new party was in a considerably better position than had been the case for the Greens in 1990. The differences between the western Greens and the representatives of the eastern civil rights movements paled in comparison to the conflicts between Realos and Fundis that had all but paralyzed the Greens in the past. Although the new party continued to boast a vocal left wing organized around Ludger Volmer (who in 1993 was reelected as one of the two party speakers), the left largely agreed with the pragmatically oriented direction promoted by Joschka Fischer, the outspoken environmental minister of Hesse and unofficial leader of the party. Under his influence, the Greens abandoned much of the radical rhetoric of the past in favor of a professional approach to Germany's social and economic problems that was not oblivious to the necessity of political compromise. Prime examples were the basic political guidelines included in the association treaty, which form the political consensus of the founding organizations and, as such, are more important than party platforms or election programs. The basic guidelines marked a significant departure from the Greens' traditional self-understanding.[13] Among others, they abandoned the principle of grass-roots democracy (*Basisdemokratie*), which ever since the first federal program of 1980 had been one of the Greens programmatic essentials bolstering the claim that the Greens were a new type of party. Instead, the basic guidelines stressed the importance of comprehensive human rights and civil liberties, including individual freedom and democracy, basic social and economic rights, and the right to a healthy environment, to education, and to development.[14] At the same time, the basic guidelines abandoned much of the anticapitalist rhetoric of the past. Although they continued to put heavy emphasis on the ecological crisis, the destruction of the natural environment was no longer interpreted (as was still the case in the 1990 electoral program) as the expression of a systemic crisis of capitalism.[15]

The political guidelines marked an important change in direction. They laid the foundation for the party's gradual transformation into an ecological civil rights party (*Bürgerrechtspartei*) and its ideological reorientation toward the center of the political spectrum. They also were a clear indication that, with the merger with Alliance 90, the new party had become considerably more moderate than its predecessor had ever been. The initial results were encouraging. By early 1994, Alliance 90/Greens were in coalition governments either alone with the SPD or with the SPD and the FDP (the famous "*Ampelkoalition*") in Brandenburg, Bremen, Hesse, and Lower Saxony. Throughout late 1993 and early 1994, Forschungsgruppe Wahlen polls showed Alliance 90/Greens consistently holding a steady 10 percent support. The result of the Land election in Hamburg in September 1993 largely confirmed this trend. Once an eco-socialist stronghold, the Green Alternative List (GAL) was now completely controlled by the Realos. Under the leadership of Krista Sager, the GAL gained 13.5 percent of the vote—the party's best result ever in the city-state. The success in Hamburg was followed by a respectable showing in Lower Saxony, where in March 1994 the party received 7.4 percent of the vote, 1.9 more than in May 1990.

In neither case, however, did Alliance 90/Greens manage to translate electoral gains into political power. In Hamburg, coalition talks with the SPD soon failed, and the SPD decided to form a coalition government with the STATT-party; in Lower Saxony, having gained an absolute majority of the seats in the state parliament in Hanover, the SPD decided to discontinue its coalition with the Greens and govern alone. To make things worse, in March Alliance 90 left the *Ampelkoalition* in Brandenburg. The civil rights activists were no longer willing to support the popular SPD minister-president, Manfred Stolpe, who was under investigation for alleged collaboration with the *Stasi*. Particularly, Marianne Birthler, party speaker and as minister for cultural affairs responsible for reforming education in Brandenburg, was no longer willing to dismiss politically incriminated teachers while the situation at the top remained unclear. Thus, within a few weeks' time, Alliance 90/Greens had lost their seats in two state governments.

Things hardly improved with the June election in Saxony-Anhalt. Although the party managed to return to the state parliament, its meager result of 5.1 percent of the vote was hardly cause for celebration. The fact that the SPD invited Alliance 90/Greens to form a minority government, which for all practical purposes would depend on external support from the PDS, created new problems for the former civil rights activists who ran the risk of being crushed between SPD and PDS.[16] However, June also provided some reason for celebration. In the European election, Alliance 90/Greens attained their best result ever in a national election. With 10.1 percent of the vote (11.0 percent in the West, 6.9 percent in the East), and double-digit results in the city-states Baden-Württemberg, Hesse, North Rhine-Westphalia, and Schleswig-Holstein, Alliance 90/Greens clearly outdistanced the FDP and PDS, both of which failed to clear the 5 percent hurdle.

However, the effect of the excellent result in the European election proved only of short duration. The elections in Brandenburg and Saxony only a few weeks before the Bundestag election spelled complete disaster. In Saxony, Alliance 90/Greens received about 4 percent of the vote, in Brandenburg even less (2.9 percent). In both states the party suffered the consequences of internal splits and defections, which had further reduced an already slim membership base. In addition, in Saxony the party suffered the consequences of having engaged in a preelection discussion about a possible "black-green" coalition with Kurt Biedenkopf's CDU. Although these discussions remained informal, they seriously damaged the party's chances to be returned to the Landtag. As if to complete the dismal picture, the Greens attained only 6.1 percent of the vote in the Bavarian state election, .03 percent less than in 1990.

The Federal Election Campaign: Toward a "Green FDP"?

The results of the state elections were hardly reassuring with regard to the Bundestag election. They reconfirmed the results of a study on the party's electoral potential commissioned by the party's executive committee in late 1993.[17] It showed that the party's core support was not larger than 4 percent of the electorate in the West, and, perhaps somewhat surprising, 5 percent in the East. Similar to the FDP, Alliance 90/Greens thus largely depended on the behavior of "peripheral" sympathizers for whose support the party had to compete with the SPD and PDS. The study also confirmed the major dilemma faced by the party: whereas in the West, the environment still ranked as the top political concern among core supporters, in the East, unemployment far outdistanced environmental concerns. Hence, the party's position remained "precarious" not only with regard to its electoral prospects, but also with regard to the future prospects of efforts to overcome the intraparty division between East and West.

Given this precarious situation, the party decided to lead a highly pragmatic and professional campaign.[18] The driving force behind this strategy was Joschka Fischer, for whom 1994 not only marked the return to national prominence, but also solidified his position as the undisputed leader of the party. And this for good reasons. No other leading Greens politician has been as closely associated with the Greens party and its fortunes as Joschka Fischer; no one embodies the party's ups and downs, continuity and change, and its steady rise to success as much as he does. Once a Frankfurt undogmatic left-wing "sponti," Fischer was among the first on the radical left to join the alternative movement. A member of the Bundestag between 1983 and 1985, Fischer's appearance (suit and sneakers) and wittiness did much to shape the Greens' public image. In 1985 Frankfurt's "Spontifex Maximus" was sworn in as the first Greens environmental minister in Hesse. At the same time the self-declared follower of Machiavelli became the undisputed leader of the party's

Realo faction. Unlike most of the first-generation Greens, Fischer managed to survive the numerous episodes of trench warfare and various internal battles that more than once threatened to destroy the Greens project. With his most ferocious opponents from Thomas Ebermann to Jutta Ditfurth having turned their backs on the party, Joschka Fischer has finally managed to be in a position to shape the Greens party according to his ideas and transform it into a left-liberal party.[19]

Joschka Fischer set the tone for the campaign when he wrote in January 1994: "In 1994, we not only fight for the return to the German Bundestag and for Kohl's departure, but we fight above all for Germany's ecological and social renewal."[20] Unlike in the past, the party no longer contented itself with playing the role of a fundamental opposition. Under Fischer's leadership—and without much opposition from Ludger Volmer or other leading figures on the party's left—the party officially declared that it was ready to take over governmental responsibility, "if that means the prospect of a serious politics of reform." The official electoral program declared that should the election end in a "red-green" majority, Alliance 90/Greens would seek a coalition with the SPD.[21]

The party ratified the electoral program at a party conference in Mannheim in February 1994. The program's central message was contained in the slogan, "To Reform a Country." Under this motto the party proposed a comprehensive reform package designed to initiate a decisive "change of direction."[22] Its central demands were an end to Germany's nuclear energy program within one or two years, the introduction of speed limits on all roads and highways, and the introduction of an "ecological tax" (*Ökosteuer*) designed to reflect the environmental costs of production and to encourage the creation of future-oriented enterprises in environmentally sensitive fields. One of the most controversial aspects of the tax package was the call for an immediate increase of the tax on gas which would eventually raise the price per liter to five deutschmarks in order to encourage the development of more energy-efficient vehicles.

In order to combat unemployment, the party called for a "just distribution of existing work" through a drastic reduction of working hours to thirty hours per week ("less work for more people") without full compensation, and a comprehensive state-sponsored labor market policy. With regard to social policy, Alliance 90/Greens reiterated their commitment to the introduction of a need-oriented guaranteed minimum income to replace the traditional welfare programs. As in the past, the party put particular emphasis on civil liberties and feminist issues. The party called for a new citizenship law, the restoration of a liberal asylum law, as well as the introduction of a "humane" immigration law. With respect to women's rights, the party called for the introduction of a comprehensive quota policy both in the public sector and in the private economy. Finally, with respect to foreign policy, the party demanded the dissolution of the German army as part of a comprehensive process of disarmament, together with the abolition of NATO and WEU in favor of extending CSCE as the central forum for building trust and as a basis for a future system of collective security.

Whereas the electoral program still reflected much of the old radicalism of the 1980s, leading party figures increasingly stressed the party's moderate image. The goal was to attract traditionally liberal middle-class voters and turn the party into a "green FDP" by stressing the party's commitment to defending the democratic *Rechtsstaat*.[23] In order to reinforce this image, Alliance 90/Greens introduced in June a list of ten reform projects together with proposals for financing the reform package. Besides reiterating its commitment to the introduction of an ecological tax structure and a drastic reduction of the public debt, the party proposed to pay for the expenditures for social and labor market programs by raising the tax on inheritance and taxing the rich.[24] And although in its foreign policy positions the party officially held fast to its pacifist principles, some of its leading representatives indicated on more than one occasion that there was room for flexibility.[25] Thus, Joschka Fischer said that although he was committed to the party's fundamental pacifist position, the party would have to confront "the concrete situation in which acts of violence do occur."

One was reminded of the bitter and emotionally highly charged internal struggle over the Bosnian question in the fall of 1993 that split the party into pacifists and "bellicists" (those supporting UN humanitarian interventions to protect human rights). At the time, the party reaffirmed its commitment to nonviolence, even in the face of genocide. However, the episode revealed the degree of frustration on the part of some Greens for whom the party's unconditionally pacifist position with respect to the Bosnian conflict was nothing but a "helpless policy of appeasement" (Krista Sager).[26]

Besides promoting its ideas through a short ten-point program, the party commissioned a number of thematic posters carrying the party's central message. It used its free television spots to alert the public to the continued threat of xenophobia and racism in Germany.[27] Altogether, the party spent about DM6 million for its campaign. By the fall, the party appeared highly mobilized and quite optimistic to the point that some even believed they had a chance to gain a direct mandate.[28]

The Election Results

Given the Greens' defeat in 1990, the result of the 1994 election marked an impressive comeback. It was all the more impressive given the fact that by September, only a small minority of Alliance 90/ Greens supporters still believed the opposition had a chance to win the election. Eight out of ten expected a government victory.[29] Overall, Alliance 90/Greens received 7.3 percent of the vote, 3.5 percent more than in 1990. It failed, however, to secure any direct mandates. In the West, the party came close to repeating its result of 1987. In the East, however, it lost almost 2 percent compared to 1990, failing to clear the psychologically important 5 percent mark.[30] Not surprisingly, in the West, Alliance 90/Greens scored the biggest gains in its big-city strongholds and in university towns where, in 1990, it had witnessed its biggest losses (e.g., former West Berlin, Hamburg, and Freiburg). In the East, the party increased its share of the vote in only two districts, while experiencing more or less substantial losses everywhere else. On the Länder level, Alliance 90/Greens did best in the city-states (Hamburg, 12.6 percent; Bremen, 11.1 percent; and Berlin, 10.2 percent), and worst in the northeastern Länder (Mecklenburg-West Pomerania, 3.6 percent; Saxony-Anhalt, 3.6 percent; Brandenburg, 2.9 percent).

INFAS voter flow analyses showed that Alliance 90/Greens gained a net of more than 240,000 voters from the SPD, of about 120,000 voters from the Christian Democrats, and of around 120,000 voters from the FDP.[31] As in the past, the party drew a disproportionate number of their support from women, the young, new middle-class voters, and students. The election once again showed that left-libertarian politics is particularly attractive to young women. Roughly 15 percent of women ages eighteen to thirty-four voted for Alliance 90/Greens, reaffirming the notion that the party is, above all, a *Frauenpartei*. Not surprisingly, the party received relatively little support from pensioners, farmers, and blue-collar workers. Despite its call for active labor market policies, it also failed to gain higher than average support from the unemployed.

As a result of the party's poor showing in the East, the eastern civil rights movements managed to elect not more than five of their candidates to the new Bundestag. The most prominent eastern victim was party speaker Marianne Birthler, who had headed the party's list in Brandenburg. Altogether Alliance 90/Greens received forty-nine mandates. Twenty-eight of the new members are women; one new member, Cem Özdemir from Baden-Württemberg, is a naturalized German citizen of Turkish descent.

Explaining the Gap Between East and West

The result of the federal election left the eastern party in complete disarray, while considerably diminishing its relative weight within the alliance. The extent of its loss of influence became painfully apparent at Alliance 90/Greens' postelection conference in Potsdam in December 1994. With the Realo Krista Sager, leader of the Alliance 90/Greens group in the Hamburg city parliament and responsible for the party's huge gains in 1993, and the left-wing Jürgen Trittin, until mid-1994 Greens Bundesrat minister for the "red-green" coalition in Lower-Saxony, the delegates elected two western members as party speakers. The eastern candidate, the left-wing Christiane Ziller from Thuringia, dropped out of the race after losing in the first round by a slim margin to Krista Sager. This left the eastern party with only two seats in the nine-member executive committee. Eastern observers interpreted this outcome as a sign that the Greens were no different from the other parties—"a western party, where East Germans are being excluded (*ausgebootet*) like everywhere else."[32]

There are several reasons for the collapse of Alliance 90/Greens in the East. Months before the federal election, leading western Greens had warned that the eastern civil rights activists' "moral rigorism" was turning a growing number of supporters away from the party. The party's disastrous showing in Brandenburg, where Alliance 90 had led the campaign against the popular Manfred Stolpe, supported this claim. At a time when western observers noted a growing "GDR-nostalgia" in the East, most eastern Germans had little sympathy for Alliance 90 politicians who still defined themselves largely in terms of their opposition to the old regime and considered it their duty to keep the memory of the *Stasi* past alive. It was thus hardly surprising that a sizeable number of Alliance 90/Greens supporters abandoned the party for the PDS. According to INFAS, Alliance 90/Greens lost almost 80,000 voters to the PDS while only gaining some 7,000 voters from the post-Communists.

However, not everything could be blamed on the peculiarities of the situation in the East. Partly the eastern party's poor showing was also the result of the fact that, despite the Greens' merger with Alliance 90, the new party still largely retained its traditional western identity. Ever since their appearance on the political scene in the early 1980s, the Greens have arguably been the most authentic product of the former Federal Republic. Central to the Federal Republic's identity was its self-understanding as a "civilian power," whose core characteristics have been defined as the acceptance of the necessity to cooperate with others in the pursuit of international objectives, the concentration on economic rather than military means to secure national goals, and the willingness to develop supranational structures to address critical issues of international management. A second important aspect of Germany as a civilian power was its self-recognition as a "postnational democracy" whose identity rested largely on the success of its political system (encapsulated in Dolf Sternberg's well-known notion of "constitutional patriotism") rather than on national attributes.[33] Both identities appear to have been particularly pronounced among the better educated.[34]

Official Greens positions on NATO and European integration, or on asylum, immigration, and multiculturalism are an almost perfect reflection of the peculiarities of West German identity in the 1980s. However, whereas unified Germany can no longer afford to maintain this identity, the Greens have largely stuck to their line, e.g., when the party opposes an extended German role in peacekeeping missions that transcends purely humanitarian aid.

Surveys show that a large majority of Greens supporters have adopted a postnational identity. Greens supporters are generally more enthusiastic about European integration and a common European currency than the supporters of any other party in Germany. They are the least proud to be German, and most favorable toward immigrants and refugees and the prospects of a multicultural society.[35]

If this goes a long way to explain the Greens' continued success in the West, it might also explain why the party has done so poorly in the East. The party's identity is still largely grounded in western experiences and a milieu which is completely alien to the vast majority of the eastern German population. As one leading western Greens analyst has pointed out, in the East the party lacks both the social structure and the voter milieus which account for the party's strength in the West. "Caught between an eastern protest and regional party, the PDS, and an eastern tendency [to vote] for personalities, there seems to be little room left for an ecological-democratic third force, especially if it suffers from the image of being too much oriented toward the past."[36] Four years after German unification, the condition of Alliance 90/Greens thus reflects German society's continued difficulties with overcoming the many walls which still divide the country.

Alliance 90/Greens 1995: From Red-Green to Black-Green?

Since the disaster of 1990, Alliance 90/Greens has come a long way. Yesterday's antiparty party has turned into "a normal, bourgeois party" (Konrad Weiss) threatening to replace the FDP in the German party system. By late 1994 the party was well on its way to becoming a left-liberal civil rights party following not only the vision of prominent Realos like Joschka Fischer or Antje Vollmer, but, ironically, also that of the eastern civil rights activists.[37] With this transformation Alliance 90/Greens has managed to escape from the danger of being squeezed to death between the SPD and the PDS. At the same time, however, it has exposed itself to new potential problems.

Nothing could have better symbolized the party's transformation than the main point of contention at the party's Potsdam conference —whether Alliance 90/Greens should seriously consider the possibility of entering coalitions with the Christian Democrats on the state and national levels. This was hardly a moot point given the fact that Antje Vollmer had been elected vice-president of the Bundestag with the votes of the CDU and against bitter SPD resistance, and that on the local level, a growing number of "black-green" coalitions" had already begun to "change the political landscape."[38] Although the majority of the delegates at the party conference voiced its opposition to any closer cooperation with the Christian Democrats, the issue had hardly been settled. In fact, a survey published shortly after the election showed a considerable proportion of the German public to be favorably disposed toward some kind of cooperation between CDU/CSU and Alliance 90/Greens. Moreover, more than half of the respondents thought it possible that Alliance 90/Greens would in the future assume the FDP's traditional role as provider of a majority for coalitions (*Mehrheitsbeschaffer*).[39]

Despite these encouraging results, the party's new strategy promises to create new problems. With its move to the center, Alliance 90/Greens has opened itself to the charge that it has lost, or given up, much of what set the Greens apart from other political parties—in short, its identity. As a recent article put it, "What do they want, what do they stand for?"[40] More serious than that is the question to what degree the Greens milieu will follow the party's tactical maneuvers. The party's experience in Saxony serves as a serious warning. In the West, too, at least the more radically left-wing party supporters might decide to abandon the party if Alliance 90/Greens becomes too much a part of the German political establishment. This, in turn, might open up new opportunities for the PDS, particularly if the latter manages to transform itself into a New Left party. Whatever the outcome of these maneuvers, one thing appears certain: at least for the foreseeable future, Alliance 90/Greens will remain a central factor in the new German politics.

Notes

1. For an exhaustive analysis see Hubert Kleinert, "Die Grünen 1990/91: Vom Wahldebakel zum Neuanfang," *Aus Politik und Zeitgeschichte,* B44/91, 25 October 1991, pp. 27–37; and Kleinert, *Aufstieg und Fall der Grünen* (Bonn: Dietz, 1992).

2. Christian Joppke and Andrei S. Markovits, "Green Politics in the New Germany," *Dissent,* spring 1994, p. 235.

3. Joachim Raschke has provided a lucid analysis of the party's internal structural problems. In his view, the party's fundamental problem is that it never managed to reconcile legitimacy and efficiency: "What is legitimate is not efficient, what is efficient is not legitimate." See *Krise der Grünen* (Marburg: Schüren, 1993).

4. See "Völlig irre," *Der Spiegel,* no. 16, 16 April 1990, pp. 42–47.

5. Interview with Joschka Fischer, *Der Spiegel,* 14 January 1991, p. 40.

6. E. Gene Frankland and Donald Schoonmaker, *Between Protest and Power: The Greens Party in Germany* (Boulder: Westview Press, 1992), 226; Thomas Poguntke and Rüdiger Schmitt-Beck, "Still the Same with a New Name? Alliance 90/ The Greens after the Fusion," *German Politics* (III,1): 98.

7. Joppke and Markovits, "Green Politics in the New Germany," p. 236.

8. Jürgen Hoffmann, *Bündnis 90/Die Grünen: Ein schwieriges Bündnis in der Bewährungsprobe* (Sankt Augustin: Konrad-Adenauer-Stiftung, 1994), 12; Antje Vollmer, Wolfgang Templin, and Werner Schulz, "Grüne und Bündnis 90," *Aus Politik und Zeitgeschichte,* B5/92, 24 January 1992, p. 33.

9. See *Assoziationsvertrag zwischen BÜNDNIS 90 und DIE GRÜNEN,* Hanover, 17 January 1993; and Bündnis 90/Die Greens, *Politische Grundsätze,* Bornheim, 1993.

10. See the interview with Vera Wollenberger and Konrad Weiß, *Der Spiegel*, no. 16, 15 April 1991, pp. 26–30; "Emotional gespalten," *Der Spiegel*, no. 7, 10 February 1992, pp. 27–30; Hoffmann, *Bündnis 90/Die Grünen*, pp. 33–35.

11. "Vorwärts und vergessen," *Der Spiegel*, no. 39, 26 September 1994, pp. 23–25; Joppke and Markovits, "Green Politics in the New Germany," pp. 236–7; Hoffmann, *Bündnis 90/Die Grünen*, pp. 35, 39–40; for the party's interpretation see Bündnis 90/Die Grünen, *Politische Grundsätze*, pp. 10–12.

12. See Elisabeth Weber, "Stasi-Einflußagent mit Einfluß bei den Grünen?" *Kommune* (X, 2), pp. 35–39.

13. For an extended discussion of this point, see particularly Hoffmann, *Bündnis 90/Die Grünen*, pp. 13–14.

14. Bündnis 90/Die Grünen, *Politische Grundsätze*, p. 22.

15. Die Grünen, *Das Programm zur 1. gesamtdeutschen Wahl 1990*, Bonn, 1990, pp. 4–9.

16. Hoffmann, *Bündnis 90/Die Grünen*, pp. 37–39; "Drinnen bellen," *Der Spiegel*, no. 28, 11 July 1994, pp. 25–27.

17. See Rüdiger Schmitt-Beck, "Wählerpotentiale von Bündnis 90/Die Grünen im Ost-West-Vergleich. Umfang, Struktur und politische Orientierungen," in Lothar Probst, ed., *Kursbestimmung: Bündnis 90/Grüne Eckpunkte künftiger Politik* (Cologne: Bund-Verlag, 1994), 192–235. For a short version of the results, see Poguntke and Schmitt-Beck, "Still the Same with a New Name?", pp. 99–109.

18. See "Alte Positionen geräumt," *Der Spiegel*, no. 49, 6 December 1994, pp. 118–20; Tissy Bruns, "Bündnis 90/Die Grünen: Oppositions- oder Regierungspartei," *Aus Politik und Zeitgeschichte*, B1/94, 7 January 1994, pp. 29–31. For an opposing viewpoint, see Hoffmann, *Bündnis 90/Die Grünen*, pp. 16–26.

19. See Jürgen Leinemann, "Der Patriarch der Grünen," *Der Spiegel* no. 38, 9 September 1994, pp. 40–47.

20. Joschka Fischer, "Bündnis 90/Die Grünen vor der Entscheidung," in Probst, ed., *Kursbestimmung*, 33.

21. *Nur mit uns: Bündnis 90/Die Grünen*, Programm zur Bundestagswahl 94, Bornheim, 1994, p. 6.

22. Werner Schulz, "Politik der Reformen und Reform der Politik," *Aus Politik und Zeitgeschichte*, B15/94, 15 April 1994, pp. 29–32; and interview with Joschka Fischer, *Rheinischer Merkur* no. 40, 7 October 1994, p. 4.

23. See interview with Fischer, *Rheinischer Merkur*, and "Rückzug realissimo," *Der Spiegel*, no. 19, 9 May 1994, p. 22.

24. See Bündnis 90/Die Grünen, *"Ein Land Reformieren: 10 Reformprojekte und ein Finanzierungsvorschlag,"* Bornheim, 1994, pp. 23–24.

25. See "Draußen wie drinnen," *Der Spiegel*, no. 32, 8 August 1994, pp. 20–21.

26. See interview with Joschka Fischer, *Der Spiegel*, no. 33, 15 August 1994, pp. 24–27; Jürgen Hoffmann, *Bündnis 90/Die Grünen*, pp. 30–31; Hans-Joachim Noack, "'Es zerreißt mich'," *Der Spiegel*, no. 40, 4 October 1993, pp. 38–44; Jost Schröder von der Brüggen, "Bekenntnisritual zum deutschen Sonderweg," *Kommune* (XI, 11), p. 16.

27. See *Grüne Seiten: Bündnis 90/Die Grünen,* Bündnis Grüne Zeitung zur Bundestagswahl, p. 4.

28. "Die große Grüne," *Der Spiegel,* no. 35, 29 August 1994, pp. 25–27; "Mit Esel und Folklore," *Der Spiegel,* no. 40, 3 October 1994, p. 24.

29. Hans-Joachim Veen et al., *Die Bundestagswahl vom 16. Oktober 1994—eine erste Analyse,* (Sankt Augustin: Konrad-Adenauer-Stiftung, 1994), B9.

30. See Forschungsgruppe Wahlen, *Bundestagswahl 1994, Eine Analyse der Wahl zum 13. Deutschen Bundestag am 16. Oktober 1994,* Mannheim, 1994.

31. See *Focus,* Wahlspezial, 18 October 1994, pp. 22–25.

32. Konrad Weiss, "Risse im Bündnis," *Rheinischer Merkur,* no. 49, 9 December 1994, p. 5; see also Peter Ziller, "Filmkulissen und ein schwarz-Grünes Gespenst," *Frankfurter Rundschau,* 5 December 1994, p. 3; Wolfgang Stock, "Die Realpolitiker feiern Erfolge," *Frankfurter Allgemeine Zeitung,* 5 December 1994, p. 3.

33. Heinrich August Winkler, "Rebuilding of a Nation: The Germans Before and After Unification," *Daedalus* (123, 1), p. 107; Hanns W. Maull, "Germany and Japan: The New Civilian Powers," *Foreign Affairs,* 1990/91 (69, 5), pp. 92–93.

34. See the suggestive study by Richard Jurasek and Rainer Brämer, "The New Federal Republic of Germany as Trauma: German Unification from the Student Perspective," *German Politics and Society,* fall 1994, pp. 85–104.

35. See, for example, Ulrich von Wilamowith-Moellendorff, *Meinungstrends im Vorfeld der Europawahl,* (Sankt Augustin: Konrad-Adenauer-Stiftung, 1993); and ipos, *Einstellungen zu aktuellen Fragen der Innenpolitik 1993 in Deutschland,* Mannheim: institut für praxisorientierte sozialforschung, 1993.

36. Huber Kleinert, "Die Rückkehr der GRÜNEN ins Hohe Haus," *Frankfurter Hefte/Die Neue Gesellschaft* (41, 11) 1994, p. 1004.

37. See the interview with Antje Vollmer, "'Ist das unser Staat oder der Staat der anderen'," *Frankfurter Rundschau,* 2 January 1995, p. 4.

38. "'Sepp, bleib an dem Thema dran'," *Der Spiegel,* no. 49, 5 December 1994, pp. 73–79; see also "'Schwarz-grün' bleibt auf der Tagesordnung," *Kommune* (XIII, 1) 1995, pp. 32–33.

39. "Die politischen Schlagzeilen und ihre Nachwirkungen beim Bürger," *Frankfurter Rundschau,* 1 December 1994, p. 12.

40. Gunter Hofmann, "Was wollen sie, wofür stehen sie?" *Die Zeit,* no. 12, 24 March 1995, p. 5.

11

THE RETURN OF THE PDS

GERALD R. KLEINFELD

The Party of Democratic Socialism, which had sprung from the ruling Communist Party of the German Democratic Republic, was a central focus of the elections throughout 1994. Renate Köcher, who heads the important polling center, the Institut für Demoskopie, Allensbach, claims that "Every election has a central theme that defines its results. In 1990, it was German unity. This time it is the PDS."[1] The PDS had continually lost membership since German unification, and 1994 opened with expectations that it would lose more voters as well and fail to be represented in state legislatures (Landtage) in the East and in the Bundestag. In the European Parliament elections in June, however, the PDS achieved 22.5 percent of the vote in the East, where it held onto its position as the third strongest party, and won a dramatic 4.7 percent nationwide. Some eastern districts showed 45.7 percent (Berlin/Marzahn), 42.3 percent (Halle), and 36.7 percent (Potsdam). The Alliance 90/Greens and the FDP suffered great losses in the East. In local and state (Land) elections, the PDS achieved similar results, gaining over 1990.

The June Landtag elections in Saxony-Anhalt created a unique situation. The CDU barely edged out the SPD as the largest party, and the FDP failed to gain the minimum. Without its Liberal ally, the CDU had no majority. The SPD's putative ally, the Alliance 90/Greens, survived by only a hair (5.1 percent), and the PDS returned to the Landtag as the third largest party. Thus, an SPD coalition with the Alliance 90/Greens also had no majority. Only a Grand Coalition of the CDU and SPD could govern, unless the PDS would cast its votes for an SPD-led coalition with the Alliance 90/Greens. SPD state leader Reinhard Höppner made his decision and formed a government resting on the votes of the PDS. In a federal election year, Höppner's decision was certain to intrude on the Bundestag campaign.

The PDS had certainly not departed. Despite defections of members, it had mobilized voters and threatened to return to the Bundestag into which it had barely crept in 1990 due only to a special ruling of the Federal Constitutional Court that it, for that one time only, need not meet the minimum requirement of 5 percent of the votes. Now, after June, all parties thought that the PDS had a real chance at gaining the full 5 percent minimum for representation in the Bundestag, and the national election campaign was fought on that basis. Given such obvious strength in the East, the PDS might achieve 5 percent nationwide if it only succeeded in obtaining about 1.5 percent in the West. Alternatively, the party could enter the Bundestag with as few as three directly elected representatives, again possible with its strength in the East. Then, it would achieve a percentage of seats corresponding to its share of the vote, negating the 5 percent hurdle. Some polls showed the PDS capturing five seats directly. In the end, the party was unable to cross the line for the Bundestag, gaining only 4.4 percent nationwide and 0.9 percent in the West, but success in the East did carry the PDS into the chamber, with four seats directly elected. The PDS polled 19.8 percent of the vote in the East, including eastern Berlin, and 34.7 percent of the vote in eastern Berlin itself. Gregor Gysi, parliamentary leader of the party, would be the leader of thirty deputies in the Bundestag.

The elections of 1994 did more than bring the PDS into the Bundestag again. They revealed the PDS as a continuing and, perhaps, growing force in the East, and tumbled the eastern Landtage generally into a three-party mix that made for problems for the CDU and SPD alike. The CDU succeeded with an absolute majority in Saxony, and the SPD in Brandenburg, but coalitions were the rule elsewhere. The PDS was more than a fingertip on the scale in the East. Either there would be Grand Coalitions, or the PDS would decide who governed, maybe even entering the state cabinets. In local elections, the PDS was even stronger, making cooperation with the party in some city councils unavoidable, even for the CDU. The FDP shrank almost into meaninglessness, and the Alliance 90/Greens were shocked into rethinking their future in the East. Many questions were on the table.

The 1994 elections revealed two German political contexts: in the West, the return of the Alliance 90/Greens and the tentative survival of the FDP meant a scene only perhaps the same as before; in the East, the Alliance 90/Greens and the FDP had disappeared in state legislatures (except in Saxony-Anhalt), and a three-party system of CDU, SPD, and PDS had emerged. This chapter will seek to analyze the structure, program, and appeal of the party, the PDS campaign, the election results for the Bundestag in 1994, and the party's response to its victory.

What kind of party is the PDS, and who determines its positions? Is it still an unreformed Communist party? Who makes up the membership, and who votes for it? Most importantly, why did so many easterners vote PDS, just a few years after the end of the SED dictatorship? Did the PDS just mobilize their remaining voters, or did they add new supporters? What will be the result for Germany of the continuation of the PDS on the political scene? These, and a myriad other questions dominate the landscape in the East and afford sleepless nights to the entire remainder of the German political spectrum. Not only Germans are asking whether the party can become permanent, attract adherents in the West, and become a long-term actor on the political scene. For the PDS, the Bundestag elections of 1994 may have been a triumph, but they were only a way station. The strategy for success saw the elections of 1994 as one battle won.

Origins, Membership, and Structure of the PDS

The PDS sprang directly from the Socialist Unity Party (SED), the governing Communist Party of the German Democratic Republic, which had itself been a product of the forced union of the Communist and Social Democratic parties in the Soviet zone of occupied Germany. The SED stared dissolution in the face when the German Democratic Republic was shaken by popular revolt in October 1989. In other Eastern bloc countries, like Hungary, the Communists split into a reformed group and a group that became a Social Democratic Party. No such split took place in the GDR, because an East German SPD was founded that very month, blocking this path for the SED.[2] Instead, members fled the SED in droves. The new East-SPD was also very cautious, and attempted to avoid permitting membership to anyone who had been in the SED. Two options were open for the SED. The party could reform itself, or appear to reform itself, and survive. Or, the party could dissolve, and reform-minded members could found a new party. An important motive for not taking the latter path was the desire to retain, as much as possible, the great wealth accumulated through years of total power in the GDR.[3] Therefore, the party simply renamed itself, first as SED/PDS, and then as PDS. The SED assets, said Social Democrat Richard Schröder, were "too good to give up."[4] It elected a new leadership, but members continued to flee.

In the autumn of 1989, the SED had had 2.3 million members. By 1994, the PDS counted only 130,000—few of them newcomers. The core of the PDS membership came from the SED. It is also not a workers' party, but largely a party of former government officials, civil servants, functionaries of all kinds, and academics. It is important to distinguish between the membership of the party and its electorate—those who vote for it—but the nature, size, and character of the membership (see figure 11.1) is important for party policy.

Membership in the East has developed as follows:[5]

Land	1990	1991	1993
Berlin	61,426	31,200	27,000
Brandenburg	59,202	24,998	23,000
Mecklenburg-			
West Pomerania	50,079	21,903	18,920
Saxony	86,591	45,245	39,876
Saxony-Anhalt	55,745	23,180	22,115
Thuringia	37,539	25,301	19,780
Total	313,043	146,526	130,911

FIGURE 11.1

SED/PDS SOCIAL STRUCTURE

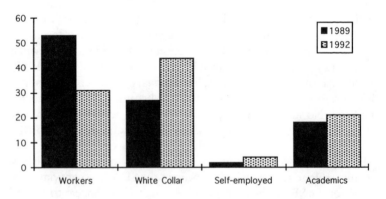

Source: Official statistics.

The PDS is an aging party, whose members were largely in the SED. It is also not necessarily a party whose members are the "losers" in German unity, but rather includes a high percentage of persons who found employment, even in the civil service. The membership, however, is too small to be a voting base, and the party leadership understood that the potential of former SED membership, those who were no longer members, formed a basic underlying resource in elections. It was necessary to retain the support of these people, but it was also clear that that support would not be enough to survive for the long term.

The PDS election campaign was managed by its Election Office (*Wahlbüro*) and led by its parliamentary leader, Gregor Gysi. The structure of the PDS is complicated and supports a number of groups with clearly different perspectives. The old SED structure could not be maintained in a democratic Germany, and it had to be adapted for a democratic society. The transitional leadership under Hans Modrow, Gregor Gysi, and André Brie saw this as the GDR moved towards democracy, and set out to change the party structure even as German unity began to take place. Modrow and Gysi were enormously popular in 1990, the former even among many non-SED members who were attracted by his apparently moderate stewardship of the German Democratic Republic before the democratic elections to the Volkskammer in March of 1990. This popularity helped them introduce changes into a party whose membership was rapidly dissipating. However, it should not be assumed that the changes resulted in a new, or even a reformed, party which would become attractive to new members who were not formerly in the SED. In short, the party was changed, reorganized, but not genuinely reformed. The result was a post-Communist party, whose members largely continued to regard themselves as Communists.[6] The leadership gathered around themselves a number of younger élites, organized into *Arbeitsgemeinschaften* (AGs), or working groups, and *Plattformen*, or platforms, each of which represented interest groups on specific themes. There is a Communist Platform (led by Sahra Wagenknecht) and a platform on ecology.[7] Most of the AG/platform groups were created by the Party Executive (*Parteivorstand*) and exist nationwide parallel to the Land, district, and communal regional party organization, although there are also some local and regional AGs. Some of these organizations exist on paper only, while others have a significant number of members.

This structure is classically that of a Communist party. The various groups, AGs, platforms, committees (such as the eastern Committees for Fairness), and the like are typical organizations for extraparliamentary activity designed to expand the party's influence in a variety of areas, while also offering opportunities to undermine existing social and political organs in the society. Their goal is to exacerbate the conflict potential in society. The main point is not that the individuals who may be addressed by the groups should accept the party program, or even that the groups represent a uniform party concept, but that these individuals are contacted and mobilized for the PDS. The AGs offer an opportunity for the party to present a diverse image and to work in a concentrated fashion on various interest constituencies. Contradictions are accepted. They appear to tolerate differences of opinion. Thus, the Communist Platform might exist alongside a Committee for Fairness which does not sound Communist and seeks non-Communist members. A Coordination Office at PDS headquarters in Berlin helps to coordinate activities of the AGs. Structurally, the AGs have no power within the party, but the speaker of an AG or a platform can be individually linked to the party executive, as is the case with the Communist Platform. The election campaign utilized regional and local organizations, as well as the existence of these AGs and platforms. It is the program which is intended to be a unifying factor.

The PDS Programs

Handouts in red, white, and black reinforced the party's new image in 1994. "The Program of the PDS: A Socialist Party in Germany" stressed three points. First, that a vote for the PDS was not a vote thrown away. The party reminded the voters that they had a real chance of getting into the Bundestag by the 5 percent clause. If not, the pamphlet realistically gauged, three directly won seats were possible. That would mean a total Bundestag delegation of between thirty and forty. Second, "What is the PDS?" "Honestly speaking," it answered, "some call it the successor to the SED. Others call it a socialist party in Germany." Here was another main tactic. Knowing that the opponents would bring home to the voters the origin of the PDS, Brie's people hit upon the countertactic of admitting it first. Certainly, this is what we were, the pamphlets admitted, but we are now a new party, a socialist party. We are "that active part of the SED which broke with Stalinism, and which—along with the other political movements of the autumn of 1989—wanted a comprehensive reform of the GDR." Third, "the PDS includes people of different philosophies, ideologies, and religions whose common ground lies in their intentions to try to introduce fundamental social change."[8] There follows a list of apparent specifics, which turn out to be populist platitudes. It would be improper to regard the brochures of any party as a definitive reproduction of the party's program.

The PDS leadership made no effort to disguise either their own or their party's heritage in the SED. To do so would be folly, since the party is a transmutation of the SED, and they are demonstrably former members of the governing party of the German Democratic Republic, some even of the State Security Police (*Staatssicherheit*) or *Stasi*. Thus, they admit this publicly, a step which scarcely fails to win points for honesty. "We are the only 'clean' party," claimed Gysi in a speech in Frankfurt am Main in September.[9] Less obvious is the nature of reform or change in the party ideology, and where the party stands today.

The 1990 program was written in the heady days of February in that year, when the population of the GDR was enraptured by market economy, and it would have been difficult to swim against the stream. Even so, the 1990 program sought to demonstrate on behalf of socialism that it was not as efficient, but more humane than capitalism. It represented the party's search for a new identity, separate from that of the SED, and an effort to create a program that was workable in the new Germany. The program strongly endorsed the party's heritage from Marx, Lenin, Rosa Luxemburg, Karl Liebknecht, and Antonio Gramsci, but also August Bebel and Eduard Bernstein. It also included a mixture of feminism, ecology, and direct democracy elements. Many of the positions in the program of 1990 were clearly contradictory, such as the references to the heritage of Bernstein and Lenin.[10] Bernstein was a "revisionist" Social Democrat in the Empire who believed in democracy and challenged orthodox Marxism, while seeking better conditions for workers without a revolution. Lenin demanded total power for his party within the state. The PDS acknowledges both, but they are clearly incompatible. The program heaps such incompatibilities on top of one another without seeking resolution. While mass parties do contain contradictory elements, the level of incompatibility in the PDS suggests a failure to reconcile democracy with the party's goals.

What was needed in the program of 1990 was something that could keep what in the past could be saved and could seek a new identity, prevent people from leaving, win new supporters, and adapt to a changing Germany. At that time, Gysi described the party's tactics as designed more to foster problems for the new forces coming to power in the East—more or less obstructionist tactics—than as serious descriptions of policy for government itself.[11]

The 1993 party program was written when many eastern Germans had become disillusioned about a market economy, or uncertain of their role in it, and unsure or insecure in their changed country. It retreats from some of the necessities of 1990, and speaks of overcoming the domination of capitalism, while explaining that the "capitalist character of modern society is responsible for endangering human civilization and culture, for the militaristic character of international relations, for the crisis in the ecosphere, and for indescribable misery, particularly for those who live in the southern hemisphere."[12] "We are," the program continues, "united in the belief that capitalist domination must be overcome." The humanistic and democratic traditions within the socialist idea, on the other hand, must not be surrendered. Despite the errors and crimes committed in its name, socialism provides the guide for the future. It would be wrong, the program argues, to capitulate before the self-proclaimed victor of history. The capitalist metroplexes of the world are centers of destructive market economy, where massive unemployment, repression of women, and a general collapse of culture go hand-in-hand with antiyouth and antichildren policies, antiforeigner attitudes, anti-Semitism, racism, bureaucratic domination, the gradual elimination of democracy, social alienation, and other evils of society.

On the other hand, the attempt to introduce socialism in the German Democratic Republic, continues the program, "has decisively influenced" the people in Germany's East. After 1945, "millions of people tried to find a better form of social order." Their experience in the GDR includes "the elimination of unemployment, far-reaching triumph over poverty, a universal system of social security, meaningful elements of social justice, including a high measure of equality of opportunity in education and health as well as in culture, and, not least, new rights for women and young people." Attempting to explain why the GDR economy failed, the PDS maintains that East Germany developed under continuing poor economic conditions imposed from outside, suffered by having to be responsible for 96 percent of German reparations, and by being separated from the rest of Germany. The "embargo of the Western powers" blocked the GDR from world trade outside of the Eastern bloc. Nor was there a "beneficial economic development within that bloc." "Forced by the Western powers to devote part of its economy to armaments," the GDR suffered still more. However, its foreign policy was highly "moral," the 1993 program insists. The GDR was a state which had "broken with the German great-power chauvinism." While not specifically condemning the *Stasi*, the party admits that its existence was a mistake. Socialism must be democratically based. Any attempt to create socialism that is not accepted and supported by the great majority of the population, and which does not guarantee the liberties of the people, must fail—sooner or later.[13]

The GDR, in other words, was created with high ideals, but failed to live up to them. According to the program, the underlying concept of socialism was, nevertheless, valid. That of a market economy is not, nor is the political system of the Federal Republic of Germany that is founded upon a market economy. The central message of the 1993 program is a "fundamental rejection" of the political and social system of the Federal Republic of Germany.[14] The goal of the PDS has been described as a gradual overcoming of constitutional democracy by a rather diffuse socialist order which sees itself as the descendant of Marx and Engels, although the program itself also adds Lenin. The 1993 program rejects the social market economy, and fails to explain how the party conceives of a German democracy under socialism.

German political parties have not only a general party program, but also an "election program" specifically for the election campaign under way. Given that there were nineteen elections scheduled for Germany in 1994, the PDS Election Convention brought out special election programs in March for the European elections of June and the federal elections of October. The program for the elections to the European Parliament rejects the Treaty of Maastricht as seeking a European "Union for the big corporations, for the banks, the insurance companies, and the firms who control capital." The European Union under Maastricht would be undemocratic and led by those who put interest income and profit above the needs of the people. The PDS calls for a "European Social Union."[15] In the program for the Bundestag election, the PDS proclaims itself "a socialist party [which] takes radical-democratic and anticapitalist positions in the social and political debates in the Federal Republic of Germany."[16] We want "a different Germany, a democratic, social, civil, ecological, and antiracist renewal of the FRG."[17]

The program combines specifics with general goals. The PDS is for a guaranteed right to a job, against the strangulation of East German agriculture, for defense of the land reform in the GDR of 1945, against a retreat from social benefits, for equality for women and for abortion, for codetermination of workers and management in companies, against nationalism and great-power politics, and for a new constitution in Germany. Jobs can be created by a general reduction in the work week. Two million jobs can be created, the

PDS argues, by a general adoption of a thirty-five-hour week. In addition, new work rules can actually reduce the work week below thirty-five hours. In the case of inadequate corporate funds to pay for this, the state can provide salary subsidies. Firms must adopt a minimal quota for employment of the handicapped. Job training must become a legal part of the regular work week. In order to ensure that workers have rights to their jobs, there must be longer notice given before layoffs are permitted, and a longer period of employment before layoffs are effective. Workers who have family members incapable of caring for themselves must be given even longer notice before layoffs are permitted, and must be given preferential treatment when jobs are available. Regional economic policy should prevent the elimination of industry in an entire region. The state must promote research and economic activity that will help smaller firms. State support should also lead to 1.5 million jobs in the service industry affecting social, cultural, and ecological needs within twelve months. No explanation is offered about how this is to affect German productivity or competitiveness in the world economy, where the high cost of production in Germany is already a serious problem. The PDS is against a "commercializing" of the health industry and medicine, and for a new health policy that makes health care independent of "the pocketbook." The party wants more public housing. In agriculture, the PDS rejects privatization of East German collectives, and suggests that these be transferred to the communes. All of this, including the remainder of the PDS proposals, is expected to cost no more than DM300 million per year and be financed by higher taxes on the wealthy, growth in the economy, cutting the defense budget ten percent yearly, taxing speculation, and by the tax payments of the newly employed.

The PDS Bundestag Election Campaign

The PDS campaign was an effort to gain both first *and* second votes under the German dual voting system.[18] The first side of the ballot is the election for an election district representative in the Bundestag, and the candidates for that district are identified by name and by the party under whose aegis they are running. They do not have to be members of the party, and the PDS selected several persons to run who were described as "nonparty." It is the second side of the ballot, the second vote, which is the party list, where voters choose a party for the proportional share of Bundestag seats. The party is assigned seats according to the percentage of votes and the individuals chosen for the Bundestag are taken from this list. Assuming that it might be difficult to gain the required 5 percent nationwide that would allow the PDS their proportional share and entry into the Bundestag, the party also elected to attempt the alternate route. They could get in by winning three seats in the first vote. That meant targeting a minimum of three districts with candidates who could actually win the district vote. Thus, the PDS strategy was twofold: 1) to seek the 5 percent minimum, and 2) to capitalize on regional concentration in the East and seek at least three direct seats.

As a part of the plan to do this, the PDS assembled a list of Bundestag candidates to which it referred as "Gysi's *bunte Truppe*" (Gysi's motley band). The motley band were twenty individuals of obviously varied background designated to run in specially targeted districts. Among them were many who were reasonably well known, even in the West, and who might have a personal appeal beyond former SED members. The most prominent and those given the best chance were:[19]

Stefan Heym	*	(nonparty)	Berlin Center/Prenzlauer Berg
Gregor Gysi	*	(PDS)	Berlin Hellersdorf/Marzahn
Christa Luft	*	(PDS)	Berlin Friedrichshain/Lichtenberg
Günter Maleuda		(nonparty)	Neubrandenburg/Altentreptow
Rolf Kutzmutz		(PDS)	Potsdam
Wolfgang Methling		(PDS)	Rostock
Barbara Höll		(nonparty)	Leipzig North
Manfred Müller	*	(nonparty)	Berlin

* actually elected to the Bundestag on the first ballot

Heym is a noted author, a Jew who fled the Nazis, wound up in the United States and took American citizenship, served in the U.S. Army, emigrated to the GDR, and renounced his American citizenship. His occasional criticism of the GDR did not extend to renunciation of the privileges extended to him, and he was able to use his considerable dollar income to purchase consumer goods in the West and to live well in the GDR, a fact criticized in the campaign. He never joined the SED. The district chosen for Heym was that represented by Wolfgang Thierse, a popular and outspoken East German member of the SPD, after the East-SPD had joined the West-SPD, and a party vice-president. Gysi's was a safe district, comparatively speaking, one inhabited by a large number of ex-SED functionaries. Luft had been economics minister in the Modrow cabinet. Maleuda had been head of the German Farmers' Party, one of the puppet parties of the GDR, and a vice-president of the Council of State, along with Erich Honecker. Kutzmutz, who had worked with the *Stasi*, had run for mayor of Potsdam and barely lost to a coalition of democratic parties. Müller is a Berlin labor union official. Methling is a veterinarian. The others included Count Heinrich von Einsiedel (who campaigned urging voters to "call me Heinrich"), a great-grandson of Bismarck; Gerhard Zwerenz, a West German author; Ruth Fuchs, an SED representative in the Volkskammer and winner of two Olympic medals; and Franz Christoph, a self-proclaimed champion of the handicapped who is confined to a wheelchair. The motley band was supposed to show the party's openness and its broadly critical attitude towards the dominant forces in German society. Thus, it would appeal to voters who shared a critical view and might not look to the program behind the party.

The PDS election program, adopted at the Third Party Congress in Berlin on 13 March 1994, gave flesh to the slogans used in the campaign. It announced that Germany needed a strong leftist opposition "and resistance," and stated unabashedly that the PDS had sprung from "tens of thousands of reform-minded SED members."[20] The PDS carries on a "self-critical discussion of its own history." It "warns against the threat to German democracy" that has erupted in German politics in recent years. This threat comes "not only from the far right," but is far more general. The GDR was "annexed" to Germany, the PDS claims, and citizens in the East have been "victims of inequality, destruction of industry, agriculture, science and culture, unconstitutional mishandling of their rights, including rights to pensions and salaries and threats to their rights to property." One-third of all Germans who are capable of work were "locked out of employment," and the East has become an "experimental territory for the shrinking of social benefits and democracy in the entire country." "All over Germany" democratic, social, and legal rights "are being called into question."

André Brie headed the Election Office, and was chief strategist. Brie had been forced to resign his post as Berlin Land chairman because the PDS then regarded his *Stasi* connections as a liability, but he reemerged to head the Election Office when his background was no longer seen to be a problem. The PDS received DM10.6 million in federal funds for the election campaign under Germany's state funding plan for elections (the SPD received DM88.74 million and the CDU/CSU DM91.8 million, while the FDP took in DM14.38 million).[21] Other money was available from PDS resources and contributions. Vera Wollenberger, eastern civil rights activist and Bundestag member for the Alliance 90/Greens, has estimated the total wealth of the PDS at DM900 million.[22]

Brie's strategy called for an active media campaign, partly focused on Gysi, who has become a media megastar. While Gysi appeared often in the East, he was a larger part of the campaign in the West and in the national media, particularly television.[23] Posters showed a picture of Gysi with the theme "Gysi is electable! Give the PDS your second vote nationwide!" Gysi was so much an election draw, that the newsmagazine *Der Spiegel* took to calling the PDS the "Gysi Party."[24] Gysi was such a dominant figure on the airwaves and in talk shows, that *Der Spiegel* also dubbed him "Terror of the other parties."[25] Gysi is not the PDS, however. "If the PDS could be reduced to Gregor Gysi," the Alliance 90/Greens leader, Joschka Fischer, claims, "many debates would be very different."[26]

Gysi was the show horse. He spoke all over the country and accepted numerous invitations to appear on television talk shows. Intelligent, witty, often ironical, and quick, he made all the same points as the posters, the placards, and the flyers while presenting a figure of great contrast with the elderly, often wooden leaders of the GDR, whose speech cadence often seemed to fit with a state dubbed the "gray republic" by its own people. His wit charmed eastern as well as western Germans.[27] He played his image carefully. In 1990, television reporters interviewing Saxon Minister-President Kurt Biedenkopf, a former university professor, thought it a wonderful trick to throw open the doors in the middle of the interview and bring in Gysi as guest questioner. To everyone's surprise, the brilliant and no less wily professor turned the tables on his hosts and took Gysi down. After that, the PDS star was more cautious. For the 1994 elections, behind-the-scenes struggles often took place over which persons might be permitted to share the TV cameras, lest Gysi not appear. Civil rights activist Freya Klier was "dis-invited" forty-eight hours before she was scheduled to appear alongside Gysi and Heym on the television talk show "Talk im Turm." Why? "Because otherwise they would not have come," she was told.[28]

Civil rights activists in the East were among the bitterest opponents of the PDS. Gerd Poppe of Alliance 90/Greens gave an impassioned speech in the Bundestag as the PDS deputies entered the debate on the Enquete Commission Report (examining the activities of the SED regime).[29] He admonished his colleagues not to forget what the party still professes while its deputies seemingly acknowledge their past. Bärbel Bohley, a figure scarcely remembered from the early days of the fall of the SED regime, later commented that the easterners would remember what the PDS actually stood for only after they ever came to power. Gysi sees these activists not only as critics, but as too credible for comfort. Newsmagazines devoted cover stories to Gysi's media persona, describing how the PDS politician monopolized the camera and combined excellent rhetoric while avoiding direct answers to specific questions. With a combination of critique and logic, Gysi looked modern and populist.[30] He was a draw and an asset to the party in changing its image. Like Lothar Bisky, party chair, he was determined to establish the PDS as a long-term participant in the German political scene. This was not only a question of image, but of membership, voting support and, above all, of structure and ideology. The elections of 1994 were not only about seats in the Bundestag. They were about permanence and power.

Brie, Bisky, and Gysi understood clearly what was at stake. It was essential to run a campaign that was designed to attract new voters without turning off the traditional support, which might not even be enough were there to be a low turnout in the East. The motley band was a part of this. So was Gysi's persona. The party campaigned in the West, hoping to pull the needed votes for 5 percent nationwide and to build for the future. Also, it needed to avoid giving to westerners the image that it was a purely eastern party, while simultaneously telling the easterners that it was their representative because the other national parties were western-based. In short, it had to appear to be a national party, while seeming to the easterners that it represented them best. Second, it had to appear to be a modern party, something that would help it dissociate itself from the SED, and everything clever, colorful, and witty would help that image. On the other hand, it could not turn off those former SED members who would certainly vote for it. In other words, as Helga Welsh writes elsewhere in this volume, it had to represent both continuity and discontinuity. Third, it had to appear constructive and not seeking a return to the GDR. Fourth, it had to appeal to voters of various age groups, expressly including the young, because its membership was seriously aging and faced a biological end. Fifth, it needed to claim that all of the other parties were part of the establishment, for which the PDS represented a socialist alternative and leftist opposition. The PDS should be seen as the representative of the man or woman in the street—the other parties of the established order and interest groups. Sixth, it needed to demand an end to certain clear, national problems, such as unemployment and pollution, while avoiding answers on details. Thus, for example, one poster showed an unemployed worker, fingers in his mouth, whistling loudly, with a superscript headline—"Send Jobs Here!"

Thus, the PDS election campaign was fought on several levels. In addition to populist slogans, attacking problems without offering workable solutions, presenting a socialist image and unabashedly seeking to be "left-radical," the party relied as well upon its chief candidates to create a varied image of differentiated perspective united in opposition to the establishment. The poster campaign was colorful and omnipresent, in both West and East. In the West, many different posters hit the theme "Change begins with Opposition." While this theme was also used in the East, it was often combined with the word "we" emblazoned even more prominently. Thus, three points were made at the same time. PDS opposition could produce change, positive change. Second, "we" meant "us" in the East, and "we" in the East were represented by the party advocating this change through opposition. The third point was an acknowledgement that they would not likely form part of a government majority, but would remain in the opposition. This, however, should not be regarded as a dead end, but as a tool of change. The young were especially courted. They were wooed by a poster of an attractive young couple with lips about to touch. The party advised, "When kissing, keep your eyes closed; when voting, keep them open. The first time—PDS!"

This was recognized only too well by the other parties. In 1990, the PDS had secured representation in eastern state legislatures, but governments were formed without their participation, and both the Alliance 90/Greens and the Free Democrats were also substantially represented. The 1994 state legislature elections in the East were different. Continuing their decline, the FDP failed to make the 5 percent of the vote necessary to gain representation in one state legislature after the other. With the exception of Saxony-Anhalt, so did the Alliance 90/Greens. This left the PDS as the third party in all state legislatures in the East. Should either the CDU or the SPD fail to achieve a majority, the PDS became the deciding factor. The first state legislature in which this occurred was Saxony-Anhalt, where the Alliance 90/Greens barely squeaked in, in June. The resulting four-party legislature found the SPD and Alliance 90/Greens without a majority. The only obvious majority was a Grand Coalition of the CDU and SPD. Reinhard Höppner, SPD leader, chose a different course. He elected to form a minority government with the Alliance 90/Greens, resting on the toleration of the PDS. Most voters in the West were shocked. The CDU was outraged. Some anti-SED civil rights activists in Alliance 90 were chagrined, but the decision held.

Given the relationships in any coalition-governed state legislature, new Minister-President Höppner had clearly invited the PDS to share government planning and decisions. By this path, he had avoided a Grand Coalition, a governmental solution disliked in general by most Germans, and chosen what seemed for him the lesser evil. Since polls revealed that most easterners had no apprehensions about the PDS sharing government coalitions and responsibility, Höppner felt that the Saxony-Anhalt decision was correct. The CDU reacted rapidly.

Using Saxony-Anhalt as an example, the CDU counterattacked, lest the SPD build a multiparty coalition in the Bundestag. If the SPD could be associated with the PDS, as Höppner was allowing in Saxony-Anhalt, traditional CDU voters could be mobilized in the West and hesitant easterners, who might not want a national government with links to the former rulers of the GDR, might back the chancellor once again. Refusing to take as definitive SPD assurances that the Saxony-Anhalt model would not be followed in Bonn, and mobilizing the considerable antipathy towards the SED and its successor in both West and East, the CDU/CSU undertook a campaign against the "red socks." Posters and speeches raised before the voters the specter of an SPD launched into power in Bonn through the "red socks." Chancellor Helmut Kohl, quoting SPD postwar idol Kurt Schumacher's description of the Communist Party, described the PDS as "red-painted fascists." As is indicated elsewhere in this volume, the campaign galvanized Union supporters and many westerners in general. As such, it was successful. However, it was not vastly popular in the East, even amongst the CDU, since it helped the PDS portray itself as a victim, as a party the government coalition in Bonn was seeking to drive out of existence, and as a left-socialist party which only wanted to participate in the democratic process, but which was being denied this.

Playing on the sympathy vote in the East, the PDS attempted to gain voting support from those who felt that the Union campaign was unjust. Soon, the PDS was distributing red socks as a campaign gimmick, attempting to turn the tables on the conservatives. Undoubtedly, the CDU picked up support in the East from those who were anxious to prevent the PDS from preserving itself in the new Germany. It remains unclear, however, how many were motivated in the opposite direction. Some politicians of all parties maintain that the PDS did pick up support from the red socks idea, but that the CDU also gained some votes.

It was not only by the poster campaign, the media, and a superstar campaigner that the PDS made its election effort for the October ballot, but by ward politics in a style that would have warmed the hearts of party machines familiar to many an American city. The 130,000 PDS members, although they were only a fraction of the earlier total, still vastly outnumbered every other party in the territories of the former German Democratic Republic, swamping the size of the SPD and the FDP, not to mention the CDU. Added to that, PDS members could count on the support of many who had dropped out of the party. Party Chairman Lothar Bisky stressed in his speech before the Election Convention of 1994 that the membership should not underestimate the value of working hard on the local level.[31] Through local contacts, door-to-door, and other ward politics work, the PDS was able to maximize the value of their membership and of their contacts, not only within the former membership base of the SED, and make the kind of effort and individual care for citizens that is recognizable in successfully functioning machine politics.[32] Especially for easterners unfamiliar with the new forms of united Germany, with the new society and its laws, regulations, and requirements, the PDS often found people ready to help. Some former bureaucrat was often there to help those who needed assistance with forms originating in an unfamiliar society. This kind of campaign work meant more to the insecure than the sometimes distant promises of a national leadership of another party.

The PDS campaign and election work had a polished and well-funded image, but never seemed to lose contact with discontent and protest. In the West, the party savored its isolated position. In the East, it tried to capitalize on it. While relying on the membership, and those who had left the party but would still vote for it, the PDS had set its sights on a broader appeal. As election day approached, speculation still grew over whether it would achieve 5 percent and whether it would gain more than three seats directly chosen.

The Bundestag Election Results: Who Voted PDS and Why?

The elections brought the PDS 695,539 more votes in the East than in the elections of 1990, 70 percent more than the first all-German Bundestag elections, and 242,562 votes more in the West, the latter figure representing a tripling of their vote. The party did best in Mecklenburg-West Pomerania, with 23.6 percent of the vote, and the Bundestag election fell there on the same day as state legislature

(Landtag) elections, where the party also did well. In Thuringia, where there were also Landtag elections, the party gained 8.8 percent over the previous federal elections. In larger cities in the East, the PDS polled 28 percent, and in the eastern districts of Berlin reached 35 percent. In those communities in the East where the population was under 5,000, the PDS achieved only an average of 13 percent of the vote.[33]

The PDS won few voters in the West with its election strategy and program, but its best showing was in Bremen, where the party pulled 2.7 percent of the vote, and in Berlin. Bremen is a depressed area, and has been so for years. In western Berlin, the "alternative" scene has developed ties to the PDS. The best districts for the PDS in the second ballot in the West were:

5.3 percent—Berlin/Kreuzberg/Schöneberg
3.6 percent—Bremen/West
3.4 percent—Hamburg/Center
3.2 percent—Berlin/Tiergarten/Wedding/North Charlottenburg
3.0 percent—Bremen/East

The PDS achieved 15 percent of the vote in Berlin as a whole, and 34.7 percent in eastern Berlin, where it was the strongest party, followed by the SPD with just under 33 percent. On that basis, future governments in the German capital could either be formed on the basis of a Grand Coalition, or an SPD coalition with the PDS. The SPD district mayor for Berlin/Kreuzberg, Peter Strieder, came out for cooperation between the SPD and the PDS immediately after the election.[24] A vigorous debate erupted within the Alliance 90/Greens in the capital on their future relationship to the PDS. Most former eastern civil rights activists were opposed. On the alternative scene, especially in the West, numerous voices urged cooperation.

Although Bisky had hoped to achieve 1.5 percent generally in the West, and rise above the 5 percent level nationwide, the PDS failed to do this, and settled in at 4.4 percent. The party's appeal in the West rested on a number of factors. These included those who supported the concept of a socialist party to the left of the SPD and believed that they saw this in the PDS, remnants of the Communist Party supporters in the West,[35] and those who believed that Gysi and his "motley band" represented a challenge to the established parties. "In the West, they want to put themselves at the pinnacle of the whole left scene, including … the women's movement and … protest voters," writes Daniel Deckers.[36] This includes the Berlin alternatives, who had been linked to the Greens.

In Cologne, for example, the PDS local Bundestag candidate was Heike Krause, former attorney for the Red Army Faction terrorists Christian Klar and Wolf-Klement Wagner. The PDS Cologne office address is shared with the GNN (*Gesellschaft für Nachrichtenerfassung und Nachrichtenverbreitung*—a fringe group on the left), the Leftist Peoples' Front, and the League of West German Communists, on whose board sits the PDS press officer for Cologne.[37] Krause has not repudiated terrorist or other violent acts against the civil order, and her position is mirrored by that of Angela Marquardt, head of the AG Junge GenossInnen (Young Women Comrades), who was quoted on ARD German television on 15 July 1994 as stating that it is naive to talk about whether or not one carries out violent acts against the civil order. Marquardt was elected in January 1995 to the PDS Party Executive. The GNN publishes the newsletter "Kurdistan Letter," which supports the Kurdish separatist political party PKK. The PKK is also a Communist party. The PDS and the PKK have organized joint demonstrations, for example in Hanover.[38] In Lower Saxony, members of the German Communist Party ran on the PDS Land list on places three, four, and seven. Three of the thirteen Land list candidates in Bavaria were members of the German Communist Party. These were the norm, not exceptions. After the October elections, state constitutional protection authorities in Berlin and Thuringia put the Communist Platform of the PDS under observation.[39] Links between Communists in the West and the PDS are numerous. Since the PDS includes a Communist Platform, this is normal and to be expected. However, such close ties with western Communists do not fit in with the plans of the party leadership. With several western districts under such obvious Communist control, the leadership has been forced into extraordinary measures in order to institute policies that can broaden the party's appeal. This meets heavy resistance both in the East and West from those who do not want a weakening of the Communist elements. Here again, there is a difference between the membership and those who have voted for the party in 1994.

In the West, the PDS did best in districts with a higher percentage of the population with a university or Hauptschule diploma and a low percentage of Realschule graduates or, alternatively, where there was a very high level of unemployment. In short, where higher education loomed largest and lower level education was smallest. This is the "educated" or "intellectual" left. Otherwise, where unemployment was greatest, such as Bremen, a city-state which also has a university. Jürgen Falter and Markus Klein see three characteristics of

districts in the West and East where the PDS did well: 1) high population density, 2) relatively high percentage of population in service
sector, and 3) relatively high unemployment rate.[40]

The election campaign itself, the appearances on television, and
the reports in the media, including issues that focused on Gysi and on
the party in *Focus* and *Der Spiegel*, all helped to draw attention to the
challenge offered by the PDS. Among the strongly negative factors in
the West were the campaign of the CDU against the "red socks,"
identifying the PDS with the SED, and calling for the SPD to repu-
diate coalitions or state governments supported by the PDS. These
campaigns of the CDU had a broad effect among some voters in the
West, but enhanced PDS support among those who saw the party as
antiestablishment. In the West, Gysi clearly won some of his support
by portraying his PDS as a kind of "SPD+," not wanting the old
GDR back, but seeking to bring a more critical tone to the opposition.[41] In the East, the Gysi-effect was less potent because a number
of other factors were more prominent, but Gysi was an effective draw
in the West.[42] The appeal of the PDS in the East was much broader,
of course. To some, the PDS was an *Ostpartei*, a party which represented the East. The Allensbach Institute had taken a poll before the
election and asked voters whether they thought, when the PDS was
attacked by other parties, this was principally an effort to prevent the
East from being better represented in the Bundestag. Only twelve
percent of westerners agreed with this, and 68 percent disagreed. In
the East, the percentages were reversed. Thirty-five percent agreed,
and only 45 percent disagreed. The remainder were undecided.[43]

The PDS drew 20 percent of the vote in the East, including many
who did not consider themselves Communists, and including many
younger voters. The basic voting strength of the party was its membership and those former members and members of the SED who
had got lost in the transition from GDR to the united Germany.
Those eastern Germans who described themselves as long-term
adherents of the PDS constituted, as a group, almost 70 percent of
the PDS voters in the Bundestag election.[44] Many of these had formerly been in the SED. It is often forgotten how large the SED was,
and how many people were directly involved with the Ministry of
State Security, the *Stasi*, or were higher functionaries in the GDR and
were not able to cross over into acceptable positions in the new Germany. These individuals did not see the "western" parties as representing them, and looked to the PDS to represent their interests, as
the party indeed did. PDS policies attempted to break or halt steps
against former *Stasi* officials and other GDR and SED functionaries

and to seek rehabilitation and favorable treatment on pensions, employment, and housing. In addition, 27 percent of white-collar workers and 35 percent of civil servants voted PDS, an indication that these people had retained party loyalty after having successfully negotiated similar positions or keeping their old positions after unification.[45] Such individuals as represented in these groups, therefore, formed a basic reservoir of support for the PDS. Falter and Klein see this as indicating good chances for a longer-term survival of the PDS, since they clearly form a committed base of support.

On the other hand, this base was far from enough to achieve 20 percent of the vote. Bisky, Gysi, and Brie were correct when they understood the support reservoir to be biologically limited. That is, these aging supporters must be supplemented by others, and especially by younger voters, or the party would simply die as the supporters did. In their view, the PDS must not, therefore, be a CSU, but a new left-socialist party.[46] In eastern Germany, about one-fourth of voters between the ages of eighteen and forty-five voted PDS. When compared with the age of the membership of the party, this is a considerable success of an aging party in attracting younger voters. It also shows, as do other statistics, that the voters of the PDS do not always reflect the party membership. This means that the party has succeeded in attracting voters who were not SED, and indicates that the party must adjust its policies to keep them and to attract growing numbers of them. This is the Bisky-Gysi-Brie direction. There is a danger here for the PDS. Of younger voters in the East, 70 percent believe that unemployment is the greatest problem and 24 percent believe that neither a CDU- nor an SPD-led government can solve that problem. Should eastern German unemployment decline, this group is still endangered for the PDS.

A second factor in gaining votes in the East was the ward activity of long-term supporters. Both in large cities and in the countryside, membership and supporters drew upon their experience to assist neighbors and to remind them that the party was a party which cared for them.[47] At an election rally in Waren, a local PDS candidate told her audience, "I want to represent you, because more women should get into politics, and because I know what the real interests of our people here are."[48] The enormous advantage of membership which the PDS had over the CDU and SPD, not to mention the FDP and the inadequately organized Alliance 90/Greens, gave the party an opportunity of direct action which helped turn into support among citizens who were unsure, insecure, or turned to them for assistance in adjusting to the new society. The party was also able to capitalize on local contacts, and by a widespread view in the East that "not every SED member was a bad person." As Helga Welsh points out, this was a continuity which residents could accept and recognize as familiar in a world which was still strange and which did not offer the same kind of security that they had experienced under the totalitarian, all-encompassing comfort of the GDR. Alienation contributed to it.

PDS voters in the East were characterized by several decisive differences from other voters. One characteristic was geography. As we have seen, urban situations predominated, and there was a South-North gap—high PDS votes in Berlin, and much higher in Mecklenburg-West Pomerania than in Saxony. Second, there is a distinction on level of education. There is a direct correlation between level and nature of education and likelihood to vote PDS. Third, there is the obvious correlation between former party allegiance. SED members are more likely to have voted PDS. Fourth, there is a correlation between occupation and likelihood to vote PDS. Civil servants, white-collar workers, retirees, and young people in certain categories supported the PDS in 1994. The PDS is decisively not the party favored by the working class, or by those who are underprivileged from the standpoint of income, education, or social standing.[49] Fifth, also with respect to the often-heard assertion that the PDS is the party of the losers in unification, certainly the PDS represents those who describe themselves as politically active and interested, and are simultaneously most unhappy with the German political and economic system, and most pessimistically view its potential.[50] The polling institution Forsa describes 82 percent of PDS voters as being unhappy with the German political system.[51] But they are not necessarily losers in the unification. They include business people and managers. The business publication *Wirtschaftswoche* reported on the eve of the election that western business managers were more "black" (i.e., conservative) than those in the East, and 6 percent of eastern business managers were voting PDS.[52] This was an increase from 1 percent in 1992, and is ascribed by the publication as due to "frustration" with Bonn's economic policies.

The loser designation is far broader than the term suggests. It applies to these voters' rejection of the system, not necessarily that they have failed to be employed in it. It can mean that they have a new and different employment than in the GDR, with either lower or higher status, though it can also mean that some are genuine losers, in the sense that they have not found a place. Richard Schröder describes the PDS as a "milieu party with elements of a self-help group, kept together by a common feeling of protest."[53] It is "no workers party, but rather one of civil servants and academics; no party of the unemployed, but rather one of pensioners and early-pensioners."

Many PDS voters are insecure about the changes since 1990. For 80 percent, the "joy of unification has been overshadowed by concern for the problems which unification has brought," even though half of these believe that the decision to opt for a western political system was correct.[54] Nevertheless, 80 percent of PDS voters believe that socialism has much to offer. Only 29 percent of all eastern German voters agree. About a third of PDS voters in the East describe themselves as far left (very left), and a further 55 percent as somewhat left. This is a self-description that is significantly further to the left than Greens or SPD voters. Further, 94 percent do not belong to any faith. While 40.6 percent of eastern German CDU voters were working class and 35.1 percent of SPD voters, only 14.7 percent of PDS voters in the East were working class.[55] PDS voters in the East have a generally far more pessimistic view of the economic situation and of their own personal economic future than other eastern Germans. They also have a far more negative perception of German political institutions, especially the government and the Bundestag.[56] Falter and Klein find this astonishing in view of the fact that it was only possible for the PDS to gain entry into the Bundestag in 1990 through a decision of a federal institution, the court in Karlsruhe.

In eastern Germany, those persons who most lack confidence and trust in political institutions are most likely to vote PDS. Similarly, the more negatively a voter judges political parties and the role of political parties, or suggests that parties have lost contact with the people, or decries corruption, the more likely that voter is to choose PDS. Those who responded to pollsters that parties have no goals other than to gain votes and secure power selected PDS two-to-one over other parties. Fifty-five percent of those who responded that they were "very unhappy" with the state of democracy voted PDS.

The PDS mobilized its membership and former membership, including as many of the former members of the SED as possible. But, to these, there were others added. Ernst-Michael Brandt, writing in *Die Woche*, contends that the younger voters and left intellectuals in the East who voted PDS would not have supported the SED and did not long for a return to the GDR.[57] They wanted to give western Germans a reason to think twice about the state of the nation and, particularly, the East. Verena Raduk complained that "we easterners are the new Jews of united Germany. I was never in the SED, was happy to be in the West, and wanted to take part in a new society. Those here who succeeded best in doing that were those who were fellow travellers before." Alliance 90/Greens floor leader in Saxony-Anhalt, Hans-Jochen Tschiche, put it this way: "The intellectuals and academics who support the Greens in the West vote for the PDS in the East, because they count themselves among the losers in unity."[58] Numerous polls have called attention to the strength of perceptions in eastern Germany that westerners look down on them and that the overall eastern economic situation is worse than it is.

While Raduk's view is extreme, a perception of being looked down on by the West does exist in the East, and is matched by a perception of some in the West who believe that they have already given much and expect more appreciation of having done so. Much has been given and is continuing to be provided. The economy in the East is growing faster than that in the West. However, the general level in the East has not yet matched that in the West, and many in the East have not enough background in understanding market societies to compare carefully. Such perceptions are normal in this kind of situation. Nevertheless, they give rise to a protest vote on both sides.

There is nothing in common between these voters and the Communist Platform in the PDS, a strong reason why the PDS program is so contradictory. Some eastern Germans in all parties were put off by the CDU campaign against "red socks" and "red-painted fascists." That seemed to put everybody who had been in the SED into one pot, it appeared to them. A number of analysts suggest that this increased a "sympathy vote" for the PDS. There is no question that the PDS pressed for a sympathy vote bonus. A majority of easterners, across all parties, did want to see the PDS in the Bundestag as a kind of representative of the East itself. The PDS played on this strongly in the campaign, and the CDU campaign against the PDS as an enemy of German democracy also is viewed by some analysts as having produced something of a backlash.

More easterners see the PDS as a democratic party than westerners. Asked if they think the PDS is democratic or whether they have doubts about it, Germans responded:[59]

	West German States (percent)	East German States (percent)
Normal democratic party	20	46
Doubtful	54	40
Not sure	26	14

Allensbach found that easterners are less likely to think that democracy as represented by the Federal Republic of Germany is the best form of government one can develop.

	West German States (percent)	East German States (percent)
Democracy best	76	31
There are others	9	28
Not sure	15	41

To the question whether socialism is a good idea, but one which has been improperly carried out in the past:

	West Germans (percent)	East Germans (percent)	PDS-Supporters (percent)
Yes	36	74	95
No	45	15	3
Not sure	19	11	2

The candidacy of Stefan Heym in the election district held by Wolfgang Thierse was a media spectacle which brought a number of issues to the fore. Why did Heym seek the seat, held by an active SPD eastern German who had successfully risen in his party since unification and was an outspoken voice for the East? Why did he run for the PDS as part of Gysi's "motley band"? Why would the voters choose this nonpolitician, an elderly author, to represent them? What would Heym do if elected to the Bundestag? To those questions, the erudite and intelligent writer flatly declined any answer. Answers to such questions were not only irrelevant, but beside the point or beneath him. In an interview with *Stern*, Heym queried: "If you say that the wrong people are voting for me, then I'll say to you that they're voting for the right man." "The PDS is really a new party." Why? "Because they put themselves behind me." If Honecker had listened to Heym, the GDR would still exist, he chortles. A lady in the audience asks Heym what his goals are. "Ah," he replies, "I have goals, but I left them at home and didn't bring them with me today." A couple of days later, he was still upset about that question. Why? "Because everybody knows my goals, and they know them fifty years now." The eastern German Konrad Weiss of Alliance 90/Greens blurted out in total frustration, "Do you think we East Germans are so dumb that we are content with this kind of pop answer?" Days later, Heym is asked again what he stands for. He responds: "Look at what kind of crazy things people ask me!" "My goals! For fifty years I have been writing books, and these are on shelves in my apartment. That's why I keep saying that I left my goals at home." Afterwards, asked if he couldn't just digest them or list them for the questioner, Heym replied that it was such a long list of goals, and he had never learned them by heart like Thierse, his SPD opponent, who memorized such things like a good schoolboy. "Aber ja, wie ein Shulbub." But, the interviewer asked, doesn't that sound arrogant? "Really, did it sound like that? Well, then, it was right." "Does this mean Heym is Heym—you just vote for Heym?" "Yes, that's about right."

The Israeli author Henryk M. Broder, writing in *Die Woche* under the pseudonym Sarah Silberstein, responded with dripping irony to dozens of Heym interviews, bemoaning the failure of politicians, analysts, political scientists, and others to come up with a satisfactory explanation for the total collapse of the GDR when Stefan Heym has it at hand. Heym has said, "The state did the contrary of what I had advised, and thereby destroyed itself."[61] Heym drew the votes. He was elected. So was Thierse. As many knew, Thierse would be elected anyway—on the SPD Land party list. By voting for Heym, they got both.[62] Heym was the critic, the "in your face" opposition. He also gave the PDS prominence, an image of being open, an anti-Stalinist image, all that the PDS needed to have in the election campaign. He served the party well. Asked if he would attend Bundestag sessions, Heym was not certain if he could be there very often. It would be onerous to participate in committee meetings.

The election of Heym in a district with a relatively large number of PDS members was less significant than the effect of his candidacy on voters nationwide, or especially in the East. Heym also personified the ambiguities in the PDS. He was a useful part of the "motley band," and the purpose in selecting him was to display the openness in the present, the self-criticism of harsh Stalinism in the GDR past, and to emphasize populist criticism of the established parties and the present state of Germany and its government. Heym has no influence within the party and represents no faction. As oldest member of the newly elected Bundestag, he delivered an opening address in the preliminary session of that body. There was much apprehension that he would say something outrageous, but the speech was merely a recitation of problems afflicting easterners, an endorsement of some further adoption of eastern traditions in the united Germany, and a plea that Germans, West and East, recognize each others' contributions. It was greeted with relief.

Long-Term Survival and Changes in the Party

The success of the PDS in the Bundestag elections gave impetus to the leadership under Bisky which sought to create conditions for the party's long-term survival. Bisky, Gysi, Modrow, and Brie were among those who understood that the dual strategy of 1994 might not be successful in 1998. It might not be possible to win enough directly elected seats again in the East. The districts which they had won had held a very high concentration of former SED members. Biologically, time was against them there. They could not count on that portion of their votes which came over from the former SED members over the long haul, either as absolute numbers in the districts they won directly or as a percentage of the total eastern vote. As these votes fell off, they would simultaneously lose directly elected seats and a portion of the eastern vote generally, unless those voters were replaced by others. Even without the directly elected Bundestag seats, they might hold on to regional influence for a longer period, but to remain in the Bundestag at all they needed votes in the West. Like the FDP, they would need to leap the 5 percent hurdle in order to survive. For national elections, those votes were in the West. There, however, the party had to reckon with the survivors of the DKP, the Communist Party, and with the other Communist groups who were active in the membership. Unless the PDS were to win more adherents from the socialist intellectual left and similar constituencies in the West, where the votes were, winning 5 percent in the next Bundestag elections would be hopeless.

Acknowledging that many of those who voted for the party did not reflect the party's actual membership, Bisky immediately called for a party congress in January 1995 which should burnish the PDS's image as a left-socialist party. Specifically, he wanted to have the congress reject Stalinism and remove the Communist Platform from the leadership. Others, who went further, wanted to have the conference declare the party open to anti-Communists as members. These included the newly elected Bundestag deputy Zwerenz, who described himself as an "ex-Communist anti-Communist."

The party congress opened in Berlin on the weekend of 28 January. Bisky, the only candidate, was elected party leader with 317 of the 383 possible votes. Although he was the only candidate, the opposition to his reelection was significant. He had declared that he would only stand for the post if the congress enacted a basic document that addressed the crucial theme of further expansion in western Germany and changes necessary to do that. He wanted the Communist Platform removed from the party leadership, as well as a repudiation of "Stalinism." This was essential if the party were to continue to attempt to present a left-socialist image.

Sahra Wagenknecht, leader of the Communist Platform, refused to back down. The party leadership had prepared a position paper with ten theses for the congress to discuss.[63] These were criticized as "too social democratic," and had to be withdrawn, lest a "fiasco" develop.[64] There were bitter discussions, and Zwerenz threatened to resign his seat in the Bundestag if anti-Communists were not specifically permitted to remain in the party.[65] Bisky, Modrow, Gysi, and Brie represented the broader course, but it was not smooth sailing. Brie failed to be elected as federal party manager, and over a third of the delegates voted for Sahra Wagenknecht. Gysi was photographed by the press sitting dejectedly in front of a poster that railed against the "cult of personality," obviously intended as a criticism of him.

The congress decided to compromise. Five points replaced the ten theses. The points stressed the "socialist" character of the PDS, its oppositional character until a "change" in Germany along "democratic, social, ecological, and civil-societal" lines is effected, its commitment to pluralism, as well as the party's relationship to its past and to possible cooperation with the SPD and the Alliance 90/Greens.[66] The Communists were not elected to the leadership. In the final document, nationalist, chauvinist, racist, anti-Semitic, and also anti-Communist perspectives were declared incompatible with membership in the PDS.[67] "Stalinism," however, was repudiated. The PDS "declared itself open for democratic-communist positions," whatever that meant.[68] It was decided to have another party congress six months later in Bremen, in the West, where they had done so comparatively well in 1994.

Bisky's position, supported by Gysi and Hans Modrow, holds that the PDS has genuine chances of winning support in the West and of holding on as a permanent fixture on the German political scene. In the West, Bisky sees the possibility of picking up voters who see the party as a left-socialist alternative to the Social Democrats, even among Social Democrats who might be concerned that there are too many pressures on their party to move towards the center-right in order to win the chancellorship. In the view of these Social Democrats, a left-socialist party might act as a weight, pulling the party back towards the left. At the same time, the FDP is in genuine danger of disappearing. With successive losses in Land elections, followed by a poor showing in the Bundestag election, the party has been greatly weakened. Seeing this, some CDU/CSU politicians have been urging a new look at the Alliance 90/Greens as a potential coalition partner. These have also been casting interesting glances at the Union parties. In 1994 Joschka Fischer made a number of speeches and wrote several articles in which he took foreign policy positions close to those of the government in many respects. Should the

Alliance 90/Greens move closer to the Union, then they might continue to gain support from voters of the failing Liberals while losing at the same time some of their more fundamental adherents, who would then be candidates for absorption by the PDS. This is not as far-fetched as it might have seemed a year ago. How the PDS would extend as a national party into the West and still keep its perspective to most easterners as an eastern party would be a difficult balancing act for the leadership. Yet, this is their goal. Angela Marquardt, however, and others in the PDS, see a different goal. For them, contacts with the Alternative List in Berlin and with others in the fundamentalist left offer a better opportunity. The party congress failed to set a clear direction for the party, except to expand in the West. Reconciling differences was postponed.

Given the precarious situation of the FDP, the increasing Liberal support for the Alliance 90/Greens, and the desire of some Social Democrats to accept the existence of the PDS as a left-socialist pressure element on their party, there is a small chance for the PDS in the West. With some Social Democrats seeing a possibility of a grand alliance left of the Union parties, and most eastern voters viewing the PDS as a party with no less a right to participation in government than the established parties, some other alternatives for the SPD arise with permanence of the PDS, however dangerous they are. In a way, the futures of the FDP and the PDS are also linked. Should the PDS survive in the West and absorb left-socialist or fundamentalist elements from the Alliance 90/Greens, that party would be drawn even further to the center, attracting even more Liberals from the FDP. If this took place, the FDP would shrink further, while the Alliance 90/Greens would become increasingly attractive to the CDU as a coalition partner. Thus, the survival of the PDS in the West could also affect the future of the FDP. These, however, are issues of electoral geometry and do not take account of the PDS program and its goals, merely its potential electorate.

The PDS is not only a socialist party, but a socialist party which has endorsed "democratic communism." Repudiation of Stalinism is hardly a revolution. Although the fourth party congress revealed considerable disagreement, the PDS is also still not a democratic party. Karin Dörre, member of the party Federal Executive, criticized the PDS leadership in 1994, complaining that the party is governed "just like the SED."[69] The party, she claimed, is becoming less democratic rather than more, the Federal Executive plays no meaningful role, and had nothing to say in who would be a candidate for the Bundestag. Dörre worries that the inner leadership is thoroughly permeated with old *Stasi* personnel, and that major decisions are taken by a very small group of individuals. On the other hand, even that group has faced strong opposition from the party membership, which clearly is not wholly sympathetic with a reformist course that would take it further from its original Communist base. Rainer Eckert, a scholar at the Humboldt University in Berlin, maintains that the "influence of reactionary-Stalinist forces in the PDS has [actually] increased."[70]

Conclusion

Despite inner contradictions, the Party of Democratic Socialism has thus far been able to mobilize a voting base among former supporters and members of the SED and combine these with new voters in the East and in the West in its effort to avoid a biological death and win election not only to the Bundestag but to state legislatures in the East. The party leadership is determined to guarantee permanence on the German political scene, and to assure a possible breakout beyond the old SED voter base that will propel it to the level of coalition partner in Land governments as it expands in the West. It has already achieved victories in city council and mayoralty elections. Therefore, it is highly concerned about both a democratic appearance and an aggressive populist stance that enables it to criticize and to initiate. The most obvious hindrance to the efforts of the leadership is the party membership. Although it is unlikely that the party will split, a significant segment of the membership and the active cadres remains opposed to weakening the SED tradition and the principles of Marxism-Leninism and is not supportive of the democratic German state.

The PDS has broken out of the SED. It has made inroads among younger voters, and enjoys a left-socialist and populist stance that belies the underlying communism of many of its traditional voters and which is attractive to SPD voters and even to some of the Greens. Hans-Jochen Tschiche laments cautiously that there is no room on the German political scene for *two* reform parties to the left of the SPD.

Some adherents of the SPD see it as a useful, or at least unavoidable, part of German electoral geometry. Others, such as party leader Rudolf Scharping, urge a harder stance that would keep it isolated. Will it survive and achieve permanence? Will it remain both an eastern regional party and succeed simultaneously in becoming a national party? These are questions that cannot now be answered. However, the leadership is aware of the dangers and is steering the party towards what it considers the best way to permanence. Not all of the Communist backing for the party is elderly. Neither Sahra Wagenknecht nor others in the AG fit this stereotype. Thus, the PDS remains the party of German communism just as much as it is the party of "democratic socialism."

Notes

1. *Frankfurter Allgemeine Zeitung*, 31 August 1995, p. 5.

2. "Die PDS als Verführung für die Unzufriedenen," by Prof. Dr. Richard Schröder, *Frankfurter Allgemeine Zeitung*, 16 September 1994.

3. In 1992 the PDS had assets of DM438.7 million, followed by the SPD with DM276.8 million, and the CDU with DM109.2 million. See *This Week in Germany*, 20 January 1995, p. 5.

4. Richard Schröder, "Hemmungslos populistisch," in *Die Zeit* 29 (15 July 1994).

5. Manfred Gerner, *Partei ohne Zukunft? Von der SED zur PDS* (Munich: Tilsner, 1994), 116, 127.

6. Patrick Moreau and Viola Neu, *Die PDS zwischen Linksextremismus und Linkspopulismus* (Sankt Augustin: Konrad-Adenauer-Stiftung, 1994), 19, who cite the work of Willy Koch and Oskar Niemeyer in Leipzig, *Parteimitglieder in Leipzig* (Mannheim, 1991) and Patrick Moreau and Jürgen Lang, *Was will die PDS?* (Frankfurt a.M: Ullstein, 1994).

7. See Sahra Wagenknecht, *Antisozialistische Strategien im Zeitalter der Systemauseinandersetzung* (Bonn: Pahl-Rugenstein, 1995).

8. See *Das Programm der PDS: Eine sozialistische Partei in Deutschland.*

9. *FAZ*, 22 September 1994.

10. Manfred Gerner, *Partei ohne Zukunft? Von der SED zur PDS* (Munich: Tilsner, 1994), 222–25.

11. Interview with the author, February 1990.

12. *Programm der Partei des Demokratischen Sozialismus (PDS)*, January 1993, p. 1.

13. *1993 Programm*, 2–3.

14. Ibid., p. 70.

15. *Europa braucht Frieden, Arbeit, und Demokratie*, Election Program for the European Parliament, in *Pressedienst* 11/12, p. 27.

16. *Wahlprogramm der PDS 1994*, 4.

17. Ibid., 3. The program uses the initials BRD (Bundesrepublik Deutschland). During the existence of the GDR, it was common practice in the GDR to use initials for both states, to emphasize equality between the two. In the West, initials were generally used only for the GDR, and the words "Bundesrepublik Deutschland" were almost always written out, to distinguish between the two, and to oppose any idea of equality. The PDS continues to follow the practice of initials. The newspapers in the West owned by Axel Springer referred to the GDR only in quotation marks ("DDR"), something retained until only months before the fall of the Berlin Wall made unification possible. Such forms, sometimes scarcely understood in the United States, were common in serious discussions of the German Question, maintaining the legal and formal distinctions that held open the issue of unity, denied the existence of separate GDR citizenship, and made it possible for eastern Germans to claim a passport from Bonn as a right.

18. Lothar Bisky, quoted in *Frankfurter Allgemeine Zeitung*, 13 September 1994, p. 4., and public letter from Gregor Gysi to voters, "Mit Ihrer Zweitstimme," n.d.

19. *Linke (wieder) im Bundestag* (Bonn: Bundestagsgruppe PDS, 1994).

20. *Wahlprogramm der PDS 1994*, 3–5.

21. See report of Rita Süßmuth, President of the Bundestag, as cited in *TWIG*, 20 January 1995, p. 2.

22. *Welt am Sonntag*, 19 June 1995, p. 26.

23. Interview with Sylvia Kaufmann, Vice-Chair of the PDS, Berlin, November 1994.

24. 10 October 1994, p. 23.

25. 4 July 1994, title page.

26. *Stern* 41 (6 October 1994): 190.

27. *Nordkurier*, 8 August 1994, p. 11.

28. Interview in *Focus* 48 (18 November 1994): 25.

29. Poppe is a constant critic of the PDS and of Gregor Gysi. See *Wochenpost*, 10 November 1994, p. 9.

30. Schröder, *Die Zeit*, 29 (15 July 1994).

31. Bisky's speech, *Auf daß der Wind sich drehe*, is printed in *Pressedienst PDS* 11/12 (25 March 1994): 3–14. He concludes, "Schnallt euch fest, Girls und Boys!"

32. See "In Hundorf herrscht die PDS," in *FAZ*, 13 October 1994.

33. *Bundestagswahl 1994: Eine Analyse der Wahl* (Mannheim, Forschungsgruppe Wahlen e.V., 1994), No. 76, 21 October 1994, Second Edition, 70.

34. *Berliner Morgenpost*, 13 November 1994.

35. The Communist Party has about 7,000 members and did not offer candidates for the Bundestag election in order to assist the PDS. See *Frontal*, 20 September 1994.

36. Daniel Deckers in *FAZ*, 8 October 1994, p. 3.

37. German television program *Report*, 7 July 1994.

38. *Hannoversche Allgemeine Zeitung*, 6–7 August 1994, p. 13.

39. *Deutsche Presse Agentur (DPA)* news report, 2 February 1995.

40. Jürgen W. Falter and Markus Klein, "Die Wähler der PDS bei der Bundestagswahl 1994," in *Aus Politik und Zeitgeschichte*, B51–52/94 (23 December 1994): 24.

41. *FAZ*, 22 September 1994.

42. Interview of the author with Sylvia-Yvonne Kaufmann, Vice-Chair of the PDS, in Berlin, November 1994.

43. *FAZ*, 31 August 1994, p. 5.

44. Falter and Klein, 24.

45. *Forschungsgruppe Wahlen*, 70, and Falter and Klein, 24, have very slightly different figures.

46. See efforts of the PDS to retain kindergartens, issues surrounding choice of county seat, and other examples of local activities of the PDS in Thomas Falkner and Dietmar Huber, *Aufschwung PDS: Rote Socken—zurück zur Macht* (Munich: Knaur, 1994), 58ff. Also, *FAZ*, "An der Seite der Bekümmerten," 8 August 1994, p. 8.

47. *Nordkurier*, 26 August 1994, p. 11.

48. Falter and Klein, 28.

49. *Forschungsgruppe Wahlen*, 71.

50. Cited in *Tango, Fremd im eigenen Land* (1995), 34.

51. 17 October 1994, p. 17.

52. Schröder, *FAZ*.

53. *Forschungsgruppe Wahlen*, 71.

54. Ibid., 22.

55. See Falter and Klein, p. 28.

56. 16 June 1994, p. 6.

57. *Der Spiegel* 38 (1994): 26.

58. *Allensbach-Archiv*, IfD-Umfrage 5109/19, June 1994, cited in *Institut für Demoskopie Allensbach*, "Ein demoskopisches Portrait der PDS-Anhänger von Elisabeth Noelle-Neumann. The next questions and responses are taken from this survey as well.

59. *Stern* interview with Heym, 41 (6 October 1994): 196ff.

60. *Die Woche*, 25 August 1994.

61. Local interviews with the author.

62. *Neues Deutschland*, 6 December 1994, pp. 13–14.

63. Lorenz Maroldt, "Wie man künftig demokratisch sein wird," in *Das Parlament*, 3 February 1995, p. 9.

64. *Disput*, 3/4 1995, 1/2 Februarheft, pp. 53–57.

65. *Neues Deutschland*, 14/15 January 1995, p. 5.

66. *Deutsche Presse Agentur Bericht*, 28 January 1995.

67. *Neues Deutschland*, 30 January 1995, p. 1.

68. "Wie in der SED," in *Der Spiegel* 37, pp. 23–25.

69. *Focus*, 13 February 1995, p. 38. See also Armin Pfahl-Traughber and Jürgen P. Lang, "PDS im Wandel?," im Deutschland Archiv 28/4 (April 1995), p. 375.

70. *Focus*, 13 February 1995, p. 38.

12

WHAT'S LEFT OF THE RIGHT?

THE NEW RIGHT AND THE SUPERWAHLJAHR 1994
IN PERSPECTIVE

MICHAEL MINKENBERG

Introduction

After their electoral failures in 1990, the short and turbulent
career of the far-right party Republikaner seemed over.[1] However, only two years later, they became the third largest party in the
state parliament of Baden-Württemberg (10.9 percent of the vote).
In the same year, the Deutsche Volksunion (DVU), a more outspo-
kenly right-wing extremist party, entered the parliament of Schleswig-
Holstein (6.3 percent). Thus, by the beginning of Superwahljahr, the
parties of the New Right were present in three state parliaments (the
DVU had entered the Bremen Bürgerschaft in 1991 with 6.2 percent) and the European Parliament (the Republikaner had gained 7.1
percent in 1989). Moreover, Republikaner delegates were elected
into numerous city and district councils in a variety of West German
local elections (e.g., North Rhine-Westphalia 1989, Bayern 1990,
Berlin 1992, Hesse 1993). These electoral developments were
accompanied by corresponding support patterns in public opinion:
beginning with a surge in public support in January 1992 and until
early 1994, around 4 to 5 percent of the public expressed an intention
to vote for the Republikaner, whereas the share of those expressing
"sympathy" for them was almost twice as large.[2]

However, with the Hamburg state elections in September 1993
(the last election before 1994), a decline set in for the New Right parties that ended in their complete electoral insignificance throughout
the Superwahljahr. The Republikaner—not to mention the Deutsche
Volksunion and the Nationaldemokratische Partei Deutschlands

(NPD)—suffered massive defeats and failed to enter or reenter parliaments in *any* of the state, national, or European elections. In fact, the actual results in the most important of these elections document a steady decline for the Republikaner: 4.8 percent of the vote in the Hamburg elections in 1993 (plus 2.8 percent for the DVU); 3.7 percent in the Lower Saxony elections in March 1994 (up from 1.5 percent in 1990); 3.9 percent in the European elections in June 1994; 3.8 percent in the Bavarian elections in September 1994, and 1.9 percent in the Federal elections in October 1994. Also, on 16 October 1994, most Republikaner delegates lost their seats in city and district councils in North Rhine-Westphalia after this state's local elections. What are the reasons for this sharp drop? Did the Germans finally learn a lesson and return to democratic normalcy?

An attempt to answer these questions must take into account that, in obvious contrast to other chapters in this volume, this essay is faced with the challenge of addressing a nonevent. Given the electoral results and a comparatively thin body of data on the right wing's performance in 1994, a focus on the Superwahljahr alone—and on the campaign and strategy of the Republikaner—limits our understanding of the outcome and its meaning. Instead, I have chosen a perspective that puts the rise of the Republikaner and their decline in 1994 into a broader historical context.

In this essay, I argue that the New Right was electorally insignificant in 1994 because of the substantial diminishing of their opportunity structures, i.e., their place in the structure of the German party competition.[3] However, this does not mean an end to right-wing politics in Germany. The rise of the New Right—embodied by the electoral successes of the Republikaner, the NPD, and the DVU since 1989—is a structural phenomenon and different from previous waves of right-wing extremism in Germany. A new cleavage and new lines of partisan conflict have resulted in a weakening of voter loyalties to all established parties and a partial realignment to new parties. The opportunity structures of the New Right were diminished in 1994 by the dialectical relationship between the New Right and the established parties, i.e., a radicalization process in which the latter moved to the right along the new conflict dimension. As a result, the internal problems of the New Right, such as organizational disarray, became highlighted and more consequential in 1994. For the time being, right-wing politics is executed from within the political establishment. But the structural changes which brought about the rise of the New Right have not disappeared. There is still a considerable right-wing vote potential, and for how long the New Right has been contained remains an open question.

I elaborate this argument by first putting the rise of the New Right into the context of the parameters of right-wing politics in Germany and the structural electoral changes in Western democracies which began *before* the fall of the Berlin Wall but were accelerated by the consequences of 1989. Then I will highlight the role of unification for right-wing politics in Germany before discussing the structural and strategic limitations for the New Right in 1994.

The Nature of Right-Wing Politics in Germany

There is widespread evidence of a sizable right-wing potential in the West German public since the founding of the Bonn Republic. The first comprehensive public opinion survey measuring right-wing attitudes, conducted only thirty-five years after the end of the Nazi regime, revealed that 13 percent of the West German public (eighteen years or older) had a coherent right-wing ideology and that a third of the population could be categorized as authoritarian.[4] Likewise, other studies have shown a considerable degree of anti-Semitism, xenophobia, and racism in the West German public.[5]

In fact, some have argued that all fast-growing industrial societies have a latent right-wing potential, as a "normal pathological condition" which is mobilized in times of accelerated change. People that cannot cope with the dynamics of rapid cultural and socioeconomic change react to the pressures of readjustment with rigidity and closed-mindedness. These reactions can be brought out by extremist movements or parties offering political philosophies that promise an elimination of pressures and a simpler, better society by scapegoating and referring to romanticized images of the country's past.[6]

In the case of West Germany, some peculiarities must be taken into account. First, the Nazi past puts considerable constraints on openly mobilizing a right-wing electorate. These include political constraints, such as taboos and commitments to democracy among major political actors, and institutional constraints, such as the German electoral law's 5 percent hurdle or the Constitutional Court's possible outlawing of extremist parties. As a result, the right-wing vote potential in the Bonn Republic was usually absorbed by the major parties. The CDU/CSU, unlike other conservative parties in Western democracies, remained particularly concerned with appealing to the right wing and absorbing this vote potential.

Only once, in the second half of the 1960s, did an extreme-right party manage to organize a "national opposition" to the Bonn system parties and exploit an anti-system effect in the context of the Bonn Republic's first major economic crisis. The Nationaldemokratische Partei Deutschlands, NPD, attracted mainly troubled members of the old middle class in areas which had given disproportionately high support to the NSDAP during the Great Depression. Quite a few members and functionaries of the NPD had been Nazis themselves in the Third Reich.[7] But the NPD's sudden rise was followed by a sudden collapse both in terms of electoral failure and organizational breakdown.[8]

Second, right-wing politics in Germany operates on the basis of a particular concept of nationhood in which national identity is still defined in terms of an ethnic German *Volksgemeinschaft*. As a consequence, the German nation has been and still is a variant of a "*Kulturnation*" in which membership can only be acquired through belonging to the ethnically and culturally defined community of Germans. In contrast, the French or American concept is that of a "political nation" in which membership is defined in terms of the adherence to political principles and a particular history and tradition, regardless of the ethnic or religious makeup of the people.[9] This German peculiarity is not only identifiable in persisting patterns in the German political culture and racist attitudes in the German public.[10] It is, above all, anchored institutionally in the German citizenship laws which define what it means to be German in ethnic or blood-related terms of the *ius sanguinis* (Article 116 of the Basic Law). This concept of "citizenship as social closure" (Brubaker) institutionalizes the exclusion of non-Germans from the German citizenry and legitimizes the continuation of a *völkisch*, or ethnically based, nationalism not just among splinter groups, but across the larger political spectrum and major parties.

The New Right in Comparative Perspective[11]

Efforts to reaffirm this traditional concept of German nationhood and the related rise of the New Right took place in the context of fundamental social and cultural changes that affected various Western democracies during the 1970s and 1980s. The transition of Western capitalism into a phase of advanced industrial capitalism, or "postindustrialism"; the exhaustion of the welfare state; and a cultural shift which challenged established social values, lifestyles, and institutions brought about a new dynamism in Western politics that opened up opportunities for new parties on the left and right, with the latter mobilizing the "normal pathological" right-wing potential. The decline of blue-collar and agrarian occupations in a continuously shrinking productionist sector of the economy, along with the rise of white-collar occupations and the service sector, resulted in a weakening of the class cleavage. Social class-based voting patterns and corresponding partisan conflicts between left and right were further neutralized by an intergenerational value change. Large portions of younger, better-educated cohorts developed so-called "postmaterialist" value priorities, defined as personal freedom, democratization of political and community life, and a less impersonal society, over "materialist" values of general economic growth, wealth, and the maintaining of political order. Progressive, largely postmaterialist, new social movements and new parties emerged, defined here as a "New Left," which opposed the Vietnam War, struggled for women's and minority rights and new lifestyles, and promoted environmentalism and grass-roots democracy.[12] Particular effects of the emerging new value-based cleavage on party politics included a weakening of voter loyalties, an increase in issue-based voting, and voter volatility, especially among younger, postmaterialist voters.[13]

As a response to the rise of postmaterialism and the New Left, influential élites and a large proportion of Western publics have "turned" to the right in a Mannheimian sense.[14] They "rediscovered" traditional and materialist values and the Old Politics agenda of economic growth, technological progress, and a stable order (as their political philosophy.) The novelty of this mounting conservative response does not lie in the issues or the underlying philosophy itself, but in the fact that it is an alliance of traditionally left-of-center groups, both at the élite and at the mass level, with traditionally conservative groups against the challenge on the new, value-based conflict axis, i.e., the New Politics dimension. This "neoconservatism" reflects the materialist end of the new cleavage. It is not simply the revival of traditional conservatism in the Old Politics sense—i.e., opposition to the welfare state and to the redistribution of income, or the return of church-based religious traditionalism—but a new coalition of forces which see their common enemy in the postmaterialist New Left and its political agenda.

The parties of the New Right radicalize this neoconservative reaction and fuse its tenets with a populist, antiestablishment, and antiparty thrust. Thus, the New Right is not simply the extension of conservatism towards the extreme right but the product of a restructuring of

the political spectrum and a regrouping of the party system. Constituencies of established parties tend to realign according to the
New Politics cleavage rather than the Old Politics cleavage. In the
context of European politics, the immigration issue serves as a signi-
fier for this radicalization to the right around which significant portions of the electorate can be mobilized.[15]

The Changing Discourse on German National Identity

The emergence of the New Right in Germany took place in the context of a related but larger cultural change that resulted in a more
"Westernized" political culture. Among the new, postmaterialist generation that was raised under the conditions of economic well-being
and stable democracy, demands arose for more democracy and new
forms of citizen involvement in politics, thereby enriching the democratic project in West Germany. The student rebellion of 1968 and
the subsequent march through the institutions, new social movements, citizen groups, and finally the new party of the Greens, i.e.,
the New Left, challenged established political and cultural norms, in
particular, traditional German patterns of authoritarian culture and
élite-directed politics, and introduced a debate on integrating foreigners and multiculturalism.

In the context of new economic uncertainties and the emergence
of the "two-thirds society" in the early 1980s, neoconservative cultural and political élites launched efforts to define German national
identity in opposition to the New Left's approach to a postnational
identity and a "constitutional patriotism" by emphasizing the traditions of a German *Kulturnation* and a *völkisch* nationalism. The
promises of the Kohl government, after its takeover in 1982, to introduce a spiritual and moral turn of the country, the Bitburg incident
and similar government actions, and the efforts to make the German
past relative in the *Historikerstreit* all illustrate the recourse to an all-
German history in order to recreate a national consciousness that
was not confined to the republican principles of the Basic Law and to
the Federal Republic. As Michael Stürmer, historian and advisor to
the chancellor, put it blatantly: "In a land without history, the future
is won by those who supply memory, shape concepts, and interpret
the past."[16]

These efforts were accompanied by a political debate on immigration, asylum, and foreigners in Germany which served the purpose of defining a German identity by fighting the concept of

multiculturalism, by denying the reality of immigration, and by raising fears among Germans of being "swamped" by aliens and their cul-
tures. This debate was seasoned with statistics on the rising numbers
of illegal aliens, the exploding costs of immigration and asylum, the
dramatic increase of crime and violence as a result of foreigners in the
country that fueled the public rage long before the rise of the Republikaner, the fall of the Wall, and a new wave of East-West migration.[17]

In fact, this debate produced the terms of a political discourse
which later served the Republikaner as a platform for political mobilization and further radicalization to the right and shaped the public's interpretation of post-unification immigration. In the interplay
of conservative élites and mass media, foreigners and asylum seekers
were defined as a "problem" in which refugees functioned as a threat
rather than a responsibility.[18] In the course of the 1980s, the pejora-
tive term *Asylanten* came to signify a grouping of asylum seekers as
people not characterized by their political status but by distinctions
such as skin color. From here, it was only a short step to "naturalize"
various cultural differences (religion, customs) into implicitly racial
ones which were impossible to reconcile with the German *Volk*.[19] In
the end, this also meant downplaying the legitimacy of Turkish guest
workers on the grounds of their "otherness" who, unlike *Asylanten*,
had been credited as contributing to the German economy.

In various respects, the year 1989 stands as a watershed year in
West German history. A new public discourse had emerged that
addressed a fundamental question of national identity: would the
Bonn Republic follow the universal and republican principles of its
political traditions and constitution and arrive at a postnational identity, thus recognizing a multicultural society and a new concept of
citizenship? Or would the neoconservative approach to recast the
Bonn Republic and its political culture in terms of an all-German history and an ethnically and exclusively defined national identity pre-
vail? As it turned out, it was not the West German electorate but the
East Germans in the GDR who gave the answer with their call for the
restoration of the German nation-state—the *demos* ("*Wir sind das
Volk!*") giving way to the *ethnos* ("*Wir sind ein Volk!*").

The New Right as a Structural Phenomenon in German Politics

The discourse on German national identity and the role of immigration was fed by, and fed back into, the rearrangement of the West

German party system in which the emergence of a postmaterialist New Left was countered by the rise of a New Right. Already in the early 1980s, there were two quite distinct ideological dimensions in the German mass public reflecting Old Politics and New Politics concerns based on changing cleavage structures. At the right-wing end of the Old Politics dimension, old conservatism clearly reflects concerns of traditional CDU/CSU voters, that is, the old middle class and Catholics, whereas in the New Politics dimension a "neo-conservatism" was mostly determined by low levels of education and materialist value orientations that cut across party lines.[20]

By 1989 the ties of these "neoconservatives" to the established parties had weakened to a degree that many were ready to vote for the Republikaner. The demographic profile of the supporters of the Republikaner and of those voting for the NPD or DVU stresses the notion that these parties had mobilized the right-wing pole of the New Politics conflict axis, which includes working class and middle class, union and nonunion voters alike. The cross-cutting nature of the New Right vote is demonstrated by the fact that even in the 1989 Berlin and European elections, about 40 percent of the Republikaner voters had previously voted for the CDU/CSU, 20 percent for the SPD.[21] This pattern of previous party affiliation among voters for the New Right continued into the time after unification.[22] Along with support from union members and Catholics, the disproportional attractiveness of the New Right to members of the younger generation is another structural feature not present in earlier waves of right-wing extremism in West Germany.

New Right voters can be characterized by a more general sense of insecurity, exacerbated by fears of social and economic marginalization and of the "threat" of immigration, together with materialist value orientations and political alienation, rather than by traditional cleavage factors, such as social class, religiosity, or bread-and-butter issues.[23] These voters represent the "normal pathological condition" in Western democracies (see above) and are driven by their own feelings about problems of adaptation to modernization processes and a fear of losing status and entitlements in a more dynamic and complex world. In their electoral choice, xenophobia and racism mix with this defense of social entitlements, or *Wohlstandschauvinismus*.

In sum, the mobilization of electoral support for the parties of the New Right in West Germany as well as in other Western democracies is a consequence of a structural change. The rise of the New Right differs from previous waves of right-wing extremism in Germany because of its different personnel and demographic support patterns which draw voters from CDU/CSU *and* SPD. This characteristic has an important impact on the place in the structure of German party competition. Unlike in earlier waves when the exchange of voters happened primarily between the CDU/CSU and the radical right, *both* major parties are affected and under pressure to react. Moreover, the CDU/CSU is now in a position to strategically play the New Right card against the SPD by putting pressure on it to conform to right-wing policies.

The Dialectics on the Right I: The New Right and Unification

By coopting part of the New Right agenda instead of fighting it, the established parties SPD and CDU/CSU have moved the political spectrum to the right along the New Politics dimension. The first occasion for cooperation for the established parties was the process of German unification in 1989–90. Before 1989, the Republikaner tried to establish themselves as the party of German unification and traditional German national identity and, thereby, find their place in the political spectrum.[24] With unification, the Republikaner lost their original theme to the Bonn government and have since focused more on immigration issues.

However, unification hurt *and* helped the New Right after 1990. It hurt the New Right by undermining the momentum it had acquired in 1989 and providing for the subsequent failures in the 1990 elections. Moreover, with unification, the New Right faced a structural constraint in the addition of an East German electorate which, despite its high levels of xenophobia,[25] was less receptive to the New Right than the West German one. As in the series of elections in 1990, the Republikaner, contrary to their initial expectations, scored significantly lower in eastern than in western state and countywide elections throughout 1994. Moreover, the Republikaner failed to build up an effective party organization in the East, with only about 2,000 members as compared to more than 20,000 members in the West.[26]

The Republikaner's limited electoral appeal in the East stems from a variety of factors. In general, despite some signs of economic recovery in the new Länder, party politics four years after unification is still more distrusted in the East than in the West.[27] While lower turnout in the East has benefited the PDS, it did not translate into a rise in the vote for the Republikaner. It has been suggested that the GDR's antifascist regime ideology has produced an immunity in the East

German public's receptivity to right-wing propaganda and a resistance to voting for the New Right because of their links with the Nazi past.[28] Such a view, however, does not explain the similarly high levels of xenophobia in East and West and the reportedly higher levels of right-wing violence. Nor does it take into account the different natures of the right-wing electorate in East and West. The Republikaner, in terms of their West German voters' concerns and despite their activists' rhetoric, are the party of a West German defensive nationalism. Far from expressing national solidarity with the easterners and a willingness to sacrifice, the Republikaner voters in the West see the newly added East German cocitizens and their massive financial and other needs as a threat, rather than as an enrichment (or even fulfillment) of national dreams. Besides Greens party and PDS voters, and for very different reasons, it was and is above all Republikaner voters who look at unification and its consequences with skepticism rather than joy.[29]

Comparisons between eastern and western German right-wing voters or the right's electoral potential in both parts of the country, confirm this point. The eastern "ideal type" of a right-wing voter is most often male and significantly younger, has fewer denominational preferences and a comparatively higher level of education, and is more worried about losing his job than his western counterpart.[30] The proportion of eastern German right-wing voters is significantly smaller than the western portion, as is borne out in all public opinion surveys since unification and, in particular, the electoral results in 1994. Thus, the all-German performance of the Republikaner is structurally hampered by its lower appeal in the East.[31]

In the West, however, unification reinforced those dynamics which brought about the rise of the New Right and reaffirmed a traditional sense of German nationhood. The solution of the German question and the 1990 restoration of the *Staatsnation* of Bismarckian heritage coincided with a new wave of immigration to Germany. Rather than restoring the public's confidence in the established parties, the policy of unification and its consequences have only added to the perceived lack of competence. The discussion about the *Steuerlüge* (tax lie), the confusion in financing unification, and the hysterical debate on immigration and the asylum law demonstrate this. The pressure on the established parties to react reached its high point at the end of 1992, after a series of antiforeigner attacks (most notably the riots in Rostock and the arson murder in Mölln) and the

New Right parties' electoral successes in the state elections of Schleswig-Holstein and Baden-Württemberg.

The Dialectics on the Right II: The New Right and the Asylum Debate

The major parties' handling of the asylum debate in 1992–93 demonstrates most tellingly the political spectrum's shift to the right on the New Politics dimension, thereby diminishing the political space in which New Right parties in Germany can legitimately operate. After unification it appeared that the established right and the New Right were in an antagonistic relationship, competing for the same potential vote. But the nature of the New Politics cleavage suggests that they were in a dialectical relationship into which the SPD was also drawn, since it too had an electorate susceptible to the parties of the New Right.[32] The New Right used more extremist rhetoric and politicized the asylum debate to a degree where the CDU's own hard-line position seemed a legitimate compromise. This made it difficult for the SPD to reject it. The alternative discourse on German identity, articulated before 1989 by the New Left in both the SPD and the Greens, was abandoned by the SPD. A de facto Grand Coalition of CDU/CSU, FDP, and SPD reached a compromise in late 1992 and amended the Basic Law's asylum paragraph in 1993. Thus, the SPD gave in to the right-wing interpretation of the asylum issue and gave up its insistence on linking a change in the Basic Law on asylum with a liberalization of citizenship and immigration policies.

Though asylum and immigration were just one set of issues relating to German national identity, they were particularly appropriate to the agenda of the right. *Asylanten* helped delegitimize the entire project of multiculturalism and integration and were successfully linked to rising crime und unemployment.[33] Both the alleged crime rate of foreigners and the right-wing excesses in 1992–93 served as a reinforcement of law and order policies by the Bonn government, again with open and tacit support of the SPD.[34] Moreover, CDU/CSU leaders continuously tried to cater to nationalists by emphasizing the priority of national interests, at times in contradiction to the government's official European policy.[35] Corresponding to these policy and rhetorical shifts, "foreigners" have been replaced by "unemployment" as the western German public's number one problem since late 1993.[36] Thus by 1994, the political opportunity structures for the parties of the New Right had been substantially diminished.

The New Right's Homemade Constraints: Ideology and Organization

As a result of the shrinking opportunity structures of the New Right, its resource problems in ideology and organization became more visible in 1994. A comparison of the Republikaner's five party platforms from 1983 to 1993 reveals that the party walks a line between pro-system and anti-system positions. Their official commitment to the Basic Law is seasoned with calls for the direct election of the federal president and for national referenda.[37] This seemingly democratic orientation contrasts with the repeated stress on the priority of the German people—the ethnically defined *Volk*, its nation and the state—over special group interests, individual rights, and party loyalties. This essentially antiliberal and antipluralist thrust is hardly reconcilable with various republican principles of the Basic Law. Moreover, the rejection of local and other voting rights for non-Germans (including EC citizens) and the call for an immediate stop of immigration reflect underlying xenophobia that wants a German state for ethnically defined German citizens. Finally, the 1993 platform does not recognize the German-Polish border of 1990 but calls for a "completion" of German unification with the eastern territories. The platform repeatedly refers to the five new Länder as "*Mitteldeutschland,*" or Central Germany, and to unification as "partial reunification."[38]

Clearly, the New Right voters' right-wing views, which consist of a large dose of political alienation, racism and xenophobia, extreme national pride, and a rather apologetic view of Germany's Nazi past, corresponded to many of these or other positions that the New Right has to offer.[39] However, besides its irrelevance to eastern Germans, the New Right's ideology, without the immigration issue and with the established parties' tougher image on law and order, has lost most of its distinctiveness and legitimacy in the West, as well. At the same time, its more controversial aspects, such as its questionable commitment to democracy and a strategic drift to the right, have become more visible. Thus, during the 1994 campaign, Schönhuber decided to sharpen his party's profile and moved further to the right by sharing his anti-Semitic and revisionist views with the German public and by reaching out to the more extremist DVU and their chief, Gerhard Frey.[40]

The relationship between the Republikaner and the DVU highlights another resource problem for the New Right: its organizational disarray. As the Hamburg elections in 1993 most vividly demonstrated, Republikaner and DVU are largely competing for the same electorate. So far, there have been no successful attempts to overcome the fragmentation on the far right. The Republikaner themselves have suffered a tremendous lack of internal solidarity and numerous leadership quarrels. For example, in 1993 alone, sixty-three of the then 136 groups in district and city councils broke up, diminished in numbers, or disappeared altogether. In one year, the overall number of Republikaner delegates declined from 402 to 289 due to dissolutions of their groups, the building of new right-wing Rathaus factions, or party cross-overs.[41] Moreover, the position of Schönhuber as the party's leader has never been very secure. This became obvious during the 1994 election campaigns. Schönhuber's desperate attempt to overcome the self-defeating fragmentation of the right-wing spectrum by reaching out to the DVU's chief Gerhard Frey backfired within his own party. Schönhuber was ousted by the Republikaner leadership three weeks before the federal elections and a new leadership quarrel ensued.[42] This is a dramatic contrast to the French scenario where a more charismatic Le Pen keeps his party together and himself on top.[43]

Conclusions and Outlook

In the "super election year," all the problems of the New Right in resources, voter appeal, and opportunity structures accumulated, and the Republikaner may finally be at their end. However, the dialectical relationship between the New Right and the established parties means a continuation of right-wing politics in the New Politics dimension. In the 1970s, the voters who had voted for the NPD in the 1960s were largely won back by a CDU that turned to the right when forced into opposition after 1969. In the 1990s, there are few indicators that the voters who had voted for the parties of the New Right have returned to democratic normalcy. Continuously low turnout, a record low of trust in the government since 1982, and the reluctance to vote the SPD into power indicate a continuation of those structural conditions which, along with the changing cleavage patterns and the new right-wing discourse of the 1980s, have laid the ground for the rise of the

New Right in Germany. Moreover, the vote for the New Right parties was never a simple protest vote but a mixture of ideological convictions with a sense of alienation from the political system and particular issue concerns, such as immigration and law and order.[44] For the time being, the issues are taken care of by the major parties.

The development of the New Right and its ups and downs reflect a sequence of shifts to the right by the entire spectrum and the search for a new profile on the right. In 1990, one of their main issues, reunification, was taken away by the East Germans and Kohl's handling of the process. In 1994, their main theme, immigration, was again coopted by the established parties. But the political constellation remains volatile: a fragile coalition might invite new controversies and damage a new public trust in the political institutions, the citizenship and immigration issues are likely to return, the European issue is still on the horizon. A reorganized New Right might capitalize on these issues and fuse them with the ones that already make them stand out from the rest of the political spectrum: anti-Semitism and the question of the eastern border. It remains to be seen if the New Right returns by 1996 and if the major parties, again, react by further shifting Germany's political center to the right.

Special thanks to Margaret Kohn, Cornell University, for her research on the asylum debate.

Notes

1. See Dieter Roth, "Die Republikaner. Schneller Aufstieg und tiefer Fall einer Protestpartei am rechten Rand," *Aus Politik und Zeitgeschichte*, 1990 (B37–38/90), pp. 27ff. It should be remembered that next to the Republikaner, the NPD made substantial headlines in 1989 when they won seats in Frankfurt's city council in the Hesse local elections.

2. Jürgen Falter, *Wer wählt rechts?* (München: Beck, 1994), 27.

3. The concept of "opportunity structures" was developed in the context of social movement research and, so far, has not yet been systematically applied to extreme right parties and movements; see Herbert Kitschelt, "Political Opportunity Structures and Political Protest: Anti-Nuclear Movements in Four Democracies," *British Journal of Political Science*, 1986 (16), pp. 57–85. For an excellent overview of the literature on the far right in Germany, see Thomas Saalfeld, "Xenophobic political movements in Germany, 1949–1994," paper prepared for

presentation at the 89th Annual Meeting of the American Sociological Association, Los Angeles, 5–9 August 1994.

4. Sinus-Institut, *5 Millionen Deutsche: "Wir sollten wieder einen Führer haben..." Die SINUS-Studie über rechtsextremistische Einstellungen bei den Deutschen* (Reinbek: Rowohlt, 1981), 78, 83, 93.

5. See Richard Stöss, *Die Extreme Rechte in der Bundesrepublik* (Opladen: Westdeutscher Verlag, 1989), 49.

6. See Erwin Scheuch and Hans-Dieter Klingemann, "Theorie des Rechtsradikalismus in westlichen Industriegesellschaften," *Hamburger Jahrbuch für Wirtschafts- und Gesellschaftspolitik*, 1967 (12), pp. 11–29.

7. See Reinhard Kühnl et al., *Die NPD. Struktur, Ideologie und Funktion einer neofaschistischen Partei* (Frankfurt/Main: Suhrkamp, 1969); Stöss, *Die Extreme Rechte*, 135–40.

8. See Eckart Zimmermann and Thomas Saalfeld, "The Three Waves of West German Right-Wing Extremism," in Peter Merkl and Leonard Weinberg, eds., *Encounters with the Contemporary Radical Right* (Boulder, CO: Westview Press, 1993), 60.

9. See Peter Alter, *Nationalism* (London: Edward Arnold, 1989); Rogers Brubaker, *Citizenship and Nationhood in France and Germany* (Cambridge: Harvard University Press, 1992).

10. See Michael Minkenberg, "German Unification and the Continuity of Discontinuities. Cultural Change and the Far Right in East and West," *German Politics*, August 1994 (3, 2), pp. 169–92; Manfred Küchler, "Germans and 'Others.' Racism, Xenophobia, or 'Legitimate Conservatism'?" *German Politics*, April 1994 (3, 1), pp. 47–74.

11. For an elaboration of the following, see Michael Minkenberg, "The New Right in West Germany. The Transformation of Conservatism and the Extreme Right," *European Journal of Political Research*, July 1992 (22,1), pp. 55–81; Michael Minkenberg, *The New Right in Comparative Perspective: The USA and Germany*, Western Societies Paper, Ithaca, NY: Cornell University, 1993.

12. The term "New Left" has various meanings, from specific revolutionary or Marxist cadre groups in the wake of 1968 to the whole array of social movements and new parties on the left in the 1970s. In this essay, the term is applied to such new social movements, new parties or wings within (old) left parties which are characterized by new middle-class instead of working-class support, postmaterialist instead of materialist value priorities, and an élite-challenging instead of an élite-directed political style. For an informative overview, see Andrei S. Markovits and Philip S. Gorski, *The German Left. Red, Green and Beyond* (New York: Oxford University Press, 1993), Introduction.

13. See Russell Dalton, *Citizen Politics in Western Democracies* (Chatham, NJ: Chatham House, 1988).

14. See Karl Mannheim, "Das konservative Denken," in *Archiv für Sozialwissenschaft und Sozialpolitik*, 1927 (57), pp. 68–142, 470–95.

15. See Hans-Georg Betz, *Radical Right-Wing Populism in Western Europe* (New York: St. Martin's Press, 1993).

16. Michael Stürmer, "Geschichte in geschichtslosem Land," *Frankfurter Allgemeine Zeitung*, 25 April 1985, reprinted in Rudolf Augstein et al., *"Historikerstreit." Die Dokumentation der Kontroverse um die Einzigartigkeit der nationalsozialistischen Judenvernichtung* (München: Piper, 1987), 36–38.

17. See Dieter Oberndörfer, *Die offene Republik* (Freiburg/Br.: Herder, 1991), 64–72.

18. See Klaus Bade, *Ausländer, Aussiedler, Asyl* (München: Beck, 1994), 100. See also Jürgen Link, "Medien und Asylanten. Zur Geschichte eines Unwortes," in Dietrich Thränhardt and Simone Wolken, eds., *Flucht und Asyl* (Freiburg/Br.: Lambertus, 1988), 53.

19. For an instructive analysis of this discourse of "new racism" in the context of British politics, see Martin Barker, *The New Racism: Conservatives and the Ideology of the Tribe* (London: Junction Books, 1981). See also Pierre-André Taguieff, *La force du préjugé. Essai sur le racisme et ses doubles* (Paris: Éditions La Découverte, 1987).

20. See Minkenberg, "The New Right in Germany," pp. 62–70.

21. See Richard Stöss, *Die Republikaner* (Köln: Bund Verlag, 1990), 97.

22. See Falter, *Wer wählt rechts?*, 44–60.

23. See ibid., chapter 6.

24. The very founding of the party in 1983, in response to the CDU/CSU's perceived selling out of the national interest, i.e., the billion DM loan to the GDR negotiated by CSU chief Franz Josef Strauß and the continuation of *Ostpolitik* by the Kohl government, illustrates the initial thrust of the party.

25. See Küchler, "Germans and 'Others'"; also Minkenberg, "German Unification and the Continuity of Discontinuities," op. cit. pp. 183, 186f.

26. See Armin Pfahl-Traughber, *Rechtsextremismus. Eine kritische Bestandsaufnahme nach der Wiedervereinigung* (Bonn: Bouvier, 1993), 46ff, 235ff.

27. See Oscar Gabriel, "Institutionenvertrauen im vereinigten Deutschland," *Aus Politik und Zeitgeschichte*, 22 October 1993 (B43/93), p. 9.

28. See for example Lilly Weissbrod, "Nationalism in Reunified Germany," *German Politics*, August 1994 (3, 2), p. 231.

29. See Michael Minkenberg, "The Far Right in Unified Germany," in Frederick Weil, ed., *Research on Democracy and Extremism*, vol. 3 (Greenwich, CT: JAI Press, 1995) (forthcoming).

30. See Falter, *Wer wählt rechts?*, 61–106.

31. In fact, the East-West difference in the Republikaner vote raises questions about all theories that postulate a direct link between economic performance, in particular levels of unemployment, or status deprivation and the far-right vote. The eastern German economic crises is by far worse than the western German recession after unification. Yet, those eastern Germans who are particularly hit by the consequences of the economic transformation show a remarkable resistance to voting for any extreme right parties. In fact, it has been argued that high levels of unemployment do not benefit extreme parties (see Hans Rattinger, "Unemployment and Elections in West Germany," in H. Norpoth et al., eds., *Economics and Politics* (Ann Arbor, MI: University of Michigan Press, 1991). The continuously high levels of unemployment in the East and the eastern public's preoccupation

with the "unemployment issue" seem to confirm directly those (western German-based) findings.

32. See Falter, *Wer wählt rechts?*, 23–26. In the Hamburg elections of 1993, the New Right parties were particularly successful among the working class, a sixth of which voted for the Republikaner or the DVU; see *Der Spiegel*, 27 September 1993 (39), pp. 29–33.

33. For a critical discussion of these alleged links and other "myths" about asylum seekers in Germany, see Rainer Geissler and Norbert Marissen, "Kriminalität und Kriminalisierung junger Ausländer," in *Kölner Zeitschrift für Soziologie und Sozialpsychologie*, 1990 (4), p. 664.

34. See Martin Klingst, "Mit dem großen Raster," *Die Zeit*, 7 October 1994 (41), p. 2.

35. The nomination of CDU hard-liner Manfred Kanther as Minister of Interior in 1993, Wolfgang Schäuble's agenda to revitalize the German nation and nationalism, and Bavarian Prime Minister Edmund Stoiber's attack on European integration are particular indicators for the CDU/CSU's shift to the right in the New Politics dimension. See *Der Spiegel*, 12 July 1993 (28), pp. 26ff.; 8 November 1993 (45), pp. 18ff.; 14 March 1994 (11), p. 32.

36. Data for 1993 and 1994 presented by Manfred Küchler, "Xenophobia and the German Elections 1994," guest lecture, Cornell University, 1 November 1994.

37. Die Republikaner, *Parteiprogramm 1993*, Augsburg 1993, p. 5.

38. For an examination of Republikaner platforms, see Wolfgang Gessenharter, *Kippt die Republik? Die Neue Rechte und ihre Unterstützung durch Politik und Medien* (München: Knaur, 1994), 157–69. See also Hans-Gerd Jaschke, *Die Republikaner. Profile einer Rechtsaußenpartei* (Bonn: Dietz, 1990), 90–106.

39. See Falter, *Wer wählt rechts?*, chapters 6 and 7.

40. See *Der Spiegel*, 11 April 1994 (15), pp. 18ff.; *Berliner Morgenpost*, 25 August 1994, p. 4.

41. See Claus Leggewie, *Druck von rechts. Wohin treibt die Bundesrepublik?* (München: Beck, 1993), 104. See also *Der Spiegel*, 16 May 1994 (20), pp. 54–59.

42. See *Der Spiegel*, 20 June 1994 (25), pp. 32–35; *Der Spiegel*, 15 August 1994 (33), p. 50. On the mediocrity of the Republikaner's personnel in the 1994 campaign, see Gisela Dachs, "Die Banalität des Radikalen," *Die Zeit*, 29 October 1993, (44), p. 5.

43. See Leggewie, *Druck von rechts*, 100–3.

44. See Falter, *Wer wählt rechts?*, 136–53.

13

REBUILDING THE GERMAN WELFARE STATE

IRWIN L. COLLIER, JR.

*In order to avoid the vicious circle of an expansion of social spending
that leads to a fall in investment with a subsequent loss of jobs that
in turn leads to financial bottlenecks in the provision of social services,
one must rebuild the welfare state. The single most important principle
has to be that social security does not represent a zero deductible, zero copayment policy covering all the risks of life.*
Klaus Murmann,[1] President of the Federal Union of German
Employer Associations

*It is completely naive to believe that the current system will remain
solvent if the terms of the generation contract remain unchanged after
the coming demographic shift. Such belief defies economic logic—even
worse, it is criminal negligence.*
Edzard Reuter,[2] Chairman of the Board of Daimler-Benz

*The German welfare state is not some carnival stand that you put up
or take down at will ... Businessmen should not keep constantly thinking
about things to dismantle. They should be working on new inventions.
... We are dealing here with a bunch of blow-hards who talk big and
accomplish little....*
Norbert Blüm[3,4] Federal Minister of Labor and Social Affairs

Only two days after the Bundestag election of 16 October 1994,
the president of the Federal Union of German Employer Associations (BDA), Klaus Murmann, released a sixty-two page brochure
published by his organization entitled *Sozialstaat vor dem Umbau—
Leistungsfähigkeit und Finanzierbarkeit sichern* (Rebuilding the Welfare State: Securing Efficiency and Solvency). This brochure
represents an attempt by the BDA to basically reform the German

system of social security, health care, and social assistance into the new legislative agenda.[5] The timing of this brochure's release was no coincidence. Nothing could have served the SPD electoral campaign better than the publication of this brochure just one or two months earlier. With a chance to play the noble champion of social justice against the mean forces of reaction, the SPD campaign would have been given a much clearer focus—as James Carville could have conceived the Scharping campaign, 'It's the entitlements, stupid!' In addition to such tactical electoral considerations, the timing of the release of this brochure probably reveals a deeper strategic motive. The cause of fundamental reform of the welfare state would have been badly served by a preelection publication date, because *all* political parties would have been pushed into the categorical denial mode in anticipation of election day.[6] Cutting social benefits or subsidies is at least as dangerous to a person's political health in the Federal Republic as is raising taxes or cutting social security pensions in the United States. The window of opportunity to discuss cutting entitlements is open, if only a crack, immediately after a major election.

If the German public seems on the whole more satisfied than not with the present condition of the German welfare state, one might wonder why democratically elected politicians should do anything other than deliver what the public wants? At issue here is whether the Federal Republic of Germany has indeed ordered, and continues to order, more welfare state than its economy can sustain as a long-run proposition.[7] Quite distinct from the feasibility of a continuation of current social policy is the issue of its efficiency, e.g., whether the present methods of financing social benefits are indeed the cheapest way of providing current benefit levels in the long run. The reformer's dream is to improve the efficiency of the system; the reformer's nightmare is to find that the system is fundamentally infeasible.

The BDA brochure *Sozialstaat vor dem Umbau* has already caught the German public's attention in a political culture full of so many fascinating distractions. However, public discussion is not much closer to the goal proclaimed in the brochure's preface of beginning a dialogue between business, labor, and other groups in the society about the future of the German welfare state. Instead the public has largely been treated to a ritualistic exchange of insults and demands for apologies. But the issues raised are bigger than the political egos involved. This brochure, while neither the first nor last word on the subject, is a very convenient point of entry into the debate about future directions for the German welfare state.

To help the reader follow this debate in the New Politics of Germany, an abstract of *Sozialstaat vor dem Umbau* is presented below, followed by a brief summary of the counterarguments it has provoked. The chapter closes with an attempt to distill the debate to its economic essentials.

Sozialstaat vor dem Umbau—An Abstract

The purpose of social insurance is to stabilize income in spite of the most significant risks of life: those associated with sickness, disability, unemployment, and old age. While social insurance constitutes a fundamental component of the social market economy, it must always be considered within a larger context, in particular in relation to the economic base which supports it. At the present time, the burden of the combination of tax *and* social contributions together, measured as a share of a nation's output, has reached a historic high in Germany.[8] During the first half of the twenty-first century, demographics alone will drive this burden even higher, as will presumably a relative cost explosion in the provision of both medical services and long-term care[9]—that is, unless needed fundamental changes in the structure of social entitlements and the methods to finance them are implemented in the meantime.

The growing trend in social insurance contributions required to finance the German social welfare system can be clearly seen in table 13.1 which has been expanded in both directions from a table in *Sozialstaat vor dem Umbau*.[10] Over the course of the last quarter century, the combined rate for all social insurance contributions together has increased from about one-fourth to two-fifths of employee pay. It is estimated that the cost to employers of both legally required and contractual benefits for employees has gone up from 50 percent of earnings in 1970 to 84 percent in 1993. A breakdown of employer provided benefits is given in table 13.2. This wedge between labor costs (the total package) and labor earnings gross of taxes is viewed by the BDA as the result of a longer trend which has been recently accelerated by the social burdens of German unification.

More alarming than the present size of the wedge between labor costs and labor earnings is the projected growth of that wedge, given the demographic structure of the population, the current structures of benefits, and the methods of financing those benefits. Ninety-five percent of social security benefits in Germany are unfunded programs run on a pay-as-you-go basis. This means that either social insurance contribution rates will have to rise to match future increases in social benefits paid per worker, or the scale of those benefits will have to be cut back so that contribution rates can remain constant. The percent of the population aged 60 years and over will grow from currently 20 percent to about 35 percent by the year 2030. Maintaining current benefit levels would require that contributions be raised from 19.2 percent to 27 percent for old-age and survivors' insurance, from 13.4 percent to 17 percent for health insurance, and from 1.7 percent to at least 3.4 percent for long-term care by 2030. Thus, even allowing for some reduction in unemployment insurance rates in the next century, the social insurance wedge will grow over one-fourth larger than it already is, i.e., to at least 50 percent of earnings.[11]

TABLE 13.1

CONTRIBUTION RATES FOR SOCIAL INSURANCE IN THE FRG
(PERCENT OF COVERED EARNINGS)

	Employee Pension Insurance	Health Insurance (average)	Unemployment Insurance	Long-Term Care	Total
1950	10.0	6.0	4.0		20.0
1960	14.0	8.4	2.0		24.4
1970	17.0	8.2	1.3		26.5
1980	18.0	11.4	3.0		32.4
1990	18.7	12.8	4.3		35.8
1994	19.2	13.2	6.5		38.9
1995	18.6	13.1	6.5	1.0	39.2
1996	19.1	13.0	6.5	1.7	40.3

Sources: 1950–60 from Helmut Winterstein, *Das System der Sozialen Sicherung in der Bundesrepublik Deutschland* (Munich, 1980), p. 158. 1970–90 from *Sozialstaat vor dem Umbau*, p. 59. 1994–96 updated from *Jahresgutachten 1994/95 des Sachverständigenrates zur Begutachtung der gesamtwirtschaftlichen Entwicklung*, p. 143.

Before discussing proposals for specific reforms of individual components of the social budget,[12] the BDA presents three general principles to guide the reform of the welfare state. The first principle, already previewed in the Murmann quotation that begins this chapter, is that the welfare state should not be seen as total insurance for all of life's risks. The BDA wants to shift the emphasis from the principle of solidarity that lurks behind all compulsory social insurance schemes to a greater role for the principle of subsidiarity which demands greater individual responsibility.[13] The BDA does not expect people to face less risky lives in the future, rather that they will make private, responsible provision for those risks themselves. This is not just a matter of expanding the role of private insurance, but also the increased use of deductibles and copayments for all forms of social insurance.

TABLE 13.2

COSTS OF EMPLOYER PROVIDED BENEFITS AS A PERCENT OF EARNINGS FOR WORK PERFORMED FRG (1993) AND U.S. (1988)

	FRG (DM)	FRG %	US 1988%
Total	36,950	84.0	34.6
Cost of legally required benefits	16,452	37.4	—
Employer contribution to social insurance (incl. private insurance)	10,733	24.4	19.1
Paid holidays and other down time	2,375	5.4	3.2
Sick-pay	2,243	5.1	1.2
Other mandated indirect labor costs	1,100	2.5	—
Cost of negotiated and company specific benefits	20,498	46.6	—
Vacation pay plus vacation bonus	9,062	20.6	4.7
Bonuses, incl. 13th month salary	4,311	9.8	—
Company-plan pension contributions	3,871	8.8	3.8
Savings and thrift plans	572	1.3	0.7
Other benefits	2,683	6.1	2.0

Sources: FRG data are for businesses with more than forty-nine employees in energy, water supply, mining, manufacturing, and construction (i.e., excluding agriculture, fishing, services and government). *Sozialstaat vor dem Umbau,* p. 61.

U.S. data refer to private industry. U.S. Bureau of Labor Statistics, cited in Ronald G. Ehrenberg and Robert S. Smith, *Modern Labor Economics,* 4th ed., (NYC: Harper-Collins Publishers, 1991), p. 398.

Note: the individual United States items have been assigned to the corresponding individual items for Germany for comparison. Because of differences between the United States and Germany regarding which benefits are statutory and contractual, the subtotals for the United States are deliberately omitted since they would not be comparable.

The German economy is fully capable of shifting at least some of the responsibility back to most individuals and their families as can be seen in two measures of private German wealth. Almost DM4 trillion in financial assets are held by private households, which amounts to nearly four times the size of the annual social budget. This is approximately DM110,000 per household in East and West. More than DM100 billion of wealth is inherited each calendar year, indicating that there are significant resources at the disposal of the senior population.

The second principle that recurs throughout *Sozialstaat vor dem Umbau* is that the welfare state must stop using revenues obtained from social insurance contributions to finance those public policies, the benefits from which extend beyond those who work in jobs covered by the social insurance system. In particular, the inappropriate use of social insurance programs to implement family policy, to redistribute income from the top to the bottom of society, and to finance the enormous start-up costs of the economic integration of the new federal states have been important reasons for the disproportionate growth of labor costs in Germany.

The third principle the BDA offers to guide the reform of the welfare state is that benefit structures must maintain reasonable incentives for an economic use of both household resources and social benefits. To support work incentives, society must guarantee that there is a clear and significant difference between income from public assistance and paid work. The BDA considers disincentives, an entitlement mentality, and the abuse of social benefits, such as the illegitimate use of paid sick leave, as intimately related problems. This is why it argues for policymakers to worry less about expanding enforcement (though it does specifically suggest tighter controls, particularly in the area of paid sick leave) and to worry more about introducing sensible incentives, such as sick leave at reduced pay or only after a one- or two-day waiting period.

HEALTH INSURANCE

Ninety percent of the German population is covered under the statutory health insurance system. There are 51 million paying members (of whom 29 million are pensioners) and 22 million nonpaying family members. The average contribution rate has increased from 8.2 percent of covered employee earnings in 1970 to over 13 percent at the present time.

Consistent with the BDA's desire to expand the role for individual responsibility in what it considers a relatively rich society is its recommendation for a narrower definition of "medically necessary" procedures and treatments to be covered by the statutory health insurance system. "Elective" treatments, such as those provided in resort spas, should be financed either out of employee pockets like any other form of consumption or through private supplementary health insurance policies.

Another way to lower the contribution rate for worker health insurance recommended by the BDA would be to stop using the statutory health insurance system for redistributive purposes. Currently, the statutory health insurance system involves an intergenerational redistribution (part of the "generation contract"), since pensioners receive approximately 80 percent more in health benefits while paying about 50 percent less in premiums than those working. There is also a redistribution that takes place based upon family status—health benefits are extended to nonworking family members without any change in the insurance rate for the employee. Finally, certain medical benefits are provided for lower income workers, such as the complete elimination of any copayment requirement whatsoever (e.g., for prescription drugs). These kinds of redistribution result in higher health insurance rates for employees. The BDA argues that such redistributive measures should be financed through general tax revenues rather than the health insurance premiums that are levied on covered employment alone.

To improve the incentives to limit the demand for health services, *Sozialstaat vor dem Umbau* argues for a greater use of copayments. The amounts suggested by the BDA are really quite modest with a suggested maximum for copayments in lower income groups of 2 percent of the income ceiling used to calculate health insurance contributions. The proposed maximum copayment for higher income groups would be up to 4 percent of the income ceiling. The BDA also proposes that medical costs should be paid by recipients and then reimbursed rather than financed with direct payments to service providers by the sickness funds, so that the ultimate recipients of health care will become better aware of the actual costs involved.

One section of *Sozialstaat vor dem Umbau* that has provoked an extremely hostile reaction is the BDA's demand for changing the sick leave benefit. Employers in Germany are obliged to provide full pay during the first six weeks of sick leave. In 1993, 5.6 percent of the work force or 1.7 million employees were sick on an average work day. The average duration of spells was about fifteen days. Adding in the employer payments to social insurance during an employee's sickness, paid sick leave amounted to DM63 billion of employer-provided benefit in 1993. Paid sick leave is the single most expensive direct social benefit employers provide.

Two particular statistical regularities indicate that factors besides physical illness are behind the incidence of sickness of German employees. In the first place, the number of sick days is positively correlated with the business cycle, i.e., employees are less frequently sick during recessions. In the second place, the incidence of sick days peaks just before and after weekends, holidays, and vacations.[14] The practical question is how to distinguish between sickness and health at lowest cost and with greatest respect for privacy. The BDA rather sarcastically notes that the medical services of the sick funds only double-check one of sixty cases of reported employee illness during the first six weeks, i.e., when employers pay the sick leave benefit. However, one out of four cases are double-checked by the sick funds after six weeks, which is when they start paying the sick leave benefit.

The BDA wants to see a significant reduction of sick pay below 100 percent of an employee's normal pay as it is the case in all other parts of the social insurance system where lost labor earnings are not replaced on a one-for-one basis. Either a graduated percent reduction or the reintroduction of a waiting period before sick leave benefits begin (*Karenztage*) are considered by the BDA to be appropriate ways of adjusting the incentives to hinder the abuse of this social benefit that works to increase the cost of labor.

OLD-AGE AND SURVIVORS' INSURANCE

Old-age and survivors' pensions make up about 30 percent of the social budget (about 10 percent of GNP). The west-to-east transfer for this item alone in 1993 (i.e., the difference between contributions gathered and pensions paid in the new states) was about DM9 billion and is expected to grow to about DM14 billion annually over the next several years. Thanks to the pension reform law of 1992, contribution rates have been stabilized through 2010.[15] However, the demographic times of trouble will still begin around the year 2015. From that point on, contribution rates will have to increase steadily to the end of the current planning horizon of 2030, when 27 percent of earnings will be required to finance the old-age and survivors' insurance program alone.

Given the low probability of much being done about the old-age and survivors' insurance for the remainder of the decade, the BDA stakes out a completely safe position for itself (at least for now) as a staunch defender of the current pay-as-you-go, contribution-based pension system. Other reform models that have been proposed are critically discussed, however.

The BDA argues *against* the introduction of a guaranteed minimum old-age pension financed out of general tax revenues (as opposed to employee contributions) that would be supplemented by individual, private savings in fully funded old-age and survivors' insurance plan. The first potential danger of a guaranteed minimum pension system is that it could easily backfire and actually encourage further growth in the entitlement mentality rather than promote greater individual responsibility. The second potential danger seen by the BDA is that such a minimum guaranteed budget system would move such an important entitlement from off-budget to on-budget. The BDA clearly fears that the guaranteed minimum pension would become subject to the demands of electoral politics (grant now, tax later) at a time when retired folks will become the fastest growing segment of the electorate.

A shift from pay-as-you-go to full funding of the statutory pension system (with or without a guaranteed minimum pension) is indeed the proper way to insulate the pension system from adverse changes in the age distributions as will happen during the next century. The BDA points to what it regards to be an insurmountable practical problem in such a shift. The transition to full funding would take decades in order to accumulate the necessary reserves. In other words, the current generation would have to pay for the old-age income of the previous generation and to save for itself as well.[16] Needless to say, there is no perceptible groundswell for this double burden.

WORK-INJURY INSURANCE

Premiums for this insurance paid by employers depend upon relative occupational danger and total employee earnings. The average contribution in 1993 was DM14.4 per DM1000 of employee earnings. *Sozialstaat vor dem Umbau* has only one major suggestion for reforming work-injury insurance. Travel accidents are making up a rising portion of work-injury claims, as workplaces have become increasingly safer. The BDA argues that travel to and from the workplace is something over which employers have no control but which falls under work-injury insurance nonetheless. Such risks would be better covered either by an employee's health insurance or, alternatively, by private accident insurance or car insurance.

FEDERAL LABOR INSTITUTION

The contributions to statutory unemployment insurance finance the budget of this organization responsible for German labor policy. Spending by the Federal Labor Institution nearly tripled between 1990 and 1993, rising from DM40 billion to DM110 billion annually. This was mostly due to the collapse of production in the new states following unification. The Federal Labor Institution's deficit skyrocketed from DM2 billion in 1990 to almost DM25 billion in 1993, this in spite of an increase in the contribution rate from 4.3 percent to 6.5 percent. For the years 1990 through 1993 combined, there was a cumulative west-to-east transfer of DM65 billion from the cash-flow surplus from contributions of western German employees subject to the unemployment insurance contribution less benefits paid in western Germany.

The BDA argues that unemployment compensation and payments for involuntary short-time work should continue being financed out of the Federal Labor Institution budget as they are now. However, other human resource programs, in particular the temporary public employment projects (ABM) and worker-training programs which amount to about DM40 billion annually, should be financed from general revenues. The BDA emphatically stresses the point that the shift from unemployment insurance contribution financing to tax financing should *not* be allowed to change the aggregate tax burden. Unfortunately, *Sozialstaat vor dem Umbau* nominates *no* pork barrels outside of the social budget for elimination.

REHABILITATION

In 1991, DM47 billion was spent to help the integration or reintegration of sick or disabled into work and society. The BDA points to the following trend: since the decade of the 1980s these benefits have grown twice as fast as the rest of the social budget. Half of the cost of these social benefits is paid from the health insurance system while the remaining expenditures are financed through the other branches of German social insurance. No particular reforms for rehabilitation programs are proposed in *Sozialstaat vor dem Umbau*. The BDA merely expresses its hope that the relative trend of expansion will stop and that efforts to increase the efficiency at the present scale of benefits will increase.

LONG-TERM CARE

The fifth supporting column of German social insurance[17] is introduced this very year. Starting January 1, an additional 1 percent of labor earnings has been collected to finance the new social insurance for long-term care. Long-term home care benefits will commence on April 1st. Beginning in the second half of 1996, the long-term care insurance contribution rate on labor earnings will be increased to 1.7 percent and benefits will be expanded to include stationary care as well. Benefits for the 1.65 million people in Germany requiring long-term care at the present time are projected to cost approximately DM17 billion annually for home care and DM12 billion annually for stationary care. Like the other four columns of German social insurance, this program is unfunded, i.e., contributions gathered in each period will be used to pay for the benefits provided in that period.

The BDA strongly disapproves of the decision to use pay-as-you-go funding of this program in light of the demographic burdens already programmed for the next century—an opinion shared by leading German economists.[18] A further shortcoming in the implementation of long-term care insurance criticized by the BDA is the use of a tax on employment earnings to finance insurance for what is definitely not a work-related risk. Since the risk of needing long-term care is faced by everyone, and not just by covered employees, the BDA believes it should be financed by everyone, i.e., from general tax revenues or through personal insurance.

Given the new long-term care insurance entitlements, the BDA hopes to limit future damage by freezing both the benefit levels to those currently mandated for the next two years and the maximum contribution rate at 1.7 percent of employee earnings. Unfortunately, this genie has escaped from the lamp.

WELFARE

The topic of public assistance receives only two pages in *Sozialstaat vor dem Umbau*. Two million western Germans and three hundred thousand eastern Germans were receiving public assistance at the end of 1992, at a net cost of DM35 billion. The BDA notes what it considers to be a disturbing trend, the basic benefit levels have grown more rapidly than net income from work since 1980. In reforming the German system of income maintenance, the BDA strongly recommends reestablishing the 1980 gap between social assistance and labor earnings in the lowest pay-grades to strengthen work incentives. Besides legal mandates to reduce public assistance for refusal to accept a job placement, a tighter control of welfare to eliminate abuse is also recommended.

There is one specific direction for welfare reform that the BDA explicitly discourages. The introduction of a *Bürgergeld* (i.e., a demogrant, or minimum income entitlement) is disapproved on the grounds that it would essentially fix a minimum wage that employers would have to pay to make work more attractive than the demogrant. On philosophical grounds, the BDA brochure rejects demogrants as supportive of the entitlement mentality that is part of the problem. Advocates of a demogrant welfare program point out that the elimination of means-testing for a guaranteed minimum income vastly simplifies the administration of public assistance. The BDA believes that greater transparency can be achieved by consolidation of institutions providing public assistance and harmonizing means-tests throughout the social insurance system. Nonetheless, elements of a negative income tax in housing and family allowances are recommended in *Sozialstaat vor dem Umbau* in order to reduce the implicit marginal tax rates of social benefits that have worked to discourage recipients from accepting paid work.

EUROPE AND THE WELFARE STATE

The BDA brochure closes with a gratuitous page on European social policy. With regard to social policy within the European Union, the BDA sees no necessity for harmonizing social systems across member countries. The (EU) principle of subsidiarity should be applied here, especially given the differences in fundamental beliefs and desires that make a harmonization of social policies inappropriate. Nonetheless, the BDA does support binding minimum standards in the particular case of worker safety regulations within the European Union.

Sozialstaat vor dem Umbau—The Critics

Will the German welfare state bankrupt itself and does it genuinely constitute a clear and present danger to *Standort Deutschland*? One-third of that nation's product now being sucked into the social budget and social insurance taxes of 50 percent projected for the first half of the next century certainly sound like impending doom. But before granting the surgeon permission to cut, it is prudent to obtain a second opinion.

The SPD speaker in the Bundestag on questions of social policy, Rudolf Dreßler, vigorously denies the validity of many of the theses of *Sozialstaat vor dem Umbau*.[19] His critique consists mainly of the following points:

- The ratio of social budget to GNP *overstates* the actual scale of social policy expenditure because the social budget is inflated with several items such as pensions and health benefits for civil servants, tax savings from income splitting for married couples and family allowances. Most of those benefits go to the upper two-thirds of society anyway.[20]
- The ratio of social budget to GNP has actually *stagnated* rather than increased during the decade of the 1980s.[21]
- The increase in the ratio of social budget to GNP in the 1990s does not demonstrate the inevitable workings of a deeply ingrained entitlement mentality, but rather reveals the conscious

shifting of part of the fiscal burden of German unification onto the social insurance system.

- The DM49 billion annually spent on public assistance is not the result of a welfare system gone wild, but rather the result of a structural crisis aggravated by the failure of the government to promote economic growth and employment.
- The problem is not work-shy recipients of unemployment compensation or welfare, but risk-shy businesses who are hustling for government subsidies instead of market share.
- The government should not slash social benefits for the needy to lower labor costs to attract investment; rather, its task is to help foster productivity growth by increasing its efforts in education, research, and development.

From no less a pulpit than that of the federal president has come the rather remarkable claim that one of the attractions of *Standort Deutschland* to investors is precisely its welfare state.[22] What Federal President Herzog probably meant with this odd assertion was more clearly expressed by Labor and Social Affairs Minister Blüm: "Those who want to demolish the welfare state are a risk for Germany's competitive position—social peace is a big locational advantage for Germany."[23] It is hard to find two words more sacred in German political rhetoric than "social" and "peace." Serious debate will not be easy.

A Leaner, Meaner Welfare State?

Examining the historical path taken by the ratio of spending for transfers and social benefits to the German gross domestic product (figure 13.1), one discovers that the relative growth of social spending has been far less uniform than one would have thought after reading *Sozialstaat vor dem Umbau*. While there indeed occurred a distinct upward jump in that ratio during the first half of the seventies, one is struck by the equally distinct downward trend that followed, especially during the pre-unification years of the Kohl government. Just as one would expect, the social costs involved in the integration of the new states have added disproportionately more to the numerator than the East German gross domestic product has added to the denominator of the ratio plotted in figure 13.1. For those who share an optimistic view of the future reconstruction of the new states,[24] the upward shift in figure 13.1 after 1990 could be interpreted as a large but *temporary* deviation from a long-range, gradual downward trend. In other words, the upwardly sloped dashed line in figure 13.1 is merely an indication of the *scale* of East German reconstruction rather than proof of the inexorable *growth* of a welfare Leviathan.

FIGURE 13.1

TRANSFER PAYMENTS TO PRIVATE HOUSEHOLDS AND SOCIAL INSURANCE BENEFITS (PERCENT OF GROSS DOMESTIC PRODUCT)

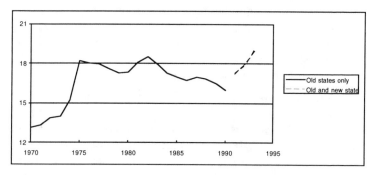

Source: Calculated from data in *Jahresgutachten 1994/5 des Sachverständigenrates zur Begutachtung der gesamtwirtschaftlichen Entwicklung*, pp. 350, 368–9.

FIGURE 13.2

POPULATION OVER 60 YRS. PER 100 PERSONS 20–60 YRS. OLD AND NEW STATES OF GERMANY

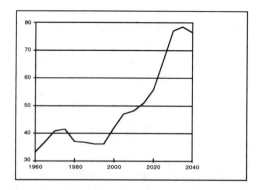

Source: 1960–1990 (actual) *Statistisches Jahrbuch der Bundesrepublik Deutschland 1993*, p. 64. 1995–2040 (forecasts) Verband Deutscher Rentenversicherungsträger, quoted in Rudolf Kolb, 'Rentenversicherung: Der Generationsvertrag vor unlösbaren demographischen Belastungen?' in Martin Lambert, ed., *Umbau der Sozialsysteme* (1994), p. 52.

The critical shortcoming of figure 13.1 is that by stopping at the present, it generates a false sense of (social) security. The real problems, as though the reconstruction of the new states of Germany does not pose a big enough challenge to the social market economy already, are yet to come. In figure 13.2 actual and projected ratios of the German population over sixty years of age to the population between twenty and sixty years have been plotted for the eighty-year span beginning in 1960. The demographic mountain of seniors after 2015 constitutes a genuine, long-range threat to the feasibility of the existing German welfare state.[25] The BDA is completely justified in wondering whether the working generations in the middle third of the twenty-first century will accept the responsibility for the extraordinary burden that the present working generations apparently intend to leave them.

One faint hope exists for the current German welfare state to survive the crossing of that demographic divide in the next century. The relative burden of supporting a nonworking population depends both on the productivity of the working population and its relative numbers. There is always the chance that the *deus ex machina* of productivity growth will ultimately save the German welfare state.

At least two good reasons can be given why younger generations in the German work force should not count that unhatched chicken in their own life-cycle planning. The first reason is that Germany, like the United States,[26] has experienced a slowing down in productivity growth over the past two decades that has led to a slowdown in the growth of living standards, both those financed from households' net earnings and those financed from transfer payments (table 13.3). The future trend of productivity growth is impossible to predict—at least professional economists have few illusions here. One thing is certain, however: the present trend of productivity growth will not get the German welfare state where it needs to go. The second reason to doubt the timely arrival of a sustained burst of productivity growth is the general lack of flexibility that characterizes the institutional framework of the German economy. This inflexibility is the result of increasingly complex social and economic regulations that, whatever the original intent behind them might be, have had the cumulative effect of inhibiting new investment and the creation of new jobs.[27]

Originally "the principle of solidarity" that provided the justification for social insurance schemes meant the solidarity of healthy with sick people, or the solidarity of the active working population with the retired senior population. For many people now, the notion of solidarity has expanded to include a "solidarity" between those fortunate to have large incomes with those unfortunate to have low incomes. There are two practical difficulties lurking behind this expanded notion of solidarity.

TABLE 13.3

AVERAGE ANNUAL GROWTH RATES, PRODUCTIVITY, REAL NET EARNINGS, AND REAL SOCIAL BUDGET

	Productivity	Real Net Earnings per Employee	Real Social Budget per Employee
1960–69	4.2%	3.4%	5.8%
1970–82	2.3%	1.6%	4.1%
1983–90	2.0%	0.7%	0.5%

Source: Author's calculations from data in *Jahresgutachten 1994/5 des Sachverständigenrates zur Begutachtung der gesamtwirtschaftlichen Entwicklung* and Bundesminister für Arbeit und Sozialordnung, *Hauptergebnisse der Arbeits- und Sozialstatistik 1993*, Bonn, 1993.

The first difficulty is whether the solidarity expected from the rich for the poor should be confounded with the solidarity expected from, say, the healthy for the sick. In other words, is it more effective to fight poverty and the risks of sickness in separate programs or both within a single program? While one could conceivably design a tank to fly, it is unlikely to be a very good tank or airplane. This point is essentially behind the many BDA proposals to shift financing of important social programs from a social insurance contributions basis to general tax revenues.

The second practical difficulty is how to target benefits to those who deserve them (offset bad luck while not rewarding vice) and to distribute the burden fairly (avoid kicking people when they are down while not punishing virtue). The implicit assumption behind the narrow and extended notions of solidarity is that *both* sickness and fortune are wholly undeserved fates—as though smoking and hard work are independent of human volition. The antithetical assumption, that fate is wholly deserved (blame the victim and hail the victor), would imply that solidarity is completely unnecessary. The truth is that both chance and choice matter in people's lives and that it is often difficult or impossible to separate the relative impact of the two, even for those we know personally. Nonetheless, it is extremely important to try to distinguish between those who deserve solidarity and those who do not. The greater the accuracy of targeting benefits to those who deserve them, the lower will be the ultimate burden of solidarity and the greater will be the willingness to bear that burden.

The English economist Sir Dennis Robertson once posed the question, "What does the economist economize?"[28] His answer, a surprise to most people, was "Love." What Robertson meant was that for those important instances where market outcomes are inconsistent with human dignity, society will have to count on voluntary altruism or compulsory solidarity to set things right. Robertson believed that the social value of competitive markets and economic incentives is that they can indeed help society from literally overtaxing its scarcest of human resources—individual altruism and collective solidarity.

Average German working people are already carrying a heavy burden of taxes and social insurance contributions (table 13.4). While the size of the *average* tax and social insurance contribution wedge is what most people see on their pay slips, it is the size of the *marginal* tax and social insurance contribution wedge that affects economic incentives. From table 13.4 we can see that the burden from combined taxes and social insurance contributions is both heavy and increasing.

As far as the long-run viability of the German welfare state is concerned, the unexpected shock of East German reconstruction has not been particularly significant—at least when compared to the certain demographic shock to occur in the twenty-first century. It seems ironic then that the 7.5 percent solidarity surtax reintroduced in January 1995 has provoked not only a further outbreak of *Ossi*-resentment in the West, but even a significant wave of people quitting German churches to avoid the 9 percent church surtax.[29] These are indications that the high burden of taxes and social contributions in Germany have met or exceeded the limits of solidarity felt by the average German citizen. Thus, we can expect to find little, if any, "wiggle room" on the solidarity side of the social insurance system to accommodate the coming demographic shock. In the absence of an unprecedented explosion in productivity growth, German social policy, sooner or later, will require not just the *Umbau* (rebuilding) but indeed an *Abbau* (demolition) of parts of the welfare state as it now exists.

Reading the coalition contract of the CDU, CSU, and FDP,[30] especially the section devoted to "Lean Government," one senses that the German polity is engaging in one of those moments of wishful thinking that could, but seldom do, lead to real change. The problem is that the main cuts will have to be made where the bulk of entitlements is to be found—right around the middle of the body politic. A slim coalition in the Bundestag, an opposition-dominated Bundesrat, and an electorate that shows little enthusiasm for sacrificing any entitlements are hardly optimal conditions for the serious reform of the German welfare state. To complicate matters, there are other concerns in political life—the pace and modalities of further European integration, the terms of German participation in international peace-keeping operations, and issues of law and order—that can easily crowd legitimate concerns about the years after 2015 off the agenda.

TABLE 13.4

COMBINED TAX AND SOCIAL INSURANCE BURDENS IN GERMANY BY MARITAL STATUS AND EARNINGS, 1975 AND 1996 (EST.)

| | Single employee | | Married employee, 2 children, sole earner, taxes filed jointly | |
	Average earnings	Twice average earnings	Average earnings	Twice average earnings
Gross labor earnings per employee				
1975	DM21,900	DM43,800	DM21,900	DM43,800
1996	DM52,300	DM104,600	DM52,300	DM104,600
Marginal tax & social contribution rate				
1975	45%	47%	35%	34%
1996	53%	51%	47%	32%
Average tax & social contribution rate				
1975	31%	38%	18%	24%
1996	41%	43%	24%	33%

Note: The figures for 1996 were calculated assuming 3 percent annual increase in gross pay in 1995 and 1996.
Source: *Jahresgutachten 1994/5 des Sachverständigenrates zur Begutachtung der gesamtwirtschaftlichen Entwicklung*, pp. 142–6.

A century ago, the tax structure of the German Reich was completely ill-equipped for the fiscal demands of the coming twentieth-century, in particular the costs of waging (and losing) a modern war. The German welfare state at the close of this century is no less challenged by the prospects of the coming century. As of this writing, the furor provoked by the publication of *Sozialstaat vor dem Umbau* shows no signs of subsiding. This is a good omen. The question is whether this furor will lead to reform that requires cooperation across the political spectrum or whether it will simply dissolve into parliamentary games of coalition versus opposition. Rebuilding a welfare state could turn out to be as difficult as transforming a socialist economy without the solidarity of a richer, bigger partner.

Notes

1. *Tagesspiegel,* 31 December 1994.

2. *Tagesspiegel,* 29 January 1994.

3. Interview with *Welt am Sonntag,* quoted in *Handelsblatt,* 24 October 1994.

4. *Handelsblatt,* 28 December 1994.

5. Almost exactly one year earlier (18 October 1993), the Ludwig-Erhard-Stiftung held a symposium on this precise topic. The proceedings of the conference, *Umbau der Sozialsysteme,* ed. by Martin Lambert (Krefeld, SINUS-Verlag, 1994), must have provided, at the very least, inspiration for the BDA brochure.

6. Cf. Labor Minister Norbert Blüm's (CDU) gloves-off response cited at the very beginning of the chapter to the particular suggestions of Murmann. Also Federal Health Minister Horst Seehofer (CSU) was quick to call the Murmann proposals "complete nonsense." The SPD's social expert Rudolf Dreßler referred to them as a "catalogue of horrors." For these last two responses, see *Tagesspiegel,* 20 October 1994. For an instance of how political competition between the parties has led to an escalation of social benefits, see Hans Günter Hockerts, "Vom Nutzen und Nachteil parlamentarischer Parteienkonkurrenz. Die Rentenreform 1972—ein Lehrstück," in Karl Dietrich Bracher et al., *Staat und Parteien. Festschrift für Rudolf Morsey zum 65. Geburtstag.* Berlin, 1992.

7. Very similar concerns in the United States led to the establishment of the thirty-two member Bipartisan Commission on Entitlement and Tax Reform. While the findings presented in its August 1994 Interim Report were supported by thirty-one of its members, the committee was unable to agree in its December final report on how to resolve the long-term imbalance between entitlements and the funds to pay for them.

8. Over 43 percent of gross domestic product in 1993 compared to 33 percent in 1960.

9. Today there are about sixty retirees being supported by one hundred working people in Germany. The relative number of retirees is expected to almost double by 2030. It is interesting to note that the United States Social Security Trustees'

Report projects that there will be one retiree per two covered workers in the United States in 2030, more favorable than the present situation in Germany.

10. Almost 70 percent of the German social budget is financed through the social insurance contributions of employers and employees.

11. Note, as in table 13.1, this does *not* include the wedge between earnings and disposable earnings due to income taxes.

12. The social budget of the German federal government is an accounting framework for the revenues and expenditures of social insurance programs first calculated in 1969. Social benefits are classified according to functional aspects (e.g., family, health, employment, old-age) and also according to institutions (old-age and survivors' insurance, health insurance, work-injury, etc.) and the revenues are classified according to the nature of the revenue (e.g., contributions from insured, from employers, or from general revenues) and by source (e.g., business, federal government, state government, etc.). Ideally, these accounts would be a set of satellite accounts to the national income and product accounts (GDP and national income), but full compatibility between these two sets of accounts is still lacking.

13. Many readers will have encountered a related principle of subsidiarity mentioned in the debate concerning the division of authority between European and national governments in the process of European unification. This is not really the same thing. The *Subsidiaritätsprinzip* in German social policy debate, the notion of a nested hierarchy of personal and social responsibilities from individuals through their families and ultimately to the level of society, is taken from Roman Catholic social thought, in particular, the papal encyclical of 1931, *Encyclica quadragesimo anno.*

14. Not mentioned in *Sozialstaat vor dem Umbau*, but consistent with the point being made here, are the lower rates of employee sickness in the new states compared to the old. A gradual convergence of sick rates between East and West has already been observed. According to statistics from company sickness funds, in 1991 employees reported on average 26 days per year sick in western Germany compared to only 10 days in eastern Germany. By 1993 the number had fallen to 21 days in western Germany (recession!) and increased to 18 days in eastern Germany. *Handelsblatt*, 13 December 1994.

15. Up through the year 2008 current estimates are for rates of 20–21 percent.

16. Or the current generation of pensioners could be "expropriated" by canceling their pensions—an unconstitutional act to be sure.

17. The four existing columns have already been discussed: old-age, health, work-injury, and unemployment insurance.

18. This is best seen in the special report on long-term care insurance published as appendix 4 to the *Jahresgutachten 1994/95 des Sachverständigenrates zur Begutachtung der gesamtwirtschaftlichen Entwicklung*. Deutsche Bundestag Drucksache 13/26, 21 November 1994.

19. *Tagesspiegel*, 29 December 1994.

20. On the other hand, the social budget does not include subsidies to producers that should be counted as part of aggregate social policy expenditure.

21. Indeed the ratio has dropped from 33 percent at the beginning of the decade to 30.4 percent by 1989, the eve of German unification. *Hauptergebnisse der Arbeits- und Sozialstatistik 1993*, Bundesminister für Arbeit und Sozialordnung, Bonn, October 1993, p. 115.

22. Federal President Roman Herzog in an interview with *Bild am Sonntag*, reported in *Tagesspiegel*, 2 January 1995.

23. *Handelsblatt*, 28 December 1994.

24. For example, Irwin Collier, "German Economic Integration: the Case for Optimism," in Michael G. Huelshoff, Andrei S. Marcovits, and Simon Reich, eds., *From Bundesrepublik to Deutschland* (Ann Arbor: University of Michigan Press, 1993), 93–113. Also Michael Burda and Michael Funke, "Eastern Germany: Can't We Be More Optimistic?" Economics Working Paper, Humboldt University, August 1994.

25. For comparison: the trustees of the United States Social Security System figure that by 2030 there will be 36 people over the age of 64 for every 100 working age Americans. United States policy analysts view this as extremely dangerous for the viability of the United States social security system. Germany will have about double that ratio of seniors to working population in 2030!

26. The consequences of this trend-break in productivity growth has been analyzed in the readable account of Paul Krugman, *The Age of Diminished Expectations* (MIT Press, 1991).

27. To its credit, the CDU/CSU/FDP coalition has put together a working group to implement the recommendations of the expert commission for the simplification of planning and approval procedures as quickly as possible. Proposals from this working group are to be worked out before the legislative break this summer.

28. The essay is published in Dennis Robertson, *Economic Commentaries* (London: Staples Press, 1956).

29. In an interview with the *Berliner Zeitung*, 30 January 1995, Bishop Wolfgang Huber of the Evangelical Lutheran church of Berlin-Brandenburg explicitly blamed the simultaneous introduction of new long-term care insurance premiums, the 7.5 percent solidarity surtax, and the elimination of the last vestiges of West Berlin pay supplements for the doubling of the church's quit rate. Almost 4,500 have left the Berlin-Brandenburg Lutheran church during the last two months of 1994.

30. Printed in *Das Parlament*, 25 November 1994.

14

IN SEARCH OF STABILITY
GERMAN FOREIGN POLICY AND THE PUBLIC IN THE 1990s

WOLFGANG-UWE FRIEDRICH

Anyone who reads German newspapers today, or chances to look at television or listen to the radio, gains the impression that Germans are extremely interested in foreign affairs. Even small local newspapers, such as the *Hildesheimer Allgemeine Zeitung*, report about the outside world in a detailed, comprehensive fashion. Not only is the quantity of this information impressive, but also its sophistication. The casual observer cannot fail to assume that Germans see foreign affairs as something of genuinely great importance, especially for their country. Long ago, in the eighteenth century, Goethe warned us not to take such things at face value. In *Faust*, he wrote: "I know of nothing better on a Sunday or a holiday, than chat of wars and warlike pother. When off in Turkey, far away, the people clash and fight with one another. We stand beside the window, drain our glasses."

Is foreign policy for today's Germans what Goethe would have called "Sunday and holiday entertainment"? The Oprah Winfrey of German television? Frankly, Germans nowadays are more serious when they talk about economic matters, or finance, or social questions. This is especially true when it comes to election campaigns, and the October elections in 1994 are a good example. A disappointed Foreign Minister Kinkel told the Bundestag in September that "I thought that we would be having a major debate on foreign policy during the budget discussions. We are now at the high point of the election campaign.... Alas, there is a silence, an eerie silence in the forests of our land, when it comes to debating foreign policy."[1] Apparently, foreign policy issues were not important enough to interest the voters. Or could one counter that this was so because German foreign affairs were in such good order, as Chancellor Kohl was fond of asserting, since at no time before the present were "the relations between Germany ... and Russia, the United States of America, Great Britain, and France so excellent as today"?[2] The chancellor's view is shared by all political parties, and it is generally assumed that there is no serious danger to the country's security any longer. The government continually asserts that Germany is today surrounded only by friends and partners. Therefore, it seems perfectly normal for people to believe that all significant international issues that have any bearing on their country have been solved. All that is left are those "wars far away," while the German citizen, in Goethe's words, says "Blessing with joy sweet peace and peaceful days."

On the one hand, it is clear that Germans are well informed about foreign affairs and that German society insists that such information is a permanent feature of the media. On the other, criticism is rising that people have decided that the subject does not affect them much, and they are not much concerned about it. In order to analyze this problem more thoroughly, one has to ask fundamental questions. The first of these involves asking what the main features and structures of German foreign policy have been since unification. What is the status of German integration into supranational organizations? Further, what are the goals of the government and of the parties? Finally, how does the public see foreign policy issues?

The Federal Republic found its foreign policy fulfillment in the Western security system. By means of a high level of integration into this system, West Germany succeeded in returning to the position of a powerful actor on the European and, remarkably, on the global scene. The preconditions for this integration were democracy, a market economy, and acceptance of a limited function as a conventional military power on NATO's eastern border. This success, unprecedented in German history, was founded upon the creation of a liberal, pluralistic democracy and the building of Europe's richest economy, rising to the level of the second largest trading nation in the world, with the second most important reserve currency. By the end of the 1970s at the latest, no economic or financial decisions could be taken within the European Community nor military decisions within NATO without the approval of the Federal Republic of Germany. This veto power was achieved by following a policy of full integration within these two bodies. At the same time, the new German status as a power with primary significance for all policy decisions took on a multilateral framework. This can be seen in Bonn's efforts on behalf of the European Union and of a global environmental policy, of the Helsinki Process and the CSCE, as well as of

GATT and the WTO. The structure and content of Bonn's foreign policy as well as West German membership in various supranational organizations also helped to make unification possible.

General Principles

The underlying principles of Helmut Kohl's foreign policy—integration of united Germany both in the European Union and the Atlantic Alliance—have contributed markedly to the achievement of Western institutional stability. Neither organization could survive without Germany. When the nation was granted its sovereignty in the 2+4 Treaty, it began immediately to exercise that sovereignty in fully anticipated directions. In other words, Bonn was *reliable* and *calculable*. The GDR disappeared along with the structures, the content, and the institutions of its foreign policy. The new foreign policy of united Germany is Bonn's old foreign policy. It seeks stability through widening and deepening of the European Union and the interlacing of the former Communist states with western Europe through treaties and supranational organizations. The first of these is promoted by the Treaty of Maastricht and its projected economic and currency union. Germany is prepared to bring the mark into a European Currency Union under conditions of strict criteria of stability. Although Maastricht also projects a common foreign and security policy as a goal, there is as yet no sign of this. Instead, there have been efforts to revive the West European Union, to be rebuilt and widened as the European arm of NATO. The Bundeswehr will be almost totally absorbed into new multinational units, including the Eurocorps with its German-French core. In short, German foreign policy continues to be based upon stability and seeks the further development of supranational organizations.

Former Communist states are being woven into ever deeper networks of treaties and organizations with the West. At the end of 1990, Germany had already signed a raft of treaties with the Soviet Union and, by 1992, with many other eastern European countries. Their official purpose has been to "finally put an end to the past" in order to "build a new Europe, united by common values." Essentially, these treaties are intended to encourage better consultation and closer cooperation. Of necessity, trade and culture are the foci.[3] Bonn promised not only consultation and cooperation, but also assistance in getting these countries "brought up" to the EU level. Tying them to the Western security structures included the new

NATO Cooperation Council and the NATO treaties on "Partnership for Peace." The Berlin Republic is going the way of its Bonn predecessor, not that of Weimar. In matters of security policy, Germany is following a *multilateral path* exclusively.

The integration of the Federal Republic into the Western community is the result of common interests and is founded upon common values. The much-cited community of values is firmly anchored in the Basic Law and the 2+4 Treaty, and finds expression in the plethora of treaties and political initiatives of German policy. The Preamble of the Basic Law states that the Federal Republic "must serve the peace of the world in a united Europe." The newly amended Article 23 now reads that "in order to realize a united Europe, the Federal Republic cooperates in the development of the European Union, and in connection therewith is obliged to uphold the democratic and legal principles of a state under law, including the social and federative bases of the Union and those of subsidiarity, while guaranteeing fundamental rights as maintained in this Basic Law." The broadened Article 88 provides for transferring competences of the Bundesbank to a European Central Bank. Article 24, Section 2 expressly permits the limitation of sovereignty, insofar as this serves the purpose of "a peaceful and long-term order" and is conditioned upon the coordination of Germany in a "system of mutual collective security." The unchanged Article 25 places international law as a part of federal law, and Article 26 forbids any kind of aggressive war. The 2+4 Treaty has the force of international law. With that treaty, all rights of the victor powers derived from their victory in World War II were dissolved. The signatories recognized the right of the German people to self-determination and the unification of "Germany as a state with final boundaries." Those boundaries were delineated as the current boundaries in the East. Normative continuity is one of the largely accepted principles of German foreign policy. Is the new Berlin Republic able and willing to fulfill these norms and goals?

Germany's New Power

The Berlin Republic is a regional great power, which demonstratively seeks cooperative efforts to serve its national interests which are primarily: social and economic well-being, stability and peace throughout Europe, free trade, and global cooperation. The preferred means for any goal is always multilateral. Therefore, the foreign policy of united Germany tries to secure stability through institutional continuity and cooperation within NATO and the European Union. However, both of these crucial organizations find themselves in a period of transformation. It is not at all clear what the results will be. Germany needs to square the circle, to combine institutional stability with structural change. NATO appears threatened by a gradual wasting away. The EU seems to be threatened by a collapse of efforts at deepening, while widening is pursued with success. The result there might be a relapse into a free-trade zone. The whole metamorphosis is being affected by the dynamics of European and international politics and the collapse of the Soviet Empire. No one could have predicted this epochal development. Equally unexpectedly, Germany united and was presented with an entirely unwelcome increase in its own power. What is the basis of that power?

With 80 million inhabitants, Germany has the second largest population of any country on the European continent. The Bundeswehr is dropping below the allowable limit of 370,000, but remains third largest, behind Russia and Ukraine. Nevertheless, if one considers training and quality of material, it is probably the strongest. United Germany is a key factor in any combination of forces, the new arbiter of Europe's balance of power. No European nation's economy comes close. The gross domestic product of DM3157 billion (1993) is almost as much as that of France and Great Britain together, and the total value of exports trails only the United States. With the exception of Luxemburg, Germany is the key trading partner of all neighboring states, but also of other countries, such as Russia, Ukraine, Turkey, and South Africa. For others, such as the United States, Japan, South Korea, China, Taiwan, Indonesia, Thailand, India, Argentina, Brazil, and Mexico, it is the most important European trading partner. Germany possesses the second largest gold and hard currency reserves in the world. At 20 percent of the total, the Deutschemark is the world's second reserve currency. As a creditworthy state for investment, the Berlin Republic holds fourth place behind only Switzerland, the United States, and Japan. Germany bears 28 percent of the EU budget. Germany's net transfer amount is DM19.6 billion, far ahead of Great Britain (DM4.8 billion) and France (DM2.9 billion). Added to that, it is second among paymasters of NATO and third of the United Nations. For Russia, Germany has become the key partner in terms of economic support, finance, and political assistance. All of these are key elements of power. How the Berlin Republic uses these depends on national interests, political norms, and on other actors in international politics.

German politics today, in the aftermath of the Hohenzollern Empire and the Third Reich, avoids, however, the use of the term "power." Politicians may have gradually come to speak openly of national interests, but this is quickly surrounded with an almost ritualistic acknowledgement of the country's duties and responsibilities. "Seeking power over others has led us along the wrong path throughout our history," observed Hans-Dietrich Genscher as Foreign Minister just a year before the fall of the Berlin Wall.[4] One of the favorite words of Bonn's diplomats is *Verantwortungspolitik*, policy based upon a sense of responsibility.[5] At the same time, Genscher knew how to use Germany's power to exclude Poland from the 2+4 Treaty negotiations. He also used it to arrange for the early recognition of Croatian independence. And, in combination with public opinion, it was used to sabotage the German policy of Margaret Thatcher. The French were saved from having the franc drop out of the European currency system. The Berlin Republic's economic power altered the traditional foreign policies of Scandinavia and the East Central European states.

Foreign policy is power politics. But this does not address the question of means. The means can be military, but they can also be economic, financial, or idealistic. As a trading nation, Germany draws its considerable means from its economic and financial strength and exerts influence on other states. In this, Bonn has been successful. Human rights and protection of the global environment are high on the public priority list, and they also have become elements of the country's foreign policy. Here, success has been elusive. Failures only reinforce the desire to return to a multilateral approach, not out of altruism, but because this has seemed the only effective means for German policy to serve national interests. There is a strong consensus that national interests are best served by a policy of peace through stability, especially in Europe. Foreign Minister Kinkel has stressed that it lies in German interests "to strengthen the European Union and the stability of all of Europe. In these questions, German and European interests are the same. Germany's future lies in Europe."[6] As the "central power in Europe,"[7] Germany needs a foreign policy debate free of idiosyncratic concepts of power that does not shy away from critically examining what the goals of foreign policy ought to be, what the national interests are, and what limitations exist—a debate which is fully conscious of the problems posed by a nonnuclear status, economic vulnerability, and the weight of past history.

Limitations of Power

One significant limitation on power is the decision forever to forego possession or use of ABC weapons. At the same time, there is a kind of structural weakness as a nonnuclear state alongside nuclear-power neighbors, such as France and Great Britain, not to mention the most powerful ally—the United States, and the potentially again-powerful former opponent—Russia. However, there is a kind of balancing advantage here, for those European neighbors would be extremely uncomfortable with a Germany that entered the nuclear club. An increase in power, such as that brought by unification, causes no distress to the United States, which shares an interest in stability and peace in Europe. In return, the United States continues to provide a security umbrella after the end of the Cold War against nuclear threat or intimidation, and this is less expensive and simpler than creating a substitute. Russia's future is too uncertain to give this up. Therefore, nobody even mentions giving up nonnuclear status. It is a dead issue. On the contrary, there is a general consensus for extension of the nuclear nonproliferation agreement.

A second significant limitation results paradoxically from economic strength, namely the dependence upon exports. Practically one-third of the domestic product is connected in some fashion to the export market, in contrast to 10 percent in the United States and 11 percent in Japan. Not one of the other G-7 states is faced with such an "eccentric foreign economic position."[5] In order to remain prosperous, it is necessary to meet international competition while simultaneously maintaining good relations with the United States and Japan. This means defending what is termed *Standort Germany* —the domestic manufacturing base. A Eurocentric focus before 1993 had led to ignoring the potential of an active East and Southeast Asia policy. Kinkel began an effort to remedy this by an official visit to China in 1992, the first by a federal foreign minister since 1988. Talks between Tokyo and Brussels began in 1991, but have yet to show any convincing results. Germany and Japan seem to have a number of interests in common, wholly aside from the competition of the marketplace. Working together could be profitable for both. Bonn was successful in helping work out a GATT compromise and in establishing the new World Trade Organization (WTO). Finally, there is still far to go in achieving a German global environmental policy and a policy of sustainable development.

A third limitation on German power is the heavy burden of history. Not only is the relationship with Israel a factor here, but that with Poland, the Czech Republic, the whole Balkan peninsula, and other countries as well. This kind of limitation may appear to be primarily of a moral nature, but it has power-political components as well. Symptomatic was the course of the debate over Maastricht in France. Those in favor claimed that only through such agreements could German power be restrained. The Socialist Paul Rocard warned that "Germany will find its historical inclinations once again." The EU would bind its most powerful member and prevent any danger. Opponents of Maastricht argued that Germany would dominate the Union, and only by maintaining her independence could France preserve her freedom.[9] Other examples are the nonnuclear status, the manner of integration of German forces within NATO and—as the French debate over Maastricht shows—in treatment by neighbors. This is why many small states want the United States to remain in Europe and, in turn, is one reason why the American presence is of crucial significance for Germany. Integration into Western structures has not only served as a component of mutual defense, but also to bind German power. Financial obligations arising from history's burden include payments to individuals and to Israel, which had reached DM93 billion by 1993.[10] In September 1993, a special agreement was reached at the Jewish Claims Conference on "hardship" terms for victims of National Socialist tyranny that would continue payments through 1999.

The measure of mutual understanding that has been reached in these fifty years cannot be estimated highly enough. One indication was the public support for unification in Europe and the United States. Another was the participation of two hundred German soldiers of the Eurocorps in a parade down the Champs Elysée in Paris on Bastille Day, 14 July 1994. The Germans and the French do not perceive each other any more as arch enemies, as they did in the past, but as very close, if not the closest, allies.

With varying intensity, these restraints on German foreign policy are continuous. Germany has learned to live with them, even in a constructive fashion. Integration in Western structures has helped immeasurably, and the search for stability has been assisted by the positive attitude Bonn has taken towards them. These structures have been seen to have positive value. The new global challenges mean that some changes are necessary, affecting the EU and NATO above all. For the latter, there is the apprehension that it will atrophy and lose its meaning unless there is fundamental reform.

Demands, Debates, Decisions: The Security Policy of the Berlin Republic

Hopes for a new world order, shared by the Germans, have not been fulfilled during the last five years. Reform of the United Nations is still on the agenda. Germany has asked for a permanent seat in the Security Council, which it joined as a nonpermanent member in 1995. Kinkel explained shortly, "Increased responsibility means an increased role in the decision process."[11] The United States and a number of Third World countries are supporting this effort, but France and Great Britain have reacted with considerable restraint. However, since the failures in Bosnia and Somalia, sobriety has set in. Public opinion no longer sees the UN as a device to create a new world order founded on justice for all. Reform has dropped on the priority list. The same has been the case with the CSCE.

When the "Charter of Paris" was signed in November 1990, Genscher waxed eloquent about a Europe united "on the basis of a community of values of law, self-determination, and responsibility."[12] Bonn pushed the further development of the CSCE process. On 1 June 1993, a German diplomat, Wilhelm Höynck, became first secretary general of the CSCE. Alas, developments have proven that fifty-three members make the CSCE far too large and diverse to accomplish much, and its structure has already proven too bureaucratic and complicated. It is more a mini-United Nations or, worse, a League of Nations in that it takes a decision on the part of a Great Power to act for something to get done. If that is not present, be it in Bosnia or Chechnya, then success is not possible. In December 1994 the CSCE Conference in Budapest agreed formally on a new document entitled "The Way to a Genuine Partnership in a New Age." At the same conference, an attempt to condemn Serbia failed due to a Russian veto. It was a poor beginning for the new OSCE, as the CSCE is now called. The Organization for Security and Cooperation in Europe has to prove that it can earn confidence. It is no wonder that hope rests with the proven organizations of the West, with NATO and the EU.

NATO was and is the decisive organization for security. It was the guarantor for forty years, protecting western Europe against the Soviet Union and binding West Germany into a defensive alliance. NATO provided security and stability. Its core was Article 5, collective defense. The collapse of the Soviet Empire raised the obvious question whether the Alliance was still needed. The new enemy was harder to see, harder to explain to the public. Its name—as President Bush described it—was "unpredictability and instability."[13] The tendency in Germany in 1990 was to say that NATO had outlived its usefulness, and to deny that any extension eastward was desirable, even to the extent of bringing in the New Federal States. Germany's neighbors saw the situation more clearly, especially as it concerned the Balkans. Only gradually have Germans begun to appreciate the validity of Bush's words, only slowly have they begun to appreciate what has happened. The security "establishment," however, knew from the start and have been patiently waiting for public opinion to catch up. The 1994 White Book proclaimed that the Alliance remained "the basis for the security of Germany. It incorporates the strategic unity of the North American and European partners."[14] However, with the attention of the general public elsewhere, the process of reform had already begun.

In November 1991 a NATO conference in Rome brought a "New Strategic Concept." Defense structures were streamlined, and increasingly organized on a multilateral basis. Arms reduction was pursued, and nuclear components drastically reduced. At the meeting of the Nuclear Planning Group in Gleneagles in 1992, the old concepts were thrown overboard. Cooperation with the East was on the horizon. In December of the same year, the North Atlantic Cooperation Council was established. This was supposed to make a breakthrough in collaboration with Russia. Somewhat more concrete is the concept of Partnership for Peace from 1994. Both the NACC and the PFP represent a policy of networking, binding eastern European states within a network of arrangements, even if they do not include membership in NATO itself. This framework is based upon the same common values (human rights, democracy, peace) that underlay the western Alliance in the first place, including the Charter of the United Nations and the various CSCE documents. PFP treaties define five areas of cooperation: transparency of national defense planning and budgeting; democratic control over the military; cooperation in UN and CSCE actions; common planning and joint training exercises with NATO for the purpose of preparation for international operations (including peacekeeping and humanitarian operations); and the long-term creation of forces with which NATO can cooperate.[15]

The Partnership for Peace has three objectives. The first is a transfer of stability to the East. Second, the Visegrad states must see it as a stage towards membership in NATO. Third, Russia must not be given the impression of encirclement by the West, but there must also be no thought of a Russian "veto" over membership. Actually, membership in NATO has become the crucial issue. When membership comes, it must be credible. A security guarantee for Poland, for example, must be a credible guarantee, accepted as such by all members, and leading to the appropriate collective defense if needed, including American nuclear protection. But this is as far as NATO could possibly go. An eastward expansion of NATO must also be seen as useful to the United States. There is no possibility of taking in Estonia, Latvia, and Lithuania, because the three Baltic states realistically can not be defended. They, and other eastern European states, must be covered by the OSCE. Therefore, some further development of that organization must be possible. Finally, it is one thing to view NATO as a collective defense for threats in Europe. It is another to view it as having a role beyond the region.

The United States is a global power, for which NATO may be interpreted as a military arm. Only a very few Europeans see things that way. Germans would only accept any global engagement of NATO under the UN as a "roof." Combining the questions of European peace and stability with global peace and stability presents extremely difficult problems for Germans. The horrors of the Bosnian conflict and the failure in Somalia have pointed to the limitations of military intervention. Both have increased the number of skeptics, and not only in Europe. What is clear is that, whatever results, it is important to have a functional military force.

There has been no significant step toward a fundamental rethinking of NATO. If it remains a purposeful and useful goal of NATO to hold Europe and North America together in a meaningful way, then it is high time for a new Atlantic Charter. Article 2 of the Washington Treaty already speaks of "solidarity" and "prosperity," including economic cooperation. It should be possible to use this as a jumping-off point to build a second pillar of cooperation besides the military one. Such a second pillar could have economic and societal elements. It should lead to an institution in which Europeans and Americans could work together in four areas: economic and finance policy, environmental protection, Third World development policy, and cultural cooperation (including science and research). NATO needs its own "Agenda 2000."

Much energy has been expended in the past several years on revitalizing the West European Union. The reason for this was the ambitious project of building the EU. The Maastricht Treaty speaks of a common foreign and security policy. The WEU is supposed to become an integral entity of the EU and have its own security identity. The

1954 version of the WEU Treaty states clearly that "the creation of a parallel organization to the military staffs of NATO is not desired." The German government spares no rhetoric to assure all and sundry on every possible occasion that this means only that the WEU will become the "European pillar" of NATO. In point of fact, however, the United States is reorienting its own foreign and security policies following the collapse of the Soviet Empire. Both the United States and Europe are in agreement that Europe should be able to act. The question lies in the degree of independence of action. The French "Livre Blanc sur la Défense" of 1994 points clearly in the direction of an independent role for the WEU, in order to deal "autonomously" in crisis situations. This means a gradual easing of the United States out of Europe. The Petersberg Declaration of the Council of Ministers of the WEU of 19 June 1992 also points in this direction.[16] Petersberg marks the beginning of a new attempt to formulate a western European security identity. It places the WEU under the roof of the UN and, especially, the CSCE as a regional entity. In a new European security architecture, the WEU should take its place and play a "military-operative role" alongside of NATO as a "defensive component of the EU." For this purpose, a WEU Satellite Center was established in Torrejon in Spain. This will make the WEU independent of American satellites. According to Petersberg, military units representing the broad spectrum of conventional arms should be organized under the WEU for the purposes of conventional defense, peacekeeping missions, as well as "military operations to deal with crises, including measures to bring about peace." This allows the WEU to take military measures without geographic restrictions. For now, this has only meant participation in the naval blockade of Serbia/Montenegro in the Adriatic. The WEU Council and the Secretary-General have been moved to Brussels. A WEU Institute for Security Studies has begun functioning in Paris. The Eurocorps that was established in November 1993 is the first WEU unit that has simultaneously been placed under NATO. It is possible to use this device to bring France back into the military side of NATO. It is also possible that this could lead to a rupture of the North Atlantic Alliance. What finally will happen depends mostly on German decisions.

The federal government views the efforts to vitalize the WEU as a positive development. Still, it can have unpleasant aspects. France has succeeded in using the WEU to gain some control over German arms, while retaining full decision-making capacity over its own nuclear forces. If the WEU develops contrary to German wishes as a competitor of NATO, Germany could lose the American nuclear guarantee without gaining the French in return. German national interests lie in giving NATO a clear preference over the WEU. Unfortunately, there is virtually no discussion in the public forum over this development.

Instead, the Bundestag hears continually positive reports over NATO developments.[17] Kohl called the 1994 NATO agreements a "milestone on the road to a new security order for Europe," and congratulated himself on the close relationship with the United States that they demonstrate. The Balkan developments, Kohl stressed, show how important it is for Europe to find a security system, and the WEU must be its arm.[18] He pleaded for multilateralism, and spoke proudly of German reliability and responsibility. Kinkel described NATO as a "cornerstone of the future security architecture for a united Europe," in which the most important goal should be the prevention of conflicts. The Atlantic, he said, must not become wider. There must be new mechanisms. He also emphasized economic, societal, cultural, and environmental goals. Germany, the foreign minister stressed, was the "representative" of the interests of her eastern neighbors. The future of European security was based upon—and there followed the full acronymic puzzle—NATO, NACC, WEU, EU, UN, CSCE, OSCE. It was a mouthful, and the inner contradictions were blithely swallowed as if the whole delicious experience made up the difference. Defense Minister Rühe took up the chorus with his own perspectives. While the chancellor spoke of the principle of opening NATO to the East, Rühe declared that this "lies fully in our vital interests." Impressed by Rand's—basically wrong—"Out-of-area or out-of-business" study, he laid out two main functions for NATO: not only collective defense, but also the "capability to take part in international efforts to extinguish crises." The latter was so important that it must be included if the Alliance were not to become dead in the water. The WEU was a European pillar of NATO, for therein the Alliance would remain "the decisive consultation forum for security issues in Europe." Hans-Ulrich Klose, then speaker of the SPD, agreed largely with the government. However, he observed that it was important that no new tensions be created by NATO. The Alliance was important as a system of collective defense. Europe did, of course, also need to build a collective security system, but that was "*Zukunftsmusik*" (something for the future). Karsten D. Voigt of the SPD had already gone further. For him, the Petersberg Declaration was leading down the wrong road, because it seemed to be trying to make western Europe, by means of the WEU, into some kind of "European interventionist power."[19] This view was shared by the Greens. Vera Wollenberger of the Alliance 90/Greens spoke out further for a continuation of the American presence in Europe. "American troops are an insurance [policy] against attempts by Germany or Russia to dominate Europe." Adding additional members limits nationalist aspirations and foreign policies. In principle, however, she thought that a way should be left open for Russia to join. But in its present form of a military alliance, it inhibits this development, and therefore a reform in the direction of collective security is very desirable. Andrea Lederer spoke for the PDS, condemning "the strong tendency towards militarizing Western foreign policy."

It is not quite usual that major political decisions result from constitutional court pronouncements. Not so in the Federal Republic. The Federal Constitutional Court issued a formal decision on 12 July 1994 in the matter of the use of the Bundeswehr on foreign soil. It was responding to a request of the Bundestag members of the SPD and the FDP for an interpretation of the Basic Law as to whether the participation of Bundeswehr units in the WEU Adriatic Sea blockade, the NATO AWACS flights over Bosnia, and the UN Somalia action were constitutional. Could Germany do these things? Failure to participate in the Gulf War had cost more than DM10 billion and political isolation. After that, the government had to make a "course correction," and attempted limited participation in various international activities, which had then produced the SPD/FDP petition. The course correction had limited support from the FDP, but opposition from the SPD, the Alliance 90/Greens, and the PDS. It had consisted of various actions, varying from humanitarian aid to Kurds in Turkey and Iran, medical support for Blue Helmet units in Cambodia, helicopter units for UN control sanctions in Iraq, to participation in the actions indicated above. The SPD first tried to deal with this by means of a constitutional amendment, allowing the Bundeswehr to be used "only for peacekeeping measures without military action" and for humanitarian or environmental aid, specifically stating that troops were only to carry light weapons for self-defense. Each of these actions would require separate Bundestag approval.[20] In 1992, the Greens brought their own proposal for a constitutional amendment, in which the Bundeswehr could take part in peacekeeping operations of the UN, provided that the Bundestag approved them with a two-thirds majority and the UN was reformed to eliminate the veto powers of the permanent members of the Security Council.[21] The PDS followed with their unrealistic proposal for an amendment that would strictly prohibit the use of the Bundeswehr for any purpose but self-defense.[22] Finally, the CDU/CSU and FDP proposed that Germany be permitted to participate in peacekeeping *and* peacemaking measures on the basis of decisions of the Security Council of the UN, and with a simple majority in the Bundestag, or on the basis of Article 51 of the UN Charter, which would then require a two-thirds majority.

The debate spilled over into the media in the early summer of 1994, while the Bundestag election campaign was going on. According to pollsters, the public was split into two about equally divided groups. All these proposals became obsolete with the Court decision. The Constitutional Court issued its opinion amidst widespread anticipation that the chancellor's view would be confirmed. Basing its decision on Article 24, Section 2, the Court held that Germany is permitted "in safeguarding peace" to participate in collective security, including use of the Bundeswehr outside of the country and of NATO. "Peace troops, and peace-securing measures, are part and parcel of a system of collective security under the United Nations, as the practical application of the UN provisions have developed and to which Germany has acceded in 1973 in a lawful manner."[23] Participation in these activities, ruled the Court, requires parliamentary approval.

The government reacted swiftly, with pleasure. A special session of the Bundestag was called at once, and Foreign Minister Kinkel praised the decision for its "definitive rejection of a German 'Sonderweg'" (isolated direction in foreign policy). SPD chancellor candidate Scharping called the whole session "superfluous." Voigt, however, described the decision as a "turning point." The majority of SPD deputies voted for the government's position, declaring that they hadn't been against the policy itself but solely against the decision making procedure. Gerd Poppe of the Alliance 90 called the session an election maneuver. Gregor Gysi of the PDS urged a negative vote. The results brought 424 "yes" and 48 "no" votes, with 16 abstentions.[24] In the end, it became obvious that there is, in fact, a broad consensus on foreign and security policy.

Widening and Deepening: The Berlin Republic and the European Union

European integration is the core of German foreign policy. The Treaty of Maastricht outlined the project of a European Union and is based upon three fundamental elements: an economic and currency union, a common foreign and security policy, and a common legal and internal policy. The three have different weights. For the European Community, the primary element was economic, which included the common market, the long sought-after currency union, common decisions on trade, a common agricultural policy, and structural policies dependent upon such matters. The four "basic freedoms" of the common market were free transport of goods, persons, services, and capital. They were the essence of the Community. Germany wants more than that—a deepening of the Union to include the other two elements. That is why achieving Maastricht became an essential part of German policy. Yet, this is not moving forward quite as hoped.

We have seen the problems of WEU in the security realm. It is far from becoming a power factor on the international scene. A common foreign policy seems only to emerge where little can be done, such as in the Middle East. Elsewhere, such as in the Balkans, there is not even consensus, much less a common policy. Widening the Union, expansion, is another subject on which there is less than consensus.

On internal policy, a major problem has been the asylum question. In 1992 Germany accepted 440,000 people. Great Britain, on the other hand, took only about as many as Hamburg. The result was the "Three State System," by which the Bundestag effectively reduced the flow through Poland. There are more problems. Britain is opposed to the social policy urged by the continental members. There is a loud silence from the membership on environmental issues. Still, Germany wants to deepen the Union and finds Britain its chief obstacle, aided by Denmark. The four southern members—Portugal, Spain, Italy, and Greece—are so weak economically, that they hinder rather than strengthen any process of deepening the Union. Therefore, deepening depends largely upon the attitude of France.

Mitterand and Kohl have launched several successful joint initiatives to tighten the EU, but the French president has not endorsed everything, and his term has expired. France does not favor a strengthening of the European Parliament, is dragging its feet on a common system of justice and other internal policies, and is not willing to grant Germany parity in the area of common foreign and security policy. The reason is clear. Just as multilateralism and integration are general principles of German foreign policy, national sovereignty is one for the French. The future will hold a rich store of problems.

Such future problems were seldom discussed in the Bundestag. Kohl explained Maastricht to the deputies by emphasizing its effect as a peace guaranty.[25] Conceding that the treaty was a compromise, the chancellor brought up the old saw that the European community buried old hatchets, and kept them buried, and how his country needed this. He stressed how the unity of Europe was one of Germany's most fundamental interests. Raising the grisly specter of his people's "geopolitical" situation, and all the fears and anxieties that that involved, he pleaded that, whatever its deficiencies, Maastricht was today's most possible arrangement and laid the foundations for everything else necessary. Kinkel followed and played the same tune, elaborated through reference to the new Article 23 of the Basic Law, reminding the deputies that European integration was enshrined in the constitution as a goal for the state. Finance Minister Theo Waigel spoke for the CSU and completed the illustration by talking about economic and political stability that was guaranteed through Maastricht. All the right buttons were pushed. Secretary General of the SPD Günter Verheugen spoke for his party, urging a united Europe, and raising concerns about those who would seek the federalist path. Small countries, he warned, would view that with "anxiety and mistrust," something Germans should spare them. No "Europe à la carte," he explained, whereby everyone would try to select what elements of united Europe they wanted to choose and support only those. His colleague, Heidemarie Wieczorek-Zeul, criticized the lack of democracy in the entire EU structure. Like Kohl, she wanted more power for the Parliament. But unlike the chancellor, she warned also against a "Europe moving at two separate speeds" towards unity. FDP and Alliance 90/Greens also saw positive aspects in the pact. Hans Modrow explained why the PDS was opposed. The whole treaty, he declared, made the way clear for the strongest state to dominate. That state was the newly larger Germany, which would dominate Europe. Finally, the Bundestag voted overwhelmingly with 543 "yes," 16 "no," and 8 abstentions. Polls showed that the general public, in this particular case, had a totally different view.

Manfred Brunner, former chief of staff to EC Commissioner Martin Bangemann, who had resigned his post in opposition to Maastricht, now brought the Treaty to the Federal Constitutional Court, claiming that it ran contrary to the Basic Law. The Court disagreed, and threw out the case. Its decision of October 1993, however, brought little joy to the government. Maastricht and the Union were, said the Court, basically an intergovernmental agreement on what is "basically an economic community," on the order of a customs union with other attributes. The other aspects, such as foreign and security policy, internal affairs, and justice were essentially of an intergovernmental character.[26] In short, the Court's view of the EU was considerably less than that seen through the rose-colored glasses of the government coalition and the SPD.

The EU was widened on 1 January 1995 through the admission of Austria, Finland, and Sweden. Norway had declined. Deepening is still far away. On 1 September 1994, the CDU/CSU Bundestag Chief Wolfgang Schäuble and the Bundestag Foreign Political Spokesman Karl Lamers presented their colleagues with a sobering assessment of the state of the European Union. They called it "Considerations on European Policy." The authors describe the EU as an "Element of Continental Order." They propose to move integration forward. Key measures would include a strengthening of the Parliament, reform of various institutions, and a greater emphasis on subsidiarity, EU-jargon for transferring decision authority from Brussels to the individual states. The public is becoming fed up with EU bureaucracy, and Schäuble and Lamers want to deal with that. Under a heading called "intensifying German-French relations," they want to gain French support for strengthening the European Parliament and, hopefully, get France to come closer to NATO. They suggest that some regions in Europe are especially ripe for the common foreign and security policy. At the same time, they want to "reorient" the transatlantic partnership whereby a transatlantic policy on global challenges can be developed. The most controversial part of the paper refers to their suggestion of a further development of the "core" of the European Union. In order to avoid a "Europe à la carte" or an "intergovernmental arrangement," they see a Europe moving at different speeds, a kind of "variable geometry," in which some states can move more quickly than others towards the ultimate goal. This would mean that those which wished to move more rapidly would not be blocked by a veto or by the inability of others to keep up. Article 109 of Maastricht allows this. A "core-Europe" would take the fast track. In any case, Schäuble and Lamers assured their readers, Germany's interests lay in Europe.

A media storm erupted, not only in Germany. Rome was furious. Italy did not want to be excluded from the core. Premier Berlusconi called the chancellor personally.[27] Although French Prime Minister Balladur had already spoken about a "Europe of Three Circles," Paris was also not complimentary about the "Schäuble-Lamers Paper."[28] Domestic comments ran the gamut, with the majority being critical. Some very unpleasant truths were laid bare. If anything, the Paper stripped rhetoric and camouflage from reality. Through September and October 1994, as the election campaign reached its climax, the clamor did not cease. Amidst the budget debate, the Bundestag took up the Paper on 7 September. Klose warned that a "core-Europe" concept endangered unity. Scharping criticized it bitterly, complaining that it divided the continent into "first- and second-class states." Schäuble defended the theses, and Kohl suggested that they were merely "proposals to engender critical thought" about significant issues. In the end, it could have been a real debate about the genuine issues, but nobody seemed to have the courage. It seemed that the deputies were simply lifting slogans off their various election placards and building them into lengthy speeches. Kinkel summed it up: "Let's not be divisive. Let's integrate. Hold the course!"[29] The deputies having satisfied themselves with mouthing the right phrases and ignoring the real issues, the debate on the Schäuble-Lamers Paper closed. The issues it raised did not. At the latest, they will revive at the Maastricht Revision Conference of 1996. Then, they will once again be asked what kind of union should emerge—a political union, or a "common market" with "intergovernmental agreements."

Ambivalence and Common Sense: Foreign Policy and Public Opinion

The discussions on NATO and the EU show clearly the gap between foreign policy and public opinion. The public is interested in foreign policy, but considers it—as the debate on European unity shows—not extremely important. A few polls show this in crystal clarity. An Allensbach inquiry in 1985 reported the general tendency: 45 percent thought foreign policy to be "less important," 24 percent to be "scarcely important," while 48 percent said that they were "interested" in it.[30] Most people want their country to be some sort of Switzerland. An impressive majority of 61 percent (1991), in contrast to the views expressed by their chancellor and foreign minister, want to see reluctance or disengagement as a hallmark of foreign policy, and only 23 percent want more responsibility on the world stage. Among the élites in politics, the economy, and the media, these statistics are exactly reversed. About three-quarters think that more, rather than less, responsibility should be the essence of the united country's foreign policy.

Every year, the Secretary General of the United Nations comes to Bonn and appeals for more engagement. This seems only to interest the élites. The ordinary citizen is thinking about his or her wallet, job, and personal freedom and security. More engagement means that the Bundeswehr should be involved in UN actions. In 1991, only 39 percent of westerners and 19 percent of easterners wanted to see this happen. The horrors of war have bored deep into the national psyche. The result is an ambivalent relationship to the entire concept of military power. People favor defense if attacked. Beyond that, pacifism is not totally unpopular.

There is yet a certain ambivalence about foreign policy. Another poll shows that 88 percent have heard of the Security Council of the UN, and 64 percent think that Germany should be a permanent member. Two-thirds to three-fourths want to remain in NATO (considerably less in the East). The great majority supports alliance with the United States and likes "the Americans." In the Gulf War, 47 percent in the West wanted to support them, and 52 percent said that Germany should help Turkey if Iraq attacked. Asked about the lessons of history, 36 percent said that their country should "never again" take part in a war, but 50 percent said that one "had to" fight against dictators, if nothing else were successful. The demonstrators against the Gulf War were a small group, and they spoke only for a minority of the people. In March 1992, 45 percent did support the idea of German participation in UN Blue Helmet actions, 37 percent against (in the East: 26 percent for, 57 percent against). In August of 1992, 54 percent supported the Adriatic action of the WEU, and only 23 percent were opposed. At the same time, 50 percent were in favor of participating in peacekeeping troops in the former Yugoslavia.

Especially interesting are the figures for European integration. For years, Germans have been everybody's best example of widespread popular support. A very considerable skepticism has lately reared its head. In December 1993, 25 percent said that their country was being exploited by the EU. Just before the European elections in 1994, 83 percent said that, in the future, their country should seek to represent its own interests more strongly. In 1989, 58 percent of westerners said that the integration process should not be slowed down. In 1991, only 34 percent held this view. Those who wanted a slower pace grew in the same years from 21 percent to 38 percent (actually, the same level for the East in 1991 as for the West). In 1994, 52 percent (West) and 45 percent (East) said that EU membership is a "good thing" (EU average = 54 percent; France, 50 percent; Great Britain, 43 percent). Manfred Brunner's "Bund freier Bürger" (League of Free Citizens) received only 3.9 percent of the vote, a real defeat. Germans are not tired of Europe. They are skeptical.[31]

What conclusions can we draw from this data? For one, foreign policy themes are important, but are pushed into the foreground only by major international crises. Previously, Germany was generally on the sidelines when it came to such occasions. The majority does not want this to change. Germans do not want to play a leadership role. It is very important to point out that the political culture of the country is still divided. In the East, the whole issue of *Westbindung*, the connection to the Western community, western Europe, and the Atlantic Alliance, is much more skeptically seen than in the West. On the other hand, people are ready to become engaged internationally. This means that they are ready to accept all rights *and* obligations of UN membership. Even though a pacifist impulse rushed to the top in the great crises of the post-Communist era, like the Gulf War and Bosnia, this was largely due to a lack of leadership. The élites want the country to do its duty, but they have not yet learned to lead the people in this direction.

Conclusion

Goethe's words are a warning to the German public and élites alike. The public is too complacent. The élites are not yet ready to lead. But the future is here. The Berlin Republic is now. There are three obligations ahead.

First, in times of change the search for stability is growing, but it cannot rest upon continuity alone. Normative continuity is of highest importance, a continuity of style or approaches is very useful, because it makes politics calculable. The Berlin Republic tries both in a good known way, to secure peace through multilateral cooperation. The basic organizations of the West, however, have to change as much as the needs and the challenges change. Every member state of the European Union has to reconcile its place as a member with its national interests. The same is true for NATO, which needs to achieve a second, civilian structure for transatlantic cooperation. Security, economic, and other interests are by necessity bound up in membership in the two most important and most successful organizations: the EU and NATO. Sovereignty and independence of actions is today nothing more than an atavistic notion.

Second, the Berlin Republic is not ready to deal with global challenges, such as migration, environmental protection, sustainable development together with Third World partners, and the global promotion of democracy and human rights. It is also unable to export stability to its eastern neighborhood by itself, as is France in the case of the Mediterranean, or the United States south of the Rio Grande. One might say that the West won the Cold War, but now it's definitely becoming a loser, too. Germany is no exception. What is desperately needed is a common Western policy vis-à-vis the most important global challenges. The United States, Germany, and Japan have to coordinate their resources together with other partners, such as Britain, France, South Korea, and Australia, to develop a common policy. Otherwise there will be no success.

Third, widening and deepening the European Union is the squaring of the circle. It is most unlikely to get a functioning Union together with such weak partners as, for example, Greece. Therefore, the EU will either relapse to a free-trade zone or succeed through different speeds. Britain sooner or later will reconcile its European policy, and so will France. Together with Germany, Belgium, Luxemburg, and the Netherlands, the six could become a core-Europe. But even such a core-Europe needs the United States as a partner and arbiter. The United States, however, focuses ignorantly on domestic issues. The Berlin Republic, on the other hand, is neither ready nor strong enough to show leadership—what almost nobody wants from the Germans anyway. Germany's search for stability, therefore, can only lead to success when its diplomacy convinces Washington and Paris and London and Tokyo to develop a new and broad strategic concept. It is a question of *Staatskunst*.

Notes

1. *Deutscher Bundestag*, 12. Wahlperiode, 242. Sitzung, 7 September 1994, p. 21460.

2. Ibid., 1436.

3. "Das deutsch-sowjetische Vertragswerk vom Herbst 1990," in *Europa Archiv* 46 (1991): 3, D 63–D 90.

4. Hans-Dietrich Genscher, *Wir wollen ein europäisches Deutschland* (Berlin: Goldmann, 1992), 170.

5. Ibid., 12, 210.

6. *Deutscher Bundestag*, 12 Wahlperiode, 216. Sitzung, 10 March 1994, p. 18591.

7. Hans-Peter Schwarz, *Die Zentralmacht Europas, Deutschlands Rückkehr auf die Weltbühne* (Berlin: Siedler, 1994).

8. Dieter Senghaas, "Deutschland ist ein 'Handelsstaat,'" in *Eichholz Brief/Zeitschrift zur politischen Bildung* 31 (1994) 2, pp. 30–39.

9. *Archiv der Gegenwart* 62 (1992): 37165ff.

10. *Jahresbericht der Bundesregierung 1993* (Bonn: Presse- und Informationsamt, 1994), 247.

11. *Deutscher Bundestag*, 12. Wahlperiode, 240. Sitzung, 22 July 1995, p. 21168.

12. *Bericht der Bundesregierung 1990* (Bonn: Presse- und Informationsamt, 1991), 14.

13. *USPIT*, 26 February 1992, p. 11.

14. *Weißbuch 1994* (Bonn: Federal Ministry of Defense, 1994), 50.

15. Reader *Sicherheitspolitik*, ed. the Federal Ministry of Defense, Documentation VIII, *Ergänzungslieferung*, 1–2/1994.

16. In *Europa Archiv* 47 (1992) 14, D 479–D 485. Also, Erich Vad, "Die WEU—'europäischer Pfeiler' oder Konkurrent der NATO?" in *Europäische Sicherheit* 1/1994, pp. 28–31. In 1995, the WEU states included Belgium, France, Germany, Great Britain, Greece, Italy, Luxembourg, Netherlands, Spain, and Portugal. Associated members since 1992 are Iceland, Norway, and Turkey, and, since 1994, Bulgaria, the Czech Republic, Estonia, Hungary, Latvia, Lithuania, Poland, and Slovakia. Observers are Austria, Denmark, and Ireland.

17. See *Deutscher Bundestag*, 12. Wahlperiode, 126. Sitzung, 2 December 1992, pp. 10838ff.

18. *Deutscher Bundestag*, 12. Wahlperiode, 202. Sitzung, 13 January 1994, pp. 17412ff.

19. *Deutscher Bundestag*, 12. Wahlperiode, 126. Sitzung, 2 December 1992, p. 10838.

20. *Deutscher Bundestag*, 12. Wahlperiode, Drucksache 12/2895.

21. *Deutscher Bundestag*, 12. Wahlperiode, Drucksache 12/3014.

22. *Deutscher Bundestag*, 12. Wahlperiode, Drucksache 12/3055.

23. Das Urteil des Bundesverfassungsgerichts vom 12. Juli 1994 zu den Organstreitverfahren Adria, AWACS und Somalia (UNOSOM II) in *Neue Juristische Wochenschrift* 1994, Heft 34, pp. 2207ff.

24. *Deutscher Bundestag*, 12. Wahlperiode, 240. Sitzung, 22 July 1994, pp. 21165ff.

25. *Deutscher Bundestag*, 12. Wahlperiode, 126. Sitzung, 2 December 1992, pp. 10183ff.

26. Das Maastricht-Urteil des Bundesverfassungsgerichts vom 12. Oktober 1993, in *Europa Archiv* 48 (1993) 22, D 460–D 476.

27. Konrad Adenauer Stiftung, ed., *Das Schäuble-Lamers-Papier. Nationale und internationale Reaktionen. Dokumentation* (Sankt Augustin: 1994).

28. *Le Figaro*, 30 August 1994.

29. *Deutscher Bundestag*, 12. Wahlperiode, 242. Sitzung, 7 September 1994, pp. 21409ff.

30. These, and the following, from Elisabeth Noelle-Neumann and Renate Köcher, eds., *Allensbacher Jahrbuch der Demoskopie*, vol. 9, 1984–1992 (Munich: Saur, 1993), 642, 956–63, 1088–95.

31. Gerd Langguth, *Suche nach Sicherheiten. Ein Psychogram der Deutschen*, (Stuttgart: DVA, 1954), 198ff; Hans-Wolfgang Platzer and Walter Ruhland, *Welches Deutschland in welchem Europa? Demoskopische Analysen, politische Perspektiven, gesellschaftliche Kontroversen* (Bonn: Dietz Nachfolger, 1994); *Allensbach-Archiv, IfD-Umfragen* 5029, 5035, 5059.

APPENDIX

TABLE A.1

BUNDESTAG ELECTIONS SINCE 1949
PARTY PERCENTAGE OF THE SECOND VOTE

Year	Percent Voting	CDU/ CSU	SPD	FDP	Greens- A. 90/Gr.[a]	PDS	Other Parties[b]
1949[c]	78.5	31.0	29.2	11.9	–	–	27.8
1953	86.0	45.2	28.8	9.5	–	–	16.5
1957	87.8	50.2	31.8	7.7	–	–	10.3
1961	87.7	45.3	36.2	12.7	–	–	5.7
1965	86.8	47.6	39.3	9.5	–	–	3.6
1969	86.7	46.1	42.7	5.8	–	–	5.5
1972	91.1	44.9	45.8	8.4	–	–	0.9
1976	90.7	48.6	42.6	7.9	–	–	0.9
1980	88.6	44.5	42.9	10.6	1.5	–	0.5
1983	89.1	48.8	38.2	7.0	5.6	–	0.5
1987	84.3	44.3	37.0	9.1	8.3	–	1.4
1990	77.8[d]	43.8	33.5	11.0	3.8/1.2[e]	2.4[f]	4.2
1994	79.1	41.5	36.4	6.9	7.3	4.4[g]	3.5

The data in this and the following tables come from the election reports published by the Federal and State Statistical Offices in Germany, from the statistical overviews in Peter Schindler, ed., *Datenhandbuch zur Geschichte des Deutschen Bundestages 1949 bis 1982,* and its continuation, *1983 bis 1991,* as well as from the election studies done by the Forschungsgruppe Wahlen e.V.

[a]In 1990, the Greens won 4.8 percent of the vote in the West, amounting to 3.8 percent in the enlarged Federal Republic. The separate Alliance 90/Greens won 6.2 percent in the East, which amounted to 1.2 percent in the entire Federal Republic. Under the special arrangement for 1990, which divided the Federal Republic into two electoral areas (East and West), the eastern Alliance 90/Greens won parliamentary representation by passing the 5 percent minimum, but the western Greens did not. By 1994, the two had merged as an all-German party with the name Alliance 90/Greens.

[b]In 1949, including BP (Bavarian Party) 4.2 percent, Center Party 3.1 percent, DP (German Party), 4.0 percent, DKP and DRP (German Party and German Reich Party) 1.9 percent, KPD (Communists) 5.7 percent, WAV (Economic Reconstruction Union) 2.9 percent, and independents 4.8 percent. In 1953, including BP 1.7 percent, DP 3.3 percent, GB/BHE (a new refugee party) 5.9 percent, and KPD 2.2 percent. In 1957, including DP 3.4 percent, and GB/BHE 4.6 percent. In 1961, including GDP (a merger of DP and BHE) 2.8 percent, and DFU (German Peace Union) 1.9 percent. In 1965, including DFU 1.3 percent, and NPD (National Democratic Party 2.0 percent. In 1969, including NPD 4.3 percent. In 1972, including DKP (Communists) 0.3 percent, and NPD 0.6 percent. In 1976, including DKP 0.3 percent, and NPD 0.3 percent. In 1980 and 1983, including DKP 0.2 percent, and NPD 0.2 percent. In 1987, including NPD 0.6 percent. In 1990, including

NPD 0.3 percent, and Republikaner 2.1 percent. In 1994, including Republikaner 1.9 percent.
[c]In 1949, a one-vote ballot only.
[d]In December 1990 the voter turnout was 74.5 percent in the East and 78.6 percent in the West.
[e]See footnote a.
[f]In December 1990, the PDS won parliamentary representation by netting 11.1 percent of the vote in the East. In the West, the PDS received only 0.3 percent.
[g]In October 1994, the PDS won 4.4 percent of the vote nationwide, based on close to 20 percent in the East and 0.9 percent in the West.

TABLE A.2

DISTRIBUTION OF BUNDESTAG SEATS SINCE 1949

Year	Total Seats	CDU/ CSU	SPD	FDP	Greens- A. 90/Gr.[a]	PDS	Other Parties[b]
1949	402	139	131	52	–	–	80
1953	487	243	151	48	–	–	45
1957	497	270	169	41	–	–	17
1961	499	242	190	67	–	–	–
1965	496	245	202	49	–	–	–
1969	496	242	224	30	–	–	–
1972	496	225	230	41	–	–	–
1976	496	243	214	39	–	–	–
1980	497	226	218	53	–	–	–
1983	498	244	193	34	27	–	–
1987	497	223	186	46	42	–	–
1990	662	319	239	79	8[c]	17[d]	–
1994	672[e]	294	252	47	49	30	–

[a]In 1990, under the special arrangement which divided the Federal Republic into two electoral areas (East and West) for that year's Bundestag election only, the Alliance 90/Greens won a parliamentary representation of eight seats by passing the 5 percent minimum in the East. The western Greens fell below 5 percent in the West that year. By 1994, the two had merged into a new party with the name Alliance 90/ Greens, which competed throughout the Federal Republic.
[b]In 1949, BP (Bavarian Party) 17, Center Party 10, DP (German Party) 17, DRP (German Reich Party) 5, KPD (Communists) 15, SSW (Danish minority party) 1, WAV (Economic Reconstruction Union) 12, and independents 3. In 1953, GB BHE (a refugee party) 27, DP 15, and Center 3. In 1957, DP 17.
[c]In 1990, the eastern Alliance 90/Greens only. See footnote a.
[d]In 1990, the PDS (Party of Democratic Socialism) won parliamentary representation by netting 11.1 percent of the vote in the East (including East Berlin). It received only 0.3 percent in the West, resulting in a total of 2.4 percent of the vote in the entire Federal Republic.
[e]In 1994, the CDU/CSU won twelve and the SPD won four "additional seats" or Überhangsmandate, an unprecedented high number. As a result, the CDU/CSU-FDP government coalition's majority margin was raised from 2 to 10 seats in a Bundestag of 672 rather than 656 seats.

TABLE A.3

THE BUNDESTAG ELECTION OF 1994 IN THE LÄNDER
PERCENTAGE OF THE SECOND VOTE BY PARTY (1990 RESULTS IN BRACKETS)

Land	Percent Voting	CDU/ CSU	SPD	FDP	Greens- A.90/Gr.	PDS	REP[a]	Other Parties
The West								
Baden-Württemberg	79.7 (77.4)	43.3 (46.5)	30.7 (29.1)	9.9 (12.3)	9.6 (5.7)	0.8 (0.3)	3.1 (3.2)	2.6 (3.0)
Bavaria	77.0 (74.4)	51.2 (51.9)	29.6 (26.7)	6.4 (8.7)	6.3 (4.6)	0.6 (0.2)	2.8 (5.0)	2.9 (3.0)
Berlin: West only[b]	79.6 (83.9)	38.7 (47.8)	34.6 (30.2)	7.2 (9.9)	12.3 (6.4)	2.6 (1.3)	2.0 (3.0)	2.6 (1.4)
Bremen	78.6 (76.5)	30.2 (30.9)	45.5 (42.5)	7.2 (12.8)	11.1 (8.3)	2.7 (1.1)	1.7 (2.1)	1.6 (2.3)
Hamburg	79.8 (78.2)	34.9 (36.6)	39.7 (41.0)	7.2 (12.0)	12.6 (5.8)	2.2 (1.1)	1.7 (1.7)	1.7 (1.7)
Hesse	82.4 (81.1)	40.7 (41.3)	37.2 (38.0)	8.1 (10.9)	9.3 (5.6)	1.1 (0.4)	2.4 (2.1)	1.2 (1.8)
Lower Saxony	81.9 (80.6)	41.3 (44.3)	40.6 (38.4)	7.7 (10.3)	7.1 (4.5)	1.0 (0.3)	1.2 (1.0)	1.1 (1.2)
North Rhine-Westphalia	81.9 (78.7)	38.0 (40.5)	43.1 (41.1)	7.6 (11.0)	7.4 (4.3)	1.0 (0.3)	1.3 (1.3)	1.4 (1.6)
Rhineland-Palatinate	82.3 (81.7)	43.8 (45.6)	39.4 (36.1)	6.9 (10.4)	6.2 (4.0)	0.6 (0.2)	1.9 (1.7)	1.1 (1.9)
The Saar	83.5 (85.1)	37.2 (38.1)	48.8 (51.2)	4.3 (6.0)	5.8 (2.3)	0.7 (0.2)	1.6 (0.9)	1.6 (1.4)
Schleswig-Holstein	81.0 (78.6)	41.5 (43.5)	39.6 (38.5)	7.4 (11.4)	8.3 (4.0)	1.1 (0.3)	1.0 (1.2)	1.0 (1.1)
The East								
Berlin: East only[b]	77.2 (76.6)	19.5 (24.3)	33.1 (31.3)	1.9 (7.7)	6.9 (8.8)	34.7 (24.8)	1.7 (1.5)	2.3 (1.6)
Brandenburg	71.8 (73.8)	28.1 (36.3)	45.0 (32.9)	2.6 (9.7)	2.9 (6.6)	19.3 (11.0)	1.1 (1.7)	0.9 (1.8)
Mecklenburg-W. Pomerania	73.0 (70.9)	38.5 (41.2)	28.8 (26.5)	3.4 (9.1)	3.6 (5.9)	23.6 (14.2)	1.2 (1.4)	0.9 (1.5)
Saxony	72.0 (76.2)	48.0 (49.5)	24.3 (18.2)	3.8 (12.4)	4.8 (5.9)	16.7 (9.0)	1.4 (1.2)	1.1 (3.8)
Saxony-Anhalt	70.6 (72.2)	38.8 (38.6)	33.4 (24.7)	4.1 (19.7)	3.6 (5.3)	18.0 (9.4)	1.0 (1.0)	1.2 (1.4)
Thuringia	75.5 (76.4)	41.0 (45.2)	30.2 (21.9)	4.2 (14.6)	4.9 (6.1)	17.1 (8.3)	1.4 (1.2)	1.1 (2.6)

[a]The right-wing Republikaner party.
[b]The East and West Berlin breakdown for 1994 is taken from table 2 in Hans-Georg Golz, "Der Wechsel fand nicht statt," in *Deutschland Archiv*, no. 11, 1994, p. 1130. The original source is *Der Wahlleiter* in Berlin.

TABLE A.4

LANDTAG ELECTIONS, 1991 TO 1994
PERCENTAGE OF THE SECOND VOTE BY PARTY
(PERCENTAGE GAINS OR LOSSES SINCE THE LAST LANDTAG ELECTION IN BRACKETS)

Land	Percent Voting	CDU[a]	SPD	FDP	Greens-A.90/Gr.	PDS	REP[b]	Other Parties
Hesse	70.8	40.2	40.8	7.4	8.8	–	1.7	1.1
20 Jan. 1991	(-9.5)	(-1.9)	(+0.6)	(-0.4)	(-0.6)	–	(+1.7)	(+0.6)
Rhineland-Palat.	73.9	38.7	44.8	6.9	6.5	–	2.0	1.1
21 April 1991	(-3.0)	(-6.4)	(+6.0)	(-0.4)	(+0.6)	–	(+2.0)	(-1.8)
Hamburg	66.1	35.1	48.0	5.4	7.2	0.5	1.2	2.6
2 June 1991	(-13.4)	(-5.4)	(+3.0)	(-1.1)	(+0.2)	(+0.5)	(+1.2)	(+1.6)
Bremen	72.2	30.7	38.8	9.5	11.4	–	1.5	8.2[c]
29 Sept. 1991	(-3.4)	(+7.3)	(-11.7)	(-0.5)	(+1.2)	–	(+0.4)	(+3.6)
Baden-Württem.	70.1	39.6	29.4	5.9	9.5	–	10.9	4.8
5 April 1992	(-1.7)	(-9.4)	(-2.6)	(0.0)	(+1.6)	–	(+9.9)	(+0.6)
Schleswig-Holst.	71.7	33.8	46.2	5.6	4.97	–	1.2	8.2[d]
5 April 1992	(-5.7)	(+0.5)	(-8.6)	(+1.2)	(+2.1)	–	(+0.6)	(+4.1)
Hamburg	69.6	25.1	40.4	4.2	13.5	–	4.8	11.9[e]
19 Sept. 1993	(+3.5)	(-10.0)	(-7.6)	(-1.2)	(+6.3)	(-0.5)	(+3.6)	(+8.8)
Lower Saxony	73.8	36.4	44.3	4.4	7.4	–	3.7	3.7
13 March 1994	(-0.8)	(-5.6)	(+0.1)	(-1.6)	(+1.9)	–	(+2.2)	(+2.9)
Saxony-Anhalt	54.9	34.4	34.0	3.6	5.1	19.9	1.4	1.8
26 June 1994	(-10.2)	(-4.6)	(+8.0)	(-9.9)	(-0.2)	(+7.9)	(+0.8)	(-1.9)
Brandenburg	56.2	18.7	54.1	2.2	2.9	18.7	1.1	2.3
11 Sept. 1994	(-10.9)	(-10.9)	(+15.8)	(-4.4)	(-6.3)	(+5.3)	(-0.1)	(+0.4)
Saxony	58.4	58.1	16.6	1.7	4.1	16.5	1.3	1.7
11 Sept. 1994	(-14.4)	(+4.3)	(-2.5)	(-3.6)	(-1.5)	(+6.3)	(+1.3)	(-4.3)
Bavaria	67.9	52.8	30.1	2.8	6.1	–	3.9	4.3
25 Sept. 1994	(+2.0)	(-2.1)	(+4.1)	(-2.4)	(-0.3)	–	(-1.0)	(+1.7)
Meckl.-W. Pom	73.1	37.7	29.5	3.8	3.7	22.7	1.0	1.6
16 Oct. 1994	(+8.4)	(-0.6)	(+2.5)	(-1.7)	(-2.7)	(+7.0)	(+0.1)	(-4.6)
The Saar	83.5	38.6	49.4	2.1	5.5	–	1.4	3.1
16 Oct. 1994	(+0.3)	(+5.2)	(-5.0)	(-3.5)	(+2.9)	–	(-2.0)	(+2.5)
Thuringia	74.7	42.6	29.6	3.2	4.5	16.6	1.3	2.3
16 Oct. 1994	(3.0)	(-2.8)	(+6.8)	(-6.1)	(-2.0)	(+6.9)	(+0.5)	(-3.3)

[a]CSU in Bavaria.
[b]The right-wing Republikaner party.
[c]Includes 6.2 percent for the right-wing DVU (German People's Union).
[d]Includes 6.3 percent for the DVU (German People's Union).
[e]Includes 2.8 percent for the DVU, and 5.6 percent for the populist *Statt Partei* (Instead Party).

Select Bibliography

The following list is limited to publications in the English language, except for the book edited by Wilhelm Bürklin and Dieter Roth. Readers who wish to consult additional German language works may wish to start with the bibliographies provided by several chapters in *Das Superwahljahr*.

Anderson, Christopher, Karl Kaltenthaler, and Wolfgang Luthardt, eds. *The Domestic Politics of German Unification*. Boulder: Lynne Rienner Publishers, 1993.

Ash, Timothy Garton. *In Europe's Name : Germany and the Divided Continent*. New York: Random House, 1993.

Betz, Hans-Georg. *Postmodern Politics in Germany: The Politics of Resentment*. Basingstoke and London: Macmillan, 1991.

Braunthal, Gerard. *The German Social Democrats Since 1969: A Party in Power and Opposition*. Boulder: Westview Press, 1994.

Bürklin, Wilhelm, and Dieter Roth, eds. *Das Superwahljahr*. Cologne: Bund-Verlag, 1994.

Cerny, Karl H., ed. *Germany at the Polls: The Bundestag Election of 1976*. Washington, D.C.: American Enterprise Institute, 1978.

Cerny, Karl H., ed. *Germany at the Polls: The Bundestag Elections of the 1980s*. Durham: Duke University Press, 1990.

Clemens, Clay. *Reluctant Realists: The CDU/CSU and the West German Ostpolitik*. Durham: Duke University Press, 1989.

Conradt, David P. *The German Polity*. 5th ed. New York: Longman, 1993.

Dahrendorf, Ralf. *Society and Democracy in Germany*. London: Weidenfeld and Nicolson, 1968.

Dalton, Russell J. *Politics in Germany*. New York: Harper Collins, 1992.

Dalton, Russell J., ed. *The New Germany Votes*. Providence: Berg Publishers, 1993.

Frankland, Gene, and Donald Schoonmaker. *Between Protest and Power: The Green Party in Germany*. Boulder: Westview Press, 1992.

Geipel, Gary, ed. *Germany in a New Era*. Indianapolis: Hudson Institute, 1993.

Hamilton, Daniel. *Beyond Bonn: America and the Berlin Republic*. Washington, D.C.: Carnegie Endowment for International Peace, 1994.

Hancock, M. Donald. *West Germany: The Politics of Democratic Corporatism*. Chatham, N.J.: Chatham House Publishers, 1989.

Hancock, M. Donald, and Helga A. Welsh, eds. *German Unification: Process and Outcomes*. Boulder: Westview Press, 1994.

Hanrieder, Wolfram F. *Germany, America, Europe: Forty Years of German Foreign Policy*. New Haven: Yale University Press, 1989.

Huelshoff, Michael, Andrei S. Markovits, and Simon Reich, eds. *From Bundesrepublik to Deutschland: German Politics After Reunification.* Ann Arbor: University of Michigan Press, 1993.

James, Harold, and Maria Stone, eds. *When the Wall Came Down: Reactions to German Unification.* New York: Routledge, 1992.

Jarausch, Konrad H. *The Rush to German Unity.* New York: Oxford University Press, 1994.

Jesse, Eckhart. *Elections: The Federal Republic of Germany in Comparison.* Oxford: Berg, 1990.

Katzenstein, Peter. *Policy and Politics in West Germany: The Growth of a Semisovereign State.* Philadelphia: Temple University Press, 1988.

Kolinsky, Eva. *Parties, Opposition and Society in West Germany.* London: Croom Helm, 1984.

———. *Women in West Germany: Work, Family and Politics.* Oxford: Berg, 1989.

———. *The Federal Republic of Germany: The End of an Era.* New York and Oxford: Berg, 1991.

Markovits, Andrei S. *The Politics of West German Trade Unions.* Cambridge: Cambridge University Press, 1986.

Markovits, Andrei S., and Philip S. Gorski. *The German Left: Red, Green, and Beyond.* New York: Oxford University Press, 1993.

Merkl, Peter H. *German Unification in the European Context.* University Park, Penn.: Pennsylvania State University Press, 1993.

Merkl, Peter H., ed. *The Federal Republic of Germany at Forty.* New York: New York University Press, 1989.

Padgett, Stephen, and Tony Burkett. *Political Parties and Elections in West Germany: The Search for a New Stability.* London: Hurst & Co., 1986.

Padgett, Stephen, ed. *Parties and Party Systems in the New Germany.* Brookfield, VT.: Dartmouth, 1993.

Paterson, William E., and David Southern, eds. *Governing Germany.* New York: Norton, 1991.

Pond, Elizabeth. *Beyond the Wall: Germany's Road to Unification.* Washington, D.C.: The Brookings Institution, 1993.

Schneider, Peter. *The German Comedy: Scenes of Life After the Wall.* New York: The Noonday Press, 1991.

Smith, Gordon, William E. Paterson, Peter H. Merkl, and Stephen Padgett, eds. *Developments in German Politics.* London: Macmillan, 1992.

Smyser, W. R. *Germany and America: New Identities, Fateful Rift?* Boulder: Westview Press, 1993.

Stares, Paul B., ed. *The New Germany and the New Europe.* Washington, D.C.: The Brookings Institution, 1992.

Szabo, Stephen F. *The Diplomacy of German Unification.* New York: St. Martin's Press, 1992.

Treverton, Gregory F. *America, Germany and the Future of Europe*. Princeton: Princeton University Press, 1992.

Turner, Jr., Henry Ashby. *Germany from Partition to Reunification*. New Haven: Yale University Press, 1992.

Verheyen, Dirk. *The German Question: A Cultural, Historical, and Geopolitical Exploration*. Boulder: Westview Press, 1991.

Verheyen, Dirk, and Christian Søe, eds. *The Germans and Their Neighbors*. Boulder: Westview Press, 1993.

Wallach, Peter H., and George K. Romoser, eds. *West German Politics in the Mid-Eighties*. New York: Praeger, 1985.

Wallach, Peter H., and Ronald A. Francisco, eds. *United Germany: The Past, Politics, Prospects*. Westcourt, Conn.: Praeger, 1992.

UNITING GERMANY
Documents and Debates, 1944-1993

Konrad H. Jarausch and Volker Gransow
Translations from the German by **Allison Brown** and
Belinda Cooper

The unification of Germany is the most important change
in Central Europe in the last four decades. Understanding
this rapid and unforeseen development has raised old fears as well as
inspired new hopes. In order to make sense out of the bewildering process
and to help both expert and lay readers understand the changes and the
consequences, an American historian and a German social scientist put
together this collection of central texts on German unification, the first of
its kind. An invaluable reference tool.

From the Contents: The New Germany: Myths and Realities – Division,
Cold Civil War and Détente – Exodus, Opposition and Immobilism –
Awakening, Fall of the Wall and Bankruptcy – National Turn and Fears of
Unity – Economic Union and International Breakthrough – Unification
Treaties and Accession – Post-Unity Problems and Perspectives

*"The first comprehensive documentation in English of the German
reunification ... a good chronological range of sources ... The editing is not
only expert but also user-friendly ... belongs in all serious academic and
major public libraries."* **Choice**

Konrad H. Jarausch is Lurcy Professor of European Civilization at the
University of North Carolina, Chapel Hill. His many publications include
The Rush to German Unity (1994) and *Students, Society, and Politics in
Imperial Germany* (1982); **Volker Gransow** is teaches in the Department
of Political Science at the Freie Universität Berlin. One of his more recent
publications is *The Autistic Walkman* (1985)

304 pages, glossary, bibliog., index
ISBN 1-57181-010-2 hardback, **$64.00/£46.00**ISBN 1-57181-011-0 paperback, **$18.95/£13.95**

165 Taber Ave., Providence, RI 02906 • Tel: 401-861-9330 • Fax: 401-521-0046
E-Mail: BerghahnBk@aol.com

Bush House, Merewood Ave., Sandhills, Oxford OX3 8EF • Tel: (01865) 742 224 • Fax: (01865) 744 978
E-Mail: BerghahnUK@cityscape.co.uk